LOGIC AND LOVE

JDV Philosophy Series - 7

LOGIC AND LOVE

Reflecting on Professor John Vattanky's Contribution to Indian Philosophy and Spirituality

Editors:
Thomas Karimundackal, SJ
Kuruvilla Pandikattu, SJ

Jnana-Deepa Vidyapeeth

&

Christian World Imprints

First Published in 2019 by

Jnana-Deepa Vidyapeeth
Ramwadi, Nagar Road, **Pune-411014**
jdvoffice@jdv.edu.in
www.jdv.edu.in
Phone: +91 20 41036111

&

Christian World Imprints
Christian Publishing & Books from India
C-3, Shop No. 14, Ground Floor
Wazirpur Industrial Area, **Delhi-110052**
cwidelhi2017@gmail.com
www.ChristianWorldImprints.com
Phone: +91 11 41526079

ISBN: 978-93-5148-371-7

"Published with the help of the Institute of Missiology – Germany"

Printed in India.

CONTENTS

JDV PHILOSOPHY SERIES - 7

Since 1893 Jnana-Deepa Vidyapeeth has been pioneering philosophy discussion and debate inspired by prominent personalities like Richard De Smet, Jean de Marneffe, Salvino Azzopardi, Cyril Desbruslais, Noel Sheth, John Vattanky, etc. It has been in the forefront of promoting Indian philosophy and making philosophical thinking relevant for contemporary times. In its effort to reach out to like-minded scholars, JDV Philosophy Series has been visualized as a catalyst for interdisciplinary thinking and contemporary exploration on social issues fostering holistic liberation, integral development and creative engagement.

JDV Philosophy Series

1. Salvino Azzopardi: ***Epistemology and Phenomenology of Religions*** (2018)
2. Kuruvilla Pandikattu & Thomas Karimundackal (eds): ***Melodies from the Flute*** (2018)
3. Kurien Kunnumpuram: ***Freedom and Joy*** (2018)
4. Cyril Desbruslais SJ: ***Postmodernity: An Indian Christian Philosophical Appraisal*** (2019)
5. Cyril Desbruslais SJ: ***Metaphysics Philosophy of Be-ing for Today*** (2019)
6. John Peter Vallabadoss: ***Indian Thinkers: Modern and Contemporary Period*** (2019)
7. Thomas Karimundackal & Kuruvilla Pandikattu (eds): ***Logic and Love***: For Prof John Vattanky SJ (2019)
8. Fabian Jose UMI: ***Relevance of Thomas Merton's Spirituality for the Consecrated Life in India*** (2019)
9. Kuruvilla Pandikattu & PT Mathew (eds): ***Committed to the Church and the Country***: For Prof Kurien Kunnumpuam SJ (2019)
10. Cyril Desbruslais SJ: ***The Philosophy of God for Today*** (2019)

EDITORIAL

One of the most eminent contemporary Indian Christian thinkers, Prof. John Vattanky SJ, has been a pioneer in making the classical Indian logic, Navya-Nyāya, popular to the contemporary world. A professional philosopher, he was inspired by late 12th century Indian mathematician and philosopher Gangesha Upadhyaya. Throughout his philosophical search, he has been constantly seeking God. He found the fulfilment of his wish in the last days of his life in the person and spirituality of St. Ephrem the Syrian (306-373).

Throughout his life, he has been an earnest seeker: both philosophically and spiritually. He has also inspired countless people - both colleagues and students - in their pursuit of intellectual and spiritual fulfilment. So as a guide, mentor and inspiration, he has contributed significantly to Indian philosophy and Christian spirituality. Thus the title of this volume! Logic was his passion and it reflected his untiring devotion to Indian philosophy and research. Love was his devotion to God and to his mother land. Thus Love and Love sum up his entire life of devotion to scholarly commitment based on joyful spiritualiy!

It is obvious that he has been the world authority on Navya-Nyāya. While in Pune, he had the most sought after scholar, both nationally and internationally. In order to acknowledge Professor Vattanky's astounding contribution both to India and to Church, some of his colleagues and admirers have come together. While facilitating him respectfully and reverentially, we acknowledge our indebtedness to this generous personality.

It may be recalled that he returned from Pune to Kerala in June 2013. After more than a year on 30 December 2014, he had a stroke, which has left him paralysed. He is fully conscious but is totally dependent on others. We are happy that he has taken this situation gracefully and even with a sense of humour. His deep trust in God has been one of the factors that has kept him mentally agile.

So this book is a humble homage to our guru, mentor and guide. Through this book, we acknowledge Vattanky's contribution not only to the Indian philosophy and Indian Church but also at the personal level. He has personally touched and inspired us.

As for the title: Logic and Love: Reflecting on Prof. John Vattanky's Contribution to Indian Philosophy and Spirituality. It reflects Prof. Vattanky total involvement in Navya-Nyāya (logic) through a deep spiritual devotion (love). The world authority he is on Navya-Nyāya, had no hesitation to surrender himself unconditionally to the God of Love thorough a spirituality and ethics that is world-affirming and intellectually vibrant.

This book, which we humbly offer to him, is divided into four parts, reflecting Vattanky's own philosophical vision and concerns. Each of these parts deals with both Indian and Western notions and categories. This reflects Vattanky's own eagerness to dialogue with Indian and Western traditions intellectually and affectively.

The first Part deals with Logic and Nyāya, the field of Vattanky's own expertise. The article by Dr. Stephen Chundamthadam, SJ explores the person of John Vattanky, one of the rare scholars in Indian philosophy who integrated the Western rigorous method of research with the traditional Indian method of reading and interpreting abstruse Nyāya text. It shows that Vattanky's reasoning was that the theory of inference the Naiyayikas meticulously developed gave scope for the human intelligence to transcend the empirical limitations to reach the Ultimate Reality.

The next article by John Peter Vallabadoss, OFM Cap explores the liberative potential of Indian epistemology. He argues that scrutiny of *pramāṇas* along with the *tātparya*, end of knowledge reveals that Indian epistemology aims at a glimpse of truth, *Sat* and liberation from untruth leading to *mokṣa*.

The next three article deals with the role of logic in contemporary science. Stephen S. Jayard argues that necessary reliance on inductive reasoning, which unfortunately lacks the deductive certainty, is usually associated with science, seems to teach some basic lessons, not only for science but also for human life. Augustine Pamplany asks if our "search for Reality" make any sense! Based on the profound notions of neti, neti and quantum mechancis, he indicates that complete explanation of Reality-in-itself is beyond the region of physics. However, the questions emerging from the problematics of the epistemology of quantum physics are deeply rooted in the ultimate epistemological problem of the intelligibility of Reality-in-itself.

The last article in this section by Vibin Varghese Padayadan, SJ, based on Karl Popper, argues that task of social sciences is to study the unintended social repercussions of intended human actions which can enable humans to understand the even more remote consequences of possible actions.

The next Part deals with the role and significance of hermeneutics or interpretation in our thinking and living. Thomas Karimundackal, SJ applies the rich notion of *Dhvani* to an Indian approach to Biblical Hermeneutics. While the first part of his article explains the Dhvani method and its various aspects, the second part of the paper illustrates its hermeneutical application to the story of the fall. James Ponniah focuses on Noble laureate Tagore's famous poem 'Mind Without Fear,' applies Dhvani method of interpretation to understand the meaning and the relevance of such a significant poem both in the past and the present.

Raju Felix Crasta attempts a hermeneutical appropriation of the Mahāvākya '*tattvamasi*'. He shows that Vijñānabhikṣu in his erudite way explores it as every being partakers in the divine essence, a unique understanding! This penetrating inter-relatedness makes tattvamasi, a semantic axis of the Vedānta, a tool for cosmotheandric and other such holistic well-being.

In the final article, Dolichan Kollareth, SJ shows that as against traditional dichotomised psychological views, Developments in neuroscience underscore the integrated brain networks subserving emotion and cognition. All reasoning has an affective quality and all emotions have a cognitive dimension.

The third part explores the intimate relationship between God and the world, between spirituality and *sadhana*. In the first article, Ivan D'Souza highlights the relationship between human and divine which is achieved through the flute play of Kṛṣṇa. In pastoral cultures, a musical instrument is often associated with the shepherd or cowherd. Next, Chacko Nadakkeveliyil explores the perceived complicatedness of human concepts to refer to a being like God, has led to a heated discussion in analytic philosophy and in the philosophy of religion. Drawing on Alvin Plantinga's reformed "re-visioning," he shows that our God-Talk is rationally legitimate.

Isaac Parackal, OIC highlights the Spirituality of Work. According to him, work is a cosmotheandric act which helps humans to live in the 'present' and relates one with all the three dimensions of reality namely divine, human and cosmic. Work as modern Yajna (sacrifice) conjoins these three constitutive dimensions of reality. In the last article in this part Stephen Plathottathil, OIC highlights remarkable contributions of Francis Acharya, a trappist monk, on his adapted English translation of the Mosul Fenqitho, which is the first attempt in English translation and this translation work points out his unique spirituality and monastical dream.

The Fourth Part deals with dharma and ethics, topics very dear to the heart of Prof. Vattanky, and their relevance for contemporary society. Henry D'Almeida, SJ explore the semantics, evolution and the significance of the core Hindu ethical category "Dharma." He highlights the relevance of Dharma in promoting and nurturing ethics of life in the context of death dealing forces.

George Ayyaneth, OIC argues that what we need is not the political deconstruction of Hindu Dharma, but a re-discovery of the spiritual inner dynamism of Hindu Dharma. J. Charles Davis, basing himself on the Hindu understanding of human dignity, probes some crimes against the equal moral dignity propagated by the Bhagavadgītā and the law of dharma which demands right living and universal application of moral duties.

Jijo James Indiparambil, CST applies the Hindu religious roots to workforce management. According to him, the holistic managerial strategy extracted from the Hindu religious traditions focuses on individuals as the unit of analysis for moral judgments, giving employees a significant place, valuing their dignity as human persons

Nishant Alphonse Irudayadason takes up the ethical dimension in the social role of educator. Taking inspiration from contemporary thinkers like Paul Ricoeur, he shows how moral democratic space becomes inevitable in the novel path of knowledge production. Jojo Varakukalayil, CST appropriates the insights of Martin Heidegger on "poetic dwelling as ecological mindfulness." Poetic dwelling calls forth for an attitude of reverence and respect for the bio-diversity, and thus in poetic dwelling humans emerge to be dwelling 'humanly' upon this habitat as his home.

The final article by Kuruvilla Pandikattu focusses on the role of long-term thinking based on Indian philosophical thinking and Western spiritual roots. After exploring the perils of short-termism, the author looks at some of the cultural works that can promote long term vision.

The Concluding Shraddhanjali, AYUSHMAN BHAVA by Placid (Jnanadas), OIC is a tribute to the thinker, mentor and seeker that Vattanky has been for so many of his colleagues and students. Through AYUSHMAN BHAVA, we are happy to wish a long, joyous and fulfilled life!

We are grateful to the three campus houses in Pune, which has made this book possible. To the Rev. Dr. Selva Rathinam, SJ, President and Dr. Jose Thayil, SJ, Registrar, and community, Jnana-Deepa Vidyapeeth (JDV), Pune, where the three of us, including Prof. John Vattanky taught, to Rev. Edward Mudavassery, SJ, Rector, Rev. Jacob Kulangara, SJ, Minister, and community, De Nobili College, where the three of us stayed and to Rev. Bhausaheb Sansare, SJ, Rev. Vincent Crasta, SJ, Minister and community, Papal Seminary, where both the editors are currently residing. We thank these communities for the opportunity given to us for our academic and spiritual fulfilment.

We are also obliged to Kerala Province of the Society of Jesus, especially the Provincials, Rev. Fr. MK George, SJ and Rev. Fr. EP Mathew, SJ. Without their support, this venture would not have seen the light of day.

Thomas Karimundackal, SJ
Kuruvilla Pandikattu, SJ

PART ONE

LOGIC AND NYAYA

1

Theory of Knowledge and Theory of God: Vattanky's Contribution to the Development of Theism in Navyanyāya

Stephen Chundamthadam, SJ

Abstract

John Vattanky is one of the rare scholars in Indian philosophy who integrated Western rigorous method of research with the traditional Indian method of reading and interpreting abstruse Nyāya texts. He chose the *Tattvacintāmaṇi* of Gaṅgeśa, a difficult text for his translation, commentary and critical study. The existence or non-existence of God is crucial to any philosophical discourse because this fundamental question determines the theory of knowledge, ethical values and metaphysical principles. The problem of existence of God was first brought to the attention of philosophers in three sutras by Gautama in his Nyāyasūtras. Gaṅgeśa, through his classical work *Tattvacintāmaṇi* played a crucial role in the revival of Nyāya philosophical discourses in India. Both the schools - Navyanyāya of Gaṅgeśa and the Dharamkīrti school of Buddhism - were the representative of two sides arguing for and against the existence of God. Vattanky's reasoning was that the theory of inference the Naiyayikas meticulously developed gave scope for the human intelligence to transcend the empirical limitations to reach the Ultimate Reality. The underlying implication is that no theory of knowledge is possible without a corresponding theory of God.

Key words: *Navyanyāya, Nyāyasūtras, Īśvaravāda,* Philosophy of God, *Tattvacintāmaṇi*, Proofs for the existence of God, theory of knowledge, *śāstrakāra*, fragmented world.

Introduction

Prof. John Vattanky is one of the rare scholars in Indian philosophy who exquisitely integrated Western rigorous method of research with the traditional Indian method of reading and interpreting abstruse Nyāya texts.[1] After his research, back in India, he relentlessly pursued his reading of abstruse Indian classical texts under pundits and *śāstrakāra-s* for the rest of his active life. According to Gopikamohan Bhattacharya, "All these –the exactitude of his translation, the faithfulness of his commentaries, and the rigour of his studies- show that Dr. Vattanky is carrying on the traditions of the eminent scholars under whom he had the good fortune to study."[2] His wide contact in the academic world by means of lectures and paper presentations, membership in international organizations and conferences, the lectures he delivered in prestigious universities and academic centers and the books and articles he published show his deep erudition in the field of Navyanyāya philosophy. He was an authority on Navyanyāya who was very much sought after for lectures and paper presentations. He is equally known for his high respect for Indian philosophy, values and culture.

1. Fragmented world and beacon of hope

Vattanky was born and brought up in a traditional conservative Christian background. But through the Jesuit formation and Western education he could broaden his horizon of knowledge to the extent that Navyanyāya became his life and mission. Religion and creed were not barriers in his search for knowledge. At a time when the Indian sub-continent is threatened to be fragmented in the name of gods, caste and creed, language and narrow mindedness, Vattanky is a beacon of hope to all who journey through the path of truth. His rational and philosophical attempt to prove the existence of God with the support of Gaṅgeśa's *Īśvaravāda* is commendable. The fine and most accurate translation and commentary on Gaṅgeśa's *Īśvaravāda* is indeed a great achievement in the academic life of Vattanky. Reviewing Vattanky's work, Paul Griffiths wrote: "Vattanky's work is the most significant English-language resource available

1 John Vattanky was fortunate to have his M A in Oriental Studies with Sanskrit and Pali as optionals from Oxford University, England under Prof. Burow and Ph D in Nyāya from Vienna University under Prof. G. Oberhammer. He continued his reading of the NavyaNyāya text with Panditaraja Sri Damodara Pisharody a distinguished traditional scholar and a close disciple of late Ramavarma Parikshit Thampuran

2 John Vattanky, *Gaṅgeśa's Philosophy of God.* Madras: The Adayar Library and Research Centre.1984 p.vi. From the Foreword by Gopikamohan Bhattacharya.

to date for the study of the Nyāya position on God's nature and attributes, and, more especially, for the analysis of the standard Naiyayika arguments for God's existence. It is not, of course, without predecessors, but much of the earlier work is not in English and is available only in scholarly journals which are not likely to form part of the Christian theologian's regular intellectual diet."[3] Vattanky, through his lectures and publications has done a great service in promoting Nyāya philosophy, particularly Nyāya theism among the English speaking scholars on Indian philosophy. Generations of students fondly remember him for his scholarship, commitment in teaching and friendly approach to students.

2. Need for accurate translations and commentaries

Indian philosophy is known to the world due to the tireless hard work of numerous traditional and modern scholars both in the East and in the West. Still there remains vast quantity of material to be edited and published. According to Gopikamohan Bhattcharya, "What we need now is a series of studies on individual authors and commentaries on them, so that the exact contributions of those authors to the development of the system could be assessed."[4] Vattanky's pioneering works are to be understood from this context. Though Vedanta was his first choice, as was the custom of his time, he opted for Navyanyāya system of philosophy for his research. He chose the *Tattvacintāmaṇi* of Gaṅgeśa[5] a difficult text for his translation, commentary and critical study.

3. Logic the lamp that enlightens

Logic (*anvīkṣi*) is one of the four components of ancient Indian education. Kautilya considered logic as the lamp which enlightens all branches of knowledge, the means to accomplish all works and the support of all religious duties.[6] The science of correct thinking is basic to philosophizing both in the West and in the East. In the ancient India sage Gautama understood the importance of logic and developed it into a science which was further developed by Vātsyāyana, Uddyotakara and Vācāspati Miśra through their

---

3 Paul Griffiths, Review of *Gaṅgeśa's Philosophy of God*, by J. Vattanky, The Adayar Library and Research Centre, Adayar, Madras: 1984 in "Theological Studies 48 (1987) 690.

4 John Vattanky, *Gaṅgeśa's Philosophy of God.* 1984 p.V. From the Foreword by Gopikamohan Bhattacharya.

5 Gaṅgeśa Upadhyaya (c.1325 BCE) lived in Mithila in northern India. He was a well-known teacher and left behind a monumental work *Tattvacintāmaṇi* (Jewel of Reflection on the Truth) which was instrumental in reviving the Nyāya school known as navyaNyāya. The thoroughness with which he explains the Mīmāṃsaka position reveals his close familiarity with the Mīmāṃsaka philosophy.

6 Kautilya, *Arthaśāstra,* p. 11, ed. By Sri Vachaspati Gairoloa Varanasi: 1977. *Paradipaḥ sarvavidyānām upayaḥ sarvakarmāṇām sarvadharmānām śāśvad ankikṣaki mataḥ*

commentaries and sub commentaries. Vattanky after several years of reading and research was fully convinced of the importance of Navyanyāya when he said,

> All schools of Vedanta since the time of Gaṅgeśa make use of the techniques and terms of Navyanyāya.... Its unique feature lies in the fact that it studies with unparalleled rigour and exactitude of the nature, dimensions and conditions of human knowledge. And so we know the philosophical problem par excellence is the problem of knowledge. With rare insight Navyanyāya examines the problems connected with human knowledge and sets forth in detail the exact conditions in which valid knowledge is possible.[7]

For Vatanky as for Navyanyāya, human intellect and theory of knowledge are with a purpose. The purpose is to search for the ultimate cause which gives meaning and existence to everything, *i.e*, God.

4. Nyāya and Buddhism on God

Belief or nonbelief in the existence of an Ultimate Principle – God, has been a decisive criterion in philosophical formulations both in the West and in the East. In India, from ancient time, philosophical investigations were centered on this fundamental question, systems and philosophers got divided on this issue. Nyāya and Buddhism in Indian philosophy adopted a thoroughly rational approach to prove or to disprove the existence of God. The prolonged philosophical discussions on the issue of existence of God spearheaded by these two systems reveal the sharpness of arguments and ingenuity of philosophers in developing arguments for and against. Hermann Jacobi and Gopikamohan Bhattacharya in their works elaborately dealt with the trajectory of the discussions on God.[8] John Vattanky, in the first section of his scholarly work *Gaṅgeśa's Philosophy of God*, discussed in detail the different stages of development of Nyāya theism.[9]

The existence or non-existence of God is crucial to any philosophical discourse because this fundamental question determines the theory of knowledge, ethical values and metaphysical principles. The polemic between the Naiyayikas and the Buddhists on the question of the existence of God is to be analyzed from this perspective because both the schools use the best

7 John Vattanky, *Gaṅgeśa's Philosophy of God*. Madras: 1984 p. x

8 Following are the two important works: Herman Jacobi, *Die Entwicklung der Gottesdee bei den Indern und deren Beweise fur das Dasein Gottes*. Bonn: Kurt Schroeder Verlag, 1923. Gopikamohan Bhattacharya, *Studies in Nyāya-Vaisesika Theism*. Calcutta: Sanskrit College Research Series, 1961.

9 John Vattanky, *Gaṅgeśa's Philosophy of God*. 1984. The first section dealing with the historical development of Nyāya theism was later published as a separate work dealing with the historical perspective and an overview.

rational arguments for opposing each other. The problem of existence of God was first brought to the attention of philosophers in three sutras by Gautama in his *Nyāyasūtras* (IV.1.19, 20 and 21).[10] These three sutras became the foundation for the discussion on God. Vātsyāyana and Uddyotakara further developed theistic arguments to prove the existence of God.

5. Absence of invariable concomitance

Dharmakīrti, one of the most brilliant philosophers in the Buddhist tradition vehemently opposed the line of thinking of the Nyāya philosophers on God by arguing that the inference to prove the existence of God is fallacious.

> The basic argument of Dharmakīrti against the Naiyayikas is that the reason in their inference to establish the existence of God is fallacious, that is, in the example there is no sādhya which they want to establish by means of their reason. In other words, no example of a thing can be given which has been produced by an omniscient being. This means that there is not invariable concomitance of the sādhya in the reason of the inference which has been adduced by the Naiyayikas to establish the existence of God. Therefore the whole inference is invalid. [11]

Dharmakīrti argued that there is an inner contradiction in Naiyayika's concept of God who is the cause of the World. At the time of creation God undergoes a change, from being non-cause to a cause. Whatever undergoes change is non-eternal, so God is non-eternal. Creation of the world makes Naiyayika's God non-eternal. According to Dharmakīrti, the only way to save the eternity of God is by denying the creatorship of world. Dharmakīrti's sharp philosophical arguments had been a source of inspiration and guidance for later Buddhist philosophers like Śāntarakṣita, Kamalāśila, Ratnakīrti in their fight against Naiyayika theism.

Vācaspati Miśra, in response to the Buddhist argument of the absence of invariable concomitance in sādhya, argued that this principle cannot be applied in the case of creation of the world. After seeing a potter making a jar, later when a man comes across a jar, he can infer that this jar is also made by a potter because there is invariable concomitance. But, the same logic cannot be applied in the case of universe. Because we haven't seen another universe

---

10 God is the cause because we find fruitlessness in the actions of men, *Īśvarh kāraṇam puruṣakarmaphalyadarśanāt)* (*Nyāyasūtra* IV.1.19

It is not so because no fruit appears without the actions of men, *Na puruṣakarmabhave phalaniṣpatteḥ. Nyāyasūtra* IV.1.20

This reasoning is not correct since it is influenced by him (God). *Tatkāritatvadahetuḥḥ, Nyāyasūtra* IV.1.21 (translation is from Vattanky's *Development of Nyāya Theism*, p. 2

11 Vattanky, *Development of Nyāya Theism*. New Delhi: Intercultural Publications, 1993 p. 3

being made. Later, Nyāya scholars Udayana and Gaṅgeśa further developed and followed the arguments of Vācaspati Miśra.

6. Logical proofs for the existence of God

Udayana, one of the best philosophers in the Nyāya history, elaborately discussed proofs for the existence of God in his works.[12] In *Nyāyakusumāñjali* he presented more than twenty logical proofs for the existence of God. *Nyāyalīlavati* of Vallabha and *Īśvaravāda* of Śaśādhara are two other important works in the development of Nyāya theism. Because of the close similarities between Śaśādhara and Gaṅgeśa one can come to the conclusion that the latter heavily depended on the former for the development of theism in Nyāya. Vattanky writes:

> It may be asserted with a fair amount of certainty that the work of Śaśādhara is the first treatise on the existence of God in post-Udayana *Navyanyāya* which exhibits the systematic plan of first discussing the *pakṣa, sādhya and hetu* of the syllogism proving the existence of God in the *pūrvapakṣa* and then establishing in the *uttarapakṣa*, the author's own *pakṣa, sādhya and hetu* of the syllogism. [13]

Nyāya-Vaiśeṣika philosophers, in general, were of the opinion that there is nothing more to be discussed about the existence of God after Udayana. Because his treatment of the subject in *Nyāyakusanjali* was thoroughly comprehensive and complete. Whatever has to be said on Nyāya theism had already been said by Udayana in his *Nyāyakusumanjali*. Herman Jacobi the famous Indologist could not find anything new in Gaṅgeśa's *Īśvaravāda*[14] which was not there in Udayana. But, later researches have proved the 'hollowness' of Jacobi's statement and at the same time proved the philosophical creativity and originality of Gaṅgeśa.

7. Gaṅgeśa's creativity and originality

Gaṅgeśa's brilliant philosophical career started at a time when Buddhism was in the process of disappearing from the land of its origin. In the absence of great Buddhist philosophers Gaṅgeśa introduced a new method and new concepts in philosophizing in India in his monumental work *Tattvacintāmaṇi.* According to the famous Indologist Stephen H. Philips:

---

12 *Atmatattvaviveka, Nyāyakusumanjali* and *Kiraṇāvalī* are the three philosophical works of Udayana which deal with the proofs for the existence of God.

13 Vattanky, *Development of Nyāya Theism*. 1993 p. 10

14 Herman Jacobi, *Die Entwicklung der Gottesdee bei den Indern und deren Beweise fur das Dasein Gottes*. Bonn: Kurt Schroeder Verlag, 1923 p. 63 as quoted by Vattanky in his *Development of Nyāya Theism.* P. 10

> It contains reflection distilled from generations of earlier philosophy both within Nyāya and Vaiseka and outside. Gaṅgeśa's originality is in fact less than traditionally implied. Udayana appears to be the innovator of several positions characteristic of the new Logic movement, as Gaṅgeśa himself acknowledges. Nevertheless, Gaṅgeśa refines and polishes Nyāya theories, developing new lines of argument. Clearly, he is recognized as the founder of New Logic. And his text stands at the center of subsequent centuries of philosophy in the Nyāya school.[15]

Vattanky based on his study and research in Nyāya theism re-established the philosophical worth of Gaṅgeśa's contribution. Vattanky writes:

> These studies establish with certainty that Gaṅgeśa show considerable originality not only in the organization of the matter that was available to him in the Nyāyavaiśeṣika tradition, but in some respects, even in the development of thought itself. The syllogism which Gaṅgeśa brings forward to establish the existence of God is remarkable from the point of view of philosophy and the history of Nyāyavaiśeṣika theism.[16]

Because the syllogism does not address the difficulties raised by the Mimasakas and the Buddhists, Gaṅgeśa reformulated the syllogism to enable it to answer the questions raised by these schools.

> Gaṅgeśa's formulation of the inference show the carefulness and accuracy with which he fought against the Buddhists and the Mīmāṃsakas. For, according to them, the world is produced by ordinary individuals by means of the unseen which they have acquired. This just means that the world comes into existence because of our merit. The formulation of the inference, particularly the enunciation of its subject and sādhya, is aimed against the Buddhists and the Mīmāṃsaka-s[17]

Gaṅgeśa formulated the syllogism with the 'intuition that the heart of the problem of the proof for the existence of God lies in the nature of the invariable concomitance of 'having-a-maker' with 'being-an-effect.' Because the Buddhists argued that 'the invariable concomitance of an invisible agent cannot be cognized in 'being-an-effect.'

8. Gaṅgeśa's Īśvaravāda

Gaṅgeśa through his monumental work *Tattvacintāmaṇi* could effect a new beginning, i.e., *Navyanyāya* in the history of Nyāya philosophy. A thorough study of the text *Tattvacintāmaṇi* is inevitable for the proper understanding of *navyanyāya* and other systems of Indian philosophies. Though some eminent

---

15 Stephen H. Phillips and N. S. Ramanuja Tatacharya. *Epistemilogy of Perception.* New York: American Institute of Buddhist Studies, 2004 p.7.

16 Vattanky, *Development of Nyāya Theism.* 1993 p. 10

17 Vattanky, *Development of Nyāya Theism.* 1993 p. 11

scholars have undertaken critical study and translation of *Tattvacintāmaṇi* of Gaṅgeśa, the *Īśvaravāda* section remained untranslated, except a Sanskrit manuscript by Pragalbha. Vattanky understood the tedious work of accurate translation and critical commentary of Īśvaravāda section. His use of the Prgalbha manuscript, careful study of the original text, accuracy of his translations and the extensive commentaries make this work original and creative. He is justified and rewarded in his selection of this important work for his reading and research. Gopimohan Bhattacharya says, "And contrary to earlier beliefs that in the Nyāya tradition everything connected with the problems of God has been already said by Udayana in his *Nyāyakusumāñjali*, Dr. Vattanky has shown conclusively that Gaṅgeśa has made original contribution on important topics."[18]

The credit goes to Vattanky for highlighting the original and creative contributions of Gaṅgeśa on Nyāya theism. Vattanky through his systematic and hard work traced the development of Nyāya theism starting form Gautama's *Nyāyasūtra*. A unique feature of Vattanky's *Gaṅgeśa's Philosophy of God* is that the author with the support of the theory of knowledge clearly presented the arguments for the existence of God and in this process he brought to the attention of the scholars a number of other issues on logic, epistemology, metaphysics, ethics and religion.

9. Revival of Nyāya discourse by Gaṅgeśa

Gaṅgeśa, through his classical work *Tattvacintāmaṇi* played a crucial role in the revival of Nyāya philosophical discourses in India. There is an enormous amount of literature in Navyanyāya by means of commentaries and subcommentaries on *Tattvacintāmaṇi*. Many of them are inaccessible to scholars who are not familiar with Sanskrit. However, any serious study of *Navyanyāya* will be incomplete without a thorough understanding of the *Upamānakhanda* and *Śabdakhanda* of *Kārikavali, Muktāvali* both by Visvanatha Pañcanana and their commentaries *Dinakari* and *Rāmarudri* by Dinakara and Rāmarudra respectively.

A systematic translation and accurate interpretation of these works was a felt need of the research scholars both in India and abroad. "In fact, anyone who carefully and systematically studies these treatises will marvel at the precision and depth which the Naiyayikas show when they deal with the various problems of Philosophy. And yet no systematic translation and interpretation of these books are available in any modern language."[19] Vattanky has done a

18 John Vattanky, *Gaṅgeśa's Philosophy of God*. 1984 p.vi

19 John Vattanky, S.J. *Nyāya Philosophy of Language,*Delhi: Indian Book Centre. 1995 p.vi. Vattanky further added the motive behind undertaking this important work: "In this context with a view to make available the richness of thought contained in these works to all those who are interested in Indian Philosophy in general and in *NavyaNyāya* in particular,

great service to the study of Indian philosophy particularly to *Navyanyāya* by bringing out a volume of translation, interpretation and commentaries faithful to the tradition on these works under the title *Nyāya Philosophy of Language.*

Conclusion

Vattanky was able to integrate the Western method of philosophizing with the Indian method of reading a text with a traditional pundit or *Śāstrakāra*. Thus he could bring in the insights from two philosophical traditions for the benefit of researchers and scholars. He is more than a translator and a commentator because, while himself being faithful to the tradition he was able to transcend the limits of tradition by his creative and critical thinking. He was courageous enough to take up *Navyanyāya* for his research which was abstruse and less popular while the study of Vedanta was more easy and common at his time. When Udayana was considered a more original and creative thinker in Nyāya School, opting Gaṅgeśa and *Tattvacintāmaṇi* was a more daunting task which he intelligently managed through his critical commentaries and accurate translations.

Both the schools - *Navyanyāya* of Gaṅgeśa and the Dharamkīrti school of Buddhism - were the representative of two sides arguing for and against the existence of God. Both were rational and logical with fine arguments for and against. So Vattanky's study of Nyāya theism was like walking on the edge of a sword where he had to accept the proofs for the existence of God because of the theory of knowledge they developed and the logically convincing arguments they put forward. At the same time he had to reject the Dharmakīrti school of Buddhsist's arguments against the possibility of an Absolute Reality which gives meaning and foundation to everything in this world. How Vattanky could hold on to a theistic position logically? His reasoning was that the theory of inference the Naiyayikas meticulously developed gave scope for the human intelligence to transcend the empirical limitations to reach the Ultimate Reality. The underlying implication is that no theory of knowledge is possible without a corresponding theory of God.

I decided to translate the whole of *Kārikāvalī, Muktāvalī and Dinakarī,* and interpret them in the light of *Rāmarudrī and Subohinī.*" *Subodhinī* is an excellent commentary on *Kārikāvalī, Muktāvalī, Dinakarī and Rāmarudrī* by Parīkṣit Thampuran of Cochin, Kerala.

2

Knowing as Liberating: Indian Soteriological Epistemology

John Peter Vallabadoss, OFM Cap

Abstract

Classical schools of Indian Philosophy have dealt with analysis of right means of knowledge, *pramāṇa,* for obtaining valid knowledge, *jñāna.* Generally, *avidya,* ignorance considered as cause of bondage, is removed by knowledge. That at the dawn of *jñāna* one is liberated has been found in all Indian philosophical systems. Delving deeper into the epistemological discourses and concerns of Indian thinkers the paper attempts to unearth the purport of knowledge process. Scrutiny of *pramāṇas* along with the *tātparya,* end of knowledge reveals that Indian epistemology aims at glimpse of truth, *sat* and at liberation from untruth, *mokṣa.* Self-awareness and identity of self with truth, as upheld by some schools relate very closely process and end of knowing. That knowledge liberates, has a soteriological underpinning within epistemological discourses of Indian tradition.

Key words: *Pramāṇa* (means of knowledge), *Avidya* (ignorance), Bondage, *Mokṣa* (liberation), *Śabda* (testimony) Verification, *Tātparya* (purpose), Self-knowledge, *Mahavākyas* (atman-brahman identity statements)

Introduction

'Ignorance causes bondage and light of knowledge leads to liberation,' is a basic premise of almost all classical Indian philosophical systems. Primary objective of any epistemological activity is to obtain knowledge; however, the ultimate goal of knowing has been termed as arriving at truth, *satyā* or specifically attaining *jñāna*. Indian epistemological discourses march beyond the frontiers of arriving at knowledge of objects, be it of things or of abstracts or of consciousness. While in most Indian thinking traditions we come across equating truth with existence, epistemological concerns go deeper into the vital question of purport of knowing. The cognition is ordinarily accepted as true and reliable. On contrary, the error and falsity does not lead to what is normal and natural to human beings. What is basically specific and natural to humans is liberation. The article attempts to probe into Indian epistemological discourses by analysing the means of knowledge and validation of knowledge along with its purpose.

1. Means of Knowing, *pramāṇa* in Indian Epistemology

The mechanism of knowing involves a knower (*pramāta*), means of knowing (*pramāṇa*) and object of knowledge (*pramēya*) that give rise to valid knowledge (*pramā*). The means of knowledge generally considered are perception (*pratyakṣa*), inference (*anumāna*), comparison (*upamāna*), postulation (*arthāpatti*), non-apprehension (*anupalabdhi*) and testimony (*śabda*). A *pramāṇa* is defined as that which gives rise to the knowledge of an entity which is hitherto unknown or concealed by *avidya* and which is not sublated (not changed) subsequently. The arguments for and against one or other sources of knowing, have complexity in rejecting or defending as similar or distinct from perception and inference.[1] Most of the arguments for testimony rely on authority of trustworthy person who is sure of his/her knowledge by perception and/or inference. The testimony is considered special not merely for certain traditions who defend it for goals of their system but for defending the trustworthiness of the predecessors of their system.

The *pramāṇa-śāstra*, theory of knowing in different schools of philosophy in Indian tradition discusses various epistemological issues concerning truth and defend their position in accordance with their own metaphysical commitment. Each of the system (*darśana*), be it realist, idealist, dualist, monist, absolutist, theist or materialist, has its own justified position on knowledge and has a confrontation of positions held by other systems. Taking a position on particular theory of justification and attacking the theories of other schools, enables each

---

1 However, the theories about *pramāṇa,* are primarily centred on widely accepted knowledge-generating processes, *pratyakṣa*, *anumāna* and *śabda*. All other conceived processes are said to be reducible to one or more of the above. Even in this, school of Carvāka would contest that perception alone is trustworthy and other means of knowledge are based on it. Certain schools consider only perception and inference as basic sources.

school to defend their perspective of truth.[2] The variety of perspectives has thus been born in Indian subcontinent, presenting a richness of epistemological assumptions and attitudes, however focusing on the question of justification for each one's take on their metaphysical position and epistemological stand. Scepticism on each means of knowledge emerges from the opposition that the views expressed by certain schools are not compatible for absolute certainty of arriving at truth. Each school in a moment of non-defensiveness of its views on certain means of knowledge, tries to compromise on its tenets either with finding fault with the criticism of others or passing on to get support from other sources of knowledge which its tradition holds.[3] Hence, scrutiny of each means of knowledge becomes evident in Indian epistemology.

2. Scrutiny of Principal *Pramāṇas*

All schools accept perception, *pratyakṣa* as a means of knowledge with slight disagreement about its nature, objects, limits, etc. Perception is largely recognized as a basic knowledge source on which all other sources such as inference and testimony, etc., have their derivation. The pragmatic standard viewpoint on the importance of perception is that no other generalization that outstrips experience is possible in the process of knowledge.[4] In inference the *hetu,* the veritable reason which becomes the proof for having a new knowledge through reasoning, is also obtained in most cases by prior experience by perception. However, the knowledge derived from the observation with the naked eyes, makes a very famous dictum 'seeing is believing' and evidently is limited and not reliable always. Some try to articulate the types of perceptions as internal and external to contain this limit. There are also issues about the media of perception, internal conditions along with sensory modalities. Right perception, avoidance of illusory perception and given the inherent limitation of sensory means, gives right knowledge.[5]

Differentiating veritable perception from illusory or pseudo-perception is also an engaging issue in all the schools.[6] Perception as 'concept-free' or 'concept-laden,' is a foundational question for Yogācāra, Mīmāṃsā and Nyāya

---

2 Govardhan P. Bhatt, *The Basic Ways of Knowing*, 2nd ed. (Delhi: Motilal Banarsidass, 1989), 27-30.

3 Solomon Ester, *Indian Dialectics* (Ahmedabad: Gujarat Vidya Sabha, 1976), 26.

4 Sibajiban Bhattacharyya, *Doubt, Belief and Knowledge* (New Delhi: Indian Council of Philosophical Research,1987), 7-10.

5 Tatacharya, *Epistemology of Perception* (New York: American Institute for Buddhist Studies, 2004), 1-4.

6 Srinivasa Rao, *Perceptual Error: The Indian Theories* (Honolulu: University of Hawai'i Press, 1998), 5.

who engage deeply in that subject.[7] For Nyāya, perception in its epistemological role is concept-laden, and as a means of knowledge it helps generating belief. Beliefs are dependent on perceived objects imprinted in the mind as concepts.[8] Concept-free perception is the classical Indian realist rendering of our ability to form perceptual concepts by attending to perception's phenomenological side. Epistemologically, it plays no role, since it is itself a posit and is unverbalizable and not directly apperceived.[9] The different views of the objects of perception feed different views of inference.

Inference, *anumāna* through which one comes to know things that are not immediately evident through senses, has a universal accord as a valid knowledge source through reasoning. The common-sense inference is always accepted in everyday life, whose basis lies in the *hetu,* reasoning relating the two apparently presented facts, like hill has smoke and it must have fire. The invariable concomitance, *vyāpti* - between the fire and the smoke, is said to be established by previous knowledge through perception. Certain schools of Buddhist and Vedic schools are concerned about a valid but unsound argument which might be false and no valid knowledge might arise, even though the mediation of facts, *hetu,* could have been applied. They relate the process of knowing through the mediation of other facts. Surely for inference, mediation, the connector, *liṅga* is essential for objects beyond the range of the senses or that which cannot be directly perceived either spatially or temporally.[10]

Epistemological concerns of Indian logicians regarding *anumāna,* are on common-sense inference, establishment of their doctrines and their justification.[11] For a valid inference, Dingnāga makes a systematization of necessity of the proposed knowledge, *pakṣa* (fire on the mountain), the relator

---

7 B.K. Matilal, *Perception: An Essay on Classical Indian Theories of Knowledge* (Oxford: Oxford University Press, 1986), 321-322.

8 That is to say, according to Nyāya, that a certain knowledge as certitude turned into a strong belief, is in need of perceptual cognitions and their verbalizations. For example, to believe that there is a pot on the floor, one must possess the concepts of "pot" and "floor". Refer, Stephen H. Phillips, "There's Nothing Wrong with Raw Perception," *Philosophy East and West*, 51 (2001), 104–113.

9 Arindamm Chakrabarti, "Against Immaculate Perception: Seven Reasons for Eliminating *nirvikalpaka* Perception from Nyāya," in *Philosophy East and West*, 50 (2000), 1-8.

10 Jonardon Ganeri, *Philosophy in Classical India: The Proper Work of Reason* (London: Routledge, 2001), 68-70. Along with the logical precision, the psychological process is taken seriously by Indian logicians, especially by Dignāga and Dharmakīrti, in Yogācāra school of Buddhism.

11 Claus Oetke, "The Role of the Example in Ancient Indian Logic," In *The Role of the Example (dṛṣṭānta) in Classical Indian Logic*, Shoryu Katsura and Ernst Steinkellner, eds. (Vienna: Arbeitskreis für Tibetische und Buddhistische Studien Universität Wien, 2004), 178.

(*hetu*, smoke), and the property to be proved (*sādhya*, fire). Everyday reasoning applies informal relationships, for instance as Vātsyāyana gives an example of a flooded river with a rain upstream.[12] The invariable concomitance, *vyāpti*, connects all three terms to bring to a conclusion of a proposed inference. Although logical reasoning is best applied in inferential process it is not exempt from validation. For, wrong relating, as Uddyotakara calls it as *vyāpti-smaraṇa,* relationship of pervasion, could turn out to be a false cognition as generalization from opposite might present a counter-inference and an erroneously drawn conclusion.[13]

While most schools accept testimony, *śabda* as a valid source of knowledge, Cārvāka, Vaiśeṣika and Buddhism question testimony as an independent means of knowing. Buddhism basses its traditional teachings as founded on reasoning and personal experience, like *nirvāṇa.* Certitude of testimony depends on the knowledge of the testifier, whose source should be other than *śabda.* The speaker or the testifier has to be trustworthy and he/she should have received that knowledge through other certified means of knowledge apart from testimony, such as inference or perception. "Testimony is the statement of an *āpta*."[14] The process of testimonial knowledge begins with independent means such as perception or inference and it is communicated by the knower, *āpta* to a hearer with each one having a competence in language being expressed and understood. For defending the Vedas as *apauruṣēya,* not spoken by humans, Mīmāṃsakas, Vedāntins and some Nyaiyikas speak of someone, God, *īśvara* or author of the Veda, as having an intention of communicating and human ability to understand it.

The intention of the speaker, *tātparya,* is taken up for debate among the schools, especially of Prābhākara school of Mīmāmsā and that of Nyāya. While the former denies the relevance of the intention of the speaker, *tātparya,* the latter champions it as epistemically relevant. Although it is considered not as the trigger for testimonial knowledge, by the later thinkers of Indian epistemology, the speaker's intention has been regarded as necessary for

12 *Nyāya-sūtra* 1.1.5. Gautama, *Nyāya-sūtra,* (with commentaries by Vātsyāyana, Uddyotakara, and Vācaspati Miśra). *Nyāyadarśanam*, ed. A.M. Tarkatirtha, Taranatha Nyayatarkatirtha, and H.K. Tarkatirtha. New Delhi: Munshiram Manoharlal, 1985.

13 Jonardon Ganeri, *Logic in India: A Reader* (Richmond, Surrey: Curzon, 2001), 108-111. Later Nyāyaikas speak of *anvaya-vyatireka,* inferences based on positive and negative correlations like smoke-fire, as in kitchen applied either to mountain with smoke or to a lake having a smoke like.

14 *Nyāya-sūtra* 1.1.7. In Nyāya tradition, Gautama provides a definition of an *āpta* as a trustworthy authority with a moral dimension. An *āpta* is a person who not only knows the truth but who wants to communicate it without deception. Further Vātsyāyana brings out the egalitarian view of testimony that an *āpta* could be even from a non-Vedic authority whose accounts are testimonial with above moral dimension of verily knowing the truth and wanting to communicate without deception.

certitude of testimonial knowledge. For instance, if a parrot or a liar who has given the statement, none would consider it as valid knowledge.[15] To check the facticity of testimony discerning of *tātparya,* along with the *āptatvam,* trustworthiness of the speaker, becomes necessary.[16] Further, in comprehending the meaningfulness of a given statement, three other conditions are considered, such as expectancy (*ākāṅkṣā*), fittingness (*yogyatā*) and proper articulation (*āsatti*). needed.[17] While speaking of the connection of things mentioned, there is a reference made, *abhidhā* in the statement given as a whole, in the process of testimony. The relatedness, *anvaya,* is indicated for the references made of words and the connectedness with the world experienced.[18]

3. Analysing other *Pramāṇas*

While Nyāya, Mīmāṃsā and Vedānta schools accept *upamāna*, comparison, analogy and similarity, as a *pramāṇa,* others reject it. The exegetics and hermeneutics for Vedic injunctions, compel Mīmāṃsā and Vedānta to interpret *upamāṇa* as suitable *pramāṇa.*[19] But for Nyāya it figures in inference through cognizing similarity and dissimilarity, *sapakṣa* which as the set of positive correlations helps in arriving at knowledge. (*Nyāya-sūtra* 1.1.8) By defending it as a separate *pramāṇa,* Nyāya argues that the *sāmānyataḥ,* general similarities between the cow and *gavaya* is true, but one cannot presuppose it to be applicable to all aspects of it as *samyōga,* co-relationality between the two always. In such case, *upamāna* cannot be reduced to Inference. Gaṅgeśa's main argument there is that similarity is not uniform, and there are also obvious differences between cow and *gavaya* whose knowledge is arrived at, in this case by comparison.[20]

Postulation, *arthāpatti* has been accepted as an independent *pramāṇa,* by Mīmāṃsā and Vedānta philosophers, which is rejected by others. Nyāya reduces it as a kind of reasoning as 'negative-only' inference by correlating negative elements of Devadatta not been observed as eating at night and none

---

15 Stephen Phillips, "Epistemology in Classical Indian Philosophy," in https://plato.stanford.edu/entries/epistemology-india/, accessed on 12-3-2019. Most of the sections on *pramāṇas* and validation of knowledge are adapted from here along with the cited indirect sources.

16 Gaṅgeśa, *Tattva-cintā-maṇi*, Tr. S. Phillips & V.P. Bhatta (Delhi: Eastern Book Linkers, 2005), 329. However, while knowing the speaker's intention, *tātparya,* is not a primary element in testimony, it helps fix the meaning of the statement given.

17 K. Kunjunni Raja, *Indian Theories of Meaning*, 2nd ed. (Madras: Adyar, 1969), 149-169.

18 Annambhaṭṭa, *Tarka-saṃgraha*, Tr. Gopinath Bhattacharya (Calcutta: Progressive Publishers, 1976), 301-302.

19 Shiv Kumar, *Upamāna in Indian Philosophy*, Delhi: Eastern Book Linkers, 1980), 110.

20 Refer, Gaṅgeśa, *Tattva-cintā-maṇi,* Tr. S. Phillips & V.P. Bhatta. 2 vols. Delhi: Eastern Book Linkers, 2005.

growing fat without eating.[21] *Anupalabdhi,* non-cognition, is accepted only by Vedānta and Bhātta school of Mīmāṃsā, as that of knowing the absences of the objects. All other schools reject it as an independent means of knowledge.[22] Scrutiny and analysis of *pramāṇas* ensures right knowledge.

4. Validity of Knowledge

Knowledge has its initial credibility as its cognition is practically verifiable in immediate circumstances. Claiming of knowledge beyond the scope of immediate verification is contested and defended by different schools. Buddhist Yogācāra as well as Mīmāṃsā and Vedānta view knowledge as inherently known to be true. Prābhākara school of Mīmāṃsā considers knowledge itself as self-evidential. Every cognition has its purpose of being truthful, certified and right. Bhātta furthers this line of thought in saying that the evidence of knowledge can be found even within the process of knowledge in which it produces a feature in the object that it cognizes, 'knowability' or 'cognizedness.' Apprehending this feature in the object during the process of knowing one really 'knows' the object. Certitude is therefore claimed to be intrinsic to a cognition that is being known during the process of knowing an object.[23] Only for the knowledge of non-verifiable objects, an extrinsic certification is needed. Nyāya uses external validation, *parataḥ prāmāṇya,* for cognition. To know that one knows, requires apperception, *anuvyavasāya* which enables one to judge the projected cognition as true or false. As a result of this requirement, one cannot certify one's claim to be knowledge without verifying it.[24]

In short, concern for Indian epistemologists is to ascertain that while calling for the validation of cognition, the result of a certain process or means, one needs to check and verify the very means. None of the process of knowledge is taken for granted without scrutiny. Certification of proper conditions in a process of knowledge is very much needed as it is the source identification and validation, without which the success or failure of the cognizing activity cannot

21 The famous example of 'Devadatta eats at night for becoming fat,' is postulated by *arthāpatti*, as he is fasting during the day and becomes fat which is known by perception and/or testimony. That his growing fat does not correspond to fasting during the day, assures that it cannot be known by inference. So it is argued by Mīmāṃsā and Vedānta as having a separate *pramāṇa*. But for Nyāya, it can be by indirect inference that so long as Devadatta has not been observed to eat at night and also there is no one else is known to be like him and having been observed to eat only at night, we correlate the negatives and make a conclusion.

22 The Naiyaikas, Gautama and Vātsyāyana explain that absences are known inferentially (*Nyāya-sūtra* 2.2.2). Uddyotakara argue that we know absences sometimes perceptually.

23 Ganganatha Jha, *The Prābhākara School of Pūrva Mīmāṃsā*, reprint (Delhi: Motilal Banarsidass, 1978), 145-146.

24 Vātsyāyana, *Nyāya-sūtra* 2.1.20, 448-449.

be ascertained. Assuming that our cognition is veridical without checking the process of cognition would lead to undesired results and sometimes faulted knowledge. Not only for the everyday knowledge of physical and material world of living, even for the practical pursuits such as supreme goals of life,[25] the checks and verifications of process of knowledge becomes essential.

5. Purpose of Knowledge

Central to our study is the purport, *tātparyā,* the end of knowledge.[26] Knowledge which is cognition produced in the right fashion becomes moments of consciousness and forms dispositions and true beliefs. There are different theories of truth, but everyone sees knowledge as not only indicating the truth but arising from it.[27] Knowledge as means of liberation or knowledge is liberation. Prabhākara identifies *pramāṇa* with *prama* or valid knowledge and regards cognition as manifesting itself but not inferable from cognizedness of its object. For him, *pramāṇa* is same as *prama*. The means of knowledge and the truth they bring forth have un ultimate goal of liberation. The goal of perception as liberation, *nirvāṇa,* is best described in Yogācāra whose claim depends more fundamentally from a commitment to the possibility of a *nirvāṇa* experience. For them perceiving as it is, makes one 'awakened,' *Buddha*. Even though the schools such as Mīmāṃsā, Vedānta, Nyāya, Vaiśeṣika, Sāṃkhya, Yoga do distinguish knowledge as result and knowledge-producing process, Yogācāra claim that there is no difference between source and result, process of knowledge and effect, *pramāṇa* and *pramā*.[28] In Advaitic perspective knowing self is liberation. Self-knowledge is liberation.

The differences in goals of life as liberation are merely terminological, expressed as *mokṣa,* heaven, individual dissolution into the Absolute Brahman, blissful yogic isolation, *kaivalya,* enjoyment of God's presence or *nirvāṇa,* becoming a Buddhist *Bodhi-sattva* or a Jaina *arhat.* A common conceptions linking liberation and knowledge, even though there is a theorization of their relationship and a drawn distinction between everyday knowledge and spiritual

25 The four highest ends of human life, which is called as *puruṣārthās – artha, kāma, dharma, mokṣa* – pursuit of wealth, seeking pleasure, acting with righteousness and attaining liberation, all proceed through comprehensions of subtle objectives in human life that could go beyond the scope of one *pramāṇa,* like perception.

26 New Nyāya philosophers ascertain the meaning of a sentence, if it meets only the three conditions of grammaticality, semantic fittingness, and proper pronunciation. They take into account the overall context, "speaker's intention," *tātparya,* along with mutual "expectancy," *ākāṅkṣā,* semantic "fittingness," *yogyatā,* contiguity, or proper presentation, pronunciation, *āsatti* of the sentence.

27 Jitendra Nath Mohanty, *Gaṅgeśa's Theory of Truth,* Reprint (Delhi: Motilal Banarsidass, 2006), 69-71.

28 Stephen H. Phillips, *Epistemology in Classical India: The Knowledge Sources of the Nyaya School* (New York: Routledge, 2012), 10.

knowledge. Thinking about the world is an obstacle to spiritual enlightenment, but a proper understanding of the world helps one disengage and to know the self as separate from things and so is an aid to transcendence. Epistemic knowledge helps achieve the real goal of life, truly greatest end of world-transcendence.

6. Self-awareness in Mīmāmsa tradition

One of the philosophic problems for epistemology has to do with an alleged regress of justification on the assumption that a *pramāṇa* is required in order to know. Is the *pramāṇa* needed for a *pramāṇa*? An assumption that a *pramāṇa* is required in order to know, as for Nāgārjuna in the tradition of *sunyavāda,* leads to a problem of regression. Nāgārjuna claims that this is absurd in that it would require an infinite series of *pramāṇa*, of identification of a more fundamental *pramāṇa* for every *pramāṇa* relied on.[29] Mīmāṃsā and Vedānta philosophers argue that knowledge is self-certifying, *svataḥ prāmāṇya.* Vedāntins hold that the self (*ātman*) has 'self-illumining awareness' (*sva-prakāśa*). Mīmāṃsā epistemology asserts that *vidyā,* awareness is self-aware. Awareness itself has access to itself, its existence or its nature. Problem of knowledge as self-aware is taken up as an important issue for connecting the purpose of knowing and liberation.

According to Mīmāmsikas, 'consciousness' is not the essential attribute of the self. Rather, it is considered as an adventitious quality that emerges in particular situations. For example, while in deep sleep, consciousness is not found in the self. This is so because in this stage there will be no contact between sense organs with objects. For Kumarila there is no knowledge of self as we have the knowledge of external objects like, tree, grass, bird, etc. Self is the object of self-consciousness. When we concentrate on self we realize 'I exist'. Refuting this view Prabhākara expresses that the self cannot be the subject and object of the same knowledge. This is so because one thing cannot be both the 'doer' and the 'deed' at the same time, and in addition to that the function of the doer and the deed are opposite/contrast to each other. Thus, on the account of Prabhākara, an objective knowledge constitutes of three constituents; the knower, the known, and the knowledge. All these three constituents are known simultaneously for acquiring the knowledge of an object.[30] For Mīmāmsikas, liberation is not a state of bliss, rather a state where the self realizes its real nature and dissociated from worldly pleasure and pain. There are attachments with worldly objects which causes suffering and pain. To detract from them, Mīmāmsikas state that liberation can be attained

29 Refer, Nāgārjuna, *Vigraha-vyāvartinī,* Tr. Kamaleshwar Bhattacharya, *The Dialectical Method of Nāgārjuna*. Delhi: Motilal Banarsidass, 1978.

30 Stephen H. Phillips, *Epistemology in Classical India,* 98.

only when the self gets emancipation from the bondages of mind, body, sense organs and objects of the world. Knowledge of the objects helps in liberation. Self-awareness is liberation.

7. Advaitic Notion of Self-knowledge

Among the six *pramāṇas* accepted in Vedānta, *śabdapramāna* is hailed as high and that gives us a notion that purport of knowledge is liberation. According to Advaita, *śabda* alone is considered to be a *pramāṇa* which gives rise to Brahman-knowledge and all other *pramāṇa* deal with the material world. The other means of knowledge cannot reveal Brahman since Brahman is not an object of knowledge. Brahman cannot be known by inference because of absence of *hētu* to determine Brahman. Brahman cannot be known through comparison since there does not exist a similar second thing like Brahman. In postulation, we presume something present elsewhere; there cannot be anything else to arrive at Brahman by postulation. By non-apprehension, *anupalabdhi,* non-existence of a thing is known and Brahman being ever existent (*sat*) it is never available for non-apprehension.[31]

Further, according to Advaita, the knowledge of self or Brahman cannot be gained by perceptual cognition since Brahman can never be objectified. Since Brahman is self-evident luminous being, hence the knowledge of Brahman is known as *svarūpa-jñāna* or knowledge of nature of self as opposed to *vṛtti-jñāna* or empirical knowledge. An object perceived differently is said to be invalid cognition as in the case of rope-snake. The analysis of the process of erroneous cognition is known as 'indescribable error' (*anirvacanīya khyāti*). Bondage is an error superimposed on Brahman due to self-ignorance and hence knowledge alone is the means to liberation. Based on the indescribable theory of error, the rope-ignorance creates a 'snake' here ignorance is the material cause of 'snake'. The rope is the substratum on which 'snake' is superimposed and hence rope is the transfigurative material cause of 'snake'. The perceiver of 'snake' superimposes the characteristics of snake is frightened and tries to run away. On rise of rope-knowledge, the 'snake' vanishes and the person 'feels' saved. In this instance, there is no sorrow but still one experiences grief because of lack of knowledge of reality (rope-knowledge).[32] Advaitin states, in the same manner, the world of plurality is superimposed on non-dual Brahman due to ignorance, plurality is cause of sorrow, on wake of Brahman-knowledge plurality vanishes (just as the 'snake' vanished) and one realizes the non-dual nature of self and 'attains' bliss.

---

31 Refer, Joerg Tuske, ed., *Indian Epistemology and Metaphysics*, London: Bloomsbury Academic, 2017.

32 Srinivasa Rao, *Perceptual Error: The Indian Theories* (Honolulu: University of Hawai'i Press, 1998), 76-81.

The verbal testimony is defined as that 'sentence in which the relation among the meaning of words, that is the object of its intention, is not contradicted by any other means of valid knowledge'. According to Advaita, the purport of the scriptures is attributeless Brahman (*nirguṇa Brahman*) which is known by scrutinizing the intention of scriptures based on six indicatory marks, they are, introduction-conclusion (*upakrama-upasamhāra*), repetition (*abhyasa*), uniqueness (*apūrvata*), result (*phala*), eulogy (*arthavāda*) and logical presentation (*upapatti*).[33] A word can reveal its meaning in the primary sense and in cases where primary sense is unfitting, they are known by their secondary sense. Deriving the meaning of a word through its secondary implication is of three kinds, namely, exclusive (*jahallakṣana*), Inclusive (*ajahallakṣana*) and exclusive-inclusive (*jahalajahallakṣana*).[34] The identity statements (*mahāvākya*), according to Advaita, reveals the identity meaning by the application of exclusive-inclusive implication.

Due to self-ignorance, the nature of self and not-self is mixed up that result in bondage. The nature of self is eternal, immortal, pure, unlimited, blissful etc. The nature of not-self is non-eternal, mortal, impure, limited, sorrowful etc. The nature of not-self is falsely transferred to the self and also the nature of self, that is, existence (*sat*) and consciousness (*cit*)is falsely transferred to the not-self. This mixture is the cause of bondage, says Śaṅkara, in his introductory commentary to the *Brahmasūtra*.[35]

8. Epistemology for Soteriology

For Advaita, self-knowledge is the liberating solution. On analysis of the metaphysical categories we understand that there are two factors, Consciousness (Brahman) and Matter (*Māya*), of which matter and its products are unreal and consciousness alone is real. One who gains the knowledge that self is non-different from Brahman and the experienced plurality is unreal is free from sorrow. To enter into an enquiry of the nature of self, scriptures prescribe remote means, proximate means and direct means.[36] The identity of individual

33 Anantanand Rambachan, *The Advaita World View: God, World, and Humanity* (Albany: State University of New York Press, 2006), 64; Refer also, *The Upadesasāhasri of Śamkara: A Thousand Teachings,* Tr. Sengaku Mayeda. Tokyo: University Press, 1979.

34 Chakravarthi Ram-Prasad, *Advaita Metaphysics and Epistemology* (London: Routledge Curzon, 2002), 56.

35 Śaṅkara, *The Vedānta-sūtras of Bādarāyana, with the commentary by Śankara,* Tr. Georg Thibaut. New York: Dover Publications, 1970.

36 The remote means to knowledge is action and meditation which enhances the purity of mind. The proximate means are *vivēka* or discrimination between eternal and ephemeral, *vairagya* or dispassion towards worldly benefits, *samādiṣatkasampatti* or six-fold mental disciplines and *mumukṣtva* or intense desire for liberation. The direct means are listening to the scriptures (*śravana*), engaging in removal of doubts (*mananā*) and being established in Brahman by dwelling on the teaching (*nididhyāsanā*).

self and Brahman is revealed through the *mahāvākya* in the Upaniṣads.[37] In analysis of *mahāvākyas,* not merely the primary meaning of the words applied which is limited in intelligence, power and by space, the identity of self and the Brahman is established by secondary implication like *sāmanādhikāranya* (appositional usage), *viseśyaviśeṣana sambandha* (relation of qualified-qualifier), *lakṣyalakṣana sambandha* (relation of indicator-indicated) through which one arrives at the consciousness principle that is non-dual as the true nature of the self. One, who gains the 'identity-knowledge' through the *mahāvākya,* is a *jīvanmukta.*[38]

The continuity in unbroken tradition of certain schools, such as Nyāya, Buddhism and Vedānta have consistent and improvised defence of their epistemological arguments. Surely in the line of traditional opposing others' and defending one's own have given rise to an intellectual engagement of epistemic systems. By learning from opponents' arguments and expanding one's own thinkers in every system engaged themselves with other schools of thought. While defending the validity of a given means of knowledge Indian thinkers have in mind of accomplishing the certitude leading to Truth and thus it has been the question of the usefulness of knowledge which would in-turn serve not only for the purposefulness in daily life but also for the desired ultimate goal of liberation, *mōkṣa, kaivalya, mukti, nirvāna*, etc. Such centrality of liberation is posited even though the articulation of it has been different in every school. The paper attempts to explore into the nature of Indian epistemology with its processes and purpose and tends to focus on the liberation as its ultimate aim of knowing.

Concluding Remarks

The most striking feature of all epistemological discourse of Indian systems is that knowledge leads to liberation. More than the question of what is there and how to arrive at truth, the focus is on the choice of correct instruments of knowledge, *pramāṇa* and their validity. Indian epistemology delves deeper into picking up the effective means of knowledge, *pramāṇa,* and puts its under strict scrutiny of its efficacy in arriving at the truth. Arguments for and against each means of knowledge, accepted as *pramāṇa* in each school of thought bear witness to the careful analysis of epistemological tools. The seriousness is evident in debating on correctness of each one's choice of *pramāṇa,* defending and correcting their way of thinking down the centuries in every school of thought. For, once right tools of knowing are at hand one not only have a glimpse of metaphysical truth but achieves liberation from the bondage of

37 Among many *mahavakyas* traditionally four *mahavakyas* are enumerated, *Prajñānam brahma* – knowledge of brahman, *aham brahmāsmi* – brahman within, *tattvamasi* – you are that, *ayamatma brahma* – self as the Brahman.

38 Arvind Sharma, *Advaita Vedānta* (Delhi: Motilal Banarsidass, 2004), 45.

untruth. The vision of truth, *darṣanā,* brings forth or even equals liberation, *mōkṣa.* In evaluating the validity of knowledge we come across the study of the purport of knowing as liberation, though called by different names. The purpose of means of knowledge, *pramāṇa,* it seems to us in this study, is liberation. *Pramāṇa-tātparyam mokṣam.* The perspective of self-awareness as liberation has a soteriological epistemology in Indian tradition.

3

Inductive Reasoning: Its Inevitability and Implications for Natural Sciences and Human Lives

Stephen S. Jayard

Abstract

The debates over the validity of inductive reasoning don't seem to be settled in the near future, if not for ever. All efforts to find a solution have so far met with little success. Hume's scathing attack on the unjustfiability of inductive reasoning is an embarrassing shock to the world of science, because science is built on induction. This also unseats the popular image of science that sees science as something qualitatively different from, superior to and ideal for any knowledge enterprise. Many proposals have been made in order to save the rational face of science, either by providing some sort of rational basis for inductive reasoning or by devising alternative scientific methods. But unfortunately all such attempts have been proved inadequate. The necessary reliance on inductive reasoning, which unfortunately lacks the deductive certainty, which is usually associated with science, seems to teach some basic lessons, not only for science, but also for human life. In this short essay I intend to discuss: i) The venerable tradition of inductive reasoning, ii) The inadequacy of the various attempts to solve or dissolve the problem of inductive reasoning, iii) Its inevitability though it is unjustified, and iv) Its implications for science and life.

Key words: Inductive reasoning and difficulties; limits and limitations in science; uncertainty; science knowledge as best, not as perfect; incomprehensibility of reality and unattainability of 'truth'.

1. The Venerable Tradition of Inductive Reasoning

Aristotle was convinced of rationality of humans. In his *Prior Analytics* and *Posterior Analytics* he used both the inductive and deductive reasoning for scientific inquiry. There are proofs in the recorded history[1] to show that humans used inductive reasoning, much before Aristotle. Science, even at the era of Pre-Socratic Ionians had two major principles of 'comprehensibility' and 'objectivation'. The former, as opposed to superstitions, animistic or magical outlook towards the world, assumes that all the happenings in the world can be understood in rational terms, while the latter demands that to rationally understand anything one must at least temporarily stand apart from it and treat it as something real out there.[2] This comprehensibility in rational terms involves inductive reasoning as well. In the modern times Francis Bacon, in his *Novum Organum*, emphatically proposed that the chief method of scientific inquiry is induction. As *facts* cannot be collected from nature, but have to be constructed by some methods and that method is the method of induction. He despised induction by simple enumeration and insisted on negative occurrences in the process of knowledge acquiring.[3]

The *Principle of Induction* can be stated as follows: If a large number of *A*s has been observed under various conditions, and if all those observed *A*s with no exception possessed the property *B*, then one conclude that all *A*s have the property *B*. Of course this principle puts forward at least three essential

1 For instance, an event narrated in the Bible (book of Judges, Chapter 6, Verses 36-40) can be cited, where the method of agreement and difference of inductive reasoning is used. It was written around the 12th -11th century B.C. God chooses one Gideon to liberate the Israelites form the tyranny of the Midianites. He asks God for a proof that he will be able to deliver them. He keeps a fleece of wool out in the open ground during the night and asks God that only that fleece to be wet with dew while the ground around to be very dry. Next morning he finds exactly as he has asked. Next day, he asks God that the fleece to be dry and the ground around to be very wet and the following morning he finds exactly that way. From these miraculous events he inferred that God will deliver the Israelites through him. [See: Werner Schmidt, 1992, p. 11].

2 William T. Scott, "On Polanyi's Notion of Rationality," in J. Misiek, 1995, pp. 205-214.

3 Bacon, 1859, p. 25; as quoted by J. R. Milton, 1987, p. 58. But Bacon's own methods of exclusion and assumption presuppose a great deal of metaphysics. He assumed one-to-one relation between the nature of phenomenon and its nature of causes. He unconsciously assumed that the number of different forms to be found in nature is manageably finite. Without these assumptions he would face the same criticisms that he raises against the simple enumeration.

conditions to avoid naivety[4]: i) The Number of observation statements forming the basis of a generalization must be large; ii) The observation must be repeated under a wide variety of conditions and iii) No accepted observation statement should conflict with the derived universal law. Russell elaborates further: "The greater the number of cases in which a thing of the sort A has been found associated with a thing of the sort B, the more probable it is (if no cases of failure of association are known) that A is always associated with B; and under the same circumstances, a sufficient number of cases of the association of A with B will make it nearly certain that A is always associated with B, and will make this general law approach certainty without limit".[5]

Inductive reasoning has a longstanding, and successful history. It makes science what it is, as it gives the explanatory and predictive power to scientific inquiries. It is also perfectly acceptable and efficient for our practical needs in our daily lives. Inductive reasoning is so common-sensical that no one doubts it in ordinary circumstances, unless there is a specific reason to do so. Yet philosophers don't seem to be convinced of this. N.R. Hanson sounds rather strong in criticizing them for this. If anyone "remained unconvinced by such [inductive] arguments would either be an idiot or a philosopher, - or both. In either case, he would need therapy".[6] This practical success and the commonsense makes it rational to accept inductive reasoning against the philosophical arguments of the inductive sceptic.[7]

2. The Problematic Nature of Inductive Reasoning

Unfortunately, all is not well with induction; it could not escape attacks, quite severe in fact, from different quarters. It was Hume who woke the world up from its rationalistic slumber, by pointing out the fundamental lacuna in the inductive reasoning. He was the first one to scathe a sever attack on induction and with him the problem of induction became so popular "which might be solved, or dissolved, or by-passed, but which could not legitimately or honestly be ignored".[8] David T. J. Liley[9] lists out several possible major problems with inductive reasoning, like: inductive arguments are not valid logical arguments, as they are ampliative, i.e. going beyond the known experiences; the principle of induction cannot be logically deduced from experience; it shows the ignorance of the role of theory and metaphysical speculation in scientific

4 A.F. Chalmers, 1992, pp. 4-5.

5 Bertrand Russell, 2002, p.37.

6 N. R. Hanson, 1971, p. 239.

7 D. M. Armstrong, 1995, p. 47.

8 J. R. Milton, 1987, p. 49.

9 See: http://marr.bsee.swin.edu.au/~dtl/het704/lecture3/logfals/node5.html. Accessed on 25 Dec, 2018.

progress; theory-dependence of observation is neglected; ascribing non-zero probabilities to individual rather than universal predictions is epistemologically counter-intuitive; scientific progress is viewed as an *ahistorical acultural* process; there is a leap from the known to the unknown domain, as universal conclusions are made.

The notions of 'large number' of instances and 'variety of circumstances', which are used to define inductive reasoning, are unclear. How large that *large* should be? And how are we to decide upon what the *significant* variations are? This choice has to be made on the basis of some prior theory. "But to admit this is to admit that theory plays a vital role *prior* to observation"[10] and this is something highly objectionable to Inductivists! Further, one may give a concession that the conclusion arrived through induction need not be absolutely true but *probably* true. However this too is problematic! For, "... any observation evidence will consist of a finite number of observation statements, whereas a universal statement makes claims about an infinite number of possible situations. The probability of the universal generalization being true is thus a finite number divided by an infinite number, which remains zero however much the finite number of observation statements constituting the evidence is increased".[11] The problem of induction, therefore, is a logical problem. However large the confirming instances may be it cannot logically justify a conclusion which pertains to an infinite domain. From a finite set of individual statements, say $Ca_1 \rightarrow Ma_1$, $Ca_2 \rightarrow Ma_2 \ldots Ca_n \rightarrow Ma_n$, one cannot logically infer universal statement Vx (Cx → Mx).

Most importantly, it is interesting to note that to justify induction itself we need to involve inductive reasoning: 'So far this principle has been successfully working, so it will be always successful'. But the irony is that one can use the same inductive reasoning to show that it does not work by giving many examples where it actually does not work. For instance, merely the vast number of instances does not guarantee the success of the induction. Indurkhya gives many examples to show where induction does not work. For instance, "1 is less than 1000, 2 is less than 1000..., 999 is less than 1000, therefore all numbers are less than 1000... [so] one can inductively infer from them (the examples) that induction is not justified".[12]

3. Mixed Reactions to Inductive Reasoning

There are various reactions towards inductive reasoning. J. Wettersten sees two trends in dealing with induction; one attempts to justify induction and the other, having decided that it cannot be justified, turns to sociology and

10 A.F. Chalmers, 1992, p. 16.

11 *Ibid.*, p.18.

12 Bipin Indurkhya, 1990, p.108.

history of science. Anyway, both trends seem to strongly hold the centrality of induction for science and "if inductivism cannot succeed, then there can be no adequate theory of rationality".[13] As a result one can easily see that if once the problem of induction is solved the whole question of rationality of science is settled.

From Bacon's *Novum Organum*, till Hume's *Treatise on Human Nature* there have been varied reactions to the principle of induction, which includes complete acceptance or complete denial, and different degrees between these two extremes.[14] While Hume saw only regularities of occurrence and not any law like situations, Armstrong and Foster develop an idea of justifying induction, by which "observed regularities are best explained by hypotheses of strong laws, hypotheses which in turn entail conclusions about the unobserved".[15] They propose that laws of nature are governed by not mere regularities but by more "objective natural necessities". They prefer this strong necessity to the 'weak' Humean or mere regularity conception of laws. Amstrong has brought out sixteen criticisms, though all not original, against Humean notion of, what he calls, *naïve* regularity of natural laws. Some propose alternative methods for science, like Hypothetico-Deductive method by C. G. Hempel, or 'Conjecture-refutation-corroboration' method by K. Popper; Popper even claims to have dissolved the problem of inductive reasoning and thus makes the whole problem a non-issue.[16] C. S. Pierce tried for some justification for inductive reasoning in terms of 'abductive reasoning', i.e. from a few seemingly unrelated facts, arriving at a hypothesis with the intuitive power.[17] Such arguments are now identified by a phrase "inference to the best explanation". Hans Reichenbach[18] attempted to defend inductive reasoning with the help of the "Principle of the Common Cause", which was later developed by Wesley Salmon.[19] If p, q, r, ... are found in a series of occurrence, amidst them, there may be either mere conjunction, or there may be a common cause. Since, in many cases it will be more probable to assume a common cause for the events, it is reasonable to

13 John Wettersten, 1994, p. 719.

14 J. R. Milton, 1987, p. 26.

15 D. M. Armstrong, 1995, p. 45. See also: John Foster, 1983.

16 Popper acknowledges the problematic nature of inductive reasoning; he agrees with the Hume's criticism against it. He claims that it does not affect science, because the process of falsification does not involve inductive reasoning and by this he shows that he has dissolved the problem of induction. But due to the limitations of the theory of falsification Popper's claim is challenged. For more details of this analysis, please see my paper: "Is Popper Proper? – Reflections on Popper's Views on Inductive Reasoning in Science", in *Indian Philosophical Quarterly*, Vol. 35, No. 1-4, 2008, pp. 1-16.

17 Justus Buchler, 1940.

18 Hans Reichenbach 1956.

19 Wesley Salmon, 1978, pp. 683-705.

postulate a common cause for them. Some authors, like O' Hear,[20] try to justify it on pragmatic grounds. It may not be rational but it would not be irrational either. Others would rely on the notion of probability to defend induction; they specify factors which would increase the probability, like initial probability, large amount of positive data and conformity to already accepted theories etc. Still others vehemently argue for induction because it has worked well in various cases at various circumstances, and therefore they argue for it. But they don't seem to realize that they 'beg the question' in their argument. Yet others seem to ignore or just tolerate the problem. For instance, Russell seems to advise us that we live with the problem since, any appeal to experience can neither prove nor disprove inductive reasoning.[21]

Bayesian theorem, proposed by Thomas Bayes[22], is an attempt to supply rational basis for inductive reasoning in science. The degree of certainty of the conclusion of an experiment is measured by the probability of the conclusion. In simple words, the relationship between the empirical data (evidence) and the hypothesis is crucial, because it helps in accepting or rejecting a hypothesis. A piece of evidence can be confirming or undermining or neutral to the hypothesis under the test: Say, h – hypothesis; e – evidence, $P(h)$ – the prior probability, and $P(h|e)$ – the posterior probability; e confirms h, if $P(h|e) > P(h)$; and e disconfirms h, if $P(h|e) < P(h)$; i.e. if the posterior probability is more the evidence confirms the hypothesis and vice versa. When the confirmation is at maximum, $P(e|h) = 1$ and then h logically entails e. When the disconfirmation is at maximum, $P(e|h) = 0$ and then h is refuted. No further evidence will confirm it, unless the refuting evidence or part of background knowledge is revoked. Of course this Bayesian reasoning too faces its own difficulties; for instance, Barry Gower points out a basic problem: certainty is partly a psychological concept; people with different psychological characteristics assign different degrees of certainty to the conclusion of a probable argument, even the same person may attribute different degrees of certainty at different times. Therefore, "*There are considerations other than the logical relations* between evidence and conclusions that have an effect upon the degree of certainty a reasonable person will have in the conclusion".[23]

20 Anthony O' Hear, 1989, pp. 43-44.

21 B. Russell, 2002, p. 38.

22 Thomas Bayes (1702-61), an English non-conformist clergyman, a renowned mathematician, a fellow of the Royal Society is the source of the great epoch-making theory of probability. His seminal work on probability was posthumously published in 1763.

23 Barry Gower, p. 91; *italics mine.* For more on this, please see: Colin Howson, 1991, p. 82; Karl Popper and D. Miller, 1984, p. 434.; I. Lakatos, 1978, Vol. 1, p.1

4. Implications of the Insolubility of Inductive Reasoning for Science and Life

a) Total Comprehension of Reality – Ever Elusive!

Objective truth, if any, is never attainable in science but we need to strive towards it. A genuine scientist cannot claim that she possesses irrefutable truth; rather she too has an irresistible search for truth and that thirst for truth is what makes her a scientist. For Popper, it is the process, not the product that is more important in the enterprise of science. The fact that we are not the possessor of truth makes our search for truth more interesting and worthwhile.[24] Humanity can never be complacent to think that it has arrived at the final and sufficient knowledge, as at every stage of history, there is the possibility of being falsified. We can have only corroboration of theories and corroboration validates our preference of one theory over another. Rejecting the orthodox attitude of scientific method, Popper held that knowledge is forever provisional and it is the beauty of science to reveal the unimaginable picture of reality.[25]

That there is no pure observation is almost evident to everyone now. Thereby the very foundational claim of Inductivism is shaken and so too with science, the edifice built upon it! All observations are theory-dependent. Even in very ordinary, commonsensical observational statements too we assume some theories, without which those so-called direct statements will be impossible. So Popper explains, "'Here is a glass of water' cannot be verified by any observational experience. The reason is that the universal terms which occur in their statement ('glass', 'water') are dispositional: they 'denote physical bodies which exhibit a certain *law-like behaviour.*'"[26] As long as sciences try to understand nature conclusiveness always escapes us, as any conclusion inductively arrived may be modified or refuted in future. Nevertheless it need not make us nervous or skeptic towards the whole enterprise of inductive reasoning. As Mellor points out, "... although that (possibility of rejecting the present inductive inferences) always could happen, we can still know that it won't: namely, by inductive inferences that have as much right to 'the complimentary title "reasoning"' as deductive ones, since they have as little chance in fact of going wrong".[27]

b) Need for an Integrated Approach to Knowledge

It seems knowledge cannot be grounded *only in reason* or *only in the senses*. The rationalists and the empiricists of modern age tend to replace one sort of

---

24 Karl Popper, 1974, p. 1029.

25 *Ibid.*, 1959, p. 431.

26 *Ibid.*, 1963, p. 387.

27 D. H. Melor, 1989, p.7.

authority (a sacred text or institution) with another (a human mental capacity). Both kinds of intellectual authoritarianism are not conducive for science. There always seems to be a tension between empiricality and rationality (logic) in science. For, the empirical experience can't give universality, as it is always instantaneous. If we were to rely only on empiricality even our ordinary life would be nigh impossible. We need to transcend our immediate environment, to think about the past and to plan about future for which rationality is very essential. Today science uses lots of probabilistic and statistical theories. Once in a while some drastic failures, like the collapse of space shuttle Challenger II, do take place. By this we cannot undermine science; we undermine only the mythical picture of science. Therefore, today the reasonable position as regards science is that it *gives the best* knowledge possible but *does not give the perfect knowledge*.

We have not been, at least so far, able to overcome the problem of induction, and at the same time inductive reasoning is so essential that we cannot get rid of it either. Highlighting the need for being satisfied with probable certainty of inductive reasoning, Poincare argues that though the Newton's law has been upheld by numerous observations there is an element of chance also; for, there is at least a remote probability that in future it may fail. Due to this essential probabilistic nature of science, "in a multitude of circumstances *the physicist is often in the same position as the gambler who reckons up his chances*. Every time that he reasons by induction, he more or less consciously requires the calculus of probabilities".[28]

An integrated approach to knowledge recognizes inductive reasoning as an integral part of rationality in science. Bipin Indurkhya suggests a distinction between *the cognitive and metaphysical notions of the induction,* where the former can be solved but not the latter. Regarding the cognitive aspect, we need to understand this reasoning fully and try to avoid erroneous conclusion; but "as far as the metaphysical dimension to the problem of justification of induction is concerned, it can no more be justified than we can justify the fact that we have two eyes".[29]

As our eyes are equipped to see the light of only a certain wavelength and our ears to hear the sound of only a certain decibels, our brain has been wired by Nature (God!) that we reason out in an inductive way. For instance, more researches in Chrmotherapy[30] reveal that the principal source of energy for life on this earth is Sunlight. The different colours of this light have different powers. Every physical, mental, emotional and spiritual functions of ours seem to be

28 As quoted in Colin Howson and Peter Urbach, 1993, p. 10; *italics mine*.

29 Bipin Indurkhya, 1990, p.112.

30 Chromotherapy is an alternative therapy, which uses colours to help the body and mind to find again their natural balance, it has been used to facilitate healing since time immemorial.

light-dependent. For instance, blue colour decreases arterial diseases, purifies the blood and hearing problems and affects throat, thyroid and parathyroid glands; and yellow colour treats lung disorders, kidney problems, regulates the menstrual and other hormonal problems and so on.[31] Now one can't ask why a particular colour has only such qualities and not others. It is the way that they are. So too, I think, is the case with inductive reasoning and this fact teaches us that there are issues where we need to be at ease even though our reason is unable to obtain satisfactory explanation or justification.

c) Learning to Live with the Limits of Science

There are not only practical and technological limits in science but also essential and existential limits in science. The basic argument for the limits of science is grounded on the fact science uses many axioms, which are taken for granted by science. It is further shown that "When you use an axiom, then you start on the wrong foot. You cannot prove axioms and if you base everything on them, then you guarantee that your whole theory cannot be ultimately be proved"[32]. Robert Miller[33] argues the very concept of conscious mind lies beyond the realm of the physical description. He shows it in four steps: i) A physical system cannot observe itself; ii) Physics is not possible without making observations (or an observer); iii) Any observation essentially requires a conscious mind; and iv) Thus, it is not possible to decipher the working of the conscious mind in purely physical terms.

John Barrow[34] has done an extensive exploration into the limits of science, starting from practical limits to cosmological limits. While the former includes cost, technology, mathematical computability and the extreme complexity of the universe, the latter involves the restrictions in learning about the origins, end, nature and structure of the universe. The very position of ours in the universe, the evolutionary growth of our brain that we have achieved over millions of years lay their own restrictions. Our brain, obviously, did not evolve having science in mind. There is no way to go outside of the universe to observer and all that we learn about it has to be done from within. There is no God's point of view to see the universe as it is. (Baby fish while swimming in the ocean asked the mother fish, "what is the ocean?" – the mother fish replied, "This is the ocean, you are swimming in it", to which the baby fish replied, "Don't tell me a lie. This is only water, where is the ocean?").

---

31 For Details See: *Health Screen*, 2005.

32 See: http://knol.google.com/k/the-limits-of-science#III(2E)_Limitations_of_exact_science. Accessed on 11 February, 2019.

33 R. C. Miller, *Space, Time and Quanta*, New York: W. H. Freeman and Co., 1994.

34 John D. Barrow, *Impossibility – The Limits of Science and the Science of Limits*, London: The Random House Group Ltd, 1999.

The most fundamental limit in the cosmos is that the universe became visible only when photons were emitted from it; that happened only after 300, 000 years after the big bang expansion. Till then the universe was opaque and even light did not come out of it. To study the universe before that we need to study the neutrinos, if at all it is possible. Even then we can go back to the time of one second after the expansion. That time the universe was ten billion times smaller than what we observe now. At the most we can go back, if technology allows it, and see when the universe was 10^{32} times smaller than what it is now.

Emil Du Bois-Reymond[35] points out that the 'riddles of the material world' might be solved in future, but the 'transcendent riddles' (like the mind-body relationship!) will never be solved. Hempel further points out that ***"why is there anything at all and not rather nothing?"*** - no science or for that matter any other discipline can answer this question, because any answer or explanation would always be in terms of something that is already existing. Even to answer in terms of primary cause or uncaused cause presupposes the agency of that cause. Therefore to expect science to answer this question is a logically inconsistent requirement, as "no theory, no conceptual scheme, can explain the existence of anything without assuming the existence of something"[36]. That is why, Hempel is convinced of the notion of 'incompleteness of explanation', i.e., no explanation is ever complete; because we explain something only in terms of something else, which is already known or much simpler; but if we go on explaining this way, we cannot go ad infinitum; we need to stop at some brute facts.[37]

Conclusion

The insolubility of inductive reasoning need not bother us. For, as G. E. Moore[38] speaks about some commonsense beliefs, which are so certain that they don't need any reasons to assert them; Armstrong goes further to include these beliefs in, what he calls 'folk theories'; it would be even irrational to give any reason to believe them.[39] He invites us to trust that the principles of reasoning are the same both in the observed and unobserved domains. The inductive reasoning is so indispensable part of our beliefs that we cannot give it up. Inductive reasoning, therefore, seems to be *a species by itself.* As Rudolf

35 Emil Du Bois-Reymond, 1912, pp.441-473. As elaborated by Hempel, 2001c, in Fetzer, 2001, p. 338.

36 Hempel, 2001c, in Fetzer, 2001, p. 341.

37 More on this, please see: C. G. Hempel, " Science Unlimited?", in *The Philosophy of Carl G. Hempel – Studies in Science, Explanation and Rationality*, ed. by James H. Fetzer, Oxford: Oxford University Press, 2001,

38 G. E. Moore, 1925.

39 Armstrong, p. 46.

Carnap too reasons out that inductive reasoning may result in a conclusion which may turn out to be false, but it does not imply that the inductive procedures are incorrect.[40] Given the nature of the world, where causality, stability and uniformity are present, it is not a mere chance or coincidence that things occur but the going together is necessitated by the very nature and capacities of things, and we have a reason for having assurance in inductive inference. Of course, this kind of pragmatic justification may not satisfy Hume, as his challenge was "about the ability of induction to give true and certain knowledge, not about its utility".[41] Induction may be seen as a part of our neural wiring. No logical or deductive evidence is needed to support its working. *So science can still be rational (or reasonable?[42]) in spite of its reliance on induction.*

Induction, therefore, in my opinion, can't be lamented as 'a thorn in the flesh', nor ignored as signifying nothing. Here it is clear that it is the community that has decided to give the definite validity to the inductive reasoning. Recognition of such non-epistemic values in science makes science fundamentally social, but not weak or irrational. Science is still the best enterprise in revealing nature to humanity. While admiring science humanity needs to be aware not to be carried away by the spirit of scientism, but to realize, as Newton did, that *we just play with a pebble or two on the seashore while the vast ocean of reality lies in front of us unexplored.* This realization will, no doubt, do a great deal of good not only to science but to human society as well!

Bibliography

Armstrong, D. M., "What Makes Induction Rational?," in J. Misiek (ed.), 1995, 45-54.

Bacon, Francis, *Magna Instauratio*, Distributio Operis, 1859, Vol. IV.

Barrow, D. John, *Impossibility – The Limits of Science and the Science of Limits*, London: The Random House Group Ltd, 1999.

Bayes, Thomas, "An Essay towards a problem in the doctrine of chances", in *Philosophical Transactions of the Royal Society of London, 1763.*

Buchler, Justus, ed., *The Philosophy of Peirce* (London: Kegan Paul, 1940).

Chalmers, A. F., *What is This Thing Called Science*? (Milton Keynes: Open University Press, 1992), 2nd ed.

Foster, John, "Induction, Explanation and Natural Necessity," in *Proceedings of the Aristotelian Society*, N. S. 83 (1983), 87-101

---

40 Rudolf Carnap, "On Inductive Logic", in Baruch A. Brody, 1970, p. 473.

41 Augustine Perumalil, 2006.

42 I have elsewhere elaborated the need, role and features of the notion of Reasonableness in Science. See: Stephen Jayard, 2010. W.D. Theobald (1968) also accepts inductive reasoning as reasonable.

Gower, Barry, *Scientific Method* (London & NY: Routledge, 1997).

Hanson, N. R., "Good Inductive Reasons" in Stephen Toulmin and Harry, eds., 1971.

Howson, Colin and Peter Urbach, *Scientific Reasoning: The Bayesian Approach* (Illinois: Open Court, 1993), 2nd ed.

Howson, Colin, "The Last Word on Induction," in *Erkenntnis - An International Journal of Analytic Philosophy*, 34 (1991), 73-82.

Indurkhya, Bipin, "Some Remarks on the Rationality of Induction", *Synthese* 85 (1990), 95-114.

Jayard, Stephen, "Reasonableness: The Defining Characteristic of Human Beings", in *Satya Nilayam – Chennai Journal of Intercultural Philosophy*, 17 (2010), 123-145.

Lakatos, Imre, *Philosophical* Papers, J. Worrall and G. Currie, eds. (Cambridge: Cambridge University Press, 1978), Two vols.

Melor, D. H., "Induction Is Warranted," in *Analysis* 49 (1989), p.7

Milton, J. R., "Induction before Hume," in *British Journal of Philosophy of Science* 38 (1987), 49-74.

Miller, R. C., *Space, Time and Quanta*, New York: W. H. Freeman and Co., 1994.

Misiek, J. ed., *The Problem of Rationality in Science and Its Philosophy* (Netherlands: Kluwer Academic Publishers, 1995).

O' Hear, Anthony, *An Introduction to the Philosophy of Science* (New York: OUP, 1989).

Perumaili, Augustine, *Critical issues in the Philosophy of Science and Religion* (Delhi: ISPCK, 2006).

Popper, K., "Philosophy of Science: A Personal Report," in *British Philosophy in the Mid-Century*, C. A. Mace, ed. (London: Allen and Unwin, 1957).

___________, *Conjectures and Refutations* (New York: Basic Books, 1962); (London: Routledge & Kegan Paul, 1963) and (New York: Harper and Row, 1968).

___________ *The Philosophy of Karl Popper*, in Paul Arthur Schilpp, ed., 1974.

___________ and D. Miller, "The Impossibility of Inductive Probability", in *Nature*, 310 (1984).

___________ "Falsificationism", in *Scientific Inquiry – Readings in the Philosophy of Science*, Robert Klee, ed. (Oxford: Oxford University Press, 1999).

Reichenbach, Hans, *The Direction of Time* (Berkley and Los Angeles: University of California Press, 1956).

Russell, Bertrand, *The Problems of Philosophy* (Oxford: University Press, 2002), first pub. 1980.

Salmon, Wesley, "Why ask 'Why'?", in *Proceedings and Addresses of the American Philosophical Association*, 51 (1978), 683-705.

Schilpp, Paul Arthur, The Philosophy of Karl Popper, Book I (Illinios: Open Court, 1974).

Schmidt, Werner, *Old Testament Introduction* (Bombay: St. Paul Publication, 1992).

Scott, T. William. "On Polanyi's Notion of Rationality," in J. Misiek, ed., 1995, 205-214.

Theobald, W. D., *Philosophy of Science: An Introduction* (London: Methun, 1968).

Wettersten, John, "Discussion - William Whewell: Problems of Induction vs. Problems of Rationality," in *British Journal of Philosophy of Science*, 45 (1994), 716-42.

Magazine:

Health Screen, Feb 2005; Published by Thyrocare Technological Ltd. Thyrocare House, Thane (W), Mumbai – 400 610. (Website: www. hyrocare.com).

4

Theory of Everything or *Neti Neti*? Epistemic Unintelligibility in Quantum Physics and the Upanishads

Augustine Pamplany, CST

Abstract

This paper explores the notion of epistemic unintelligibility in both quantum physics and the Upanishadic mysticism. Given the integral nature of the ultimate reality with the thinking humans being part of it, does our "search for Reality" make any sense? This question is deeply embedded in the epistemology of quantum theory. On the basis of the new epistemological implications of quantum theory, it may be argued that a complete explanation of Reality-in-itself is beyond the region of physics. However the questions emerging from the problematics of the epistemology of quantum physics are deeply rooted in the ultimate epistemological problem of the intelligibility of Reality-in-itself. Quantum logicians have argued that the quantum revolution goes so deep that a radical amendment in the very model of reasoning is necessary, as though there is a non-human way of reasoning in the subatomic world. It is also argued that the unintelligibility and incomprehensibility of the ultimate nature of reality is also an insight advocated long ago by the ancient Indian sages. Be it the Western rationalistic or scientific or the Eastern mystical or spiritual tradition, the final outcome is an indescribable sense of wonder and silence at the face of a deep reality.

Key words: Epistemology, Unintelligibility, Quantum Physics, Aum etc.

Introduction

The marvel and amazement we feel at the fascinating phenomena in the world of our experience compel our enquiring minds to associate an element of mystery with it.[1] Thus Reality as the immediate object of our experience becomes the most real of all philosophical concepts and, given the baggage of meanings and explanations associated with it, it becomes the most puzzling and the most mysterious of all philosophical concepts. As the projection and expression of our deep-rooted natural quest for an ultimate meaning, this concept has fallen victim to the speculative analysis of philosophers and to the rigorous experimental onslaught of scientists. Generations of philosophers and scientists have expended their intellectual energy, tampering this innocent concept in an attempt to tame it. Despite all the fierce markings and fingerprints imposed on it by the serious researchers of reality, it appears to be immeasurably enigmatic, pregnant with an immeasurable amount of paradoxes, puzzles and perplexities.

The new insights of the new physics, particularly of quantum physics, into the mystery of the universe have prepared the stage for a dialogue between science and philosophy. Beyond the rigorous experimental method of science and the strict speculative nature of philosophy, there emerges a new domain where science and philosophy can join their hands to begin the great task of exploring the real.

If reality is essentially integral and if the human being - the knowing being - is essentially a part of it, does our "search for Reality" make any sense? Is it in itself a futile task? Though speculative in nature, these questions are deeply embedded in the epistemology of quantum theory. On the basis of the new epistemological implications of quantum theory, it may be argued that a complete explanation of Reality-in-itself is beyond the region of physics. However the questions emerging from the problematics of the epistemology of quantum physics are deeply rooted in the ultimate epistemological problem of the intelligibility of Reality-in-itself. Our thesis states that epistemologically quantum physics dispels an extreme pessimism as well as an exaggerated optimism. We will show that the unintelligibility and incomprehensibility of the ultimate nature of Reality is also an insight advocated long ago by the ancient Indian sages.

1 It is indeed quite fulfilling to dedicate this essay in honour of my venerable *guru*, Prof. Dr. John Vattanky. Prof. Vattanky strained his brain in applying his genius to the rigorous epistemological tools and methods of the *Nyaya* System in the Indian tradition. With this essay I wish to add a tiny small string to his epistemological adventures by reflecting over the analogical epistemic complementarity between quantum physics and the Upanishadic philosophy.

1. The Epistemic Dualism in Quantum Physics

The "epistemological dualism" of quantum physics is our starting point. Though physicists are well aware that classical concepts are inadequate at the subatomic level, they cannot but use them to describe their discoveries for they do not have a better language. Quantum physics stands in need of a new language. "The source of all quantum paradoxes appears to lie in the fact that human perceptions create a world of unique actualities - our experience is inevitably 'classical' - while quantum reality is simply not that way at all. Quantum reality consists of simultaneous possibilities, a 'polyhistoric' kind of being absolutely incompatible with our merely one-track minds."[2]

Quantum logicians have argued that the quantum revolution goes so deep that a mere replacement of new concepts with the old ones is not sufficient. To cope with the quantum facts, a radical amendment in our very mode of reasoning is necessary.[3] It seems as if the world follows a non-human way of reasoning in the subatomic world. The problems of language here are really serious. We wish to speak in some way about the structure of the atoms and not only about the 'facts' - the latter being, for instance, the black spot on a photographic plate or the water droplets in a cloud chamber. But we cannot speak about the atoms in ordinary language."[4]

Heisenberg considers this language barrier as an indication that modern physics opens its door to a wider outlook on the relation between the human mind and Reality. However, he also adds that physics cannot give up this classical use of language for the reason that any understanding must finally be based on the natural language because it is only there that we can be certain to touch Reality.[5] Herbert's creative intellect has made an interesting fantasy very well conveying the paradoxical experiences of the quantum physicists with quantum facts that reside at the root of the language barrier. We notice a mystical flavour in this imaginative description.

> One imagines Max, the famous quantum physicist, deciding on Monday morning to face the quantum facts. Donning quantum-resistant body armour, he climbs inside his bubble chamber, waves goodbye to the workaday world, and prepares to enter the mysterious realm of the quantum.... Max suddenly drops through the world's phenomenal surface into deep quantum reality. Holy Heisenberg! Centuries of Newtonian certainties vanish in an instant. Solid objects melt into the undivided wholeness as he enters the place without Separation. Max mixes with

2 Nick Herbert, *Quantum Reality* (New York: Anchor Books, 1987), p., 248.

3 See, Herbert, p. 20.

4 Werner Heisenberg, *Physics and Philosophy* (London: George Allen and Unwin Ltd., 1959), p. 154.

5 See, Heisenberg, *Physics and Philosophy,* pp. 172-173.

the mystery when his subject/object membrane dissolves. In tune with totality, Max creates a new universe faster than light wherever he turns his omnipotent gaze.[6]

The nature of this problem shows that it is not merely a linguistic problem. The problem of language is a symptom of some other basic problem. Linguistic crisis seems to be originating from some fundamental epistemological problems associated with Reality. From a limited epistemological framework, we could say that the absence of strong objectivity and the limits of our rationalism in the quantum world are the two main reasons for this problem. Despagnat thinks that true Reality is beyond pure rationalism and our rationalist approaches cannot reach out to this Reality. "To approach empirical reality by means of the system of calculation rules that ultimately constitute quantum physics does not necessarily hide some fundamental irrationality in true reality. But it shows us this only if we consider empirical reality... to be nevertheless not identifiable with ultimate reality."[7]

A response to this question from a limited epistemological framework raises a more fundamental question: if our rationality cannot reach out to the true Reality behind phenomena, shall we ever be able to know Reality-in-itself? Precisely this is implicit in Morris' anxiety: "After all, the fundamental question is not "Will physics ever be complete?", but rather, "Is an understanding of the ultimate nature of... reality something that is within the reach of the human mind?"[8] In response to this question, we find ourselves in the midst of two extreme poles. On the one side we have Philosopher Immanuel Kant with his pessimistic outlook which says that we will never know Reality-in-itself.[9] On the other side we have Hawking with his deep faith in the omniscience of the human intellect.[10] In the light of quantum theory, how shall we understand this Kantian "syndrome of unintelligibility?" Is the philosophy of modern physics in harmony with Hawking?

---

6 Herbert, pp. 55-56.

7 Bernard Despagnat, *Reality and the Physicist* - Knowledge, Duration and the Quantum World (Cambridge: Cambridge University Press, 1989), p. 173.

8 Richard Morris, *The Nature of Reality* (New York: Noonday Press, 1987), pp. 188-189.

9 According to Kant our human nature is entwined with appearance and our concepts can explain only the phenomenal aspect of the world. Since we can deal only with phenomena the nature of deep reality remains forever inaccessible to us.

10 In an inaugural lecture Hawking expressed the hope that the task of physics would be over towards the end of this century: "(T)he goal of theoretical physics might be achieved in the not too distant future, say, by the end of the century. By this I mean that we might have a complete, consistent, and unified theory of the physical interactions which would describe all possible observations." (John Boslough, *Stephen Hawking's Universe* (New York: William Morrow, 1985), p.131).

It is from the broader framework of the nature of Reality implied by quantum theory that we have to answer these questions. The epistemological limits of quantum theory are not merely a problem of vocabulary, much less a problem of the sharpness of our experimental tools. It stems from the very nature of the object of our enquiry. The real really transcends our concepts and equations. As the Reality implied by quantum theory is integral and synthetic and our role in this Reality is that of a participatory existence, it is natural that we as part of Reality do not know the whole of Reality. Reality cannot be conceived as hiding its real nature from us. Our participation in Reality is a unique participation. It implies the subject-object non-duality in Reality. If Reality is considered as knowledge itself, our non-objective presence in Reality makes a complete objectification of Reality, thereby rendering a total intelligibility of Reality impossible. It is here that we find the philosophical depth of Heisenberg's statement: "What we learn about is not nature itself, but nature exposed to our methods of questioning."[11]

Neither human nor the cosmos, nor human plus the cosmos is the totality of Reality. Since our participation in Reality is a participation in the "in-itself" of Reality and not merely participation at the phenomenal level, it means that Reality is not totally unintelligible to us. We do know Reality-in-itself but not fully. In this regard, an absolute distinction between phenomena and Reality-in-itself does not seem to be necessary. In a participatory whole of Reality such a dualism is misleading. It is from the physical that we have come to the metaphysical. If the metaphysical had not been "present" in the physical, if the metaphysical had been spatially distinct from the physical, physics would not have come to encounter metaphysics in its laboratory. Quantum theory thus implies a oneness of knowledge constituted by the totality of Reality and present in its parts in the form of intelligibility and transcends them as unintelligible. In other words, knowledge is a union of phenomena and noumena, intelligibility and unintelligibility. In this sense we could say quantum mechanics is in a way a unique "mechanics" of knowledge itself. In a philosophical context, the glory of quantum theory resides not in its ability to predict the probabilities of subatomic events well but in its inability to say why these events take place.

We could see a moderate reconciliation of the above two extremes of unintelligibility and "all-knowability" in Despagnat's understanding of quantum epistemological problems - which seems to be in agreement with our conceptions. According to him, Reality-in-itself[12] is "veiled." The epithet "veiled" is intended to indicate a midpoint between the terms knowable

11 Cited by Herbert, p. 172.

12 Despagnat uses the term "independent reality" to mean it.

and unknowable.[13] In terms of non-separability the notions "knowable" and "unknowable" are too strong words. Where the former seems to suggest that we can know things exhaustively as they are in themselves, the latter would largely underestimate our cognitive abilities. The concept of veiled Reality avoids these pitfalls. The notion that Reality is veiled means: "Knowable only as far as some of its structures are concerned, and further, without our being able to say exactly which ones of these structures are knowable."[14]

2. Unintelligibility in the Indian Perspective

In India, one wonders whether the idea of the unintelligibility of the ultimate Reality is overemphasized. The idea of the unintelligibility of Reality scientists have come across in recent times is found in the mystical wisdom of the *Vedas* and the *Upaniṣads.*

> There no eye can penetrate
> no voice, no mind can penetrate
> We do not know nor understand
> How one should teach it.[15]
> As a unity only is it to be looked upon, this indemonstrable, enduring being.[16]
> Whence all the speech turn back with the mind without reaching it (that is the Eternal Truth the *Brahman*).[17]

In India the ultimate Reality is looked upon as knowledge, bliss and existence (s*at, cit, Ānanda*) itself. This Reality is inexplicable in language. Hence the profoundness of the negative way of referring to It as *neti*, *neti* (not this, not that). A series of seemingly "fallacious," "dichotomic," and "irrational" statements resulting from this inexplicability could be seen in the Indian thought. It is what led the mystics to turn to myths, symbols and metaphors to convey their experience of the ultimate Reality which is knowledge itself. This unintelligibility and inexplicability are the underlying factors behind the Indian classification of the different states of consciousness and the different phases of knowledge.

A profound explication of the unintelligibility of the absolute and the unceasing human pursuit of the truth beyond the domains of language through meditative practices is represented in the Upanishadic *mahāvākya (Great Saying)*, *AUM*. According to *Katha Upaniṣad*, the Ultimate Reality is:

---

13 See, Despagnat, p. 171.

14 Despagnat, p. 175.

15 *Kena Upaniṣad*, 1.3

16 *Brhadaranyaka Upaniṣad*, 4.4.20.

17 *Taitiriya Upaniṣad*, 2.4. Swami Chinmayananda, tr. (Madras: Chinmaya Publication Trust, 1962), p. 147.

> Hard to know, to be meditated upon as "*AUM*"
> The word announced by all the *Vedas*,
> Proclaimed by all ascetic practices,
> The word in search of which men practice chastity,
> This word I tell thee now in brief: "*OM*" ... this is it.[18]

This *mahāvākya* states that *Brahman* is hard to know and he is to be meditated upon as '*AUM.*' Brahman is an incomprehensible reality. Like arrows shot at the moon, going up and not touching it, so will all words fall down without reaching Brahman. So what one has to do is to consider that reality as "*AUM*" and meditate over that. *AUM* here is an indicative symbol of that ineffable Reality of Brahman.

Given this profound value and meaning of *AUM*, it could be used as a means to liberation, as a yogic exercise. The basic presupposition here is that language conceals reality. To get rid of this concealment, the linguistic faculties such as the senses, *manas* (mind) and *buddhi* (intellect) must die, which in its final analysis merges into *Brahman* as he is. According to Sankara, this is the self-immersion into language. It is the dying into the real language and thorough this, death into the unreal. In this yogic exercise there are different stages of identity with the Brahman. The vedantic scholar Somaraj Gupta has made a brilliant elucidation of these stages with a profound intuitive insight.[19]

In the *Mahāvākya 'AUM,'* 'A' as the first stage of identity stands for the identity of the individual self to the universal self, where senses are submissive to the *manas*. There is however, at this stage, one temptation for the *manas*: it might start glorifying the theo-anthropo-cosmic presence, might start enjoying it, or, like artists, describing it, predicating some awe-inspiring traits of it. This way the mind gets active, loses its innocence and falls back into the riot of the senses. The mind can lose its *rājasic*, its ekstatic character only by self-submitting to the presence and getting absorbed into it. It is in this self-oblivion, in this abyss that the creative source of the world lies. This is the vision of *Hiraṇyagarbhā*, the Golden Germ, the primordial source of everything.

Thus does *AUM* reveal its second letter U, the symbol of the creator. The Golden Germ, the shining creator, gets revealed when man has been laid asleep in body, and the mind has been stilled into passivity; when *vāk* (language as *ekstasis*) and *manas* have merged into *buddhi*. The mind stilled is the creator of the world and not the active mind which ever remains at the mercy of a 'material' world, its constitutive-destructive *other*.

Thus 'U' stands for the self-submission of the *manas* to the *Brahman*. This state, too, is open to backsliding. When the senses cease to function and

---

18 *Katha Upaniṣad*, 2.15.

19 Somarj Gupta, "*The Word that Became the Absolute*: Relevance of *Šankara's* Ontology of Language," *Journal of Indian Philosophical Research*, 1989, pp. 27-41.

the *manas* gets stilled, *buddhi* which is the determinating faculty, determinates reality in terms of existence only. It cannot, in that state of innocence, determinate the given eternity-infinity in terms of non-existence, for there will be no ekstatic *manas* to move from the given to the non-given. Consciousness of *Brahman* as the sole Reality is still consciousness inflicted with intentionality, and is subject to possible backsliding into self-consciousness. Therefore, even this consciousness that *Brahman is* has to go. The intellect, in order to 'reach' *Brahman*, has to self-submit to *Brahman* as *IS* and let it, in absolute passivity, possess it and usurp it. Then alone does *Brahman*, as it really is and not as 'He is,' become one with it. It is then alone that *AUM* reveals itself as the highest *Brahman*. *Brahman* as IS is lower *Brahman*, and *Brahman*, as it really is, is the supreme *Brahman* - to which even 'is-ness' is not applicable. 'M' stands for the self-submission of *buddhi* to *Brahman*. "The Self should be realized as 'He IS,' the Self should also be realized as it truly is. To one who, of the two forms, knows that of 'He IS,' to him becomes favourably disposed the Self-in-truth."[20]

Conclusion

The unintelligibility of reality demonstrated by science and mysticism invokes us to give up our ideological solipsism. Any approach to Reality, be it instrumentalist or realist, and any description of Reality, be it philosophical, theological, sociological or whatever, can carry only a partial representation of truth. To us a philosophical system is most fitting to humanity if it is conscious of its limits. That we are able to generate philosophy is an indication that infinity is kind enough to let us taste and experience itself. As Bohr has remarked: "Part of infinity seems to lie within the grasp of those who look across the sea."[21] The insightful imagination of the Bengali scholar Brahmobandhab Upadhyay has so creatively presented the unfathomable and awe-inspiring spirit of the human pursuit after truth. Be it the Western rationalistic or scientific or the Eastern mystical or spiritual, the final outcome is an indescribable sense of wonder and silence at the face of a deep reality:

> Two birds once lived in the same nest. One spreading its wings rose up high towards the expanseless (heavens). Leaving cloud and sky behind, it pierced the planet-and-star bedecked firmament and reached the Milky Way. Immersed in the depths of the bliss in this directionless void, it said: Profound, unalloyed bliss is founded in boundless, highest space. And the other bird traversed the compass-points, north, south, east and west, in search of the infinite's abode. How much beauty, how much correlation (*sambandha*), how much cause-and-effect-begotten spelendour, did it

20 *Katha Upaniṣad*, 2.3.13.

21 Cited by Heisenberg, *Physics and Beyond* (London: George Allen and Unwin Ltd., 1971), p. 60.

see. Bemused at the vision of Nature's (*prakṛti*) grace, it concluded: The infinite's indivisibility reposes in synthesis (*samanvaya*), on conjunction, in union. The first (searcher) is the *Aryan* seer, the second the Ionian or Greek observer.

Two fish made a sacred journey to determine the true nature (*svarup*) of the ocean. One dived deep, and penetrated from depth to depth. Finally it came to the bottomless bottom and fell silent. The other gradually became obsessed with desire for catching sight of shore. Making light of the buffets of heaving swells with a strength that countered fierce currents, it swam about till it got lost in the boundless main. Bewildered, it came to the conclusion that the infinite lacked boundaries. The first is the oriental, the Hindu; the second the westerner, the German.[22]

22 Brahmabandhab Upadhyay, "The One-Centredness of the Hindu Race," J. J. Lipner, tr., *Vidyajyoti Journal of Theological Reflections,* 51 (1981), pp. 415-416.

5

The Method and Logic of Social Sciences to Popper: A Review

Vibin Varghese Padayadan, SJ

Abstract

Popper's method evolved in conversation with historicist method. He asserts that society is changing and developing. Development being non repetitive, predictions can become inaccurate. Thus he says that the task of social sciences is to study the unintended social repercussions of intended human actions which can enable humans to understand the even more remote consequences of possible actions. Situational logic analyses the situations of the acting persons to explain the actions of the persons. By his attempt to elaborate social sciences, he brought out the worth of individual into world's notice. And by stating that no theory is permanently stable, he opened new avenues for growth and further movement.

Key words: Falsification, negative force, social wholes, criticisms, social planning etc.

Introduction

Karl Popper's social philosophy emerged as reaction to doctrines like historicism, holism, essentialism, totalitarianism etc. To a large extent, his philosophy derives from the negative force of these criticisms. The term 'negative force' is never used in a belittling sense, because he gives importance to falsification[1] in the development of knowledge and understanding. Popper considered the growth of physical sciences as the best examples of the increase of knowledge that humanity has come across till date. True that Popper's methodology of sciences not only aims at promoting the expansion of knowledge but also facilitates the improvement of human conditions. This paper is an attempt to show how his work tries to unify methods in order to avoid irrational elements from social sciences. In this attempt, he was able to regain the place of the individual in the society which was lost in the totalitarian translations. To this end, I pinpoint certain facets of the method of logical sciences and take a closer look at logic of social sciences.

1. A Study into Popper's Method

1.1 The Trial and Error Method

According to Popper, the scientific method is the 'trial and error' method which consists in formulating hypotheses those are falsifiable. When any hypothesis is falsified, a new one is formulated in the light of the resulting epistemological situation. Here we analyze two aspects of this procedure as Paul Arthur explains:

> First, no hypothesis is put forward *in vacuo*: it springs from a context of existing theories regarded as provisionally established and it is intelligible only in that context. Second, a hypothesis is always advanced in a form which makes it possible for the investigator to learn from his mistakes: he does not have to start absolutely afresh each time, but puts forward his new hypothesis in the light of what he has learnt not to be the case.[2]

This scientific principle he applied to the methods of social sciences also. It is worth mentioning that the inspiration of his trial and error method is, of course, from a different point of view. Popper used, for the first time, the rubric of 'trial and error' to describe his own philosophy and posed it as an alternative to the dialectic.[3] He reaffirmed that dialectic was a good affirmation to "trial

1 Popper's 'falsificationism' reverses the usual point of view that accumulated experience leads to scientific hypotheses; rather freely conjunctured hypotheses precede, and are tested against, experience. The hypotheses that survive the testing process constitute current scientific knowledge.

2 Paul Arthur Schilpp, *Karl Popper*, (Illinois: The Open Court Publishing Co., 1971), 890.

3 Popper seemed to have had little problems with the 'dialectical view' of thought with the assumption that science and philosophy developed through a conflict between thesis and antithesis, issuing a synthesis. However popper cautions that a synthesis always does not occur and its character could not be predicted by examining thesis and synthesis.

and error… the same method as that applied by living organisms in the process of adaptation."[4]

Popper spoke of free competition of theories as essential to the scientific progress. He linked it to the struggle of political ideologies and the suggested result was 'survival of the fittest', a social Darwinian theme. In short, trial and error became scientific method permitting the survival of the fittest theories.[5] What happens to people is that they often perish with their beliefs intact. But occasionally turned against an ideology and only then weaknesses had been demonstrated. The growth of knowledge was rarely continuous, slow and steady. Explicating the nuances of trial and error method, he made it viable enough for applications to social sciences. He was in fact thinking big. "It would be best, perhaps, not to use (the term 'dialectic') at all – we can always use the clearer terminology of trial and error development."[6]

1.2 The Roles of Prediction and Prophecy

Prediction and prophecy had decisive roles in the evolution of his method of social sciences. Popper's method evolved in conversation with prediction and prophecy, very specially that of historicist method. Historicist doctrine[7] says that it is the task of social sciences to propound historical doctrines and those historical prophecies are of very much help to conduct politics in a rational way. The central ideas of historical method are these:

a) It is a fact that we can predict solar eclipses with a high degree of precision and for a long time ahead. Then the question arises that why are we not able to predict revolutions? The fundamental idea is that it should be able to predict revolutions just as it is possible to predict solar eclipses.
b) The task of social sciences is the same that of natural sciences – to make predictions. It is to make predictions about the social and political development of mankind.

---

4 Karl Popper, *Conjunctures and Refutations*, (New York: Harper and Row Publishers, 1968), 403.

5 Malachi Haim Hacohen, *Karl Popper: The Formative Years 1902-1945*, (U K: Cambridge University Press, 2002), 349.

6 Karl Popper, *Conjunctures and Refutations*, (New York: Harper and Row Publishers, 1968), 412.

7 By Historicist doctrine, Popper primarily aims at the historicist doctrines of Marxism. He criticizes Marxism for its claims like that it is a science and that it is progressive. It should be noted that by historicism he does not mean only Marxism. But he includes other hostoricist doctrines also.

c) Once the predictions are made, the task of politics can be determined. For it can lessen the birthpangs of revolutions.[8]

In short, it means to say that the story of mankind has a plot. And if we can succeed in unravelling this plot, we shall hold the key to the future.

Popper criticizes this view tooth and nail. He says that "this impression disappears once we make a clear distinction between what I shall call 'scientific prediction' on the one side and 'unconditional historical prophecies' on the other."[9] Ordinary perceptions in science are conditional.[10] Unconditional scientific predictions can sometimes be derived from these conditional scientific predictions provided the conditions in question are fulfilled. But Popper's argument is that the historicist "does not derive his historical prophecies from conditional scientific predictions. The second (from which the first follows) is that he cannot possibly do so because long term prophecies can be derived from scientific conditional predictions only if they apply to systems which can be described as well isolated, stationary and recurrent."[11] But these kinds of systems are very rare in nature. Take the case of eclipse prophecies. These prophecies are based on the regularity of seasons and are possible only because our solar system is a stationary and repetitive system. It is isolated from the influence of other mechanical systems by immense regions of empty space and it is relatively free of interference from outside. In science, these prophecies become very impressive because of the special cases of these repetitive systems.

This can never be the case with regard to the historical prophecies. On no basis we can apply unconditional prophecy to human history. For society is changing and developing. And this development is never repetitive. Of course in certain cases, as far as it is repetitive, we can make prophecies.[12] Unfortunately, most striking aspects of historical development are non-repetitive. Conditions are changing and new situations arise, especially as a consequence of new scientific discoveries. Ultimately we cannot predict revolutions as we predict eclipses. So what then is the primary task of social sciences?

---

8 Karl Popper, *The Myth of Framework: In Defence of Science and Rationality*, (London: Routledge, 1994), 338.

9 Karl Popper, *The Myth of Framework: In Defence of Science and Rationality*, (London: Routledge, 1994), 339.

10 They assert that certain changes (say, of the temperature of water in a kettle) will be accompanied by other changes (say, the boiling of water).

11 Karl Popper, *The Myth of Framework: In Defence of Science and Rationality*, (London: Routledge, 1994), 339.

12 For example, there is some sort of repetitiveness in the manner in which new religions arise or new tyrannies. A student of history may find that he can foresee such development by comparing them with earlier ones, i.e., by studying the conditions under which they arise.

1.3 The Task of Social Sciences

It is generally believed that social sciences are to study the behaviour of 'social wholes', such as groups, classes, nations, civilizations etc. It studies in the same way biology studies animals and plants. But Popper is of the opinion that these so-called 'social wholes' are 'postulates' of popular social theories rather than empirical objects. Take the name like 'middle class'. It never stands for any such empirical group. What it stands for is a kind of ideal object whose existence depends upon theoretical assumptions[13]. It is in this context Popper argues that social phenomena "should be analyzed in terms of individuals and their actions and relations."[14] This method is known as methodological individualism. This view is mainly intended to deny the holist view that superhuman factors are operative in history. Such a view is diametrically opposite to the view of Popper's Open Society too. What methodological individualism asserts is that "the functioning of all social institutions should always be understood as resulting from the decisions, actions, attitudes etc of human individuals."[15]

At this juncture Popper comes with the specific task of social sciences. He says, "the main task of social sciences is to trace the unintended social repercussions of intentional human actions."[16] It is well elucidated with the help of an example. If a man wishes to buy a house in a certain district urgently, we can surely assume that he does not wish to raise the market prices for houses in that district. But the very fact that he appears on the market, the market price will tend to rise. Popper sees our knowledge of social life and social relations itself in terms of experiments being made by the agents:

> The introduction of new kind of life- insurance, of a new kind of taxation, of a new penal form are all social experiments which have their repercussions through the whole of society without remodelling society as a whole. Even a man who opens a new shop, or who reserves the ticket for a theatre, is carrying out social experiment on a small scale; and all our knowledge of social conditions is based on experience gained by making experiments of this kind[17].

13 Karl Popper, *The Myth of Framework: In Defence of Science and Rationality*, (London: Routledge, 1994), *341.*

14 Karl Popper, *The Myth of Framework: In Defence of Science and Rationality*, (London: Routledge, 1994), 341.

15 Karl Popper, *The Open Society and its Enemies*, Vol 2. (London: Routledge and Kegan Paul, 1962), 98.

16 Karl Popper, *The Myth of Framework: In Defence of Science and Rationality*, (London: Routledge, 1994), 342.

17 Karl Popper, *The Open Society and its Enemies*, Vol.1. (London: Routledge and Kegan Paul, 1962), 162.

1.4 Initial Conditions: Milestone of Popper's Approach

At this point we should not miss the particular space given to initial conditions. Naturally, this approach of Popper reminds us of the 'theory of chaos' which speaks of the initial conditions. The initial conditions sometimes contribute very much to the further development of the phenomena. The easy example for the theory of chaos would be the claim that the flap of a butterfly can create a tornado in some parts of the world provided initial conditions are specific. Whatever be the case, Popper claims that initial conditions of a small event can even make a revolution. And the task of social sciences is to study the unintended social repercussions of intended human actions. Its practical role is one of helping us to understand even the more remote consequences of possible actions and thus help to choose our actions more wisely. This social experiment on small scale is the basic insight from which his advocacy of piecemeal social engineering derives.

Popper proposed piecemeal social engineering in opposition to utopian engineering. The utopian engineer takes the view that, along the historicist line, the real change in the society can be effected only through complete change and any attempt to partial improvement is doomed to failure. Popper contrasts this view by saying that the scientific attitude to social policies is that of piecemeal engineering "which consists in concentrating on one social problem at a time, 'making little changes and adjustments', and modifying one's subsequent interventions in the light of the outcome of one's previous interventions."[18] Popper's emphasis falls on particular institutions rather than on society as a whole. We may deal with these problems one at a time, leaving the rest of social life alone – at least for the time being.

1.5 Method of Social Sciences in Nutshell

To summarize this portion, let us say that his method of social sciences evolved as a consequence of criticism to the then prevailing doctrines. The method of social sciences is the trial and error method. And its task is to study the unintended social repercussions of the intended human actions. He vehemently criticizes the overrule of history and the damages done by it. The earlier naturalistic revolution against God replaced the name 'God' by the name 'nature'. The science of God was replaced by the science of nature. Theological determinism was replaced by naturalistic determinism and nature's omnipotence and the omniscience of science replaced God's omnipotence.[19] After that, Hegel and Marx entered the scene. They replaced goddess nature in its turn by the goddess history. And there we get the laws of

18 Paul Arthur Schilpp, *Karl Popper*, (Illinois: The Open Court Publishing Co., 1971), 890.

19 Karl Popper, *The Myth of Framework: In Defence of Science and Rationality*, (London: Routledge, 1994), 346.

history like powers, forces, tendencies, designs etc. of history. "And we learn that not God but history (the history of 'nations' or of 'classes') will be our judge... And they discovered that all standards are after all only historical facts which led to the deification of Facts."[20] If at all you need the ultimate wisdom of philosophy, appeal to the logical and moral authority of these Facts. It was to this deification Popper fought tooth and nail.

2. The Logic of Social Sciences

Before bringing out the nuances of logic of social sciences, Popper firmly believes that the grounds on which knowledge stands should be made clear. He makes use of this explanation as a starting point to his elucidation on logic. Furthermore, he dwells on the contrast between our knowledge and ignorance. He proposes two theses. These two theses lay foundation for his critical methods. First, "we have a fair amount of knowledge. Moreover we know not only details of doubtful intellectual interest, ...but also things that provide us with deep theoretical insight, and with a surprising understanding of the world". Secondly, "Our ignorance is boundless and sobering. Indeed, it is precisely this overwhelming progress of the natural sciences (to which my first thesis alludes) that continually reminds us of our ignorance, even in the field of natural sciences themselves."[21] With each step forward, we not only fall on new unsolved problems, but also we discover that the grounds (we supposed) on which we stood firm and safe are in reality insecurable and unstable. So the fundamental task of every theory of knowledge is to clarify the relation between our increasing knowledge and the increasing insight that in reality we know nothing.

And how does this knowledge arise? One might say that knowledge does not start from perceptions or observations or the collection of data or facts, but rather from problems. More precisely, this means "knowledge starts from the tension between knowledge and ignorance."[22] It is the discovery that there is something missing within our supposed knowledge.[23] It is the character and quality of the problems, which determine the value, or the lack of value of the scientific achievement. It is the same with that of the achievement of social sciences. So, the starting point is a problem and observation becomes a starting point only if it reveals a problem.

20 Karl Popper, *The Myth of Framework: In Defence of Science and Rationality*, (London: Routledge, 1994), 346.

21 Karl Popper, *In Search of a Better World,* (New York: Routledge Publications, 1998), 64.

22 Karl Popper, *In Search of a Better World,* (New York: Routledge Publications, 1998), 65.

23 It can be an inner contradiction ion our supposed knowledge or a contradiction between our supposed knowledge and facts or an apparent contradiction between our supposed knowledge and supposed facts.

2.1 The Main Theses and the Problem of Scientific Objectivity

Popper's six theses which give rise to his ideas on logic:

a) The method of the social sciences, like that of the natural sciences, consists in trying out tentative solutions to those problems from which our investigations start.Solutions are proposed and criticized. If a proposed solution is not open to objective criticism, then it is excluded as unscientific, although perhaps only temporarily.
b) If the proposed solution is open to objective criticism, then we attempt to refute it; for all criticisms consist in attempts at refutation.
c) If a proposed solution is refuted through our criticism, we propose another solution.
d) If it withstands criticism, we accept it temporarily; and we accept it above all, as worthy of further discussion and criticism.
e) Thus the method of science is one of tentative attempts to solve our problems which are controlled by the most severe criticism. It is the critical development of the method of 'trial and error.'
f) The so-called objectivity of science lies in the objectivity of the critical method; that is, above all, in the fact that no theory is exempt from criticism, and further, the fact that logical instrument of criticism – the logical contradiction – is objective.[24]

In fact, the last thesis 'the objectivity of science' lays ground for the logic. Apart from that the tension between the knowledge and ignorance leads to problems and tentative solutions. Yet tension is never overcome, because they are only tentative solutions. The idea that 'knowledge evolves' means it is possible that it will turn out to have been a mistake and therefore a case of ignorance[25].

Now, let us move on to the problem of scientific objectivity. There is a hue and cry over the notion that it is the high time for social sciences to learn from natural sciences what a scientific method is. This misguided naturalistic intervention demanded social sciences to begin with observations and measurements. That means, begin by collecting statistical data and then proceed by induction to generalizations and to the formation of theories. This is the way to shed away your subjectivity. And there is also a warning attached. Objectivity in social sciences is much more difficult than in the natural sciences. In order to be objective, one's judgments have to be 'value free.'[26] In

24 Karl Popper, *In Search of a Better World,* (New York: Routledge Publications, 1998), 66-67.

25 The only way of justifying our knowledge is just provisional, for its stability is based on the criticisms. It just means that so far our attempted solutions appear to have withstood our penetrating criticisms.

26 Max Weber coined the term 'value free'.

rare cases it is possible for a scientist to be free of the value system of his own social class and achieve value freedom.

When objectivity is talked of, Popper always brings into notice the anthropological stand which in some respects overtook sociology[27] in a period of history. Popper admits that social anthropology is one of the most successful social sciences. The anthropologists, at times, cling to the extreme ideas especially that of philosophical relativism. Philosophical relativism is the idea that there is no objective truth, only truth for this age or that age.[28] Similarly, anthropological relativism teaches that there are truths or sciences for this group or that class so on and so forth. Popper comes in here saying that this extreme position is not unimportant especially if one modifies a little. This stand of Popper also contributes to the nuances of his logic.

At another point, he deals with the fact that the objectivity of a science depends upon the objectivity of the social scientist. Popper renders his disagreement saying that it is completely wrong to believe that the attitude of natural scientist is more objective than that of the social scientist. The natural scientist is also biased as anyone else, unless he belongs to the few who are constantly producing new ideas. Unfortunately, s/he is often extremely biased favouring his own ideas in a one-sided and partisan manner. Still, the sad part of the story is that several of the most outstanding contemporary physicists have even founded schools, which set up a powerful resistance to new ideas.

Then what can be described as scientific objectivity? Popper says, "scientific objectivity is based solely upon that *critical* tradition which, despite all kinds of resistance, so often makes it possible to criticize a dominant dogma."[29] In other words, the objectivity of science is never a matter of individual scientist, but rather the social result of mutual criticism. It may be of the friendly–hostile division of labour among scientists or of their co-operation and also of their competition. Sometimes the sociology of knowledge itself has completely missed the decisive point: the fact that objectivity solely rests upon criticism. To him, "objectivity can be explained in terms of social ideas such as competition (both of individual scientists and of various schools of thought); tradition (that is the critical tradition); social institutions (for instance, publications in various competing journals and by various competing publishers; discussions at congresses); the power of the state (that is, its

27 Before Second World War, sociology was regarded as a general theoretical science and social anthropology always fell after it. But later history shows us that social anthropology slowly became general social science and sociology resigned itself to becoming one element within social anthropology. The relationship between sociology and anthropology was completely reversed. The victory of anthropology is the victory of an allegedly more objective method.

28 Karl Popper, *In Search of a Better World,* (New York: Routledge Publications, 1998), 71-72.

29 Karl Popper, *In Search of a Better World,* (New York: Routledge Publications, 1998), 72.

political tolerance of free discussion).[30] He does not completely rule out the part researcher's social or ideological habitat play, but claims that they will be eliminated in the long run as critical tradition does its duty properly.

Mutual criticism is again entrusted with another responsibility. In the question of truth in the research, there may arise various extra-scientific problems like the problem of human welfare, national defense or of nationalistic policy or industrial expansion etc. It is impossible to eliminate such extra scientific interests from scientific researches.[31] What is important here is not the elimination of this extra scientific interests, but it is the distinction between the interests which do not belong to the search for truth and which belong to truth. Though truth is one of the chief scientific values, relevance, interests and significance are also scientific values. It is difficult to draw a straight-line between the two and it is one of the tasks of scientific criticism and scientific discussion to fight against the confusion of value-spheres and to eliminate extra scientific evaluations from questions of truth.[32]

In nutshell, it is practically impossible to do away with extra scientific values from scientific activity. The situation is similar to that of objectivity. We cannot rob the scientist of his partisanship without also robbing him of his humanity. We cannot suppress his value judgments unless we destroy him as a human being and as a scientist.

2.2 Situational Logic

Without the paraphernalia of introduction, let us straightaway enter into the definition. Situational logic consists in analyzing the situation of the acting person sufficiently to explain the actions of the person.[33] Objective understanding consists in realizing that the action was objectively appropriate to the situation. Now we seem to be admitting that there are differences between agents from different backgrounds which are crucial to the explanation and interpretation of their behaviour. This difference is not merely verbal. It very much depends upon the backgrounds and attitudes of the agents involved. Without knowing the situation, we will never be in a position to know the actions of the individual. Form of life also determines what actions the agents do.[34] The situation is analyzed to know the actions. The method of situational analysis is certainly an individualistic method and yet it is certainly not a psychological one. Popper

30 Karl Popper, *In Search of a Better World,* (New York: Routledge Publications, 1998), 73.

31 It is impossible to eliminate such type of extra scientific problems from natural sciences also. For example, stem cell research, cloning, artificial intelligence etc.

32 Karl Popper, *In Search of a Better World,* (New York: Routledge Publications, 1998), 73-74.

33 Karl Popper, *In Search of a Better World,* (New York: Routledge Publications, 1998), 79.

34 Anthony O'Hear, *Karl Popper,* (London: Routledge and Kegan Paul, 1980), 164-165.

usually calls it 'the logic of the situation' or 'situational logic.'[35] Popper claims that although his analysis of society is based on individual behaviour, it is not psychologistic. It is because the behaviour of individual is governed by their social situation as much as by their individual motives.[36] We cannot explain psychologically man's social environment. Therefore we cannot look upon psychology as the basis of social science.

The explanations of situation logic are rational and theoretical reconstructions. Yet it may appear as oversimplified and overschematized. Still, "they can possess a considerable truth content and they can, in the strictly logical sense, be good approximations to the truth". If that is so, "the logical concept of the approximation to the truth is indispensable for a social science which uses the method of situational analysis."[37] More than that, situational analyses are empirically criticizable and capable of improvement.

Lastly, situational logic assumes a physical world in which we act. The physical world contains the physical resources and the physical barriers about which we know and also we do not know. Secondly, it assumes a social world inhabited by other people and social institutions. These social institutions in fact determine the character of our social environment. A grocer's shop, a university, church, state etc are all social institutions. They consist of all social realities of the social world, which correspond to the things of the physical world.

Conclusion

Popper's social science is an attempt to avoid various extremes. It is individualistic without being psychologistic. He was trying to unify the methods of natural sciences and social sciences in order to avoid irrational elements from social science. But it is great from his part to admit the situation as an essential part of any explanation. Thereby he gained a place for the individual, which was really found lost in the totalitarian explanation. Thus he brought out the worth of the individual into world's notice. We have already seen that Popper developed his social science method in opposition to the Historicist method. But, "from a cold war perspective, Popper's critique was read as an attack on communism and a warning against social planning."[38] Though we cannot blindly rule out this possibility, what Popper aimed at was an opposition to large scale planning which tarnishes individual wishes, desires, and cultures. With regard to predictions, "Popper retained autonomy

35 Karl Popper, *In Search of a Better World,* (New York: Routledge Publications, 1998), 79.

36 Anthony O'Hear, *Karl Popper,* (London: Routledge and Kegan Paul, 1980), 162.

37 Karl Popper, *In Search of a Better World,* (New York: Routledge Publications, 1998), 79-80.

38 Malachi Haim Hacohen, *Karl Popper: The Formative Years 1902-1945*, (U K: Cambridge University Press, 2002), 354.

and predictive power for science by disengaging prediction from history."[39] It is true that formulating a thesis and revising it in the light of experiments made is agreeable and trying out a new form of government on the basis of trial and error is well and good. But the problems lie in where people's views vary on particular issues whether it is success or failure. What I mean to say is that people will tend to disagree on what constitute a success. The disagreements cannot be brushed aside.

For, these disagreements may express different values springing from diverse social movements, interests and institutions. But what is noteworthy in him is his humility and courage to propose a notion that no theory is permanently stable at a time when science was seemingly giving answers to many of the problems. He was a man always searching and helped others to search constantly.

Bibliography

O'Hear, Anthony. *Karl Popper.* London: Routledge and Kegan Paul, 1980.

Popper, Karl. Conjunctures and Refutations. New York: Harper and Row Publishers, 1968.

Popper, Karl. *In Search of a Better World.* New York: Routledge Publications, 1998.

Popper, Karl. *The Myth of Framework: In Defence of Science and Rationality.* London: Routledge, 1994.

Popper, Karl. *The Open Society and its Enemies*. London: Routledge and Kegan Paul, 1962, vol. 1.

Popper, Karl. *The Open Society and its Enemies*. London: Routledge and Kegan Paul, 1962, vol. 2.

Hacohen, Malachi Haim. ed. *Karl Popper: The Formative Years 1902-1945* U K: Cambridge University Press, 2002.

Schilpp, Paul Arthur. ed. *Karl Popper*. Illinois: The Open Court Publishing Co., 1971.

39 Malachi Haim Hacohen, *Karl Popper: The Formative Years 1902-1945*, (U K: Cambridge University Press, 2002), 380.

PART TWO

HERMENEUTICS AND *DHVANI*

6

Dhvani:
An Indian Approach to Biblical Hermeneutics

Thomas Karimundackal, SJ

Abstract

Dhvani theory proposed by Anandavardhana (9th CE) in his *Dhvanyālokā* serves as a hermeneutical method to interpret a written text. The suggested or the evocative meaning, i.e. the *dhvani* meaning, invariably stands out in the interpretation of the text irrespective of its linguistic nature. There is ample room for a hermeneutical adaptation of the *dhvani* theory to the religious texts as Anandavardhana himself has shown it with the interpretation of the *Mahabharatha*. *Dhvani* theory is equally valid and adaptable to the interpretation of the biblical texts. Therefore, one possible 'Indian' way of interpreting the Scriptures in the Indian context is to follow the method of *dhvani* theory. While the first part of this article explains the *dhvani* method and its various aspects, the second part of the paper illustrates its hermeneutical application to the story of the fall in Genesis.

Key words: *Dhvani*, primary meaning, secondary meaning, expressed meaning, suggested/evocative meaning, author-centered meaning, text-centered meaning, and reader-centered meaning, extrinsic *dhvani*, intrinsic-*dhvani*, *rasa-dhvani* etc.

Introduction

Different hermeneutical methods enrich our understanding and interpretation of the Scripture text by leading readers into greater depths in appreciating the meaning, significance and the relevance of the text in the context. One possible way of an Indian interpretation of the Scriptures is to use a method developed in the traditional Indian aesthetics known as *dhvani.*[1] Anandavardhana (9th CE), a poet and critic from Kashmir has proposed this method and gives us a model by interpreting the great epic Mahabharata.[2] Through his work *Dhvanyālokā* Anandavardhana establishes his theory of *dhvani* that suggestion/evocation[3] is the soul of poetry.[4] Thus the word *dhvani,* which literally means sound, tone, echo, etc., came to be known in the aesthetic sense as suggestion. Anandavardhana defines *dhvani* as a specific feature of language wherein the primary meaning remains subordinate and hence the suggested meaning stands out prominently.[5] That means a text should be suggestive, and what is suggested should be prominent, and it should be strikingly clear to the readers. In short, *Dhvani* way of interpreting the text focuses on the meaningfulness, significance and relevance of the text based on its evocative power. The first part of this paper explains the *dhvani* method and its various aspects. In the second part of the paper, I have attempted to apply the *dhvani* theory to the story of the fall of Adam and Eve in Genesis 3.

1. What is *Dhvani*?

Anandavardhana defines *dhvani* as:

Yathārthah sabdo vā tam artham upasarjanīkrtasvārthau
Vyanktah kāvya visesa sa dhvanir ti sūribhih katitah

1 The Sanskrit word *dhvani* in grammatical literature is used to denote phonemes, the uttered syllables. This aspect was brought into discussion in the Sanskrit poetic literature by Anandavardhana, a poet and a critic from Kashmir and made popular through his work *Dhvanyaloka* in the ninth century A. D. K. Krishnamoorthy, Anandavardhana's *Dhvanyālokā*: A critical edition with introduction, English Translation and Notes, (Karnatak University, Dharwar), 1974.

2 Cf. Anand Amaladass, "*Dhvani* Theory and the Scriptural Interpretation-Dhvani Reading of the Mahabharata by Anandavardhana," *Adyar Library Bulletin*, Vol. 54, (1990), 68-98.

3 "The term *dhvani* is usually translated as 'suggestion'. Since the emotional factor involved in the *dhvani* processes is not highlighted by the term 'suggestion', 'evocation' would be the better term in English", Prema Vakayil, "An Indian Approach to John 13,1-11," *Biblebhashyam*, 27/1, (March 1979), 21.

4 Krishnamoorthy, *Dhvanyālokā*, 47-48.

5 Cf. Anand Amaladass, *Philosophical implication of Dhvani: Experiencing the Symbol Language in the Indian Aesthetics,* (Vienna: Gerald & Co, 1984), 79-80; Anand Amaladass, "*dhvani* Method of Interpretation and Biblical Hermeneutics," *Indian Theological Studies,* 31/3, (September 1994), 201.

"That kind of poetry wherein the conventional meaning renders itself secondary and suggests the implied meaning is designed as *dhvani* or suggestive poetry."[6]

As the above definition indicates *dhvani* is applied to suggestive poetry when the suggested sense predominates over the literal sense. However, it must be noted that the predominance of *dhvani* is discernible only through the existing meanings.[7] *Dhvani* literally means sound, tone, echo, etc, but in aesthetics it means evocation or a poem that evokes.[8] According to Anandavardhana *dhvani* is a specific arrangement of language, wherein the primary meaning remains subordinate in order that the evoked significance shines forth prominently and with clarity.[9]

Aleaz explains the meaning of *dhvani* in the following way:

> *Dhvani* is something like an echo or resonance creating newer and newer echoes. The term *dhvani* is used only when the suggested sense *(vyangya)* is predominant. The argument of Anandavardhana is that categories like *abhidha* (primary meaning), *laksana* (secondary meaning), *anumana* (inference), *tatparya* (import of a sentence), and various *alamkaras* (poetic usages) are not adequate to explain reality. Beyond these categories there is something real and more beautiful, which he calls *dhvani.* The main task of *laksana* is to remove the incompatibility implied in *abhidha.* It has no power to suggest any additional meaning. But *dhvani* provides an additional meaning, which is something new.[10]

Therefore, *dhvani* is basically an indication, a silent suggestion, and works more through evocation than through implication. D'Sa explains it like this:

> Whatever is implied can be arrived at merely from an analysis of the implying statement or gesture. Not so with *dhvani.* No amount of analysis can lay bare the *dhvani-effcct* if the hearer/reader does not have a special

6 Krishnamoorthy, *Dhvanyālokā*, 18-19; Prema Vakayil, "An Indian Approach to John 13,1-11," *Biblebhashyam*, 27/1 (March 1979), 20.

7 Cf. Krishnamoorthy, *Dhvanyālokā*, Op. cit. 10, 16-17,20-21 and 12,4-5 for a detailed exposition of the point.

8 The Sanskrit word *dhvani* carries from the root *dhtian* which means "to sound, to make noise" etc. cf. Monier-Williams, a Sanskrit-English Dictionary, (Delhi: Motilal Banarsidas, 1981), 522. However, according to Chempakassery, "in Sanskrit literary critical tradition it has the sense of 'to mean or to imply'. But it is not the sense we understand from the first reading, but a sense which is more refined than the literal sense and which is arrived at only at a second or third or fourth reading." Philip Charnpakassery, "*Dhvani* (Implied) Meaning of the Marcan Parable of the Sower, *Indian theological studies*, 33/1, (March 1996), 8.

9 Anand Amaladass, "*dhvani* Method of Interpretation and Biblical Hermeneutics," *Indian Theological Studies*, 31/3, (September 1994), 201

10 K. P. Aleaz, "The Sabda-Dhvani Methods of Biblical-Theological Hermeneutics," *Bangalore Theological Forum* 37/2 (December 2005), 132.

> quality that 'attunes' him to it. Whereas an implication *can* be (sooner or later) pin-pointed, and even expressed, *dhvani* (in the best sense of the word) can *never* be pin-pointed, much less can it be expressed in words. It can at best be merely pointed at through metaphor and parable but its precise content evades formulation.[11]

Dhvani is neither a meaning among other meanings nor a meaning arrived through a rational process. Anand Amaladass explains:

> *Dhvani* is not a meaning among other meanings. It is rather meaningfulness or significance attained through a meaning. Meaning and Significance are on different levels ... Hence they cannot be identified nor even put on the same level. *Dhvani* is not merely an indirect way of conveying a meaning for the sake of charm ... *Dhvani* proper is not a rational process where meaning and its implications are arrived at in the logical order. *Dhvani* is the Significance that a meaning brings about to person in the context of a deeper experience.[12]

In short, *dhvani* is said to exist only when there is a suggestion, and that suggestion stands out prominently, and it is recognized without ambiguity.[13]

1.1. The Nature of *Dhvani*

Anandavardhana explains the nature of *dhvani* through various similes and metaphors:

1. Dhvani is like the charm (*lāvanya*) *in* a young woman, which is more than the sum total of her proportionate limbs though all the limbs and the entire organism contribute to it.[14]
2. It is like a soul (*ātman*) in a body (*sarīra*). "According to this metaphor *dhvani* is the soul of poetry (*kāvyasyātma dhvanih*), the literal meaning (*vācyartha*) being its body. In other words *dhvani* is not the external structure of *kāvya* (poetics), such as words and their meaning, its style and figure of speech, but it is the atman (life principle) of *kāvya.*"[15]
3. The third metaphor used is that of lamp and the pot (*ghatapradipa nyaya*). The lamp illumines itself and at the same time reveals the pot

---

11 Francis X. D'Sa, "Dhvani as a Method of Interpretation" *Biblebhashyam*, 5/4 (December 1979), 20.

12 Anand Amaladass, *Philosophical Implications of Dhvani. Experience of Symbol Language in Indian Aesthetics*, 207

13 Anand Amaladass, "Dhvani Theory in Sanskrit Poetics", *Biblebhashyam*, 5/4 (December 1979), 266.

14 Krishnamoorthy, *Dhvanyālokā*, 6, 18-19

15 Prema Vakayil, "An Indian Approach to John 13,1-11," *Biblebhashyam*, 27/1 (March 1979), 21

> nearby. Once the light reveals the pot in a dark room, the attention is shifted to the discovered pot. That is, if the literal or expressed meaning is the lamp, the evoked meaning is the pot.[16]

About the nature of *dhvani* Anand Amaladass says:

> It comes to life in the process of being relished. For this there is no explanation other than the operation of suggestion. It is not the object of denotative language and so it cannot be circumscribed by words. *Nasaksat sabda-vyāpara-viṣayah,* as Anandavardhana puts it. But it does not mean that it is beyond the scope of words and that it cannot be communicated at all. It could be communicated but indirectly, evocatively, through pointer language symbols. *Dhvani* operates through signs which are linguistic or non-linguistic, through words, gestures, musical sounds and so on.[17]

Thus, the nature of *Dhvani* is more of intrinsic irrespective of its expressed meaning. While the expressed meaning arises from a word, the suggested meaning of *dhvani* arises from the text's entirety, such as from words, parts, sentence, style, intonation, gesture etc. Unlike the expressed meaning, suggested meaning goes beyond the rules of grammar and is influenced by the context and the reader, because, it produces different effects in different readers in different contexts.

1.2. How does *Dhvani* function?

Meaningfulness of a text presupposes a reader. A *dhvani* evocation is possible only when there is a *sahrdaya,* the one who has a heart, who is attuned to real beauty to discover and appreciate the *dhvani* meaning of a piece of literature.[18] At the *very* outset of *Dhvanyālokā,* Anandavardhana says that his exposition of *dhvani* is intended for the *sahrdaya.* In his own words:

> The ancient scholars have declared again and again that the soul of poetry is *dhvani.* Yet some insist that it is non-existent and some others say that it has only a logical existence and yet others think that (even if it exists) it is not possible to express it in words. In this situation we are trying to explain its nature and thus bring joy to the *sahrdaya.*[19]

---

16 Krishnamoorthy, *Dhvanyālokā*, 6, 9; Anand, Amaladass, "*Dhvani* Method of Interpretation and Biblical Hermeneutics," *Indian Theological Studies,* 31/3, (September 1994), 203

17 Anand Amaladass, "Poetic Quest for Truth and *Dhvani* mode of Communication," in Anand Amaladass (ed.), *Christian Contribution to Indian Philosophy,* (Madras: CLS, 1995), 9-10.

18 Philip Champakassery, "*Dhvani* (implied) Meaning of the Marcan Parable of the Sower," *Indian Theological Studies,* 33/1, (March 1996), 9.

19 Krishnamoorthy, *Dhvanyālokā*, op. cit, 2.

Now who is a *sahrdaya?* The word is a combination of *sa* and *hrdaya. Sa* is as inseparable prefix which when attached to a word means 'with', 'together with' or 'along with'.[20] Thus, *sahrdaya* means one who is with a heart. "The implication is that only a person who has a heart attuned to real beauty can discover and appreciate the *dhvani* meaning of a piece of literature."[21]

According to Anandavardhana the *dhvani* meaning transcends all other meanings. Amaladass explains:

> Ananda argues that categories like *abhidha* (= primary meaning of a word), *laksana* (= secondary meaning), *anumana* (inference), *tatparya* (import of a sentence), and various *alamkaras* (poetic figures) are not adequate to explain reality. He points out that beyond these categories there is something real and more beautiful, which he calls *dhvani.* Rather he is hinting at a wider horizon which is not circumscribed by the then known logical or linguistic categories. So he shapes a new category, *dhvani* which works through the known categories but transcends them at some stage or other.[22]

Therefore, it is clear that the suggested meaning (*dhvani*) is not to be equated with the primary meaning of a word (*abhidba*), because the primary meaning is the dictionary meaning, something fixed in the sense that whenever the particular word is heard, its fixed meaning is conveyed because of its significative power.[23] The suggested meaning (*dhvani*) is also not the secondary meaning of a word (*laksana*). *Laksana* plays a role only when the primary meaning of a word is not suitable in a particular context and so a meaning other than the usual meaning has to be assumed. However, *laksana* meaning is somehow related to the primary meaning by popular usage.[24] It is in this context *dhvani* meaning comes up with an echo or resonance creating newer and newer echoes *(anuranana).*[25]

---

20 Cf. Monier-Williams, Sanskrit-English Dictionary, 1111.

21 Philip Champakassery, "*Dhvani* (implied) Meaning of the Marcan Parable of the Sower", 9.

22 Anand Amaladass, "Dhvani Theory in Sanskrit Poetics," *Biblebhashyam*, 5/4 (December 1979): 262.

23 Ibid., 263.

24 Ibid.

25 Ibid.

1.3. Distinction between the Suggested Meaning and the Expressed Meaning

The suggested meaning (*dhvani*) and the expressed meaning (*abhidha* and *laksana*), are different though they are related.[26]

- The expressed meaning arises from the words but the suggested meaning can emerge from a word, part of a word, sentence, its style, intonation, or gestures. In other words the suggestive factor can be anything in a given context of the expressed meaning.
- The expressed meaning can be understood by anyone who knows the features of linguistics but the suggested meaning can result beyond the rubrics of linguistics sanctions.
- The expressed meaning brings a cognitive perception (*pratīti*) whereas the suggested meaning creates an atmosphere of pleasant surprise (*camatkrti*) in the hearts of the reader and leads to a thrill of discovery.
- The expressed meaning is the same for all those who know that language because it is something fixed in a context. But the suggested meaning can vary from person to person depending on each one's background.

Thus, though the suggested meaning is different from the expressed meaning, however, it can only operate though the expressed meaning and so they are closely related.

1.4. Kinds of *Dhvani*

Anandavardhana classifies *dhvani* into various kinds on the basis of the following criteria:[27]

- On the basis of the relationship of the suggested meaning to the primary sense.
- On the basis of the elements in the text which affect the suggested meaning.
- On the basis of the nature as such.

Since we are mainly concerned with the *dhvani* proper we shall take up the last way of classification viz. based on the nature of *dhvani* itself.

26 Anand Amaladass, "Dhvani Theory in Sanskrit Poetics", *Biblebhashyam*, 5/4 (December 1979), 265-266.

27 Cf. Anand Amaladass, "Dhvani Theory in Sanskrit Poetics," 266.

Dhvani, according to its nature is divided into two: extrinsic *dhvani* (*dhvani* of attribution) and intrinsic *dhvani* (*dhvani* proper). Extrinsic *dhvani* includes *vastu-dhvani* and *alamkara-dhvani* while intrinsic *dhvani* is *rasa-dhvani.* In *vastu-dhvani* what is evoked can be of the nature of an objective fact, an event or anything that could be said in words. In *alamkara-dhvani* the figure of speech is evoked by the power of the words and their meanings. *Rasa-dhvani* is the *dhvani* proper. It cannot be expressed directly. It can only be indirectly hinted or evoked. The nature of *rasa-dhvani* is such that it is not the object of denotative language but it could be evocatively pointed to, hinted at. It comes closer to the notion of symbol that points beyond itself in and through what it denoted.[28] A poet, in order to create *rasa-dhvani,* has to create a required atmosphere. He has to employ language in such a way as to make the reader experience the situation. By the power of the words and their special usage, the poet tries to stimulate reader's imagination.[29] Thus, *dhvani* proper comes into play between the evocative language of the poet and the aesthetic sensibility of the reader.

The intrinsic *rasa-dhvani* is a result of a dialogue between the reality outside and the actively responding experiencer. Ananda Amaladass notes:

> What Ananda understands by *rasa* is a reality that can be experienced and so can be located though it is not possible to bring it under the denotation of language. The nature of this reality is such that though it belongs to the appreciative level, it can be reached through perceptive reality. In other words, it is a non-space-time dimension of a space-time reality.[30]

In short, the intrinsic *dhvani,* i.e. the *dhvani* proper invites the reader to respond to the evocative meaning of the language used in the text. It involves an active interaction between the text and the reader, and the context of the reader and the text.

1.5. *Dhvani* as a Hermeneutic Principle for Biblical Interpretation

Anandavardhana's *dhvani* theory seems to be offering suggestions in the line of hermeneutic reflections rather than merely as a principle for future poets for composing poetry. *Dhvani* meaning takes us to that realm of significance, which is *rasa.*[31] The *dhvani-event* enable a communion, a communion of the

28 Anand Amaladass, "*Dhvani* Method of Interpretation and Biblical Hermeneutics,"*op.cit.*, 202-203; Prema Vakayil, "An Indian Approach to John 13,1-11," 22.

29 According to Amaladass, "The poet's expression however powerful to evoke rasa, is not without its limitations. It cannot evoke anything and everything and its power is limited by the very nature of language. But its richness depends on the capacity of the reader." Anand Amaladass, "*Dhvani* Theory in Sanskrit Poetics", 272.

30 Anand Amaladass, *Philosophical Implications, op.cit.,* 121.

31 Anand Amaladass, *Philosophical Implications, op.cit.*, 154.

mind of reader with that of the world and that is what *rasa-experience* is. In this process of communion the text evokes meanings significant for the reader's life. Consequently the essence of the text and the inner essence of the reader converge in the evocated meaning level. Thus, a convergence of the essence of things is accomplished in the *dhvani* reading of the text and thus the text becomes a guiding principle for the reader's life.

How can we use *dhvani* as a hermeneutic principle to interpret the Scriptures? By doing that, are we not reducing the Scriptures to mere poetry? Anandavardhana interprets Mahabharata with *dhvani* method and thus sets a paradigm of how one could interpret a religious text according to *dhvani* theory. The reason is that a written text is autonomous whether it is a poetry or prose, scripture or religious discourse. "Their autonomy consists in their ability to stand by themselves inviting the reader to read again and again and evoking a richness of significance in his/her open and sensitive mind."[32]

Biblical scholars will admit that there are author-centered, text-centered and reader-centered approaches to meaning. Earlier hermeneutical interest converged on the author and the author's world. Meaning was assumed to lie in the author's intention, which was formulated in terms of the social, political, cultural and ideological matrix of the author. With the modern emphasis on the autonomy of the text and the role of the reader in the production of meaning, the text has been dislodged from its historical mooring and interpreted it with an array of meanings. Text-centered approaches, in claiming textual autonomy, downplay the boundaries imposed by the world of author upon the text.[33] In the reader-centered approach the reader brings to the text a vast world of experience, presuppositions, methodologies, interests and competencies. Meaning is, thus, produced by the mutual interaction between the text and reader.[34] The text is re-contextualized through the multicoloured lenses of the reader. Today we tend to take an integrated approach to the meaning making process, i.e. three realities converge: author's, text's and reader's. Without an author there is no text, without a reader, a text does not communicate. In a real sense, an unread text carries no meaning, because it can mean nothing until there is mutual engagement between reader and text. As Randolph Tate says "[J]just as the author brings his her worldview and understanding of reality to a text, allowing the text to mirror at least some elements of that worldview and reality, so the reader brings to the text his or her worldview and conception of reality. Texts must be read and made

32 Prema Vakayil, "An Indian Approach to John 13,1-11," 25.

33 Cf. M. H. Abrams, *A Glossary of Literary terms* (New York: Rinehart & Winston, 1981), 83.

34 Edgar V. McKnight, *The Bible and the Reader* (Philadelphia: Fortress, 1985), 128.

sense of within the reader's complex and multifaceted world."[35] As we read a text we infer meaning or the text evokes some meaning to us, and that meaning is in some measure determined by our understanding of our own world. In short, the reader's world is as constitutive of textual meaning as the world of the author.[36] This is what the *dhvani* theory means to the text and to the reader. The *dhvani*-event enables a convergence, a convergence of the mind of reader with that of the text. In this process of convergence the text evokes meanings significant for the reader's life.

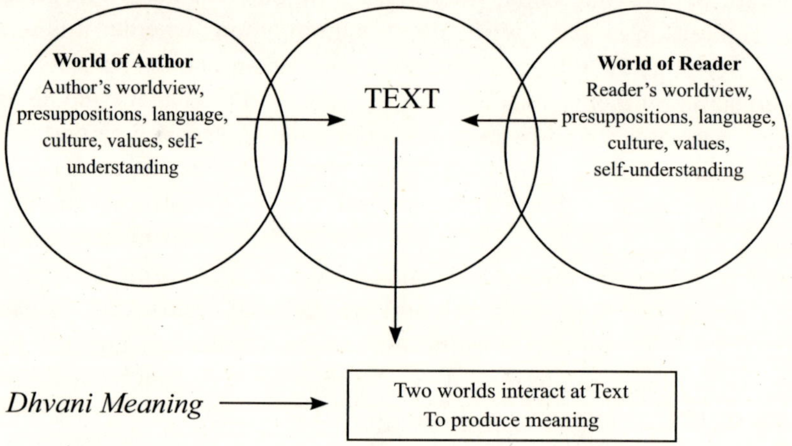

2. *Dhvani* Reading of the Fall of Adam and Eve in Gen 3:1-24

The inverted word order in v1 is quite suggestive because the writer wants to emphasize that a new figure, a snake, is now the subject of the action. The Hebrew term translated "serpent" (*hannāḥāš*; cf. Num 21:7–9; Deut 8:15; Prov 23:32) besides being the generic name for reptile, is also related in its cognate verbal form in the piel to the word for "divination" (cf. Gen 30:27; 44:5, 15; Lev 19:26; Num 23:23; 24:1; Deut 18:10). Therefore, it may suggest to the original audience the association between the serpent and the Canaanite religion both at a literal level and at an etymological level. Ellen van Wolde suggests:

> The serpent may, however, be interpreted as a magical animal of life and wisdom, which according to Vriezen, is apparent from texts like 2 Kgs 18:4 and Num 21:9, in which there is mention of a brass serpent in the temple. Because the serpent sheds its skin and renews itself each time, it

35 Randloph M. Tate, *Biblical Interpretation: An Integrated approach* (Peabody, Hendrickson Inc., 2008), 190.

36 Cf. Randloph, *Biblical Interpretation*, 190.

> is an animal of life. Consequently in the Canaanite, Phoenician, Egyptian and Babylonian world the serpent represents fertility, life-giving power or life itself. This general presentation of the serpent as an animal of life and an animal of wisdom has been used by the author of Genesis 2–3. He did so not because he agreed with this presentation but because he wanted to present a polemic contrast and challenge the image.[37]

As Park has interpreted, it may also suggest an anti-idolatry polemic against Canaanite fertility goddess Ashtoreth (a consort of Baal). He concludes: "Given these associations of snake, woman, and fertility goddess, given the intense competition between the worship of Ashtoreth and Yahweh in ancient Israel, we can see that the story of Eve and the snake, in addition to other readings, is a parody of Canaanite religion."[38] Thus, the possible connection between snake (*nāḥāš*) and "a bronze serpent" (*nāḥāš neḥōšeṯ*) in Num. 21:9, snake as "Nehushtan" (*neḥuštān*) in 2 Kings 18:4, and the Canaanite fertility goddess Ashtoreth may suggest to the original audience of Gen 3:1 a shiny and luminous object which has certain polemic elements.

The wordplay between the word *ʿārûm* and *ʿarur* is also very suggestive. The serpent is introduced as the most "crafty" (*ʿārûm*) creature of the field. However, the serpent and his wisdom (*ʿārûm*) lead ultimately to its curse (*ʿarur*) in v14. That is, he who is *ʿārûm*, "crafty" is also *ʾārûr*, "cursed" one. The most subtle of all the animals now becomes the loneliest and oddest of the animals. Similarly, the acoustical similarity between *ʿārûm*, ("crafty") of 3:1 ʿărûmîm (naked) in 3:14 (cf. 2:25) is also quite evocative. Instead of knowing good and evil, the first parents now know that they are naked. This is hardly the knowledge for which they bargained. What was formerly understood to be a sign of a healthy relationship between the man and the woman (2:25) has now become something unpleasant and filled with shame (3:14).

A careful reading of Gen 3:1-5 will further evoke the Satan's subtle way of functioning to the reader. He pretends to be interested in Eve's well-being. However, he brings about the contrary effects: 1) Firstly he deceives Eve. He disguised himself in a very attractive and appealing way: *"The serpent was more subtle than any beast of the field which the lord god had made"* (v1). 2) Secondly he raises doubts in the heart of eve: *"yea, has god said?"* (V1). 3) Thirdly he brings discontent in the heart of eve. He focuses on the negative, on the restrictions, rather than on the positives, on the privileges: he focuses on the burdens, not the blessings. *"Yea, has god said, you shall not eat of every tree of the garden?"* (V1). 4) fourthly, he denies divine judgment: *"you shall*

37 Ellen van Wolde, *Words Become Worlds: Semantic Studies of Genesis 1–11,* (Leiden: Brill, 1994), 4–5. See also F. Hvidberg, "The Canaanite Background of Gen. I-III," *VT* 19 (1960) 288–90.

38 William Park, "Why Eve?" *St. Vladimir's Theological Quarterly,* 35 (1991), 130.

not surely die" (v1). 5) fifthly, he dishonours god all he can. he would make god cruel, unfair, and much too restrictive. in the narrative he claims that god was holding back blessings from man: *"god does know that in the day ye eat thereof, then your eyes shall be opened, and ye shall be as gods, knowing good and evil"* (v1).

The very first question of the serpent in the narrative is also very evocative: "Did God really say that you shall not eat from any tree in the garden?" (3:1). Who is speaking here? Snakes do not have vocal cords. Thus, the personification of snake is also very suggestive to the reader. The question sounds innocent enough, however, not an innocent one. The reader will obviously understand the Satan's (snake's) purpose as to raise doubt in Eve's mind - doubt as to exactly what God had said as well as doubt about the fairness of God's prohibition.

In Eve's response in v2 the reader can detect the very beginnings of mankind's fall into sin. She knew that snakes can't talk. She knew also that animals have no sense of right and wrong. She should have recognized immediately that an evil spirit was involved here. And yet Eve entered into a discussion of God's Word and God's goodness with the snake. When she answered the devil, Eve restated the broad permission that God had granted (cf. 2:16), although it may be significant that she omitted the word "all" (3:2). And when she restated God's prohibition, she added "neither shall you touch it" (3:3). The reader can seen in these words an unwarranted addition to God's original command. Thus, the textual context suggests that the serpent's insinuation that God was not being faithful to her is one she should immediately have rejected.

Verses 4-5 presents the bait Satan dangled before Eve's eyes. At this moment the reader understands very clearly that Satan had sowed two poisonous seeds in Eve's heart. First, he persuaded her not to take God seriously. Second, he made her doubt God's goodness. Therefore, the text invites the reader to recognize the basic lie of Satan: "God and his will are not really good. God has known all along that eating the fruit would make you his equals, and he doesn't want that."39

Verses 6-7 show that Satan's promise to Eve turned out to be a lie. Eve and Adam did not become like God. Their eyes were opened, however, not in the way Satan had promised. They now knew *good* as something they had lost. And they now knew *evil* as something that controlled them. For the first time in their lives, they felt a sense of shame at their nakedness. They, therefore, made immediate, though ineffective, efforts to clothe themselves. Thus, as the narrative progresses the reader understands well that they were no longer able to direct them according to God's will and to his glory, but fall as victims of

39 John C. Jeske, *Genesis* (Milwaukee, Wis.: Northwestern Pub. House, 2001), 45.

deceit.[40] V6 further clearly suggests various steps in the fall, such as 1) passion: *"When the woman saw that the tree was good for food."* Sin focuses on the fleshly appetites and passion: 2) pleasantness: *"It was pleasant to the eyes."* 3) desire: *"A tree to be desired to make one wise."*4) Proselyting: *"Gave also unto her husband with her, and he did eat."* Sin is not satisfied to do its evil alone but encourages others to join in.

In v8-10 the reader sees a compassionate turn in the narrative which evokes positive feeling towards God. In their sin and shame, Adam and Eve were not looking for God, but God was looking for them. "Where are you?" (v9) is a call of God's love and concern, rather than a question of threat and anger. The creator-God is moving to restore his fallen children to himself. The reader senses an emotion of fear that Adam and Eve had never felt before in the statement: "They hid themselves." The garden had been a place of joyful fellowship with God, but now they ran from him and hid. God's second question further reveals the gravity of the consequence of the fall: "What have you done that you should be hiding?" (v11). Adam's answer, "I was afraid because I was naked; so I hid," (v10) is a half-truth. It is evasive and deceptive, and it shows the ugly effects of the damage sin causes.[41]

In v8 the verb translated "was walking" is in a relatively rare verb stem, the hithpael, usually the intensive reflexive. For the Old Testament reader the hithpael of *hālāk* may point forward to Deuteronomy 23:15 "For Yahweh your God walks about (hithpael participle of *hālāk*) in the midst of your camp" and Leviticus 26:12 where an obedient future Israel is promised, "I will walk (hithpael of *hālāk*) among you and be your God and you will be my people."[42] Thus, the hithpael of hālāk in v8 indicates God's continued presence with the humanity even after the fall.

The questions in v11–13 further reveal that there is something distressing God. "Who told you that you were naked? Have you eaten from the tree that I commanded you not to eat from?" (v11); "What is this you have done?" (v13). While Both Adam and Eve were concentrating on the sinful deed of eating, God was much more concerned about the sinful attitude that produced the sinful deed. The first question will naturally raise further questions in the mind of the reader. Is it the serpent who told Adam that he is naked? Is it the woman who told Adam that he is naked? Is it Adam's own eyes that told Adam that he is naked? In other words, whence the man's source of guilt and shame? Although the answer is not given, the reader understands the source of their nakedness. The woman's answer to God's question is similar to the man's (v13). However, she does not say "the serpent whom *you* made" nor does

40 For the above discussion, see Jeske, *Genesis*, 45-46.

41 For this discussion, see Jeske, *Genesis*, 46-47.

42 Cf. Paul J. Kissling, *Genesis* (Joplin, Mo.: College Press Pub. Co., 2004), 198.

she say "*the man* to whom you gave me." But she openly admits that she was tricked or deceived.[43] That is to say that the reader understands that Eve has made a mistake and she admits it.

One element distinguishes God's decree to the serpent from his decree to the human couple, i.e. a unique form of locomotion for the snake - he is to crawl on his belly. This posture will make him eat dust. Such a penalty matches the serpent's sin[44] He who tempted Eve to *eat* now himself will *eat* dust.[45] He who is *ʿārûm*, "crafty," (v1) is now *ʾārûr*, cursed (v14). The most subtle of all the animals now becomes the loneliest and oddest of the animals.

V15 will evoke to the New Testament reader the promise of Christ. God warned Satan: "He will crush your head, and you will strike his heel." For the New Testament reader it is easy to understand allegorically that it was through the woman's offspring that God would conquer sin and death, which brought through the first woman.[46]

V16–19 presents God's punishment to Eve and Adam. It is interesting to note that God first addressed Eve because it was she who had first believed Satan's lie that following him would bring blessing. The punishment to Eve corresponds with natural law showing that every time Eve or one of her daughters would bring a child into the world, the pain of childbirth would be a reminder that sin brings sorrow and suffering instead of satisfaction. Moreover, in the fall Eve had sought to act independently of her husband. Consequently the punishment goes against her will and act: "Your desire will be for your husband, and he will rule over you." (v16).

In order to make God's judgment serious and emphatic the cursing the author employs doublets in pronouncing sentence upon snake, Adam and his wife, For example,

---

43 The verb for "deceive" is *nāšāʾ*. It is used in the same sense in a few other instances, e.g. by Rabshakeh when he says to the people of Jerusalem, "Do not let Hezekiah deceive you, for he will not be able to deliver you out of my hand" (2 Kgs 18:29 [= Isa. 36:14]), and by the king of Assyria to Hezekiah: "Do not let your God deceive you" (2 Kgs 19:10 [= Isa. 37:10]). Jeremiah's attribution of such activity to God is electrifying (Jer. 4:10).

44 For further illustrations of the correspondence between sin and judgment in Gen. 4–11 see P. D. Miller, *Genesis 1–11,* pp. 27–37.

45 Obviously, snakes do not eat dust, and no ancient writer ever thought they did. One has to take this passage symbolically, not literally.

46 Wifall, "Gen. 3:15 - A Proto-evangelium?" *CBQ* 36 (1974) 361 - 65, allows for a messianic interpretation of Gen. 3:15, but only if the verse is seen in the context of Israel's royal ideology. For him the verse is anything but a direct prediction. I am most comfortable with Las or's use of the verse as an illustration of *sensus plenior:* "I do find the fullness of meaning (viz., of Gen. 3:15) in some as-yet-unspecified member of the human race who would destroy the satanic serpent, thus playing a key role in God's redemptive plan. In that sense, the passage is indeed the first enunciation of the good news", cf. W. S. LaSor, "Prophecy, Inspiration, and *Sensus Plenior,*" *TynBul* 29 (1978) 56–57.

- Upon your belly you shall go, and dust you shall eat all the days of your life (v14).
- I will put enmity between you and the woman, and between your offspring and hers (v 15).
- He will strike your head, and you will strike his heel (v15).
- I will greatly increase your pangs in childbearing; in pain you shall bring forth children (v16).
- Thorns and thistles it shall bring forth for you; and you shall eat the plants of the field (v 18).

V20-24 show how the fall resulted in settling Adam and Eve in another place instead of the Garden of Eden. The word play between *šālaḥ* (qal) and *šālaḥ* (piel) in v 23-24 is quite suggestive. God was concerned that the man might "put forth" (*šālaḥ* qal) his hand; so God *expelled* or put him out (*šālaḥ* piel) of the garden. "He drove out the man" (v24); "So he drove out man" (v24). This suggests refusal to leave, continued rebelling against the will of God. Another repeated verb in vv. 22 and 23 are *lāqaḥ (qal) and lāqaḥ* (pual): "take"—"lest he … take [*lāqaḥ* in the Qal] also of the tree of life" and "the ground from which he was taken [*lāqaḥ* in the Pual]." The narrative comment in v23 "The Lord God sent him forth from the garden of Eden, to till the ground" (v23) suggests the duty after the removal. It would be a cursed ground with weeds battling the productivity of it (3:17.18).

Conclusion

The theory of *dhvani* as it appears in Anandavardhana's *Dhvanyālokā* is a major contribution to the study of the meaning of the text. It goes beyond the primary or literal meaning of a sentence (*abhidha*) and the secondary or implied meaning (*lakṣana*) to postulate a third but important sphere of suggested meaning. *Dhvani* is that use of language which through the expressed meaning (*abhidha* and *laksana*) takes the reader to a depth-meaning which is experienceable but not expressible. *Dhvani* meaning challenges the readers because it depends upon evocation, and it presupposes some involvement of the reader with the text to attune himself to the *dhvani-effect.* By presenting to us a *dhvani-reading* of the Mahabharata, Anandavardhana provides us with a paradigm as how one could interpret a religious text according to *dhvani* theory. As it has been applied to the Mahabharata, *dhvani* theory can also be applied to the other scriptures, including the Bible. The *dhvani* reading of the fall of Adam and Eve in Gen 3:1-24 shows the evocative meaning and the theological depth of the fall narrative in Genesis 3. In Gen 3:1-24 we can see a convergence of the worldview of the original reader and contemporary reader with the text evoking meanings significant for their life.

7

Contemporary Reading of Tagore's Poem 'Mind Without Fear' Through *Dhvani* Method

James Ponniah

Abstract

This essay titled as 'Contemporary Reading of Tagore's Poem 'Mind Without Fear' Through *Dhvani* Method' focuses on Noble laureate Tagore's famous poem 'Mind Without Fear,' applies *dhvani* method of interpretation to understand the meaning and the relevance of such a significant poem both in the past and the present. The essay is divided into three parts. Part one enunciates the major principles of *dhvani* method of interpretation that would be employed in the essay. Part two tries to analyze the poem at various levels, besides briefly looking at the meaning of the poem during the author's life period. Part three of the essay dwells upon the relevance of the poem for our contemporary period.

Key words: Tagore, Patriotism, unity, inclusiveness, freedom, knowledge for all. dhvani

Introduction

We live in a divided-world. There is a sudden surge of bigotry and conflict in our contemporary life, often based on boundaries such as religions, cultures and nations. However, we do come across instances where appreciation for and collaboration with the different others exist. People also value and celebrate the presence of the good and the positive regardless of where it is found. We see

Bhagavad-Gita being quoted by Christians and Muslims, Bible by Muslims and Hindus, and Quran by Christians, Hindus and Sikhs. This practice of religious accommodation is encouraging and heartening. In this connection, it is in place to note that Tagore's famous poem 'Mind without Fear' is included in Christian hymnals in India and it has been sung regularly in Christian worship services for more than three decades. It is well received by the Indian Christian community, because it advocates patriotism and its core values such as unity, inclusiveness, and freedom and knowledge for all. This essay, which focuses on this poem, aims to apply *dhvani* method of interpretation to understand the meaning and the relevance of such a significant poem both in the past and at present. The essay is divided into three parts. Part one enunciates the major principles of *dhvani* method of interpretation that would be employed in the essay. Part two tries to analyze the poem at various levels, besides briefly looking at the meaning of the poem during the author's life time. Part three of the essay dwells upon the relevance of the poem for our contemporary period.

1. Revisiting *Dhvani* Method of Interpretation

Dhvani is one of the important methods in Indian theory of meaning. Its name *dhvani* literally means sound, echo, tone etc. This word owes its origin to a Sanskrit *dhvan*, i.e. to reverberate. One of the key proponents of the school is Anandavardhana whose 9 Cent C.E. work Dhvanyaloka became the key text of the school. Differing from the then two well-known functions of language recognized in the Vedic language by ancient exegetes like Jaimini and Sabara such as primary or literal meaning (*abhidhi*) and the transferred or metaphorical sense (*laksana* or *gunavada*), he claimed that there was a third potency of language, namely, suggestion (*vyanjana*), which was the proper function of poetic language.

The most fundamental premise of the *dhvani* theory is that "suggestion is a supernumerary meaning."[1] Though utterances contain their literal meaning, "they also convey further sense (*dhvanir nama arthantaram*). And the activity whereby the comprehension of an additional meaning is caused must be accepted as suggestion, because the denotative function of words can only yield the syntactical meaning and rests there having exhausted its function (*viramya vyaparabhiavt*)."[2] Once the syntactical and primary meanings come to a stalemate, what results can only be suggestion. The second important premise of this theory is that "where the suggested meaning arises, it is necessarily always the predominant element and the literal meaning subordinates itself

1 V. K. Chari, "The Indian Theory of Suggestion (dhvani)," *Philosophy East and West*, Vol. 27, No. 4 (Oct., 1977, pp. 391-399), p. 392.

2 Ibid.

to it. This is the principle of subordination (*upasarjantbhava or gunibhiva*)."[3] Thirdly, in as much as the extra meaning is obtained beyond the limits of the expressed or the secondary meaning, "it is necessarily "indirect" meaning; and indirection or concealed significance is the chief source of charm in poetry (*gopyamanasaratvat*)."[4] The suggestive mode in *dhvani* is "essentially a presentational mode, not discursive"[5] and it lies not in the syntax of words but in their evocation. That means, according to *dhvani* a literary piece or a work of art should be evocative. Only then it becomes the subject of *dhvani* theorization. Thus the evocated, suggested, additional and unstated meaning is deemed the key to the *dhvani* system. Anandavardhana makes use of many metaphors to drive home the nature and power of *dhvani*. He likens it to the charm of a young woman whose beauty is much more than the sum total of her bodily parts. So too is *dhvani*, the evoked meaning of a poem or a literary piece and its evocative power lie beyond its various components such as words, meter and figures of speech. He also compares it to the *atman* (the soul) in the body. Dhvani is the soul of poetry. One of his most powerful metaphors in this regard relates to the relationship between a lamp and the pot. The light of the lamp in the dark room shifts the attention of the people in the room from the light to objects like pots. Here, the function of the lamp is to provide visibility to the objects in the dark room and not to draw attention to itself. However, the lamp needs to be there all the time; otherwise the pot would not be seen. In a similar vein, the simultaneous presence of the literal meaning and the evoked significance of the words is acknowledged in *dhvani*. And the literal meaning of the poem acts as light or a pointer.

In Indian philosophy, *dhvani* is of three kinds. They are: a) *Vastudhvani* b) *Alamkaradhvani* c) *Rasadhvani*. The first one is used to evoke the nature of an objective fact, an event that can be expressed in words. A poet subscribes to this method to communicate his or her ideas more effectively. For instance, when one says, 'Feel free to explore the beach on your own and enjoy the waves of the seashore. A couple of days ago, two young boys got drowned at this beach,' what is intended is 'do not play with the waters as you wish' though one might say 'feel free to explore the beach'. In *alamkaradhvani* meaning is evoked through the use of figures of speech. While the first two are extrinsic *dhvani*, i.e., they can be expressed, *rasadhvani* is intrinsic *dhvani*. It means that the latter cannot be expressed but only evoked. "On the one hand, *rasadhvani* is at work in and through the power of denotative meaning and on the other hand, it cannot be directly denoted or circumscribed in words. In other words, the nature of *rasadhvani* is such that it is not the object of denotative language

3 Ibid.

4 Ibid.

5 Ibid.

but it could be evocatively pointed to, hinted at."[6] Besides, in Indian theory of meaning, two well-known types are primary meaning (*abhidha*), i.e, the literal meaning and secondary meaning (*laksana*). When the primary meaning of the text is not congruent with the sentence and context, one needs to allude to a secondary meaning. The famous example given is the phrase 'the hamlet is on the river Ganges.' The primary meaning is incongruent, as no village can be located on a river. But what is implied is the idea that the hamlet is on the banks of the Ganges. The idea of Ganges can also obtain additional meanings besides the primary and the secondary meanings. Given its cultural and religious significance, Ganges evokes the ideas of purity, sacredness and tranquillity. The latter known as *vyanjana vyapara* was not only considered separate and different from the first two, but is given a separate position and theorized by Anandavardhana to develop his theory of *dhvani*. The evocativeness of a poem or a literary piece may coincide with the import of a poem or a sentence or at times with the intention of the author. But it can also go beyond intention of the author and obtain an unintended meaning. When that occurs the text or an art speaks for itself wherein the author's role in bringing out the meaning of the text is rather minimal and no more relevant. But such a possibility requires a sensitive reader (*sahrdaya*).

The reader's background, capability, sensitivity and openness do make a difference in the process of bringing out the meaning of the text. It means a sensitive reader plays a key role in making the text come alive. This reader need not be a great scholar, nor be well trained in exegetical skills but one "who is endowed with an inborn gift, a sensitivity to be responsive to the evocations of significance."[7] She or he should not be indifferent to what happens but rather be open to the reality which is constantly disclosing itself, calling for our attention, laying its claim on us, and demanding a response from our side. One may also choose to remain blind to it and thus perceive the reality in a muted mode. For instance, the phrase 'The sun has risen' might evoke different responses from different actors. While it means to a sacristan or a *poojari* or an *imam* that it's time to open the church/ temple/ mosque and start the prayer, to a mother it means it is time to make morning coffee, and to a student it is time to get up, revise the lessons and get ready for the exam. But for a drunkard such a phrase is irrelevant as he is fast asleep. Hence he is deaf and unresponsive to the situation. Thus the evocation of the phrase or a poem is dependent on the character of the reader. It is either present or absent accordingly. "It is openness or preparedness that allows the evokers to be far-reaching. Because it is an attitude to life and to reality as a whole, a *dhvani*

---

6 Anand Amaladoss, "*Dhvani* Method of Interpretation and Biblical Hermeneutics," Indian theological Studies, Vol 31, No 3, (September 1994, pp 199-217), p. 203.

7 Ibid, 206.

attitude, that is not content with what appears, but looks for a depth dimension in reality. This process itself is a thrill of discovery of something previously concealed."[8]

While elaborating the idea of *dhvani*, Anandavardhana goes on to describe how it can become an important hermeneutical principle not only to the reading of poems but to the reading of epics and literature. While reading epics like Mahabaratha, he would maintain that a key evoker in the text can be identified. The key invoker verse is a key that unlocks the rest of the text to a new world of meaning. 'Herein the eternal Lord Vasudeva is glorified' is the key invoker in Mahabaratha as the Lord alone exceeds everything else as a permanent and supreme reality and this Lord becomes both the means and the end of human destiny (*moksha*). Similarly, in the reading of other religious or secular texts one can identify the key evoker phrase or verse that would help the sensitive reader to be open to the world of hermeneutical possibilities. In the section below we will try to identify the key evoker text in Tagore's famous poem 'Mind without Fear' and understand its meanings then and now.

Analyzing Tagore's 'Mind without Fear' Against the Context

The poem 'Mind without fear' was written by the Nobel laureate Rabindranath Tagore. The original version of the poem in Bengali titled *Chitto jetha bhoyshunyo* was published in 1910 and its English translation was included as the thirty-fifth poem in Tagore's magnum opus Gitanjali which clinched the Nobel prize in 1913 for literature. This famous and evocative poem reads as follows:

Where the mind is without fear and the head is held high
Where knowledge is free
Where the world has not been broken up into fragments
By narrow domestic walls
Where words come out from the depth of truth
Where tireless striving stretches its arms towards perfection
Where the clear stream of reason has not lost its way
Into the dreary desert sand of dead habit
Where the mind is led forward by thee
Into ever-widening thought and action –
Into that heaven of freedom, my Father, let my country awake.

The poem not only reflects the unflinching patriotism of Tagore but also expresses his desire, like that of other patriots, to have India freed from alien rule. To Tagore, freedom movement meant struggle not only against the British administration but also against the prejudices and superstitions of the people in

8 Ibid., 209.

India. Written at the time of British Raj against whom there were protests and demonstrations in the early 20th century, this poem expresses not only Tagore's unquenchable thirst for a holistic freedom but also his relentless zeal for an alternative human world.

From the point of view of English literature, this poem employs many literary styles. For instance, it adopts the technique of 'anaphora', i.e. the repetition of the same word or phrase at the beginning of successive clauses or verses. In the poem the word 'where' is being repeated in almost all the lines except in the last. This poem also employs 'alliteration i.e., the repeated use of the same consonant sound at the beginning of a word in a line or a verse. One may notice such alliterations in lines 1 ('head' 'held' and 'high'), 3 ('where' and 'world'), 5 ('where' and 'words') and 8 ('dreary' 'desert' and 'dead'). The poem also adopts the literary technique of personification. For instance, line 5 personifies the human activity of 'striving' as a living being with arms. The poem also uses the metaphor of stream for human reason in line 7.

The last line of the poem is the most important verse, because it offers the possibility for both *laksana* and *dhvani* meanings. When Tagore uses the expression, "Into that heaven of freedom, my Father, let my country awake,' the literal meaning of the verse seems incongruent. The country is not a living being which is capable of awaking from its state of sleep or dream. What is meant by this statement is that the people of the country who are in a state of ignorance and slumber need to wake up and come to their senses. This is the secondary meaning, the *laksana* function of this verse. But this verse also possesses the *dhvani* function of the meaning, as the word 'country' evokes much more than a geographical location. It evokes the atmosphere of a grim situation prevalent in the 20th century India. The status of such a situation then in the country is taken note of and described by Tagore himself in the preceding lines of the poem. These verses bring to light the desperate situation of the country. Tagore painfully recounts the existing context of the country such as the sense of fear in British India, lack of self-respect, inaccessibility of knowledge, oppressive walls of division among the people created by caste, creed, wealth and gender, circulation of hypocrisy and lies in the country, the deadweight of customs, traditions and superstitious beliefs, and the narrow-minded thought and action of the people of the country. It is from this ignominious moments that Tagore prays for liberation, and urges God to awaken his countrymen to a world of freedom wherein prevails self-dignity, freedom of knowledge, unity, truth, relentless search for perfection, reign of rationality and openness of mind that seeks new horizons in thought and action.

It is against this background that Tagore places the key evoker verse "Into that heaven of freedom, my Father, let my country awake" as the pinnacle of the poem. The rest of the poem both structurally and hermeneutically leads up to this verse. The first 9 lines of the poem that uniformly contain 'where' possess a number of statements that are made to express the positive attributes Tagore feels that India needs to achieve, while taking into account the challenges such as divisions and irrational beliefs and customs. As a poet and philosopher, Tagore's prayer to God whom he calls Father - an uncommon attribute to God in Hindu tradition - in the 11th line is for a world of freedom to which his country India should awake. The previous 10 lines are nothing but qualifiers of the 'heaven of freedom'.

Dhvani Interpretation of the Poem Today by a Sensitive Reader

How does this poem resonate with a sensitive reader living in India today? What kind of *dhvani* evocative power does it enjoy today? Does this poem strike a chord with the people of India today? Do the concerns, anxieties and hopes expressed by Tagore a century ago continue to echo in our hearts and minds in 2019? Let me briefly answer these queries in this section by re-reading the poem verse by verse as a sensitive reader.

> *Where the mind is without fear and the head is held high*
> *Where knowledge is free*

'The mind without fear,' being the title-line of the poem, is deemed to be one of the defining characteristics of Tagore's vision of India. A democratic nation ideally speaking is a fearless country in the sense that it is a nation of the people, for the people and by the people. Hence unlike other forms of government such as monarchy or oligarchy or colonial rule where people constantly live under the fear of being under someone's rule, in a democracy people stay fearless as they rule themselves through their representatives. Hence they must be able to live without the fear of repercussion of what they think, believe in, practice, eat and wear, There is no fear of physical harm meted out to them on account of such a life. That is the ideal situation of a democracy. But the people in today's India, like that of other nations in the world, live in fear as they are ruled by short-sighted fundamentalist politicians. In a polarized world today, more and more people are made to feel that they are less and less wanted. The category of the unwanted seems to grow in numbers as more and more people such as migrants, religious and ethnic minorities, the elderly, the invalid, the tribals, the dalits and the poor are pushed into this category by the dominant few and their supporters who seem to have captured the reins of power by cook or by crook. The 'heaven of freedom' Tagore prays for is a place without this fear wherein people can hold their head high as they can live with self-dignity and self-pride. Such a situation is far from being real in India today. Those who think differently from those in power are intimated, targeted and terrorized by the state and its machinery. As a result, what prevails is a regime of silencing. The self-thinking intellectuals, media persons and conscientious bureaucrats and the judiciary are forced to be resigned to a situation of intellectual and professional backwaters. Those who cannot play second fiddle to the powers that be cannot any more hold their heads high. Rather they are made invisible and inarticulate by the nefarious powers that rule the nations today. In the second line of the poem, Tagore turns to knowledge and wishes that it be made accessible to all freely without manipulation and restriction. Unfortunately and paradoxically in this information age such a situation is absent. Knowledge has become a site of politics wherein information and data are manipulated, tampered with and colored before it is disseminated as a public knowledge. Further, with the privatization and corporatization of higher education, scientific knowledge has become the commodity of the elite and the affluent while innovative knowledge systems are made inaccessible to the poor and the marginalized, blocking them from bettering their lives.

Where the world has not been broken up into fragments
By narrow domestic walls

The third and the fourth lines of the poem articulate Tagore's dream of a perfect civil society—a civil society that has overcome man-made boundaries and barriers of gender, religion, region and caste. It is an inclusive society that refuses to be divided and broken into narrow niches and dungeons. Unfortunately independent India that has survived for seven decades as a single political entity with its principle of unity in diversity is experiencing tremors created by sectarian ideologies and their insecure leaderships that have been systematically producing a range of religion-based, language-based, caste-based conflicts and cleavages in the social fabric of India for the last two or three decades. This has resulted in disagreement, disharmony and violence among people, religions, cultures and regions. Tagore's vision of a united and unbroken India is increasingly becoming a distant reality in present day India.

Where words come out from the depth of truth
Where tireless striving stretches its arms towards perfection

The fifth line of the poem, more philosophical in nature, calls for ethical propriety on the part of the Indians. In our contemporary world, where lies and fake news are in abundant supply, Tagore calls for integrity among his country men and women. The words uttered, no matter by whom, should emanate from the deep-seated truth humans have cultivated within themselves. Such an honest life no doubt comes as a huge challenge to each one of us. But Tagore wants us to come out clean, shedding away all forms of hypocrisy in our lives so that we speak out what we think and live out what we are deep inside. This harmonious life at the individual level would lead to peace and harmony at the societal level. It is this congruence between the personal and the social, the inner and the outer that Tagore subscribes to in this verse. The sixth line calls upon India, the youngest nation in the world today, to work hard. It reiterates the obvious, namely that the road to perfection is hard work and tireless striving. In whatever one does one can attain perfection when one works hard. In this regard, Tagore warns the Indians against complacency that often results in mediocrity.

Where the clear stream of reason has not lost its way
Into the dreary desert sand of dead habit

The next two lines of the poem warns us against the labyrinth of traditions, its customs and rituals. It states that the old and outdated customs and traditions are like a desert that absorbs water and brings man's reason to a halt. Very many Indians today, in spite of their achievements in science and technology, easily take to a slew of irrational beliefs and rites. Not many things that go on in the name of faith and old traditions confirm the view that education in this country has brought about enlightenment among its people. The increase of astrologer-shows on Indian television is not an encouraging sign. Does it reflect a multi-layered uncertainty the globalised world brings to the lives of modern humans? Or does it cater to the people looking for quick-fix solutions in their superfast contemporary lives? Or does it reflect quick success people want to have by earning easy money? Or does it predict the lack of self-confidence that pervades Indians today? Perhaps the popularity of astrology in India can be seen as a solution to a complex combination of many such questions. Be that as it may, the solution Tagore offered to the blind pursuit of customs is the path of reason. He compares 'reason' to a 'clear stream' in line 7. Just as a clear stream is crystal clear and offers better clarity and visibility to water, so also reason provides clarity to human mind. That clear mind is an enlightened mind that can distinguish between meaningful and irrelevant customs.

Where the mind is led forward by thee
Into ever-widening thought and action –
Into that heaven of freedom, my Father, let my country awake.

The last three lines form one unit and culminate in Tagore's prayer to God whom he addresses as Father. In the 9th verse, he asks God to lead the mind while in verse 7 above he subscribed to the guidance of reason. Thus Tagore advocates the role of both reason and faith in the lives of modern Indians. He reminds us that reason without faith is blind, and faith without reason is lame. He provides the rationale for the role of God in the lives of modern Indians today. He brings in God as God is the author of the new, the creative and the transcendent. That is why he asks God to place the human mind in the world of never-ending new possibilities of thinking and acting. Perhaps he warns the modern Indian against the supremacy of reason which loses sight of the beyond and the transcendent. Our contemporary world under the siege of fundamentalism of different kinds—be it religious, ethnic, national, racial or linguistic—has become short-sighted and does not see beyond itself. It has become inward looking and exclusive, whereas Tagore wants Indians today to become outward looking and inclusive. He wants us to remain open to the ever-widening horizons of life. He urges us to expand our little worlds to experience the new by engaging in thought and action that promote the widening of horizons. Perhaps we are well-settled with the old and the known that make us feel secure and protected. Tagore pushes us to the new levels of security and protection by exploring the new and the unknown. His project is creative, inclusive and all-embracing. This is the new India Tagore has crafted in this poem which he refers to as 'that heaven of freedom'. He places this 'heaven of freedom' in the last verse, which according to *dhavni* is the evoker verse. In this verse, he evokes his own vision of new India (which he has delineated all through the poem) that is relevant even today to which he asks God to let his country awake.

Conclusion

The values of unity, inclusiveness and equality echoed in such Sanskrit and vernacular wisdom sayings as '*vasudhaiva kutumbakam*' ('world is a family') and '*yaadhum oore yaavarum kelier* ('To us all towns are one, all humans are our kin') continue to remain ideals in India. They have not become a reality even after seven decades of India's emergence as a sovereign nation state. In spite of India's achievements in various fields, its civil society is far from an enlightened society. It suffers under the grip of a narrow mind-set, discriminatory policies, divisive politics, ignorant beliefs and a non-equalitarian ethos. To this grim situation of India, Tagore's poem offers a way forward. Written more than 100 years ago, it lays down the road-map India needs to adopt to become an inclusive and an enlightened society.

8

The Hermeneutical Appropriation of *Tattvamasi*

Raju Felix Crasta

Abstract

The *Mahāvākya 'tattvamasi'* found in the *Chāndogya Upaniṣad* is a neutral statement revealing a mysterious aspect of the scripture. In a capsule form, it can be interpreted from diverse points of view, i.e., from *Advaita*, *Dvaita* and *Dvaitādvaita* or *abheda*, *bheda* and *bhedābheda* without causing any hermeneutical violence to the text. Śaṅkara translates it as 'You are That,' Madhva as 'You are not That,' and Vijñānabhikṣu as 'You are in That.' Further, Vijñānabhikṣu in his erudite way explores it as every being partakers in the divine essence, a unique understanding than the former two. This penetrating inter-relatedness makes *tattvamasi*, a semantic axis of the *Vedānta*, a tool for cosmotheandric and other such holistic well-being.

Key words: *tattvamasi, mahāvākya, Advaita, Dvaita, Viśiṣṭādvaita, Avibhāga Bhedābheda, Vedānta, Brahman, Ātman, bheda, abheda, prakṛti, puruṣa, apṛthakasiddhi, anubhava,* Vijñānabhikṣu, tautology.

Introduction

Īśāvāsyamidamsarvaṁ yatkiñca jagatyāṁ jagat; tena tyaktena bhuñjīthā mā gṛdhaḥ kasyasviddhanam" (Īśā Upaniṣad, 1). The Lord pervades all things whatsoever live in this universe and the universe itself. One should savour by abandonment and shouldn't covet anybody's wealth. Essentially, divinity emanates from every being. All that we behold and all that we overlook, all that is manifest and all that is transcendent, is a manifestation of the divine, for it has been created not only by Him, but also out of Him like a spider weaving its web. This divinity is the linking element between every being. The potentiality to discover and realize lies in every sentients. Thus, there is an inseparable Oneness (*avicchedādvaitaḥ*) in the reality.

Scriptures reveal this complexity through various ways and means. One such concept is found in the *Chāndogya Upaniṣad* (CU), in terms of a Great Sentence (*mahāvākya*) called *tattvamasi*. The phrase *tattvamasi* occurs nine times in the Upaniṣad which contains just three words (*tat, tvam* and *asi*) forming a single word. It is also called a *mahāvākya* neither because of the linguistic or the grammatical nuances nor for its length, but due to the meaning it impregnates, *the declaration of the identity of the individual Self with the Supreme Self. Tattvamasi* is one among the four well accepted *mahāvākyas* by most of the *vedāntic* thinkers: *prajñānambrahman* (*consciousness is Brahman*, taken from the *Aitareya Upaniṣad* 3.1.3 of the *Ṛgveda*) expresses the nature of the Self, while the other three, *ahambrahmāsmī* (*I am Brahman*, taken from *Bṛhadāraṇyaka Upaniṣad* 1.4.10 of the *Śukla Yajurveda), tattvamasi* (*That Thou Art*, taken from *Chāndogya Upaniṣad* 6.8.7 of the *Sāmaveda,* and *ayamātmabrahma* (*This Ātman is Brahman*, second *mantra* in the *Māṇḍūkya Upaniṣad* of the *Atharvaveda*) express the nature of essential identity between the finite and infinite self. These are "the quintessence of *Upaniṣadic* wisdom."[1]

Though the basic issue tackled in the *mahāvākya tattvamasi* is the identity of the essence of the individual Self and the Supreme Being, various thinkers have attempted to answer it from their perspective. This is explicit in the philosophical stand taken by different *ācāryas*. In this paper, we endeavour to understand *tattvamasi* and its significance.

1. The Context, Text and Analogies of the *Mahāvākya Tattvamasi*

The *Chāndogya Upaniṣad* begins directing the priests performing their sacred duties to discern the significant wisdom in what they perform and recite as a brute ritual. This sublimating of ritualism gradually leads one to perceive the entire life system as a *yajña*. This is to recognize the reality as divine (*sarvamkhalvidam brahma,* CU 3.14.1), followed by the enquiry into what Brahman or the reality is. The answer arrived at is *tattvamasi*. Once this is realized in oneself, the person reaches the state of *idam sarvam* (CU 3.12.1 one's own divine self). In other words a leap takes place from the self-identity to leading everything eventually to the world of *becoming* (Brahman).[2]

1 M. K. Venkatarama Iyer, "The Methodology of the Upaniṣads," in *Studies in Vedānta Philosophy*, ed. R. K. Panda (Delhi: Bharatiya Kala Prakashan, 2002), 69.

2 The root word of Brahman is *bṛh*. The derivative is interchangeably used as *vṛh* or *bṛh*. *Bṛh* or *vṛh* has the meaning of '*tearing apart, to grow, to increase, to cause to grow, to nourish*'. The confusion of *b* and *v* goes back to the oldest time. See, Apte, *Sanskrit-Hindi-English Dictionary*, Delhi: Satguru Publications, 2002. William D. Whitney, *The Roots,*

1.1 Context and Story

According to Hindu *saṁskāras*, a *brāhmin* upon crossing the infant stage requires to undergo '*vedārambhaṇa*' (studentship), necessitating to study under a *guru* in a *gurukula* (resident school) for 12 long years. Śvetaketu, the son of Uddālaka Aruṇi delays in going so. Later, upon his father's insistence embarks upon the study for 12 long years and returns at the age of 24 as a proud and arrogant learned student. His father spots it.[3] Here, three words are used to describe the state of Śvetaketu: *mahāmanāḥ* (one feels greater than the other, resulting in arrogance), *anūcānamānī* (one thinks of oneself as a great orator) and *stabdhaḥ* (stubborn or obstinate and condescending behaviour). *Learning should bring humility and humility right knowledge.*[4] Often, instead of this, ego and arrogance seize over their right knowledge, and reflected in their behaviour: '*I am better than the other,*' "*I have studied,*' '*I know it all.*' This is a kind of pride Śvetaketu crammed with. The humbling experience of the *upaniṣad*[5] expected of him is not yet acquired.

In order to remove his pride, arrogance and to test his knowledge, father poses a philosophical question: "*Did you ask for that teaching, through which 'what is unheard becomes heard, what is unthought of becomes thought of and what is unknown becomes known?*" The son gets a first tremor here. He identifies his education is not yet complete and therefore, mellows down imploring for the answer, "of what nature reverend teacher is that teaching?"[6] Father replies with three metaphors, "*with a single clod of clay all that is made of clay is known, through a single ingot of gold all that is made of gold is known, through a single nail clipper all that is made of iron is known, all that perceived is but mere a name.*" Śvetaketu responds to the father, "*that thing the teachers did not know. Had they known it, why they did not tell me?*" (CU 6.1.4-6). A proud person will never acknowledge one's weakness rather will blame it on others. A good teacher always knows how much to give, whom to

---

Verb-Forms and Primary Derivatives of the Sanskrit Language (New Delhi: Motilal Banarsidass Publishers, 2006). However, the origin of the word *brahman* is controversial. The etymological meaning is not clear. That may be the reason, the word is traced to *vṛh* or *bṛh*. Śaṅkara traces it to *bṛh,* meaning *to depart.* Another meaning would be *to burn.* In this sense, *brahman* has something to do with fire and heat and thus to sacrifice. For more details on this issue, see, K. Luke, "The Term Brahman in Modern Research," *Indian Theological Studies* 30, no. 2 (June 1993): 145-170.

3 *sa ha dvādaśavarṣa upetya caturviṁśativarṣaḥ savrvānvedānadhītya mahāmanā anucācamānī sthabdha etāya taṁ ha pitovāca śvetaketo yannu somyedam mahāmanā anucānamānī stabdho 'syuta tamādeśamprakṣayaḥ* (CU 6.1.2).

4 *vidyā dadāti vinayaṁ, vinayam dadāti jñānaṁ.*

5 *upa+ni+ṣad* (near down sit), sitting at the feet of the guru and learning.

6 *yenāśrutaṁ śrutaṁ bhavatyamataṁ matavijñānataṁ vijñātam iti katham nu bhagavaḥ sa ādeṣo bhavatīti* (CU 6.1.3).

give, what to give, when to give and how to give. Gradually, Śvetaketu realizes it and entreats his father to teach. Father becomes the teacher, instructing his son by means of nine analogies.

1.2 The Text and Nine Analogies

Nine analogies of *tattvamasi* are found in the *Chāndogya Upaniṣad*, between the sections 8 to 16 of the chapter six–8.7; 9.4; 10.3; 11.3; 12.3; 13.3; 14.3; 15.3; 16.3. Each analogy ends with the phrase, "*sa ya eṣo'ṇimaitad ātmyamidaṁ sarvaṁ tatsatyam* ***sa ātmā tattvamasi*** *śvetaketo iti bhūya eva mā bhagavānvijñāpayatviti tathā somyeti hovāca.*"[7] This key sentence is called '*identifying sentence.*' Nine analogies are enlisted below.

1. Just as a bird tied to a string, after flying in various direction and finding no resting place elsewhere, takes refuge at the very place where it is tied, so also the mind tethered to *prāṇa*, after flying in various directions and finding no resting place elsewhere, seeks refuge in *prāṇa* alone (CU 6.8.2).
2. Honey collected from various kinds of flowers forms one essence and never discriminates from being a particular tree, so too upon merging with Existence, does not know where it has converged (CU 6.9.1-2).
3. Rivers upon flowing from different directions ultimately merge into the sea, and upon intermixing one cannot distinguish the sea water from the river water to which it belonged, so too creatures emerge from one Existence and ultimately become one with it (CU 6.10.1-3).
4. If one cuts a tree from bottom, middle or top, the sap exudes from everywhere, though the tree is still living. When the sap dries up in one branch, that branch desiccates and eventually the whole tree (CU 6.11.1-2).
5. Upon breaking the seeds of *nyagrodha* tree, no subtle essence of life can be detected in the broken pieces, so too the subtle essence exists in one, though unseen, still exists (CU 6.12.1-3).
6. Salt upon completely dissolved in water cannot be discovered by naked eye, but can be known with the taste (CU 6.13.1-3).
7. The blindfolded waylaid traveller when led into a remote jungle and unfolded his blindfolded ribbon and guided to his destiny, reaches back safe (CU 6.14.1-2).

7 That *sat*, so subtle, is the Self of everything in all the worlds. That is the Real. That is *ātmā*. *That thou art*, O Śvetaketu.

8. A sick person at the deathbed recognizes one's closed ones as long as the *prāṇa* is intact or is in his senses. Whence the life is gone, then will not be able to identify (CU 6.15.1-2).
9. When an accused thief is subjected to fire ordeal, the fire will burn only if the person is wrong. If one is truthful, the fire will quench. The truth will protect the righteous person (CU 6.16.1-3).

Thus, through the use of nine analogies father enlightens the son into the subtleties of life as *that thou art* (*tat-tvam-asi*). However, this has been understood, explained, defined and commented by different people from different view-points and point of views. In fact, each Vedāntic thought is a point of view, viewed from a particular 'view-point.'[8] Depending on the view-point, the beauty differs though the reality beheld is the same.

2. Three-fold Surgeries on *Tattvamasi*

2.1 The *Kevalādvaita Vedānta*

"Brahma satya, jagatmithyā jīvo brahmaiva nāparaḥ," "Brahman is truth, world is an illusion, and *jīva* and Brahman are none but the same," sums up the *Kevala Advaita* of Śaṅkara. This doctrine discloses that the true Reality is One, that the individual Self and Brahman are one. In Advaitic chorus, this is the core teaching of all the *Upaniṣads*. *Satyam*, that which exists in all the time without undergoing any change and exists in all the three states of consciousness (waking state, dream state and deep-sleep state). Therefore, the absolute Reality is birthless, deathless and changeless, referred to as '*Brahman*.' *Mithyā* refers to the world, appearing as 'real' only in the 'waking state'; but it disappears in the dream and deep-sleep states. Therefore, the world is said to be *mithyā*. *Jīva* refers to the sentient principle in all living beings, including human beings. This life-principle is the pure consciousness which is same in all beings. The all-pervading Brahman of the *Upaniṣads* is that pure consciousness present in all *jīvas* as their inner spirit.

8 View-point is that place where a panoramic view is obtained.

Śaṅkara explores *tattvamasi* chiefly in three places, viz., the *Chāndogyopaniṣadbhāṣyam*, *Vākyavṛtti*[9] and the *Upadeśasāhasrī*.[10] In all these three works, three main strategies worked upon. They are: *neti-neti marga* (method of negation), *śāstra mārga* (method of scriptural assertion) and *bhāgatyāga lakṣaṇa or jahadajahad lakṣaṇa* (reject-accept method). In his *Vākyavṛtti*, Śaṅkara states, "Having thus ascertained the meaning of the term "thou" one should reflect upon what is meant by the word "that" – employing both *the method of negation and also the direct method of scriptural assertion*" (No. 28). "In the statements like 'that thou art' etc., the *reject-accept method is to be employed* as in the sentence 'He is this man'. No other method can be applied" (No. 48).[11]

Neti-neti (*na-iti*–not-so) is a *Vedic* analytic method of negation to affirm Brahman (an equivalent to the Western '*via-negativa*'). In this method, the seeker negates one's identification of self with all the worldly things. Through a gradual process, the seeker negates the mind and transcends all the worldly experiences till nothing remains but the Self.[12] The concept expresses something "inexpressible"[13] when no other definition applies to it. This denies the body, name, form, intellect, senses and all limiting adjuncts (superimposed) to discover what remains, the true "I", like pealing the sheaths of onion, i.e., one de-sheaths the layers of *pañcakośas*[14] to reach the ultimate pure essence. The *Avadhūta Gīta* confirms this: "By such sentences as "That thou art," our own Self is affirmed. Of that which is untrue and composed of the five elements–

9 Śaṅkarācārya, "Ādi Śaṅkarācārya's Vākya Vṛtti," (Mumbai: Chinmaya Mission, 2010). http://www.astrojyoti.com/vakyavritti.htm. Part of this book is also translated by Satya Sarada Kandula and is available in his blog. See, Satya Sarada Kandula, "Tat Tvam Asi: Vakya Vritti of Sri Adi Sankaracharya," in *Old Thought*s (2010). Available at, https://oldthoughts.wordpress.com/philosophy/tat-tvam-asi-vakyavritti-of-sri-adi-sankaracharya/, accessed on 12 December 2016. In fact, there is a doubt regarding the authenticity of the authorship. Mostly, it is ascribed to Śaṅkara. It mainly explains purport of *Aham Brahmāsmī* and *Tattvamasi*.

10 Śaṅkarācārya, *A Thousand Teachings, the Upadeśasāharsī of Śaṅkara: Translation with Introduction and Note*s, trans., Sengaku Mayeda (Tokyo: University of Tokyo Press, 1979).

11 See, Śaṅkarācārya, "Ādi Śaṅkarācārya's Vākya Vṛtti". Italics mine.

12 Swami Vishnu Devananda, *Meditations and Mantra*s, 2003 ed. (Delhi: Motilal Banarsidass Publishers, 1978), 119.

13 Pavel G Somov, *The Lotus Effect: Shedding Suffering and Rediscovering Your Essential Sel*f (Oakland: New Harbinger Publications, 2010), 34.

14 The concept of *pañcakośa* (the theory of five sheaths of the self) can be found in Taittirīya Upaniṣhad (2.1.1). i. The bodily self or the *annamayakośa*, ii. the biological self or *prāṇamayakośa*, iii. the psychological or *manomayakośa*, iv. the intellectual self or *vijñānamayakośa*, and v. the spiritual self, or *ānandamayakośa*. The *ānandamayakośa*, the highest stage of individual self, consists of bliss and within all the other sheaths. The realization of *ānandamayakośa* leads to God-realization or *brahmānubhava*.

the *śruti* (scripture) says, "Not this, not this.""'[15] Thus, one dis-identifies the self to attain the union with the Absolute.

The second way to achieve the meaning of *tattvamasi* is by adopting *bhāgatyāga lakṣaṇā* or it can also be called, *jahadajahad lakṣaṇā*. Śaṅkara opts for secondary meaning, because the primary meaning cannot be adopted since two entities of opposite attributes cannot be treated as identical. Śaṅkara explains this in his *Vākyavṛtti* thus: "The direct meaning of the term *tvam* is pure consciousness with the internal organ and the reflection of consciousness in it. Likewise, the direct meaning of the term *tat* is Pure Consciousness with *māyā* and the reflection of consciousness in it. On account of the incongruity involved in one part of their import, the idea of identity of consciousness cannot be established. Therefore, by abandoning that incongruent portion which has relation to invisibility and visibility etc., there remains only Absolute Pure consciousness which is common to both *tat* and *tvam*. This speaks of the identity of *jīva* and *Īśvara,* the real purport of the *Upaniṣadic* text: *Tattvamasi*."[16] If the direct word-meaning throws up inconsistency with what is pointed out by other proofs and evidences, then the sense consistent with its word-meaning, which is intelligible suggested by the term, is to be accepted. Thus, a reject-accept method is to be employed as in the sentence, 'he is this man.'[17] In the example, both 'he' and 'this' refers to the same man. So also the example, 'the village is burnt' indicates not as the whole village burnt, but refers to the 'part of the village.'

The statement has to be, therefore, understood in its totality, *akhaṇḍārtha*,[18] as a *part-less single essence*. According to *Vedāntasāra* of Sadānanda,[19] *akhaṇḍārtha* is established by delimiting the adjuncts (*upādhi*) as in the case of *so'yam devadattaḥ*. What is delimited is the contrary meaning arising from *tat* and *tvam* from *vācyārtha*. At the end of the process of delimitation,

---

15 "*tattvamasyādivākyena svātmā hi pratipāditaḥ, neti neti śrutirbrūyād anṛtaṁ pāñcabhautikam*" (1.25). Rishi Dattatreya, "Dattatreya, Song of the Avadhut: An English Translation of the Avadhut Gita with Sanskrit Transliteration," (abhayananda@bellsouth.net, 2009). The saying, "That thou art," affirms the reality of your own true Self. The saying, "Not this, not this," denies the reality of the five composite elements. See, ibid., 30.

16 Śaṅkarācārya, "Ādi Śaṅkarācārya's Vākya Vṛtti".

17 Ibid., no. 47-48.

18 *Akhaṇḍārthavākya* is a proposition that employs demonstrative and has an indivisible meaning. Such sentences are self-complete. On the contrary, *saṁsargāvagāhivākyas* are the ones which employ descriptive, classificatory and relational expressions. They are incomplete as they do not satisfy the conditions of *ākāṅkṣā*.

19 *Vedāntasāra*, the Essence of Veda, is a 15th century Advaita text written by Sadānanda Yogendra Saraswati. It contains six chapters in which fourth chapter deals with the de-superimposition of *tattvamasi*. For translation and text, see, Swami Nikhilananda, *Vedāntasāra of Sadānanda with Introduction, Text , English Translation and Comments* (Mayavati, Almora, Himalayas: Advaita Ashrama, 1931).

akhāṇḍacaitanya is obtained that is *abheda* between *tat* and *tvam*.[20] This is the *lakṣaṇārtha*. The word '*tvam*' is meant not as the physical body, but the witness-self (*sākṣin*) of the nature of reality, consciousness and bliss. The connecting verb, '*asi*' is in the indicative mood and so the utterance is an indicative sentence as opposed to relational or qualificational meaning.

2.2 The *Dvaita Vedānta*

Madhvācārya (1238-1318 CE), the proponent of *Dvaita* Vedānta opines that Brahman, the Supreme Reality, is the only *svatantra* (independent) reality. *Jīva* and the world are eternally separate, real, and always depend on Brahman. The relationship between Brahman and *jīva* is that of *biṁba-pratibiṁba-bhāva* (mirror-image-relation). Therefore, Madhva's entire thesis is *the majesty of Brahman as the highest purport.*[21]

Keeping the above semantic axis in mind, Madhva formulates his strategy on certain presuppositions. Some of them are: i. Hari is Supreme (*Hariḥ paratarah*), Lord Viṣṇu (Hari) is *sarvottama*, *parabrahma,* can be known only through scriptures, and is different and distinct from both sentient and non-sentient beings. ii. All souls depend on Him (*jīvagaṇāḥ harer anucarāḥ*). iii. World is real (*Satyam jagat*). Iv. Difference (*bheda*) is fundamental (*Tattvatobhedaḥ*), the very nature of the entity. There are five-fold *bhedas*: *Brahman-ātman*, *Brahman-jagat*, *ātman-ātman*, *ātman-jagat* and *jagat-jagat*.

Through *tattvamasi* concept, Madhva elucidates his philosophical stand mainly by means of two techniques: *padaccheda* technique (division of words according to grammatical rule) and *prakaraṇa saṅgati* (contextual relevance). He splits the conjoined sentences as *atat-tvam-asi* (not that-thou-art) based on *savarṇadīrgha sandhi* between the final long vowel in the preceding word *ātmā* followed by the initial short vowel of the following word *atat*. According to the compound, if there is a '*a*' *kāra* (sound) in the last syllable of the first word and '*ā'kāra* (long sound) in the beginning of the next word or vice-versa, then the resulting combination '*a*' *kāra* is omitted. Hence, grammatically the formulation is read as "*ātmā-atat-tvam-asi*" (*ātmātattvamasi*). This reading is favourable since it does not necessitate the dependence on the *lakṣaṇa* (secondary meaning) for either *tat* or *tvam*. For Dvaita, *lakṣana* is optional.

20 *tasmād yathā 'so'yam devadattaḥ' iti vakyaṁ tadartho vā tatkālaitatkālaviśiṣṭa devadatta lakṣaṇasya vākyārthasyāṁśe virodhāt viruddha-tatkālaitatkāla viśiṣṭatvāṁśaṁ parityajyāviruddhaṁ devadattāṁśamātram lakṣyati tathā 'tattvamasi' iti vākyam tadarthāvā parokṣatvāparokṣatvādiviśiṣṭa caitanyaikatvalakṣaṇasya vākyārthasyāṁśo virodhād viruddha-parokṣatvāparokṣatvādi viśiṣṭatvāmśaṁ parityajyā viruddham akhaṇḍa caitanyamātra lakṣayati*. See, ibid., 169.

21 *Viṣṇu sarvottama Madhva.* B.N.K. Sharma, *Brahamasūtras and Their Principal Commentaries: Critical Exposition*, III vols., vol. I (Delhi: Munshiram Manoharlal Publishers, 1974), 22.

The secondary meaning of *tat* brings about the association, relation, being a source of another, dependence, resemblance between Brahman and *jīva*, etc.[22]

The context is vital to understand the purport of the *sūtra*. The contextual discourse itself offers a *bheda* between *tat* and *tvam*. It can be found in Śvetaketu's ego. He did not know that he was under the control of Supreme God. If one were to tell him that 'you are Brahman,' it would heighten his pride and ego. Therefore, father's declaration has to be understood as, 'you are not that' or 'you are totally under His control.' The grammatical explanation 'not that' (*atat*) doesn't go against Pāṇini's grammatical rule. Nine illustrations justify his reading. Besides, the reading, '*atat-tvam-asi*' directly and categorically conveys the truths of '*jīveśvara-bheda.*'

One has to consider the text as a whole (*akhaṇḍārtha*) from *adhikaraṇa* point of view. The whole teaching enunciates dependence of *jīva* and *jagat* on the Brahman. Nowhere it illustrates the identity. B.N.K. Sharma substantiates this in the following way, "The whole cosmos, of which we as individual souls form part, is metaphysically dependent, as reality, on One Supreme Power which sustains everything in the cosmos including the souls; that the cosmos lives, moves because of that Being and derives all its powers and potencies from that great Source, and therefore the philosophical message of the text *Tattvamasi* is the dependence of the cosmos on Braham as a reality and not its identity with Brahman."[23]

The illustration of 'the bird's coming back to rest' signifies that though the bird is in rest with the lord, it is utterly helpless without the protective benevolence of the Supreme. The analogy of 'the honey collected' exemplifies that the living beings, though existing in the *Sat* is in an inseparable relation, fail to realize and know not that they are all existing in the Supreme Being. The insentient beings may fail to recognize the dependency, but not the sentient human beings. The example 'the sap oozing from the cut tree' exhibits that bereft of the immanence of the supreme power within, the *jīvātman* (*tvam*) would be a non-living being (*jīva*). It is the Brahman who gives life to the *jīva* and makes what it is, a living being (*jīvayati iti jīvaḥ*). The presence of the Supreme has to be grasped in one's life-experiences just as the presence of salt is inferred from the taste. The case of man in the sick bed reveals the utter helplessness being experienced and thus the person is totally relying on the unseen power of God. Traveller waylaid and blindfolded manifests that rebirth causes one to be in ignorance. The grace of God, instruction of a teacher and *sādhanas* liberate the person. The analogy of robbery, theft and ordeal offer an appropriate warning to Śvetaketu and to all human beings at the end of

22 B.N.K. Sharma, *Mahātātparya of Mahāvākyas and Other Advaita Śruti*s (Bangalore: Anandatirtha Pratisthana of Akhila Bharata Madhva Mahamandal, 1999), 177-78.

23 B.N.K. Sharma, "Tat Tvam Asi," *Dharmaprakash Journa*l Vol. XI, no. 11 (1982): 18.

instruction against laying claim to any identity of essence or status with the Supreme Being.

2.3 The *Avibhāgabedābheda of Vijñānabhikṣu*

Vijñānabhikṣu, lived at the turn of 16th Century CE, proposes a fusion of *abheda* and *bheda*. According to him, the reality is *avibhāgabhedābheda*. There is non-differentiable (*avibhāga*) difference (*bheda*) and non-difference (*abheda*) between Brahman and *jīva* and *jagat*. Just as there is difference and non-difference between the spark and fire or son and father, so is the relationship between Brahman and sentient and non-sentient realities.

Vijñānabhikṣu opines that Bādarāyaṇa codified the *Brahmasūtras*, the vedāntic philosophy in *Bhedābheda* way. Therefore, the real purport of the Upaniṣadic teaching is both *bheda* and *abheda*. Moving in line with this, he reiterates that the purport of *tattvamasi* too is neither to teach *Brahma-ātma* or *Brahma-jīva aikya*, nor to denote the words '*tvam*' and '*aham*' as *ātman*. Basically, the *mahāvākyas*–'*tattvamasi*,' '*ahambrahmāsmi*,' '*so'yam*,' etc.– teach the divine essence or the spiritual nature of the Supreme Being.[24] This, therefore, needs to be understood from the context (*prakaraṇasaṅgati*). If the context is not taken into consideration, then the texts will appear contradictory. Only *aṁśa-aṁśī sambandha* (part-whole relationship) can give the purport of the *Vedānta*. He defines *tattvamsi* as 'Thou art *in* That.'[25]

According to Vijñānabhikṣu, Brahman is not the same as *ātman* in the primary meaning. The primary meaning of the word '*brahman*' refers only to Supreme Being. However, it can also denote *Ātman*, but only in the secondary sense (*gauṇārtha*). Just as the word '*paṅkaja*' popularly means lotus, and the secondary sense from its etymology imports as water-born; so too, Brahman

---

24 "“*tattvamasi aham brahmāsmi*” *ityevaṁvidhānyeva vedānta mahāvākyāni can a jīvabrahmabhedam bodhayanti. nāpyetaṣu vākyeṣu tvamahaṁ śabdārtho jīvaḥ, kintu sandhānāntargasya ṣaḍviṁṣati tattvasya madhye ko'ahaṁśabdātha ityākāṅkṣāyām pravṛttatayā 'tattvamasyādi' vākyāni brahmoddiśya tvamaham śabdārthatvaṁ vidaghati, ko ghaṭaḥ? kambugrīvādimān ghaṭa ityādivākyavat.*" Vijñānabhikṣu, *Brahmasūtra Vijñānāmṛtabhāṣya*m, ed. Kedāranātha Tripāṭhī, Prācyavidya Series (Varanasi: Banaras Hindu University, 1979), 1.1.2, p.35. (Henceforth VAB).

25 This claim comes closer to Rāmānuja's *Viśiṣṭādvaita* and Vallabha's *Śuddhādvaitic* interpretation of *tattvamasi*. If Rāmānuja interprets it as, '*You are His part*' or '*You are God's part*,' Vallabha interprets it as '*you are in essence God*' or '*Soul is an essence of Brahman.*' This is because Vallabha splits *tattvamasi* into two parts: *tattvam* and *asi*, where *tattva* refers to essence or state of *tat* (*Brahmanhood*). *Tvam* in *tattvamasi* does not refer to the second person singular form but a termination conveying the sense of state, added to *tat*. The meaning therefore is that the soul is an essence of Brahman as its part or *aṁśa*. Jethala G Shah, *Shri Vallabhacharya: His Philosophy and Religio*n (Gujarat: The Pushtimargiya Pustakalaya, 1969), 133-135.

can relate to something specific as well as something general.[26] Generally, the word *brahman* stands for the Highest Being. He is qualified positively by his attributes of greatness and negatively by without imperfections. Even in the primary meaning, there is a distinction between primary[27] and secondary meaning regarding the word '*brahman*.' The former refers to the Supreme Being (*Parabrahman*) and the latter to the Lower Being (*Aparabrahman*). The secondary sense also can typify the beings like *hiraṇyagarbha*, *puruṣa*, *ātman*, *jīva*, creator, individual soul, etc.[28] Therefore, when *tat* is referred to *tvam*, it means *tat* finding its proximity to *tvam* only in the secondary sense. Even though *ātman* is understood to be equal to Brahman, yet they cannot become one ultimate reality, just as butter and milk cannot be one. Butter in essence is from milk, yet they aren't the same.

Brahman is tranquility, without passions, without any conditioned activity, omniscient, qualityless, and eternal. It is devoid of contact with any qualities or the qualities are totally dissolved, distinct from any *jīvas*, all knowing, etc.[29] On the other hand, *jīva* and *jagat* is tainted by the impurities of *karma* and stained by modifications. If *Ātman* and Brahman were to be the same, then Brahman should be the cause of misery, pain and joy in the world. This cannot be the case. All the *kleśakarmavipākāśaya* (the impurities) are the characteristics of *prakṛti,* caused due to the union of *puruṣa* with *prakṛti*. Therefore, Brahman cannot be *Ātman*.

Parabrahman cannot be *ātman*, *jīva* or *jagat*. Brahman is the *adhiṣṭānakāraṇa*, the supporting cause of everything or the *mūlakaraṇa*, the root cause.[30] As having the nature of witness, it upholds *prakṛti*. However, it is not separate from Brahman as it is a part or *aṁśa* of Brahman. *Prakṛti* and *puruṣa* are powers of Brahman. Because of the powers of Brahman (*śakti*), *prakṛti* evolves and the *sṛṣṭi* emerges.[31] Thus, deep down in the *sṛṣṭi*

26 *etaśca jagajjanmādikāraṇatvam brahmaśabdapravṛttinimittam api bodhyam. mūlakāraṇasaiva niratiśaya bṛhattvāt. brahmaśabdaśca paṅkajādivad yogarūḍhaḥ. ato na jīvādirmukhyo brahmaśabdārthaḥ.* VAB 1.1.2, p.19.

27 This should be understood as super-primary meaning or *paramamukhyavṛttiḥ*. For more details on this notion read, Ivan D'Souza, "Role and Significance of Paramamukhyavṛtti in Dvaita Hermeneutics and Its Scriptural Application: A Probe into the Super-Primary Meaning in Mādhvavedānta" (Dissertation, Jnana-Deepa Vidyapeeth, 2017).

28 VAB. p.20,35,36.

29 *śāntaṁ, rāgādirahitam, aupādhikya apāraśūnyam ca, na tu suṣuptavad viṣaya saṁvedanarahitam, sarvajñam iti uttarāt. nirguṇam nityam eva guṇānābhimānena guṇasaṅgena ca guṇātītaṁ, gurṇānāṁ vilayādva nirguṇatvam.* VAB 1.1.2, p.19.

30 *etādṛśakāraṇatvam eva adhiṣṭānakāraṇatvam iti mūlakāraṇattvam iti ca ucyate.* VAB 1.1.2, p.17.

31 *evaṅca jagataḥ sarvaprakārakāraṇatvam api brahmalakṣaṇam kartuṁ śakyate.* VAB 1.1.2, p.18.

Brahman's permeation is always there. Since Brahman is the indwelling and immortal (*ātmāntaryāmyamṛtaḥ* BU 3.7.3), all this is verily Brahman (*etadātmyamidamsarvam* CU 6.8.7*)*; and thus, *ātman* is considered to be Brahman.

Second reason is that there is *brahmanhood* deeply engraved in all the *abheda mahāvākya śruti* texts. The *brahmanhood* is nothing but the divine essence or the "spiritual nature."[32] Vijñānabhikṣu asserts that the *abhedavākyas* in *mahāvākyas* are acclaimed due to their characteristics of removing ignorance. That is the general rule of such statements also. In fact, the first part of the verse containing the word *tattvamasi* in Chāndogya Upaniṣad *abheda* between a whole and its part, is leading to the spiritual nature of knowledge of Brahman. It is not that the first part of the sentence only declares about the essence of Brahman and latter part doesn't, rather the whole sentence affirms primarily about it. That is the reason, Vijñānabhikṣu counsels the commentators to see whole scripture as a unit from the "beginning till end," "*upakrama-upasaṁhāra-aikya*" (VAB 1.1.1, p. 3). It is the nature of Brahman to be one with the world in its quintessence, just as the pot in essence is clay. This does not imply that pot is only clay, similarly *Ātman* and Brahman are not absolutely one. There is an *avibhāga* relationship with them. In the same way, *abhedavākyas* which convey *brahmātmatāikya* should be understood according to propriety and context.

How and when this relationship is established? He posits, "The difference and identity between souls and God, which is composed of separation and non-separation, is established through the relationship between a whole and its parts. Only non-separation, because it is co-incident, essential, and eternal, is true at the beginning and at the end. Separation, on the other hand, in the middle through a limitation of parts is temporary and of a purely nominal existence. This is the distinction."[33] Thus, in the beginning and at the end (*sṛṣṭi* and *pralaya*), there is *avibhāga* between Brahman and *ātman*; and during the course of its existence in the world (*sthiti*), there is *vibhāga* as understood by *aṁśa-aṁśī sambandha*.

Vijñānabhikṣu, using this *sambandha*, expounds the *mahāvākya tattvamasi* once again. *Jīvā* and Brahman differ so far as to be divided as *aṁśa* and *aṁśī*. These two cannot be termed as one and the same. Being *aṁśa* and

32 "*brahmatāparatvam*" (VAB p. 30). John W. Borelli, "The Theology of Vijñānabhikṣu: A Translation of His Commentary on Brahma Sūtras 1.1.2 and an Exposition of His Difference-in-Identity Theology" (Dissertation, Fordham University, 1976), 63.

33 "*tasmāt siddau jīveśvarayor aṁśāṁśibhāvena bhedābhedau vibhāgāvibhāgarūpau. Tatrāpyavibhāga eva ādhyantayor anugatatvāt svābhāvikatvāt nityatvācca satyaḥ. vibhāgāstu madhe svalpa avacchedena naimittiko vikārāntaravad vācārambhaṇamātram iti viśeṣaḥ.*" VAB 1.1.2, p.32. Translation, ibid., 32.

aṁśī in their true forms, the *tat* and *tvam* stand different from each other,[34] yet they are mutually related. If the *ātman* were to be totally different from Brahman, then it would have been totally unconscious like pot.[35] *Bhagavat Gītā* also discloses *avibhāga* between *aṁśī* and *aṁśa* (*tat* and *tvam*), "know that I am the conscious principle" (BG 13.2).

One cannot be understood without the other, like son is a part of father or part is part of the whole. But then, when do we claim Brahman and *ātman* are one? As far as divine essence is concerned (*brahmātmatāvagatiphalatvāt*) between part and whole (*tvam* and *tat*), they are one. In other words, the divine nature of the world in its essential form, before the creation and after the dissolution, is the same as that of Brahman through the relation of *avaibhāga*. That's why it is said, *ātman* is Brahman or Brahman is *ātman*. This is the reason, *ātman* is considered to be the witness, chief coordinator and consciousness. In fact, these qualities are of Brahman. Since the *ātman* in essence is divine, it operates as chief-coordinator and is reflected in *tvam* and *aham* words. These words are concomitant to each other like master-slave (*sva-svāmi bhāva avagagmāt*, VAB p.31). *Yama Purāṇa* discloses this in terms of master-slave relationship between Lord Hari and his devotee respectively. They are joined together by the will of that same Lord of souls.[36]

In the perception of *ātman*, Brahman is understood. In other words, in the perception of *tvam*, *tat* is realized. But it is in the secondary sense of the term *brahman* (*Aparabrahman*). The *Aparabrahman* is perceived to be the energy of the *Parabrahman*. This insight is possible only through part-whole relationship. Therefore, it is affirmed that consciousness (*caitanya*) is the substance of *Aparabrahman*. In the same way, *caitanya* is the very substance (*dravya*) of *ātman* and not its quality (*guṇa*). Therefore, when *ātman* is perceived, Brahman is perceived, because both have the same thing as their substance. It is like upon seeing fire or light, one sees simultaneously light and that which lights (VAB, p. 33). Thus, unity is inferred.

The important point here is the relationship represented by the word '*asi*.' Only when there is co-ordination between the two (for example, I and Thou or *aham* and *tvam*), it is asseverated that I am thou or *aham* is *tvam* or *tvam* is *aham*. The activities of *ātman* are effected through speech and senses. That's the reason *prāṇa* is said to be *ātman*. In the same way, the activities of Brahman are realized through *ātman*. *Tattvamasi* statements exemplify this fact–the coordination between *tat* and *tvam*. In the statement, *asi* represents

34 *etena "eṣā ta ātmāntaryāmyamṛtaḥ sa ma ātmeti vidhyāt, tattvamasi" ityadi śrutayo vyākhyātāḥ jīvabhede'pīti mantavyam*. VAB 1.1.2, p. 30.

35 Vijñānabhikṣu quotes *Gautamīyatantram*, "*yadi jīvaḥ parād bhinnaḥ kāryatāmeti suvrata, acitkvam ca prasajyet ghaṭavat paṇḍitottama*." Exact reference is untraceable. VAB, p.32.

36 "*paramātmā hariḥ svāmī dāso'ham tasya sarvadā. svecchayā viniyoktātastasyaivātmeśvarasya hi*." VAB, p.30. Translation, Borelli, 62, 63.

this coordination. *Tat* elucidates the specific sense and *tvam*, the general sense of agent acts as a coordinator.[37]

3. Post-Surgical Application of *Tattvamasi*

3.1. Identity versus Tautology

The nature of identity is in fact a perplexing one. Wittgenstein propounds, "Roughly speaking, to say of two things that they are identical is non-sense, and to say of one thing that it is identical with itself is to say nothing at all."[38] The identity statements question the very proposition itself, "what is it being claimed to be identical in a true identity statement?"[39]

At the outset, *tat* and *tvam* seems to be identical either formally or materially. It cannot be formally, because, in its form both are different. Secondly, *tat* and *tvam* is not just a logical truth (for example, a = a) but much more than that. It cannot be materially, as the material identity deals with numerical identity (for example, a = b). Material identity pertains to two different entities or objects: it will be true, if and only if the objects are same entity, and it will be false, if one is different from the other or is not an entity at all (object). In *tattvamasi*, the identity sought is beyond formal or material one, a metaphysical one. If one considers *tat* and *tvam* to be inter-definable or one of the concepts contained in the other, then, it would be tautology in the first sense.[40]

For the Advaitins, *tat* and *tvam* are identity entities, whereas for the *bhedavādins*, it is the contra view and for the *bhedābhedavādins*, it is both. For the non-advaitins, oneness of *tattvamasi* is "neither intended nor implied."[41] If, *tat* refers to Brahman and *tvam* refers to the embodied *jīva* then one cannot talk about identity, for the former is unqualified, unlimited and unconditioned entity and the latter qualified, limited and conditioned entity in its primary meaning. And therefore, it would be a tautology. But, if one considers *tat* to be pure consciousness and *tvam* to be embodied pure consciousness, as the Advaita would refer, then the entities can be deemed identical. Therefore, the secondary meaning is important while interpreting the text. Here, as *jahadajahallakṣaṇa* understands, the primary meaning is defunct and the

37 *ahaṁ śabdārthatvena prayoktṛsaṅghāta adhyakṣatvādinā sāmānyarūpeṇaivā kāṅkṣāyām tat ityādi viśeśa rūpeṇa upadeṣa iti*. VAB. p, 30.

38 Ludwig J. Wittgenstein, *Tractatus Logico-Philosophicu*s, trans., D. F. Peers and G. F. McGuninnes (London: Routledge and Kegan Paul, 1965), 105.

39 Bina and William C Wilcox Gupta, ""Tat Tvam Asi": An Important Identity Statement or a Mere Tautology," *Philosophy East and Wes*t Vol. 34, no. 1 (January 1984): 85.

40 Ibid., 85-86.

41 Ibid., 88.

secondary meaning is active. Thus, the Advaitin understands 'the Reality is One and Pure Consciousness' as insufficient.

The point regarded here is not the tautology or identity issues, but the subject-object intricacy. There is something unchanging, permanent essence in every individual. *The person whom I saw ten years ago and behold now is the same* though there is a remarkable change in him/her. *Ghaṭākāśa* and *bahirākāśa* have something unchanging and permanent thing. Individual soul and Supreme Soul have something identical. What Śaṅkara teaches us is this unique mystical union.

3.2 Towards a New Interpretation

The hermeneutics exposed here distinguishes two kinds of relationships: i. Brahman as immanent in the *jīva* and *jagat*, expressed as *abheda* or identity, ii. Absolute transcendence of Brahman enunciated as distinction between finite and infinite.

Absolute transcendence is dangerous at least for two reasons–danger of leading towards mechanical deism and pantheism. Mechanical deism creates an unbridled gulf between Supreme Being and *jīva-jagat* undermining unity or harmony of things. Dualism and pluralism are necessary outcome of transcendence. The *Kevala Advaita* notion of *tattvamasi* regards the reality belonging to the Real and all the phenomenal existence as unreal with no human reason daring to touch and contaminate.

The immanence of Brahman comes to rescue the transcendental approach. But an undue emphasis on immanence will lead to identify Brahman with the world of experience. If this is the case, then the finite objects will be the shadows of the Brahman depriving them the independent existence. Rāmānuja's *Viśiṣṭādvaita* somehow falls into this category. The objects of phenomenal world are *viśeṣana* of the *viśeṣa*. Worldly becoming is necessary through which divine can become self-conscious. But the danger is that it might lead to materialism. Brahman's self-subsistence depends on the existence of *jīva-jagat* where the unity is sought.

Śaṅkara errs in accepting the absolute transcendence and independent existence of Brahman, thus leading us to pantheism. Instead of explaining relation between Brahman and *jīva-jagat*, he cancels out the thing to be related as branding it unreal. Further, he superimposes the related as *upādhi* (illusion). Even after counterbalancing unreality, the appearance of the finite world cannot be negated.

Neither the *bhedavāda* nor the *abhedavāda*, or neither immanence nor transcendence independently can define *tattvamasi* adequately. That is, both *bheda* and *abheda* alone are inadequate to describe the nature of Brahman and the *jīva-jagat*. Accepting one will lead to deny the other as illusion or emphasizing the other will lead to unbridgeable gulf between Brahman and the *jīva-jagat*. Even the logic fails in front of *the logic of infinity*, as the scripture says, '*My ways are different from your ways*' (Isaiah 55:8).

Where then shall we find a solution or at least a balance? The only way is as Buddhism proposes, *the middle way*, a third possibility which embraces both–the *bhedābheda* way of interpretation. Here, transcendence and immanence are reconciled to a higher synthesis. They are made associate aspect of an abiding unity in the Reality, be it proposed by *Bhedābhedavādins* like Bhāskara, Vallabha, Caitanya or Vijñānabhikṣu.

Bhedābhedavādins in general consider Brahman to be both *nirguṇa* and *saguṇa,* and real. Brahman is *nirguṇa*, appears *saguṇa* for the practical purpose. To corroborate their view, the concept of *māyā* is brought in as the power (*śakti*) of Brahman to define it as *anirvacanīya*, describing neither real nor unreal. If there is an absolute identity, then the fault of one should be the fault of the other. In other words, can either real or unreal be the power of Brahman who is real? On the other hand, if the absolute differs, then immanence is not possible, it will end up in dualism or pluralism. Therefore, just like the case of sun and its rays or sea and its waves which cannot be separated, the immanence of Brahman from its transcendence cannot be separated.

3.3 *Bhedābheda* as the Basis of *Tattvamasi*

The interpretation given for *tat* and *tvam* as Brahman and *jīva-jagat* as denoted by *abhidha* and *lakṣaṇa* are sound enough to accept without any complication. But the issue is the copulating verb '*asi*' to describe relation between the two terms.

The *Nyāya-Vaiśeṣika* system points to *samavāya* relation between two objects. On the other hand, Rāmānuja acknowledges *apṛthakasiddhi* (inseparable) relation. The former is external relation and the latter is internal relation. The external relation pointed out is between two real objects, quite distinct from each other, for example *gavaya* and *gau* (wild cow and domestic cow). But the existing relation between *tat* and *tvam* is not just external as material *gau* and *gavaya*, but a physico-transcendental one. In this respect, a well-accepted relation could be *apṛthakasiddhi* between Brahman and *jīva-jagat*. But again this relation is not conclusive. In other words, it is *avaktavyam*, (indescribable).[42]

What kind of difference-in-identity (*bhedābheda*), therefore, is to be envisaged: *aupādhika* (accidental), *svābhāvika* (natural), *acintya* (incomprehensible) or *avibhāga* (undividable) Or is it not sufficient to restrict oneself to *bhedābheda*?

42 This concept is borrowed from Jaina theory of *Saptabhaṅgīnaya* to describe the reality as indescribable.

Bhāskara's system is called *aupādhikabhedābheda* where *abheda* is real and eternal while *bheda* is unreal and accidental. *Bheda* is due to *upādhi* (accidental predicate). He gives an example of a diamond looking red due to a red object placed near it. Thus, *bheda* is unreal and unacceptable.

Nimbārka's *svābhāvikabhedābheda* considers both *bheda* and *abheda* as real. They represent the very nature (*svabhāva*) of Brahman. Therefore, this system is preferred over Bhāskara as it reconciles the apparent contradictory statements of the scriptures.

Caitanya encapsulates both the preceding views in his *acintyabhedābheda* system. If both *bheda* and *abheda* are real, they must necessarily be *svābhāvika*. The *bheda* and *abedha* is conceived between Brahman and *jīva-jagat* as whole and part, body and limb (*avayava-avayavi*) and cause and effect by Bhāskara and Nimbārka. That is, the cause or whole is both transcendent and immanent in the effect or in part. But they cannot both be one. Therefore, the reality is to be understood as incomprehensible, says Caitanya.

Yet, a better way of expressing it is *avibhāgabhedābheda* way as Vijñānabhikṣu envisages. The reality is indescribable because it is *avibhāga, bheda, abheda,* and cannot be separated like spark and fire, or wave and sea.

Basing on the context of *tattvamasi*, Uddālaka's purpose of *upadeśa* to Śvetaketu was to remove his arrogance and pride to instil in him a sense of a power greater than everything. At the same time, this power is to be found within as *kastūri* in the *nābhi* of the *kastūrīmṛga*. Nine illustrations clearly illustrate the above purport. For example, just as honey collected from various flowers remain one unit, so also the transcendental Brahman is immanent in you and you in Him. Thus, you are inseparable from Him and He from you. That you are, *tat tvamasi*.

3.4 Extrapolation of the Supreme Reality

From the dynamics of the relationship between *tat*, *tvam* and *asi*, one can infer the Supreme Reality from three ways.

i. From *anubhava* (experience): One can begin the search for the Supreme from *anubhava*. From its etymological sense, *anubhava* comes after (*anu*) the empirical reality (*bhava*). The word '*tvam*' refers to the empirical reality. It is the epistemology, leading to ontology. The knowledge of the seen reality apart from bringing awe, leads one to a sense of mystery and to experience it as divine.
ii. From *śruti* (revelation): One can also proceed the search for the Supreme from *śruti*. According the *Mīmāṁsakas*, scriptural injunctions are *codana śabda*s due to the inherent power (*śakti*) in them. The power of *sphoṭa* of the *śabda* guides one to have a mystical experience. This is the reason, the *Sāmavedic* hymns open

with the meditation on AUM, as the symbol of Brahman (CU 1.1). The word '*tat*' refers to this revelation, the revelation of Supreme Reality.

iii. From *upadeśa* (denotation): Certain things cannot be learnt without the aid of a proper Guru. It is the'point of view' of the *ācāryas* impels the disciples to construe a particular system from that 'view-point.' The Upaniṣad in this sense, is an instruction of the teacher to the student to assist the latter understand the Reality. Śaṅkara's mystical experience of Viṣṇu initiates him to perceive everything as divine, thus to define *tattvamasi* as 'You are That (Brahman).' Therefore, it is not an indirect learning, but as witness of a first-hand experience with its greater role to deepen one's faith-experience.

3.5 The Reality, a Chimera!

Mystery cannot be solved, but can be made amenable when one gets involved in it. Being an outsider, one cannot grasp the core of it. Today, science acquaints us that we can know a thing almost for sure, but not fully. This is vivid from the hermeneutics of *tattvamasi*. Different way(s) of interpreting a text indicate that the reality is a complex whole. The Advaita explains it literally, the Viśiṣṭādvaita non-literally and the Dvaita as resemblance. Still further, people like Nimbārka, Caitanya and Vijñānabhikṣu interpret the same reality from a 'holistic view.'

3.6 *Tattvamasi* as the Semantic Axis of the *Vedāntic* Philosophy

There is a possibility to bind the whole of the *Vedāntic* thought in one thread, the *avibhāgādvaitic* way of interpreting *tattvamasi*. All the thinkers very well accept the primary meaning. And there is no disagreement between them, that the divine is the thread which links God, world and Soul. Disagreement is only in the secondary meaning. In fact, this is the purport of the *Vedānta* from its etymology and *tattvamasi* proves it so. Therefore, *tattvamasi* can be aptly called the axis of the *Vedāntic* Philosophy.

3.7 *Tattvamasi* as the Cosmotheandric Inter-Relatedness of the Reality

All the commentators concur that the *mahāvākya*, *tattvamasi* refers to the Supreme Reality and its relation with the '*other.*' The '*other*' denotes the whole of cosmos. Thus, the word '*tvam'* would signify the world of beings in the cosmos apart from the Supreme Being. The relationship existing between '*tat'* (Brahman) and '*tvam'* (world of beings) is denoted by the word '*asi'* as Rāmānuja expresses it: like body and soul relation existing in the same locus (*samānādhikaraṇyam* or collocation). This is the reason, we discover the *advaitins* regard the *Gītā* in terms of '*tat-tvam-asi*:'[43] the relation between the Lord Kṛṣṇa as the Supreme Reality and the world of reality as Kaurava and Pāṇḍava, and their relationship with Kṛṣṇa.

What is to be seen here is the basic cosmotheandric unity (World-God-Man) in the form of *tat-tvam-asi*. There is a basic unity in the whole of cosmos. Human beings cannot exist without relating with other. The very fact of human beings' existence on the earth affirms their inherent relationship. Deep down, there is a power or a mysterious energy or a mystery one is part and parcel of. This mystery is expressed in the word '*tat*' in the *Upaniṣad*.

Going along with *bhedavāda* there is a mutual dependency and independency. The whole of world of reality is dependent on God for its sustenance. Thus, there is an essential unity and uniformity in the whole of '*tat-tvam-asi*' concept. Human beings, being the crown of God's creation, undergo necessarily this cosmotheandric reality to make the world a better place to dwell in. The whole reality of *tat-tvam-asi* must be experienced (*anubhava*) in one's life here on earth. One *becomes* (*bhavati*)[44] or experiences the divine one-ness through knowledge, good works, devotion, good conduct and good virtues, '*Once you know that, you become that*' (*brahmāvid brahmaiva bhavati*). Vijñānabhikṣu too testifies this, 'reality is *avibhāga Bhedābheda*.' There is only one Supreme God, called the *Puruṣa* or *Paramātman* who cannot be divided. *Paramātman* is always the same who cannot be subjected to any change or transformation or dissolution. But He is verbalized as *puruṣa*, *prakṛti* and its evolutes. However, they are different yet identical to certain extent with the *Paramātman*. The *puruṣa* and *prakṛti* totally depend on *Paramātman* in *aṁśa-aṁśī* relation or like the wave-sea relation. They exist as a potential power in God. In the same way, *tat* and *tvam* are related. The existence of *puruṣa* and *prakṛti*, manifested by its evolutionary activity, proves in itself that God is the inner-controller (*antaryāmin*), the binding force of everything. In other words, it is the *asi* of *tattvamasi*.

Conclusion

Śvetaketu must forgo his *aham* (ego) to live a practical life. He has a lot of things to learn from 'the world of experience.' In our life, we experience many miracles. Upon appreciating and experiencing can discover the beauty of merging with it. God is closer than we are to ourselves. But seldom have we experienced His closeness making it conscious part of our existence. *Tattvamasi* prompts us to experience this oneness by purging away our ego

---

43 See, Pathikonda Viswambara Nath, *Tat Tvam Asi: The Universal Message in the Bhagavadgītā*, 2 vols., vol. I (Delhi: Motilal Banarsidass Publishers, 1998; reprint, 2002).

44 The root '*bhū*' means to become. '*bhava*' is a derivative form.

and thus make the earth 'a universal family,' the family of God where everyone and everything is relational and interwoven.

References

Borelli, John W. "The Theology of Vijñānabhikṣu: A Translation of His Commentary on Brahma Sūtras 1.1.2 and an Exposition of His Difference-in-Identity Theology. " Dissertation, Fordham University, 1976.

D'Souza, Ivan. "Role and Significance of Paramamukhyavṛtti in Dvaita Hermeneutics and Its Scriptural Application: A Probe into the Super-Primary Meaning in Mādhvavedānta." Dissertation, Jnana-Deepa Vidyapeeth, 2017.

Dattatreya, Rishi. *Dattatreya, Song of the Avadhut: An English Translation of the Avadhut Gita with Sanskrit Transliteration.* abhayananda@bellsouth.net, 2009.

Devananda, Swami Vishnu. *Meditations and Mantras*. 2003 ed. Delhi: Motilal Banarsidass Publishers, 1978.

Gupta, Bina and William C Wilcox. ""Tat Tvam Asi": An Important Identity Statement or a Mere Tautology." *Philosophy East and West* Vol. 34, no. 1 (January 1984): 85-94.

Iyer, M. K. Venkatarama. "The Methodology of the Upaniṣads." In *Studies in Vedānta Philosophy*, edited by R. K. Panda, 69-83. Delhi: Bharatiya Kala Prakashan, 2002.

Kandula, Satya Sarada. "Tat Tvam Asi: Vakya Vritti of Sri Adi Sankaracharya." In *Old Thoughts*, 2016, 2010. Available at, https://oldthoughts.wordpress.com/philosophy/tat-tvam-asi-vakyavritti-of-sri-adi-sankaracharya/, accessed on 12 December 2016.

Luke, K. "The Term Brahman in Modern Research." *Indian Theological Studies* 30, no. 2 (June 1993): 145-170.

Nath, Pathikonda Viswambara. *Tat Tvam Asi: The Universal Message in the Bhagavadgītā*. Vol. I. 2 vols. Delhi: Motilal Banarsidass Publishers, 1998. Reprint, 2002.

Nikhilananda, Swami. *Vedāntasāra of Sadānanda with Introduction, Text , English Translation and Comments*. Mayavati, Almora, Himalayas: Advaita Ashrama, 1931.

Śaṅkarācārya. *A Thousand Teachings, the Upadeśasāharsī of Śaṅkara: Translation with Introduction and Notes*. Translated by Sengaku Mayeda. Tokyo: University of Tokyo Press, 1979.

Śaṅkarācārya. *Ādi Śaṅkarācārya's Vākya Vṛtti*. Mumbai: Chinmaya Mission, 2010. http://www.astrojyoti.com/vakyavritti.htm.

Shah, Jethala G. *Shri Vallabhacharya: His Philosophy and Religion*. Gujarat: The Pushtimargiya Pustakalaya, 1969.

Sharma, B.N.K. *Brahamasūtras and Their Principal Commentaries: Critical Exposition*. Vol. I. III vols. Delhi: Munshiram Manoharlal Publishers, 1974.

Sharma, B.N.K. "Tat Tvam Asi." *Dharmaprakash Journal* Vol. XI, no. 11 (1982): 17-37.

Sharma, B.N.K. *Mahātātparya of Mahāvākyas and Other Advaita Śrutis*. Bangalore: Anandatirtha Pratisthana of Akhila Bharata Madhva Mahamandal, 1999.

Somov, Pavel G. *The Lotus Effect: Shedding Suffering and Rediscovering Your Essential Self.* Oakland: New Harbinger Publications, 2010.

Vijñānabhikṣu. *Brahmasūtra Vijñānāmṛtabhāṣyam* Prācyavidya Series, Edited by Kedāranātha Tripāṭhī. Varanasi: Banaras Hindu University, 1979.

Wittgenstein, Ludwig J. *Tractatus Logico-Philosophicus*. Translated by D. F. Peers and G. F. McGuninnes. London: Routledge and Kegan Paul, 1965.

9

The Emotional Cognition of the Humans: Contemporary Attempts at Integrating Emotion and Cognition

Dolichan Kollareth, SJ

Abstract

Reflecting on the destiny of the human person in a technological world necessitates an understanding of human cognition. Traditional views dichotomizes rational thinking from emotions. Recent views, however, integrates reasoning with emotions. This article highlights the emotion-cognition integration in humans by surveying the recent developments in philosophy, psychology, and neuroscience. Premodern and modern philosophy, sharply separated emotions from reason, whereas contemporary views underscore rational processes at the heart of emotional experiences. Traditional psychological theories see emotions as irrational, whereas recent ones support an integration perspective. Developments in neuroscience underscore the integrated brain networks subserving emotion and cognition. All reasoning has an affective quality and all emotions have a cognitive dimension.

Key words: Emotion, cognition, philosophy, psychology, neuroscience etc.

Introduction

Saudi Arabia became the first country to give citizenship to a robot, which they named, Sophia. The move was part of a business plan to attract future investors into artificial intelligence. Unarguably, the future of technological revolution is developments in artificial intelligence. There is some fear that with the coming of intelligent machines like Sophia, humans may face a push back. Instead of humans, machines with super cognitive capacities may control and dominate the world. This recent scenario invites us to closely examine the human capacity for cognition.

Both in the academic and popular discourse, human rational thinking is sharply dichotomized with emotions. Decision making is at its best when emotional influences are kept at a minimum. Emotions are sometimes understood as the epitome of irrationality. In contrast, in more recent views, emotions and reason are highly integrated, thus it is neither desirable nor possible to avoid emotion in the decision making processes. All reasoning has an affective quality and all emotions have a cognitive dimension. Moreover, while it is true that emotions can degrade our decision making, they can also enhance it. This article highlights the emotion-cognition integration in humans by surveying the recent developments in philosophy, psychology, and neuroscience.

1. Philosophy: From separation to integration

Premodern philosophers near unanimously made a strong distinction between emotion (or passion) and reason. Plato and Aristotle saw them existing as two (often opposing) forces within the soul.[1] For both philosophers, humans share the capacity for passions with other animals, but uniquely are capable to exercise reason.[2] Plato propounded a tripartite human soul consisting of reason, spirit and the appetitive element. The latter two include what we today would consider the emotion – the nondeliberative drives, desires and instincts of human life. Plato argued that a person is virtuous or just when reason rules over the other two parts just as a city works most ideally when persons act appropriate to their class. Plato's student, Aristotle, likewise identified reason as the unique element in humans. As 'rational animals,' the proper exercise of reason is central to human flourishing.

The Stoics proposed the same dichotomization when they taught that the passions ought to come under control of reason. The aim of human life is to pursue happiness or flourishing through living a virtuous life as established by reason.[3] The implication for the Stoics is that one should not try to simply moderate emotions, but one should totally eradicate them.[4]

---

1 Powell, S. M. (2016). *The impassioned life: Reason and emotion in the Christian tradition.* Minneapolis: Fortress Press.

2 Plato, trans. C. D. C. Reeve (2004). *Republic.* Indianapolis: Hackett Pub Co.

3 Sorabji, R. (2000). *Emotion and peace of mind: From stoic agitation to Christian temptation.* New York: Oxford University Press.

4 Annas, J. (1993). *The morality of happiness.* New York: Oxford University Press.

Aquinas[5] made more positive connections with the passions than Augustine. Passions are an element shared with animals that need to be brought under the distinct human capacity of reason.[6] While they often act as negative forces, when they come under the control of reason they are morally advantageous. Unlike the Stoics who took the passions to be unequivocally base, Thomas recognized them as holding the possibility for good or ill depending on the passion's relation to reason. "Antecedent" to reason, Thomas argued, passions diminish the goodness of an act because it is always better to act on the judgment of reason rather than of a passion. These acts are prone to "inordinate movements" that are not moderated by reason. On the other hand, passions that are "consequent" to reason can be beneficial in two ways. First, "by way of redundance," when a passion arises from the intensity of the movement of reason. Second, "by way of choice," when a person by reason chooses to be affected by a passion in order to more readily act rightly. In these two ways, a passion can increase the goodness of an act and is thus beneficial for the moral life.[7] In summary, for Aquinas and most thinkers in the premodern period, emotion and reason are sharply dichotomized as two forces within the soul. The passions need not be antagonistic to reason, but they are always in danger of taking over. The role of reason is to keep emotions in check.

While emotion and reason were sharply separated in the premodern period, there was the possibility of emotions participating in rationality. However, in the modern period this contrast was radicalized and emotions were often presented as wholly irrational. Rather than understanding passion as an element of the soul which influences the body, the modern period shifted to seeing passions as the body acting on the soul or mind. This is particularly evident in thinkers such as René Descartes, Charles Darwin and William James.

Descartes was instrumental to a radical new understanding of the passions owing to his inverting the relationship of emotions to the soul and body. Descartes states that his goal in *The Passions of the Soul* is to discuss the passions not as a philosopher, but as a "Physicist." In this work, the body and

---

5 Aquinas, T. (1948). *Summa theologica*, trans. Fathers of the English Dominican Province, *3*, 1.

Aristotle, trans. Christopher Rowe (2002). *Nicomachean ethics*. New York: Oxford University Press.

6 Cates, D. F. (2009). *Aquinas on the emotions*. Washington DC: Georgetown University Press.

Crawford, K., & Calo, R. (2016). There is a blind spot in AI research. *Nature News*, *538*(7625), 311.

7 Dixon, T. (2003). *From passions to emotions: The creation of a secular psychological category*. New York: Cambridge University Press.

the soul are conceived as two subjects. The soul is the fundamental essence of the person while the body is but a machine. The soul can be both active and passive. The action of the soul is volition while the passion of the soul is knowledge or perceptions. The latter "passions of the soul" are defined as "perceptions or sensations or excitations of the soul which are referred to it in particular and which are caused, maintained, and strengthened by some movement of the spirits."[8] Perceptions are understood "to mean all the thoughts that are not actions of the soul, or volitions, but not when it is used only to mean cases of plain knowledge."[9] Passions can also be called sensations as "they are received into the soul in the same manner as the objects of the external senses, and are not known otherwise by it."[10] Specifically, the soul is acted on by the animal spirits which are the "liveliest and finest parts of the blood."[11] The soul passively perceives these sensations of the body. No longer is the body the passive recipient of the sense appetite, rather it is the cause of the passions. For the first time, the perception of the physiological change is the essence of the emotion.

By contrast to premodern and modern philosophers, some contemporary philosophers uphold a closer emotion-cognition integration. For Robert Solomon emotions are judgments.[12] Emotions are intentional toward an object in a specific way: they are an evaluation of that object. He stresses, they are not consequent to judgments (i.e., the bodily sensations that come from a judgment), but are the judgments themselves. They are not something that simply happens to us hydraulically, but something we do. Our emotional judgments of an object are based on certain opinions and beliefs. If a person becomes angry at someone for shoving them in the back, but then realize they tripped accidentally, usually the anger will subside. As beliefs change, so change the emotions. Emotions are judgments about our present situations, our past, and most importantly, emotions include intentions for the future, to act, to change the world, and change ourselves. If it is the case that emotions are something we do, not just something that happens to us, why do they feel passive? They feel passive because they are judgments that are often not reflective or deliberate. Usually our judgments have already been made when we come to consciously reflect on them which causes them to feel as if they are not ours.

---

8 Descartes, R. (1989). *Passions of the soul*, trans. S. H. Voss. Indianapolis: Hackett Publishing. 34

9 Ibid

10 Ibid

11 Ibid p. 22

12 Solomon, R. C. (1993). *The Passions: Emotions and the meaning of life.* Indianapolis: Hackett Publishing Company, Inc.

For Martha Nussbaum, emotions are cognitive appraisals or evaluation. By cognition, Nussbaum means any brain process that is "concerned with receiving and processing information," which does not "imply the presence of elaborate calculation, of computation, or even of reflexive self-awareness."[13] To say an emotion is cognitive does not imply conscious deliberate thought, but simply that the mind is processing information about an object. That it has to do with an object implies that emotions are intentional. Specifically, it has to do with an evaluation of the importance of an object. This evaluation is related to what one values. Nussbaum maintains, "there is something marked in the intentional perceptions and the beliefs characteristic of the emotions: they are all concerned with value, they see their object as invested with value."[14] Nussbaum finds the roots of this perspective in the Stoic idea of judgment as assent to an appearance.[15] The judgment follows a two-step process: first an object has a certain appearance to us and then we make an evaluation of that appearance. Nussbaum wants to ensure she is not misunderstood as suggesting a judgment is the cause of an emotion. No, the judgment itself is the emotion. However, a judgment is not freestanding. Both the appearance of an object and our judgment of it are affected by our biology, our common experience as humans, our individual upbringing, and by our social location.

The philosopher Robert Roberts advocates a "mentalist account" of emotion.[16] He concurs that emotions relate to with how we evaluate the world. But rather than deeming emotions to be judgments, he identifies emotions as a type of perception, namely a construal.[17] Therefore, it is possible to alter one's emotions to bring them in line with reality (to avoid "false emotions"). Just as in the famous rabbit-duck picture where we can choose to construe either a rabbit or a duck once we have both concepts "in our repertoire," when we have various concepts available to us we can voluntarily assign objects different roles and choose to construe the object differently.[18] For example, a person may see an immigrant and identify the person with the role of "an illegal" who is stealing jobs, or the immigrant can be given the role of a child of God who works hard for their family and is an asset to one's community (to give just two role options). By choosing to see the person performing different roles, our

---

13 Nussbaum, M. C. (2004). Emotions as judgments of value and importance. In R. C. Solomon (Ed.), *Thinking about feeling: Contemporary philosophers on emotions.* New York: Oxford University Press. 23

14 Ibid 189

15 Nussbaum, M. C. (2001). *Upheavals of thought: The intelligence of emotions.* New York: Cambridge University Press.

16 Roberts, R. C. (2003). *Emotions: An essay in aid of moral psychology.* New York: Cambridge University Press.

17 Roberts, R. C. (2013). *Emotions in the moral life.* New York: Cambridge University Press.

18 Ibid

construals of the person and situation change. Of course, emotions often feel involuntary as we find ourselves unable to overcome certain perceptions. This is because the concepts available at a moment depend on our history, context and physical state.[19]

Solomon, Nussbaum and Roberts, though concerned about the nature of emotion, demonstrates the close link between emotion and cognition. Emotion is not irrational, rather it is the evaluation, judgment, or perception of an object that is the essence of emotions.

2. Psychology: From universalism to constructivism

Though a more recent science, psychology propose diverse positon with regard to how emotions and cognitions interact in humans. In one strand of theories and empirical work, emotion and cognition are dichotomized such that emotions are seen as wholly irrational. By contrast, other theories support an integration perspective.

Perspectives that dichotomize emotion and cognition, in general tend to view emotions as physiological. In the mid-twentieth century, Silvan Tomkins built on Darwin[20] to propose there is an "affect program" with discreet emotions. Evolutionary mechanisms brought about innate programs in the brain that respond to external stimuli. Stimuli trigger reactions in the brain which in turn causes specific behaviors and bodily responses. These behaviors may do relatively little to further the chances of our survival today (e.g., the fear of snakes), but did serve such an end sometime in our ancestral past.[21] Tomkins proposed nine innate emotions in humans: interest, enjoyment, surprise, fear, anger, distress, shame, contempt, and disgust.[22] These nine emotions were considered as evolutionary fixed and free of any cognitive processes.

The most influential writer in recent decades on this physiological view of emotions is Tomkin's student, Paul Ekman. His career has focused on building the case for "basic emotions" which are identifiable by unique physiological reactions and behavior. Ekman most recently identifies seven basic emotions (though he expects there are more): anger, fear, surprise, sadness, disgust, contempt, and happiness.[23] The basic emotions are distinct, innate, and universal affective states shared throughout the human race. They

19 Ibid

20 Darwin, C. (1979). *The expression of the emotions in man and animals*. New York: St Martin's Press Inc.

21 Plamper, J. (2010). The history of emotions: an interview with William Reddy, Barbara Rosenwein, and Peter Stearns. *History and Theory*, *49*(2), 237-265.

22 Tomkins, S. (1962). *Affect imagery consciousness: Volume I: The positive affects*. New York: Springer publishing company.

23 Ekman, P., & Cordaro, D. (2011). What is meant by calling emotions basic. *Emotion review*, *3*(4), 364-370.

have developed because of "their adaptive value in dealing with fundamental life tasks."[24] Thus, basic emotions are accurately considered "natural kinds". Emotions are thus understood as primarily innate and shared across the human species, and more importantly free of any cognitive processes.

By contrast, alternative theories have shifted from the view of emotions as irrational to including a cognitive component. One particularly influential theory today is the appraisal theory of emotion. Here, emotions arise from a cognitive appraisal of how an event bears on one's good. Emotions are not irrational but are caused by the evaluation of an event according to what one values. Richard Lazarus, an early proponent of this view, argues that the emotional response is elicited by a complex cognitive appraisal of the significance of events for one's well-being.[25]

Yet another theory emphasizing the interaction of emotional and cognitive components are psychological constructionism. For psychological constructivists, many psychological phenomena including distinct emotions and judgments are formed from more basic psychological primitives (e.g., core affect, memory and a conceptual system, attention networks, and possibly others).[26] Capacity for core affect and the ability to create conceptual systems in which events are categorized Emotions are biologically based, yet cognitively constructed. They involve perception and interpretation of events both internal and external. Thus in psychological constructionism, emotions and in fact any psychological phenomena emerge from the interaction of cognition and emotion.

3. Neuroscience: From a modular brain to a networking brain

A common understanding among neuroscientists in the second half of the 20th century was that certain regions of the brain, especially those associated with an older evolutionary history (e.g., the "limbic system"), are the source of emotion while other regions, such as the evolutionarily newer neocortex, are associated with cognitive reasoning. Even today some subscribe to a

---

24 Ekman, P. (1994). All emotions are basic. In R. J. Davidson (Ed.), *The nature of emotion: Fundamental questions* (15-19). New York: Oxford University Press.

25 Lazarus, R. S. (1982). Thoughts on the relations between emotion and cognition. *American Psychologist, 37*(9), 1019.

26 Barrett, L. F. (2014). The conceptual act theory: A précis. *Emotion Review, 6*(4), 292-297; Barrett, L. F. (2017). *How emotions are made: The secret life of the brain.* New York: Houghton Mifflin Harcourt; Fehr, B., & Russell, J. A. (1984). Concept of emotion viewed from a prototype perspective. *Journal of Experimental Psychology: General, 113*(3), 464-489; Lindquist, K. A., & Barrett, L. F. (2008). Constructing emotion: The experience of fear as a conceptual act. *Psychological Science, 19*(9), 898-903; Russell, J. A. (2003). Core affect and the psychological construction of emotion. *Psychological Review, 110*(1), 145; Russell, J. A. (2009). Emotion, core affect, and psychological construction. *Cognition and emotion, 23*(7), 1259-1283.

similar view of separating emotion from cognition. The case for the emotion of fear can be an illustration: The emotion has neural, facial, and behavioral manifestations that served a function in our evolutionary history and today. Fear has a neurological basis with the amygdala playing a key role.[27] When the amygdala is activated, a response mechanism that assists in the avoidance of threats and dangers is initiated. Fear draws one's attention and focus to a potential danger. Fear also has a distinct facial expressions and physiological reaction characteristic to the emotion which assist in avoiding threats. Thus, expression of fear involves no cognition.

However, more recent discussions would show that this hypothesis of separate neural systems is lacking in empirical evidence. One such transition in understanding would be Joseph LeDoux's conception of the link between amygdala and the emotion of fear. In earlier work, LeDoux labeled the activity of the amygdala network as the "fear system." In LeDoux's recent work, however, he has sought to correct this common misconception of conflating the behavior and emotion.[28] In a *Cell* paper entitled "Rethinking the Emotional Brain," LeDoux argues that it is an error to equate the brain networks and behavior with emotions.[29] He proposes instead to call the circuitry connected with survival a "threat-induced defensive reaction" and the conscious feeling, "fear" proper[30] It is the latter alone that is properly thought of as an emotion. The emotion may often link to the physiological response, but consciousness must be differentiated from the survival circuit.

Neuroscientist Michael Spezio boldly asserts that the field of affective neuroscience has reached a consensus on emotion as cognition.[31] By cognition Spezio means "any kind of information processing or transformation that had relevance to measurable outcomes."[32] As emotions have to do with a response to stimuli that prepares a person for action, emotions are rightly understood as cognitive. Further confirmation of the cognitive aspect of emotion is found by Spezio in the failure of researchers to identify any circuitry in the brain for emotion that is distinct from cognition. Another neuroscientist, Richard Davidson, concurs and identifies the assumption that emotion is something

27 Feinstein, J. S., Adolphs, R., Damasio, A., & Tranel, D. (2011). The human amygdala and the induction and experience of fear. *Current biology*, *21*(1), 34-38.

28 LeDoux, J. E. (2015). *Anxious: Using the brain to understand and treat fear and anxiety*. New York: Viking.

29 LeDoux, J. (2012). Rethinking the emotional brain. *Neuron*, *73*(4), 653-676.

30 LeDoux, J. E. (2013). The slippery slope of fear. *Trends in Cognitive Sciences*, *17*(4), 155-156.

31 Spezio, M. L. (2011). The neuroscience of emotion and reasoning in social contexts: Implications for moral theology. *Modern Theology*, *27*(2), 339-356.

32 Ibid 346

other than cognitive as a great mistake in the study of emotion.[33] It is wrong to suppose that, "affect and cognition are subserved by separate and independent neural circuits."[34] Rather, Davidson insists, there is an "overlap between circuitry involved in cognitive and affective processing."[35] Spezio sums up the neuroscientific case: "the long-held divide between cognition and emotion had been breached by a failure to find such clear divisions in the circuitry of the human brain, and by the positive findings relating areas known for emotional salience processing to effective reasoning and decision making in the social domain."[36] In other words, emotions are constitutive of, and not separate from, the reasoning and decision making that people do about their own values and preferences.

Luiz Pessoa is one proponent of the integrated brain model.[37] Rather than comprising separate systems, he argues, it is better to think of the brain as a network. This is not to say there is not a phenomenological or subjective difference between a methodical thinking process and an intuitive manner. No one would deny this. But it is to say the two can never be divided in practice: even deliberate thinking is influenced by affect and affect always has a cognitive, perceptive component.

Drawing on research from the last two decades, Pessoa argues that while it is true that certain parts of the brain are vital for emotion, they are so as parts of wider, interconnecting networks. Pessoa affirms, "it is undeniable that certain brain regions play an important role in emotion. Yet, it is also apparent that they do not work in isolation and, instead, participate in distributed networks of regions that, collectively, carry out important functions."[38] The future of the brain sciences is not in distinguishing separate systems in the brain for emotion and cognition, but in understanding how deliberate thinking and emotional processes are integrated. By cognition, Pessoa refers descriptively to processes that have been thought of primarily as rational and deliberate. However, since he does not believe that cognition and emotion can be mapped onto particular domains in the brain, Pessoa does not focus on precise definitions for cognition or emotion, but attends to how different parts of the brain interact in certain behaviors. The task of the brain sciences lies with understanding the integration of emotion and cognition.

33 Davidson, R. J. (2003). Seven sins in the study of emotion: Correctives from affective neuroscience. *Brain and Cognition*, *52*(1), 129-132.

34 Ibid 129

35 Ibid 129

36 Spezio, M. L. (2011). The neuroscience of emotion and reasoning in social contexts: Implications for moral theology. *Modern Theology*, *27*(2), 339-356.

37 Pessoa, L. (2010). Emergent processes in cognitive-emotional interactions. *Dialogues in Clinical Neuroscience*, *12*(4), 433.

38 Ibid 433

To illustrate this integration, Pessoa focuses on the amygdala, a region of the "limbic system" often prototypically associated with emotion and fast processing. It has been thought that this system largely by-passed the neo-cortex associated with cognitive functions. However, "it is becoming increasingly clear," Pessoa writes, "that their connectivity affords them [subcortical structures such as the hypothalamus and the amygdala] great potential to interact with many other cortical and subcortical structures that are involved in cognitive functions."[39] Pessoa traces out the connections between the cortex, multiple subcortical regions, basolateral amygdala, extended amygdala, hypothalamus, and brainstem.[40] He concludes, "together, these architectural features allow the amygdala to be influenced by, and influence, a vast array of cortical and subcortical regions."[41] The implication is that the "cortex-amygdala" system "does not have a core function such as 'affect generation'. Instead, its particular functional state determines how it will contribute to multiple mental operations, and these involve not only arousal, vigilance, and novelty but also attention, value determination, and decision-making more broadly."[42] Particularly notable is the amygdala's function in attention to relevant stimuli. The amygdala is indeed important for emotion, but its significance arises from its role as a crucial hub in a wide network which simultaneously serves a role in many "cognitive" functions.

Thus, through integrated networks, processes typically deemed emotional have an impact on those considered cognitive. In other words, affect is essential for cognition, even when we are not aware of its influence. Feelings and emotion (conscious or otherwise) play a vital role in cognitive, deliberative thought processes. The converse is also true: emotions are influenced by cognitive processes. The implication is that to radically separate or oppose reason and emotion is problematic. James Russel affirms, "the dichotomy between rational thought and irrational emotion was long ago undermined by research showing, on the one hand, that cognitive processes emphasize economy and speed as much as rationality and, on the other, that cognitive processes are relevant to emotion."[43]

Development in philosophy, psychology, and neuroscience point to an emotional cognition in humans. Human cognition, unlike that of an intelligent machine, is not cold and merely logical. Various emotional factors might be

---

39 Ibid 437

40 Pessoa, L. (2017). A network model of the emotional brain. *Trends in Cognitive Sciences*, *21*(5), 357-371.

41 Ibid 463

42 Ibid 366

43 Russell, J. A. (2009). Emotion, core affect, and psychological construction. *Cognition and emotion*, *23*(7), 1259-1283.

anchoring and coloring an act of human cognition. Reflections on human nature will need to consider this characteristic human cognition for a richer perspective on the human destiny.

References

Annas, J. (1993). *The morality of happiness.* New York: Oxford University Press.

Aquinas, T. (1948). *Summa theologica*, trans. Fathers of the English Dominican Province, *3*, 1.

Aristotle, trans. Christopher Rowe (2002). *Nicomachean ethics.* New York: Oxford University Press.

Barrett, L. F. (2014). The conceptual act theory: A précis. *Emotion Review*, *6*(4), 292-297.

Barrett, L. F. (2017). *How emotions are made: The secret life of the brain*. New York: Houghton Mifflin Harcourt.

Cates, D. F. (2009). *Aquinas on the emotions*. Washington DC: Georgetown University Press.

Crawford, K., & Calo, R. (2016). There is a blind spot in AI research. *Nature News*, *538*(7625), 311.

Darwin, C. (1979). *The expression of the emotions in man and animals*. New York: St Martin's Press Inc.

Davidson, R. J. (2003). Seven sins in the study of emotion: Correctives from affective neuroscience. *Brain and Cognition*, *52*(1), 129-132.

Descartes, R. (1989). *Passions of the soul*, trans. S. H. Voss. Indianapolis: Hackett Publishing.

Dixon, T. (2003). *From passions to emotions: The creation of a secular psychological category*. New York: Cambridge University Press.

Ekman, P. (1994). All emotions are basic. In R. J. Davidson (Ed.), *The nature of emotion: Fundamental questions* (15-19). New York: Oxford University Press.

Ekman, P., & Cordaro, D. (2011). What is meant by calling emotions basic. *Emotion review*, *3*(4), 364-370.

Fehr, B., & Russell, J. A. (1984). Concept of emotion viewed from a prototype perspective. *Journal of Experimental Psychology: General*, *113*(3), 464-489.

Feinstein, J. S., Adolphs, R., Damasio, A., & Tranel, D. (2011). The human amygdala and the induction and experience of fear. *Current biology*, *21*(1), 34-38.

Lazarus, R. S. (1982). Thoughts on the relations between emotion and cognition. *American Psychologist*, *37*(9), 1019.

LeDoux, J. (2012). Rethinking the emotional brain. *Neuron*, *73*(4), 653-676.

LeDoux, J. E. (2013). The slippery slope of fear. *Trends in Cognitive Sciences*, *17*(4), 155-156.

LeDoux, J. E. (2015). *Anxious: Using the brain to understand and treat fear and anxiety*. New York: Viking.

Lindquist, K. A., & Barrett, L. F. (2008). Constructing emotion: The experience of fear as a conceptual act. *Psychological Science*, *19*(9), 898-903.

Nussbaum, M. C. (2001). *Upheavals of thought: The intelligence of emotions.* New York: Cambridge University Press.

Nussbaum, M. C. (2004). Emotions as judgments of value and importance. In R. C. Solomon (Ed.), *Thinking about feeling: Contemporary philosophers on emotions.* New York: Oxford University Press.

Pessoa, L. (2010). Emergent processes in cognitive-emotional interactions. *Dialogues in Clinical Neuroscience*, *12*(4), 433.

Pessoa, L. (2017). A network model of the emotional brain. *Trends in Cognitive Sciences*, *21*(5), 357-371.

Plamper, J. (2010). The history of emotions: an interview with William Reddy, Barbara Rosenwein, and Peter Stearns. *History and Theory*, *49*(2), 237-265.

Plato, trans. C. D. C. Reeve (2004). *Republic.* Indianapolis: Hackett Pub Co.

Powell, S. M. (2016). *The impassioned life: Reason and emotion in the Christian tradition.* Minneapolis: Fortress Press.

Roberts, R. C. (2003). *Emotions: An essay in aid of moral psychology*. New York: Cambridge University Press.

Roberts, R. C. (2013). *Emotions in the moral life*. New York: Cambridge University Press.

Russell, J. A. (2003). Core affect and the psychological construction of emotion. *Psychological Review*, *110*(1), 145.

Russell, J. A. (2009). Emotion, core affect, and psychological construction. *Cognition and emotion*, *23*(7), 1259-1283.

Solomon, R. C. (1993). *The Passions: Emotions and the meaning of life.* Indianapolis: Hackett Publishing Company, Inc.

Sorabji, R. (2000). *Emotion and peace of mind: From stoic agitation to Christian temptation.* New York: Oxford University Press.

Spezio, M. L. (2011). The neuroscience of emotion and reasoning in social contexts: Implications for moral theology. *Modern Theology*, *27*(2), 339-356.

Tomkins, S. (1962). *Affect imagery consciousness: Volume I: The positive affects*. New York: Springer publishing company.

PART THREE

SPIRITUALITY AND SADHANA

10

Divine and Human *Jugalbandi* through the Flute of Kṛṣṇa

Ivan D'Souza

Abstract

This article highlights the relationship between human and divine which is achieved through the flute play of Kṛṣṇa. In pastoral cultures, a musical instrument is often associated with the shepherd or cowherd. In the Kṛṣṇa narrative, though it is primarily used by him to attract the young women—gopīs—of his village, it is symbolic of many other meanings and messages. The article tries to explore various layers and levels of Kṛṣṇa's flute. It tries to delve deep into some questions such as, what is the significance of flute for Kṛṣṇa? What is the effect of Kṛṣṇa's flute play? How do the ancient writings and different literary works narrate the flute of Kṛṣṇa? What does it communicate? etc.

Key words: Flute, *Muraḷī*, Kṛṣṇa, Rādhā, *Gopīs, Vṛndāvana, Bhāgavatapurāṇa, Bhagavadgītā*

Introduction

Jugalbandi literally means "entwined twins" or "tied together." It is a spontaneous instrumental or vocal duet involving two or more musicians. This article highlights such a perfect *jugalbandi* between human and divine which is achieved through the flute play of Kṛṣṇa. In pastoral cultures, a musical instrument is often associated with the shepherd or cowherd. He uses it to call his flock together. In the Kṛṣṇa narrative, though it is primarily used by him to attract the young women – *gopīs* – of his village, it is symbolic of many other meanings and messages. The paper tries to explore various layers and levels of invitation symbol of Kṛṣṇa i.e., flute. Kṛṣṇa was born in a pastoral surrounding, among the cowherds. In most of his images and portrayals he holds the shepherd's reed. The study tries to delve deep into some questions such as, what is the significance of flute for Kṛṣṇa? What is the effect of Kṛṣṇa's flute play? How do the ancient writings and different literary works narrate the flute of Kṛṣṇa? What does it communicate? etc.

1. Flute in Indian Music

Flute is accepted as representative instrument of the *suṣira* class i.e., full of holes, hollow and perforated in Indian musicology. In Indian tradition, it is called by different names such as *veṇu, vaṁśi, muralī, bānsuri* etc. The term '*veṇu*' is derived from the root '*ve*' which means 'to weave,' '*vaṇ*' means 'to reflect,' 'to echo,' 'to play.' '*Veṇu*' stands for a bamboo, a reed, a cane, a flute pipe.[1] *Koḷalu, Kuḷal, Puḷḷānkuḷal* and *Piḷḷangovi* are the expressions used in the Dravidian languages. It is played by the fingers of both the hands, on the right side of the body. *Veṇu* is very small, not more than six inches long and has six eyes or holes, *bānsuri* has six or seven holes, *vaṁśi* is about fifteen inches long and has eight or nine holes and *muraḷī* is about eighteen inches long and has four finger holes. *Veṇu-s* have been classified into different types of wind instruments and on the basis of length of the pipe, material from which the pipe is made, number of sound holes, number of pipes used etc. The Carnatic flute is known as *veṇu* and it is used in South Indian music whereas the Hindustani flute called as *bānsuri* and it is used mostly in North Indian music. The ancient scriptures like *Vedas*, *Rāmāyaṇa*, *Mahābhārata* and *Arthaśāstra* mention flute as *veṇu*, Grammarian Pāṇinī, refers it as *nāḍi* and *Nātyaśāstra* calls it as *vaṁśi*.[2]

2. Flute of Kṛṣṇa

In the Indian philosophical and mythological texts flute is closely associated with Kṛṣṇa. Kṛṣṇa uses the flutes of different kinds, sizes and shapes. He uses the flute made up of gold, jewels, marble, hollow bamboo and even leaves. Longer *vaṁśi* of Kṛṣṇa which is made up of jewels is called as *mahānanda* or *sammohini*, still longer one made up of gold is known as *ākarṣini* and even

1 See M. Monier Williams, *A Sanskrit English Dictionary* (New Delhi: Bharatiya Granth Niketan, 2015). Also refer V. S. Apte, *The Student's Sanskrit-English Dictionary* (Delhi: Sri Satguru Publications, 1991).

2 K. L. Seshagiri Rao, ed., *Encyclopedia of Hinduism*, vol. 4 (New Delhi: India Heritage Research Foundation, 2010), s.v. "flute."

longer one is called *ānandini*. The *ānandini* flute produces enchanting melody to the cowherd group and is technically named *vaṁśuli*.[3]

There is a story about the flute of Kṛṣṇa. Everyday Kṛṣṇa was going to the *Vṛndāvana* and would express his love to all plants and animals of the forest. One day he approached a bamboo tree and said, "I want a favour from you. But I do not know how to ask you." Bamboo replied gracefully, "If it is possible I can do it for you." Kṛṣṇa asked, "I want your life. I want to cut you." After a pause bamboo requested, "Is there any way out?" Kṛṣṇa said, "No." Immediately bamboo agreed, "Take me, I surrender myself to you." Kṛṣṇa felled it, cut it and made eight holes in it. The tree cried with great pain. But it got the shape of a flute and remained all the time with Kṛṣṇa. Even the women cowherds were jealous of the flute because they could spend only few hours of the day with Kṛṣṇa whereas flute was with Kṛṣṇa all the time. Cowherds asked the flute, "Why does Kṛṣṇa honour you so much?" The flute answered, "I am hollow and empty inside. Kṛṣṇa uses me as he wants. I am filled with his breath. I offer myself fully to him. In fact who are we? I am he, we are he!"[4]

Different epithets are attributed to Kṛṣṇa, the flute-player such as *Bihari, Bānsiwāla, Gopāla, Sākṣigopāla, Veṇugopāla, Veṇudhāra, Govinda, Muraḷī, Gopīnātha, Muraḷīlola, Muraḷīdhara, Muralimādhva, Muraḷimanohara, Mohana, Madanamohana, Madanagopāla* etc.[5] The most common posture of Kṛṣṇa used in art, dance, drama and in various depictions is the *tribhaṅga* posture. In this posture Kṛṣṇa's limbs are bent in three places–his head inclines slightly to one side, the upper half of his body is bent in the opposite direction at the waist, and his right calf is crossed in front of his left shin with the ball of his right foot resting on the ground. This posture is adopted when he plays the flute, and his hands are raised beside his right shoulder.

Kṛṣṇa is called as *bhuvanasundara* i.e., beautiful in the world. Rupa Goswami (1489–1564), philosopher of the Gauḍīya Vaiṣṇava tradition mentions sixty four qualities of Kṛṣṇa in his work *Bhakti-rasāmṛta-sindhu.* Out of them four qualities stand out as very important. The four sweet features which are said to be unique to Kṛṣṇa are:[6]

---

3 A. C. Bhaktivedanta Swami Prabhupada, *Vaniquotes*, https://vaniquotes.org/wiki/There_are_three_kinds_of_flutes_used_by_Krsna._One_is_called_venu,_one_is_called_murali,_and_the_third_is_called_vamsi accessed 8 March 2019.

4 Vassanthi, "Kṛṣṇana Kolaḷina Bagge Kathe," *Human Value Blog in Kannada* (blog), (28 February 2017), https://saibalsanskaarkannada.wordpress.com/2017/02/28/, accessed 8 March 2019.

5 Alan W. Entwistle, *Braj Centre of Krishna Pilgrimage* (Groningen: Egbert Forsten, 1987), 79.

6 Tamal Krishna Goswami, *A Living Theology of Krishna Bhakti* (New York: Oxford University Press, 2012), 137.

1. *Līlāmādhurya*: Sweetness of past times especially dancing with the *gopīs* or cowherd maidens
2. *Premamādhurya*: Sweetness of spontaneous love of associates or devotees
3. *Veṇumādhurya*: Sweetness or opulence of flute melody
4. *Rūpamādhurya*: Sweetness of form or beauty

3. Kṛṣṇa: The Divine Musician

Kṛṣṇa is all in all. He is irrepressible child, graceful dancer, an enchanting flute player, irresistible lover, great hero and valiant warrior. Kṛṣṇa symbolises *prema* (divine love), *rūpa* (divine beauty) and *līlā* (divine sport). The *Rāsa*-dance (the sweet act of divine love) in the *Vṛndāvana*[7] commences with Kṛṣṇa's *veṇugīta* (song on flute). It is believed that Kṛṣṇa has the skill and power to enchant both animate and inanimate worlds through his flute-playing. According to Rūpa Goswāmi, Kṛṣṇa plays his flute for the following reasons:[8]

3.1 An Impromptu Self-expression

Kṛṣṇa is a mellow person with full of *rasa*. His flute reveals his freedom, passion, gaiety and spontaneity. He loves to play the flute and relishes the music. It is completely an independent act. He would climb a tree and play flute for himself. He himself would get attracted to the flute music. It is so attractive that it attracts the all-attractive. *Kṛṣṇa is mischievous and humorous in his approach.* He plays flute to dance with *gopīs* and to enliven the cows. He not only calls the cows individually but in different groups. He calls them by name such as *surabhi*, *kuṅkumi*, *dhavani*, *saraswati*, *śyāma* etc. Few cows are named as *mṛdaṅgamukhi* (having a sweet and chubby look like drums), *siṁhamukhi* (having the face of lion) according to their appearances. He plays the tune which makes them dizzy.

3.2 Bundle of Contradictions

Kṛṣṇa loves contradictions. There are five examples which testify that flute of Kṛṣṇa is a bundle of contradictions.

---

7 *Vṛndāvana* is a historical city in the Mathura district of Uttar Pradesh, India. It is the place where Kṛṣṇa spent his childhood days. The town is about 11 km away from Mathura, Kṛṣṇa's birthplace. It is also termed as *Goloka, Gokula, Śvetadvīpa, Vraja.*

8 I am indebted to the well-researched lecture by Amarendra Das. I have borrowed many ideas from his reflections. H. G Amarendra Das, *Why does Krishna play the flute,* (Yasodadulal das, Dec 28, 2017), https://www.youtube.com/watch?v=W1-sxiqRj7U accessed 26 Mar 2019.

a) The general view is that anything in this world which has holes is defective. But though flute has six or more holes it is more complete than anything else.
b) The flute has holes yet it is the origin and source of music. Though it is hollow it holds everything.
c) It is very hard yet it can make hard hearted soft.
d) Fourth contradiction is based on the word '*parva.*' *Parva* has two meanings, namely, cross-section and festival. Flute is a cross section of a plant yet when it is played it creates festivity. In other words, flute comes from *parva* and creates *parva.*
e) Final contradiction can be noted through word-play of '*vaṁśa.*' *Vaṁśa* refers to family tradition. Flute is called *vaṁśi*. The playing of *vaṁśi* makes the *gopīs* to leave their *vaṁśa*. They leave their dynasty and family and get united to the high class of Kṛṣṇa.

3.3 Carnival of Joy in *Vṛndāvana*

Kṛṣṇa plays the flute to create a playful world of bliss and ecstasy around. He uses his flute to please, serve and reciprocate the devotees of *Vṛndāvana*. He uses the flute for playing, calling, pacifying the cowherds. In the morning he plays the flute with excitement. During the day he plays flute to excite and entertain friends, *gopīs*, and cows. Afternoon to reciprocate with the residents in the forest. He tells animals in the forest, "Yes, I have noticed you." He plays flute for rivers, mountains, trees and communicates his presence with them. He expresses to the dancing peacocks, "I have come for you." He reciprocates all the creatures of *Vṛndāvana* with the intoxicating, mesmerizing music by satisfying their senses, minds, hearts and souls.

4. Effects of Kṛṣṇa's Flute Play

The Scriptures of *Vaiṣṇavism* and poems express the effect of music echoed from Kṛṣṇa's flute. According to Rūpa Goswami, the flute of Kṛṣṇa has eight holes with eight notes or sounds. Goswāmi's work *Vidagdha-mādhav* beautifully highlights some of the effects of Kṛṣṇa's flute play. He mentions six effects of the first note of the flute:[9]

9 Giriraj Dasa, *Krishna's flutes* (Gurgaon: 21st February 2015), Blog article, For the Pleasure of Lord Krishna, http://www.forthepleasureoflordkrishna.com/2015/02/21/krishnas-flutes/ accessed 9 April 2019.

1. Lord Śiva or *Natarāja*[10] who is dancing with his drum in *Kailāsa*[11] found the first note of Kṛṣṇa's flute so mesmerizing that he feels like dancing.
2. Four sons of Brahma[12] who sit for meditation lose their meditation.
3. Brahma in *Brahmaloka*[13] who is contemplating on how to create, forgets who he is and forgets what he has to do.
4. Tuṁburu, the best among *gandharvas* (celestial musicians who were established in music) gets astonished and forgets to sing.
5. *Ananta Śeṣa*[14] who holds heavy universe on his head feels that planets are going to slip or fall from his head in dizziness.
6. Balarāma, elder brother of Kṛṣṇa says that when Kṛṣṇa plays his flute Indra falls from his *Airāvata*[15] and bows down the direction of the flute sound. He cries in happiness and sometimes he talks loudly.

The second note of Kṛṣṇa's flute makes river Yamuna to flow backwards. It forgets the direction of its flow. The third note makes the moon to forget the direction of its movement and stuns the moon. It is stuck in amazement and wonder. The fourth note makes cows motionless. Their ears go upward, taking the shape of a vessel to be filled with the nectar of music. Unlimited nectar falls into the long ears of the cows, they forget to suck milk, forget to drink and milk flows from the side. The eyes of the cows see the form of Kṛṣṇa, their noses nuzzle up to Kṛṣṇa, their tongues try to lick Kṛṣṇa's feet, their minds think of Kṛṣṇa and their hearts embrace him. Their being overflows with zeal and zest.[16]

Kṛṣṇa calls the *Vrajagopīs* through the fifth note (*pañcamasvara*) of the flute and with the sixth note the autumn arrives. Everything becomes fresh, blooms and blossoms. Trees say, "These fruits are for you, O Kṛṣṇa." When

10 *Natarāja* means "Lord of the Dance." The Hindu god Śiva is depicted as the cosmic ecstatic dancer.

11 *Kailāsa* is the name of a mountain in the Himalayas which is believed to be the paradise of the Hindu god Śiva.

12 *Purāṇic* Scriptures state the four *Kumāras* as the four mind-born sons of Brahma, namely, Sanaka, Sanātana, Sanandana and Sanatkumāra.

13 *Brahmaloka* or *Satyaloka* is the abode of Lord Brahma, the creator god.

14 *Ananta Śeṣa* can be translated as 'the Endless One.' He is an expansion of God who appears as a serpent with thousands of heads and who serves as the bed of Lord Viṣṇu. *Ananta Śeṣa* holds all the planets of the universe on His hoods and constantly sings the glories of Viṣṇnu from all His mouths. He is the first-born among snakes.

15 *Airāvata* is the elephant who carries Lord Indra. It appeared from the churning of the Milk Ocean and has four tusks and seven trunks.

16 "*gāvaśca kṛṣṇa mukha nirgata veṇugīta pīyūṣam uttabhita karṇa puṭaiḥ pibantyaḥ śāvāḥ snuta stana payaḥ kavalāḥ smā tasthur govindam ātmani dṛśāśru kalāḥ spṛśantyaḥ*" (*Śrīmad Bhāgavatam* 10.21.13).

Kṛṣṇa touches the branch, it nods in glee. The stones melt and become like butter. Whole hill melts like mountain of butter and Kṛṣṇa eats it.[17]

The seventh note in Kṛṣṇa's flute brings together all the six seasons, namely, *vasantha* (spring), *grīṣma* (summer), *varśa* (rain), *śarad* (autumn), *hemanta* (early winter) and *śiśira* (dew winter). It signifies that everything is available through the mellow melody of the marvelous musician Kṛṣṇa. The eighth note is exclusively and extensively meant for Rādhā.

4.1 *Muraḷī's* Melody makes *Gopīs* Gleeful

The mellifluous flute of Kṛṣṇa brought ineffable joy to all his devotees. The damsels gave up their household duties, left their husbands and listened to it, the girls began to dance for its music. The needs of the children and calves at home were not met. The *gopīs* expressed, "O thou dearest one, with the nectarous flow from thy lips, do thou extinguish the fire of desire kindled by the melodious music of thy flute and by the side-long glances accompanied by bewitching smiles. Otherwise, our bodies being burnt by this fire, as well as of separation from thee, O dear one, attain your proximity by meditating on thy foot."[18]

The flute sound made the *gopīs* to forget what they were doing and what they were supposed to do. As they ran swiftly towards the direction of Kṛṣṇa's flute music, some left half-finished the milking of cows in the cowshed, one did not bother to check the milk which was kept for boiling, some of them left the babies on the floor without breast-feeding, some stopped serving the food to the family members at home, some others who were engaged in beautification and decoration of their bodies left them half done and some ran without even dressing properly or putting on wrong clothes on different parts of their body.[19]

When Kṛṣṇa returned to his village it was the happy time for villagers because they gained transcendental experience with Kṛṣṇa. But it was a sad time for the residents of the forest because they felt every moment of his absence. The missing of Kṛṣṇa for twelve hours in *Vṛndāvana* was like twelve years of *vanavāsa*.[20] The cowherds ask themselves amidst their desolation: when will this night end? When will Kṛṣṇa return to the forest?

---

17 One of the epithets of Kṛṣṇa is *Navanīta* or Butter thief.

18 P. Banerjee, *The Life of Krishna in Indian Art* (New Delhi: National Museum, 1978), 27.

19 A.C. Bhaktivedānta Swami Prabhupāda, *Kṛṣṇa: The Supreme Personality of Godhead* (A Summary Study of Śrīla Vyāsadeva's Śrīmad-Bhāgavatam, Tenth Canto) (Mumbai: The Bhaktivedanta Book Trust, 2002), 218.

20 *Vanavāsa* denotes to the lonely experience of Paṇḍavas in the forest for twelve years which is explained in the great Indian epic *Mahābharata*.

4.2 Nature's Trance, Creatures' Dance for Govinda's Songs

Kṛṣṇa attracts the whole universe, captivates the planetary systems through the tune of his flute. The flute melody expels evil powers and extends its positive effect all over. The forest is filled with a celestial cadence. The entire forest entities fell in deep love with Kṛṣṇa. The deer stood spell-bound, the peacock danced, the birds lay quiet on the trees,–all stood attentive and motionless as his sweet voice thrilled through the air. Bengali poet Rabindranath Tagore says, "O hear those sweet flute sounds as the smell of his flower-necklace fuses with the melody . . . The ripple music of Yamuna fills my ears and eyes, O look how the honey-moon smiles at him."[21] The flute which echoes and resounds in the mountains and forests is a gesture of nature's communication. *It is a* gentle, *clear, sweet, pure and simple yet rich and gratifying encounter.* When Kṛṣṇa leaves the forest the tree was burnt with the feeling of separation as if there was a forest fire.

Due to the music of the flute of Kṛṣṇa the rocks melt, the rivers flow backward, animate go inanimate and inanimate go animate, cows forget to drink, deer forgets to eat and chew grass. The hair i.e., grass in the body of *Vṛndāvana* stands up with admiration. Cows get the best opportunity to eat the grass yet worst ability to chew it. It is said that the bird in the forest remembers Kṛṣṇa at night. The tears begin to fall from its eyes. The bird which was sitting straight goes upside down. It loses its grip on branch and falls. Fortunately, it falls on the pool of water made up of its own tears.[22]

5. *Muraḷīdhara* in Ancient Scriptures

The various accounts narrated in the Scriptural texts such as *Harivaṁśa, Bhāgavatapurāṇa, Mahābhārata* etc. describe the mutual love between Kṛṣṇa and *gopīs* quite differently. *Harivaṁśa* makes the mention of Kṛṣṇa's playing of flute in the company of cowherds (*Harivaṁśa* 55.26). The herdswomen enjoy the melodious singing of Kṛṣṇa. They leave their work unfinished whether milking, cooking, serving food, suckling their babes, waiting on their husbands or decorating themselves in order to meet their beloved.[23]

In *Bhāgavatapurāṇa*, the flute music is both a sign of presence and absence of Kṛṣṇa. In other words, the love of Kṛṣṇa is experienced by the *gopīs* both as union in *Vṛndāvana* and as separation when he goes to the village. It awakens the sense of separation in the herdswomen, who feel drawn towards

---

21 Sukanya Sarbadhikary, *The Place of Devotion: Siting and Experiencing Divinity in Bengal-Vaishnavism* (Oakland: University of California Press, 2015), 188. https://www.jstor.org/stable/10.1525/ j.ctt1ffjn1f.10, accessed 7 April 2019.

22 Amarendra Das, *Why does Krishna play the flute,* YouTube video.

23 Noel Sheth, *The Divinity of Krishna* (New Delhi: Munshiram Manoharial Publishers Pvt Ltd., 1984), 119.

him. They miss him and are reminded of great days spent with Kṛṣṇa. Kṛṣṇa's flute instils devotional love and a mystical feeling of communion with nature. The whole of cosmos is captured by the mellifluous melody of flute of Kṛṣṇa. The whole nature gets the romantic and ecstatic mood. The animals, rivers, trees, creepers, birds and clouds are totally enticed, enchanted and thrilled by the music of the flute. It excites the passion of women. Even Indra, Śiva, Brahma and other leaders of the gods enthralled by the enchanting music of flute.[24]

Śrīmad-Bhāgavatam narrates the praises of milk-women towards Kṛṣṇa in the following words: [25]

> Being thus surrounded by the kine and the cow-herd boys, Kṛṣṇa entered in to *Vṛndāvanaa* where the lake-waters were rendered translucent on the advent of the autumn and where a breeze, laden with the fragrance of lotuses, was continually blowing. The trees therein were decorated with floral wealth, and the lakes, rivers and mountains rang with the humming and chirping of enraptured bees and birds. Wandering deeper and deeper into that forest, *Madhusudana* (Kṛṣṇa) grazed the cattle in company with Balarama and other cow-herds, playing charmingly on his flute. On hearing the music of his flute, the damsels of Braja came there under the spell of *Cupid* (the god of love). Some among them in the absence of Kṛṣṇa, began to rehearse unto their confidents the achievements of Kṛṣṇa. But attempting to describe his deeds, they failed to do so, remembering the dalliances he held with them.

He further says that when Kṛṣṇa plays the flute its holes are filled with the nectar which are dropped from his lips. Kṛṣṇa is surrounded by the cowherds for the scintillating melody of his flute (1-6).

> O Gopees, what act of great merit hath this flute performed in consequence of which, it is drinking the nectar from the lips of Damodara (Kṛṣṇa), without leaving the smallest particle for the Gopees, the rightful enjoyers of it? Seeing its prosperity, the rivers from which the bamboo of the flute had drawn its sap are displaying delight by the blossoming of lotuses in them, and the bamboo trees out of which the flute is made are shedding tears of joy in the form of juice, even as the elderly people of a family are delighted and shed tears of joy when a child devoted to *Narayana* is born in their family.
>
> O friends, the glory of the earth is now enhanced by *Vṛndāvanaa*, which has obtained all prosperity from the lotus-like feet of the son of Devaki

24 Sheth, *The Divinity of Krishna*, 129-130.

25 *The Srimad-Bhagavatam of Krishna-Dwaipayana Vyasa*, trans. J. M. Sanyal, vol. II (New Delhi: Munshiram Manoharlal Publishers Pvt. Ltd., 1973), (*Śrīmad-Bhāgavatam* 10.21.1-20) 87-90.

> and where on the summits of mountains the animals have ceased to move and exert, beholding the dances of the delighted peacocks to the music of Kṛṣṇa's flute. Blessed are these hinds (the females of the stags) in spite of their being born in the animal species; for listening to the notes of his flutes, they with their males, *Krishnasaras*, are approaching the son of Nanda vested in variegated garments, and are drawing adoration from him for casting lustful glances towards him. Beholding Kṛṣṇa of handsome appearance and graceful manners capable of enhancing the joys of the ladies, and listening to the music of his flute and to his melodious and faultless song, even celestial damsels,-that range through the heavens-when seated on the laps of the deities would lose all patience and become senseless coming under the spell of Cupid and chaplets of flowers fall off from their braided hair, and the *nibi* (loin-cloth) on their persons drop down. The cows drinking with their raised ears the melodious music of the flute sounded by the breath of Krishna, and the calves holding in their mouths the milk sucked from the udders of their mothers, would stand motionless as if they are paralysed; tears would roll down their cheeks for perceiving Krishna by their eyes, and they would embrace him in their minds (7-13).

The birds in the forest eagerly wait for the sight of Kṛṣṇa after listening to the melodious music of the flute sounded by Kṛṣṇa. Pleased by the songs of Kṛṣṇa the rivers take meandering courses, their force of currents and flow slows down. They even carry lotuses as presents for Kṛṣṇa.

> On seeing Krishna playing on the flute, and tending the cattle in company with Balarama and other cow-herds, in the scorching rays of the sun, the rain-clouds rose in the skies out of affection for their friends Krishna; and by their shadow they served the purpose of his umbrella, and they then cooled him by pouring down their flower-like drops. Blessed are the wives of the foresters; for though afflicted with desire excited by the sight of saffron sprinkled on grass, they hold their passion at bay by smearing their faces and breasts with the self-same saffron, which had hued the breasts of the beloved ones of Krishna.

Everything gets absorbed in Kṛṣṇa as he traversed the forest of *Vṛndāvana*. The melodious notes of flute stops the movement of the cattlefold (14-20).

6. Poetic Poses and Portrayals of *Veṇugopāla*

Various images and imaginations of Kṛṣṇa in the *Vṛndāvana* has given rise to umpteen number of poetry and paintings, creative dramas and dances and melodious music and singing in different languages over the years. The pre-Caitanya Bengal Vaiṣṇavite poet of 15th century, Baṛu Caṇḍīdāsa notes the effect of Kṛṣṇa's flute play as:

How can I describe his relentless flute,
which pulls virtuous women from their homes
and drags them by their hair to Shyām
as thirst and hunger pull the doe to the snare?
Chaste ladies forget their lords,
wise men forget their wisdom,
and clinging vines shake loose from their trees,
hearing that music.
Then how shall a simple dairymaid withstand its call
Chandidāsa says, Kālā the puppet master leads the dance.[26]

The 15th century poet Kṛṣṇadāsa Kavirāja, belonging to Bengal *Vaiṣṇavism*, proclaims in his *Śrī Śrī Caitanya-caritāmṛta*, "And the white nails in the hands of the Lord are also like so many moons. As the Lord blows His flute there, little moons dance upon the holes of the flute. They appear as if the tune proceeds not from the flute but from these beautiful nails of the Lord."[27] The sound of Kṛṣṇa's flute creates vibrations in heavenly abode too. Kṛṣṇadāsa states, "The sweet tune that the flute produces is sublime and powerful. It spreads like lightning in all directions. It penetrates into the creation and reaches the highest heaven known as Vaikuntha."[28]

Mirābai of Rajasthan (1498-1546), the great woman saint and devotee of Kṛṣṇa of the 16th Century sings:

On the bank of the Jamuna
I heard the flute
and lost my heart to him
who played it so enchantingly.
The dark Krishna
sat on a blanket
beside the dark waters of the river,
and as soon as I heard him play
I lost my consciousness.
I was like a figurine
carved out of stone.

---

26 Edward C. Dimock and Denise Levertov, trans., *In Praise of Krishna: Songs from the Bengali* (Garden City, N. J.: Doubleday & Co., 1967), 29.

27 Quoted in David R. Kinsley, *The Sword and the Flute: Kālī and Kṛṣṇa* (Delhi: Vikas Publishing House Pvt Ltd., 1975), 24.

28 Kṛṣṇadāsa Kavirāja, *Śrī Śrī Caitanya-caritāmṛta*, trans. Nagendra Kumar Ray, 2nd ed., 6 vols. (Calcutta: Nagendra Kumar Ray, 1959), 538.

Mira says:
Come quickly, O Giridhar,
and end this tableau.[29]

Further Mirābai chants to Kṛṣṇa:
Mohan has totally charmed me:
with his lovely face and lotus eyes
he has stolen my heart away.
On the bank of the Jamuna
Krishna grazes his cattle
and plays his haunting flute.

My body, soul and all my wealth
is Giridhar's
Mira is lost at his lotus feet.[30]

Surdas, a 16th century blind devotional poet of *Vallabha Sampradāya* sings in delight the enchanting impact of Kṛṣṇa's flute:

The flute has done her work.
She plunders for herself, depriving us of the nectar of Hari's lips.
Nanda's son [Kṛṣṇa] is under the influence of
her music. She has cast her spell over him.
The living and the non-living, the moving and
the unmoving, and even the God of Love are spellbound
She distracted all, even those not easily distracted.
The milkmaid says that the Lord, the crown of
the wise, has fallen into her hands.[31]

The great poet Rūpa Goswāmi addressing the Krṣṇa's magic flute as a living symbol of love and ecstasy lauds:

Friend flutelet, Krishna's best-beloved!
Art thou not full of flaws, uneven and frail?
Still how hast thou won to thy blessed bliss?
To be caressed by His hands everlastingly,
And, thrilling to His ambrosial lips' own kiss.
Call all to His feet with thy moon-melodies![32]

29 Pritish Nandy, trans., *Krishna, Krishna: The Devotional Songs of Mirabai* (Ghaziabad: Vikas Publishing House Pvt. Ltd., 1982), 31.

30 Nandy, trans., *Krishna, Krishna: The Devotional Songs of Mirabai*, 46.

31 Surdas, *The Poems of Surdas*, ed. and trans. S. M. Pandey and Norman H. Zide (Chicago: South Asia Language & Area Centre, University of Chicago, 1963), poem 60.

32 Dilip Kumar Roy and Indira Devi, *The Flute Calls Still* (Bombay: Bharatiya Vidya Bhavan, 1982), xi-foreward.

Thus, we find volumes of literature extolling and exalting the entrancing effect of Kṛṣṇa's flute.

7. *Rādhāvallabha* as the Robber of Her Heart

The impact of Kṛṣṇa's flute play completely robs the heart of Rādhā. It arouses her spirits, troubles her emotions and makes her standstill amidst the kitchen work. Baṛu Caṇḍīdāsa beautifully notes the sentiments of Rādhā in his *Śrīkṛṣṇakīrtana*:

> If I were a bird, then I would fly to his location.
> Let the earth split open, I shall hide myself within it!
> Granny, when a blaze burns down a forest, people know it;
> But my heart is like a potter's kiln, it burns discretely.
> I'm consumed inside because of loning over Krishna.[33]

Rādhā further pleads to her Granny to find Kṛṣṇa for love and merriment:

> Since I heard the music of the sweet-voiced flute, my Granny,
> listen to this tale of what I'm cooking.
> Into sour dishes I've been mixing pungent spices;
> to the brim I've drenched the greens in water…
> Thinking it was snakegourd as I listened to the music,
> in some ghee, I fried unripened betel…
> Into bitter curries I've been squeezing juice from citrus;
> setting rice to boil, I left out water.[34]

8. *Gopīs* as Thieves of *Gopīnātha's* Flute

The accounts of Kṛṣṇa speak in volumes about Kṛṣṇa's thievery. He not only steals the butter but robs everyone's heart. But the accusation of theft on Kṛṣṇa remains unjustifiable because there are narratives of Kṛṣṇa's flute being stolen by his beloved out of love for him and jealousy towards his flute.

8.1 Rādhā as the Thief

Baṛu Caṇḍīdāsa's *Śrīkṛṣṇakīrtana* is a great and second oldest piece of Bengal literature which contains the songs in praise of Lord Kṛṣṇa.[35] Out of 13 *khaṇḍas* (sections) the twelfth section is known as *Vaṁśikhaṇḍa* (episode of the flute). Rādhā plots with her great-aunt Baṛāyi (Granny, Rādhā's mother's father's sister), an aged woman to steal the flute of Kṛṣṇa. Granny puts Kṛṣṇa to sleep with incantations to steal his Flute in the banks of river Yamuna. Kṛṣṇa tries hard to get back his much played and treasured flute. Finally, Rādhā returns

33 Baṛu Caṇḍīdāsa, *Śrīkṛṣṇakīrtana* (*Singing the Glory of Lord Krishna*) translated by M. H. Klaiman (California: Scholars Press, 1984), Song 2, 238.

34 Caṇḍīdāsa, *Śrīkṛṣṇakīrtana*, Song 15, 246-247.

35 Caṇḍīdāsa, *Śrīkṛṣṇakīrtana*, 14.

the flute as a result of his repeated unfailing requests after promising to remain faithful to her. The theme of the theft of Kṛṣṇa's flute is referred for the first time by Caṇḍīdāsa.[36]

Few lines from the first song of *Vaṁśikhaṇḍa* in *Śrīkṛṣṇakīrtana* runs as follows:

> Krishna then created an enchanting flute for playing.
> It was built beyond compare. The finger holes were seven;
> Golden was its head joint, while its shaft was worked with diamonds.
> When, most energetically, he filled the flute with music,
> By its singing he could have the cosmos in distraction.[37]

Kṛṣṇa pleads Rādhā to return his flute and poet depicts his feelings of impuissance. Kṛṣṇa requests thrice, "Give me my flute, Rādhā; count it a present," "Give me the flute and let's end discussion," and "Give me the flute and fulfill what I'm seeking!"[38] After getting back his flute Kṛṣṇa blesses, "All of your mistakes, Candrāvalī, have been forgiven; furthermore, your Vanamālī wishes you no evil."[39]

8.2 Shaivya as the Thief

Krishnadas Kaviraj in his tenth chapter of *Govindalīlāmṛta* narrates the episode of theft of Kṛṣṇa's flute by the girl named Shaivya, a companion of Candrāvalī (Rādhā). Gripped by the flute of Kṛṣṇa her heart throbs in joy:

> A flute, a tuneful bamboo flute
> –or is it a fisherman's pole?–
> The name is the same and so is the goal:
> to tangle, lure, and snare.
> Hari's little bamboo flute
> makes mountain ranges shatter
> And drives me to such madness
> I could twist and shatter it!
> Hari's captivating reed
> plays deep as it plays strong,
> And on the banks of the Kālindī[40]

36 Entwistle, *Braj Centre of Krishna Pilgrimage*, 56.

37 Caṇḍīdāsa, *Śrīkṛṣṇakīrtana*, Song 1, 237.

38 Caṇḍīdāsa, *Śrīkṛṣṇakīrtana*, Song 24, 252.

39 *Candrāvalī* is another name for Rādhā which literally means 'moonbeam'; *Vanamālī* is an epithet of Kṛṣṇa which means 'wearer of forest garlands or wildflowers.' Caṇḍīdāsa, *Śrīkṛṣṇakīrtana*, Song 41, 263.

40 The name of the Yamuna River, possibly derived from *kālī nadī* (black river). John Stratton Hawley, *At Play with Krishna* (New Jersey: Princeton University Press, 1981), 115-116.

8.3 *Gopīs* as the Thieves

The *rāsalīlas* of Kṛṣṇa includes "the theft of the flute" (*bānsurī* or *banśī corī līlā*) which is one of the important scenes in the of present dramatic traditions of *Vaiṣṇavism* (*Kṛṣṇa Saṁpradāya*). He remains alive in the dramatic traditions depicted in Braj Bhāṣā, the dialect of the Hindi family that is spoken in Braj region to the south of Delhi on the river Yamuna. The plays that are enacted have come down as a tradition from at least five centuries. "The theft of the flute" depicts the effort of *gopīs* to steal the flute of Kṛṣṇa. The flute is pictured as a woman in the play. Hence, there is a quarrel among the women over the issue of flute because 'she' is with him always enjoying his intimacy.[41] The flute invites and attracts all women to dance by creating the conditions to love and simultaneously it controls them altogether by preventing them from enjoying love-play. In order to regain the independence the women rob 'her' (flute) and make Kṛṣṇa dependent upon them for a moment. "She is his grammarian, and without her he is speechless."[42]

The theft of the flute is brought to the feminine tribunal for the settlement. Kṛṣṇa does not find legitimate charges against the *gopīs*. He finds difficult to regain his flute on juridical grounds. The climax of the play is that Kṛṣṇa performs a musical proclamation expressing his sentiments of separation and loneliness without the flute. Such a confession melts the hearts of the judge Rādhā and she orders for the return of 'her' without any justification.

9. Themes of "The Theft of the Flute"

There many themes that can be culled out from the play, "The Theft of the Flute." The play speaks about an unfounded jealousy. The Kṛṣṇa's attachment to the flute makes the *gopīs* jealous. In fact the flute communicates the love of Kṛṣṇa to all but *gopīs* see it as an obstacle to express their love freely and fully. The problem of women lies in feminizing the flute and limiting Kṛṣṇa's attachment to 'her' alone.

The flute *līlā* includes the characters of cross-dressing. The sex roles are exchanged by a boy dressing as a girl or girl as a boy. Rādhā disguises herself as a cowherd and tries to test Kṛṣṇa's love for her. Even Kṛṣṇa plays this game of disguise by dressing up like a woman selling mynah birds or a dyer woman. This interchanging of sex roles illustrates two aspects of a single reality. It suggests that "even humanity and divinity are but different costumes for an un-differentiable non-dual reality."[43] This also reminds us the infancy days of Kṛṣṇa, where Yaśoda dressed him as a girl to protect him from the invisible, dark, malevolent forces. 'Ghosts fear girls but feed on boys' was

41 Hawley, *At Play with Krishna*, 108.

42 Hawley, *At Play with Krishna*, 109.

43 Hawley, *At Play with Krishna*, 111.

the prevalent belief of the people. Krṣṇa becomes the complete man (*pūrṇa-puruṣa*) by accepting the feminine look.[44] In many temples, Krṣṇa is adorned as a woman once a year which expresses his love for his mother and his milkmaid companions. Though the appearance of Krṣṇa changes the essence or reality remains the same. The core nature of our self is nothing but Krṣṇa itself. Krṣṇa himself suggests that as person removes the outer garments and puts on new ones so too human soul casts off the body and enters a new one at the time of death (*Bhagavadgītā* 2.22).[45]

The *banśī corī līlā* highlights the issue of larceny. It is a playful act of misplacement, temporary change of possession and a game of hide and seek. In this play an object is neither lost or gained, produced or destroyed. The *gopīs* try to take revenge to Krṣṇa who is a 'great thief'[46] by stealing the flute of Krṣṇa. The flute is the medium of invitation and expression of love. The theft of flute symbolizes the theft of love, for love can be manifested powerfully through mischiefs and naughty ways.[47]

The play brings out the idea of God's dependence on humankind so that humankind depends on the 'Independent One.' The human-divine are at war with each other asserting their control and command over each other in the characters of Krṣṇa and Rādhā, the beloved of the *gopīs*. This brings about harmony between the two realms of reality. The play in its climax declares the victory of music, feelings and sentiments.[48]

10. The Perennial Call of the Flute

Krṣṇa's flute is symbolic of many truths and messages. It speaks in new tunes and melodies. The poetic language and literary expressions about the flute of Krṣṇa in different writings looks like a hyperbole. Yet it conveys great lessons and makes all to realize deeper truths in life. It soothes, admonishes, warns, advises, directs, motivates, exhorts and does everything for a creative life and critical outlook.

---

44 Devadutt Pattanaik, *Shyam: An Illustrated Retelling of the Bhagavata* (Gurgaon: Penguin Random House, 2018), 50.

45 *"vāsānsi jīrṇāni yathā vihāya navāni gṛihṇāti naro 'parāṇi tathā śharīrāṇi vihāya jīrṇānya nyāni sanyāti navāni dehī" (Bhagavadgītā 2.22).* Swami Mukundananda, "Bhagavad Gita: The Song of God," https://www.holy-bhagavad-gita.org/chapter/2/verse/22 *a*ccessed *9 April 2019.*

46 There are many instances Krṣṇa's theft such as stealing of Rādhā's ring, the milk products of *gopīs*, curds and butter at home etc.

47 Hawley, *At Play with Krishna*, 113.

48 Hawley, *At Play with Krishna*, 110.

10.1 Kṛṣṇa's Flute Invites

Tukaram, the 17th century poet saint of Maharashtra chants, "When Krishna's flute doth call, I must go: though the way may be through the forest thick with thorns, go I must." The constant refrain of the melody of the flute was "Back to nature and Simplicity."[49] It calls for the simplicity of life. Flute is symbolic of God's invitation to all to come to him. Like Jesus Christ as a shepherd extends his invitation, "My sheep hear my voice. I know them, and they follow me" (John 10:27), Kṛṣṇa invites all towards him distancing the mundane and material attachments of the world.

The divine call of Kṛṣṇa reverberates, "Abandon all varieties of *dharmas* and simply surrender unto me alone. I shall liberate you from all sinful reactions; do not fear" (*Bhagavadgītā* 18.66).[50] The flute of Kṛṣṇa represents the voice of the Supreme, calling all to get attached to Him and to get detached from all evils and earthly things.

Śrīmad Bhāgavatam says, "All those hundreds of thousands of women knowing Me as their most charming lover and ardently desiring Me that way, were unaware of My actual position. Yet by intimately associating with Me, they attained Me, the Supreme Absolute Truth" (*Bhāgavata Purāṇa* 11.12.13).[51]

10.2 Holes of the Flute Calls all to be Whole

Only empty entities can be filled. If heart is full it cannot be filled. If empty heart is given to Kṛṣṇa he can fill it. The flute points to the fact, 'what is in, is what is out.' It has inner space and outer space. There is no duplicity. Everything has to be transparent and genuine. It is straightforward yet it has holes. We too have public, private and secret face in our lives. Our public face is known to all, private face is known to our family members and secret face is known only to God. The different holes in the flute invites the devotees of Kṛṣṇa to build up a wholesome personality.

The different number of holes in the flute of Kṛṣṇa is symbolic of many meanings.

---

49 Ardaser Sorabjee N.Wadia, *The Message of Krishna* (London: J. M. Dent & Sons Ltd., 1934), 110-111.

50 "*sarva-dharmān parityajya mām ekaṁ śharaṇaṁ vraja ahaṁ tvāṁ sarva-pāpebhyo mokṣhayiṣhyāmi mā śhuchaḥ*" (*Bhagavadgītā* 18.66). Swami Mukundananda, "Bhagavad Gita: The Song of God," https://www.holy-bhagavad-gita.org/chapter/18/verse/66 accessed 8 March 2019.

51 "*mat kātmā ramaṇam jāram asvarūpa vido'balāḥ brahma mām paramam prāpuḥ saṅgāc chata sahasraśaḥ*" (*Bhāgavata Purāṇa* 11.12.13). Gopiparanadhana Dasa, *Sri Brhad-bhagavatamrta*, Vol. III (The Bhaktivedanta Book Trust International, Inc., 2015), no page number.

- The flute having five holes communicates the message that persons should be receptive to those positive learnings which contribute to one's own integral growth in the world i.e, *Vṛndāvana*, by accepting only that which pleases the senses in the true sense of the term.
- The flute with six holes advices the connoisseurs of *Vṛndāvana* to remain away from *ariṣaḍvargas*.[52] Kṛṣṇa fills such good willed devotees with his sweet voice and fragrance of life.
- Seven holed flute primarily indicates seven musical notes (*saptasvara*). It is suggestive of avoiding seven kinds of addictions (*saptavysanas*). They are: womanizing (*strivyasana*); gambling (*dyūtam*); hunting (*mṛugayā*); drinking liquor (*madyapānam*); harsh talking (*vākpāruṣyam*); punishing more than crime (*ugradaṇḍanam*); extravagant spending or defiling (*artha sandūśaṇa*).
- The flute having eight holes has lot of association with Kṛṣṇa. He is considered to be the eighth *avatāra* (incarnation) of Viṣṇu. Kṛṣṇa was the eighth son of princess Devakī and Vāsudeva. Among the 16,108 consorts of Kṛṣṇa, eight of them (*aṣṭabhārya*s)[53] were prime ones.
- The flute with nine holes can be linked with nine openings in our body (*navaraṅdhras*). The body consists of nine gates–two eyes, two nostrils, two ears, one mouth, the anus and the genitals. *Bhagavadgītā* says that human body is the city of nine gates where the soul dwells. It says, "The embodied beings who are self-controlled and detached reside happily in the city of nine gates, free from thinking they are the doers or the cause of anything" (*Bhagavadgītā* 5.13). This analogy is also found in the *Śvetāśvatara Upaniṣad*. "It is He who resides in the body, the city of nine gates. He is the soul that sports in the outside world. He is the master of the whole world, animate and inanimate" (*Śvetāśvatara Upaniṣad* 3.18).[54] Only when the life

52 In Hinduism, *ariṣaḍvarga* or *anarthas* means the six enemies or vices, viz. *kāma* (lust), *krodha* (anger), *lobha* (greed), *moha* (attachment), *mada* (pride), and *mātsarya* (jealousy).

53 The eight principal queen-consorts of Kṛṣṇa include: Rukmiṇi, Satyabhāma, Jambāvati, Kaliṇḍi, Mitraviṇḍa, Nagnajiti, Bhadra and Lakṣmaṇa.

54 "*sarva-karmāṇi manasā sannyasyāste sukhaṁ vaśhī nava-dvāre pure dehī naiva kurvan na kārayan*" (*Bhagavadgītā* 5.13). Swami Mukundananda, "Bhagavad Gita: The Song of God," *https://www.holy-bhagavad-gita.org/chapter/5/verse/13* accessed 8 March 2019. "*nava-dvāre pure dehī haṁso lelāyate bahiḥ vaśī sarvasya lokasya sthāvarasya carasya ca*" (*Śvetāśvatara Upaniṣad* 3.18). *The Upanishads* (Vande Mataram Library Trust (VMLT), Gurugram & Sri Aurobindo Foundation for Indian Culture (SAFIC), Sri Aurobindo Society, Puducherry, 2019), https://upanishads.org.in/upanishads/9/3/18 accessed 8 March 2019.

breath of the Divine is inhaled into our body through the spiritual practice then body becomes the flute.

10.3 Flute Melody, the Song of Love and Joy

Kṛṣṇa is an ideal of divine love. Human heart which is empty, free and open becomes a flute in the hands of God of love to play upon. Upon listening to the flute melody there is play of love i.e., pure and passionless love, deep sensual and carnal love between Kṛṣṇa and young maidens. The love whether sportive or sexual doesn't mean immoral and indecent as long as self is seen as extension of Godhead. The joy and merriment of *gopīs* from the abundance of heart (i.e., *Vṛndāvana*) conveys their love for Kṛṣṇa. Kṛṣṇa sings love and women dance for the love song. Nature enjoys its ineffable lyrics. One of the old hymns expressing deep love of Kṛṣṇa flows thus:

Though Kṛṣṇa thousand times
In Mathura be born,
If He's not born in thee,
Thy soul is still forlorn.
The flute in *Vṛndāvana*
Will never save thy soul!
The flute in thine own heart
Alone will make thee whole![55]
Narada, the sage exclaimed ecstatically:
"You play your flute with such a divine art,
You brush the dust off from the oldest heart!"[56]

The *Upaniṣadic* teaching suggests that all beings come into existence from divine joy, they grow and live by it and are also destined for it. "He knew that bliss was Brahman, for, from bliss all these beings are produced, by bliss do these beings live. They go to bliss on departing and become one with it" (*Taittirīya Upaniṣad* 3.6.1).[57]

10.4 Nature is the Melody of Kṛṣṇa's Flute

The dance of nature for the flute song of Kṛṣṇa manifests that nature is in Kṛṣṇa himself. It is evident in the eleventh chapter of *Bhagavadgītā*, *viśvarūpadarśana* i.e., vision of cosmic form of the universe. Kṛṣṇa makes us aware that there is music everywhere in the breath, heart, river, wind, trees, stones, birdsong etc. One has to find that *Śabdabrahman* in this world and

55 A. S. P. Ayyar, *Sri Krishna: The Darling of Humanity* (Madras: The Madras Law Journal Office, 1952), xvi.

56 Ayyar, *Sri Krishna: The Darling of Humanity*, 43.

57 "*ānando brahmeti vyajanāt ānandāt hi eva khalu imāni bhūtāni jāyante ānandena jātāni jīvanti ānandaṁ prayanti abhisaṁviśanti iti*" (Taittirīya Upaniṣad 3.6.1). See Swami Chinmayananda, *Taittirīya Upaniṣad* (Mumbai: Central Chinmaya Mission Trust, 2013).

realize His presence. The world is in Kṛṣṇa, the Godhead and Kṛṣṇa Himself is the world and in the world. The following lines coming from the mouth of the flute express the cry and mourning of the flute like a dirge:

> I like the caress of his fingers
> on my warm, brown body,
> while his mouth blows into me
> (the moist air filling my very lungs).
> But I miss the bark that used to embrace me,
> the wind messing the leaves of my hair,
> the sap that wells inside me,
> gathering and forming, rising and rising,
> until the very sun explodes into tears.[58]

Thus, flute also makes us aware that we need to preserve and protect our nature while admiring it with awe and wonder.

10.5 One Flute, Many Tunes

The melody of the flute travels everywhere and heard from all distances. It transcends all kinds of barriers. It is a symphony of many tunes and sounds travelling across the lines of village boundary, river bank and forest valley. Anyone can dance for the flute play of Kṛṣṇa. The song of Kṛṣṇa is written in the universal language of mutual love, acceptance, respect, justice, concern and sensitivity. In the great dalliance (*mahārasalīla*) of Kṛṣṇa with *gopīs* there is dialogue as well as alliance.[59] It accommodates variety and multiplicity. Expecting 'one' tune from the flute amounts to 'blowing the trumpet' without considering the multi-tunes and melodies. Such an indifference and exclusion is seen Biblically in these words: *"We played the flute for you, and you did not dance; we wailed, and you did not mourn" (Matthew 11.17).* The flute promotes equality and fraternity of all by providing equal opportunities to listen to it, learn from it and become one with it. *Kṛṣṇa teaches us that we are all God's playmates and are born on earth to take part in God's play.*[60]

10.6 Flute awaits Response and Reaction

The flute of Kṛṣṇa never leaves anyone unheard nor puts anyone in a dormant state. It awaits for a natural and spontaneous reaction. It beckons us to be sportive, active, fruitful and cheerful. The response to the flute song should be an expression of overwhelming joy without falling prey to the passing passions

58 Danton Remoto, "Song of the Flute," *Ateneo Journals Online* 58 (American Theological Library Association, 2016), https://journals.ateneo.edu/ojs//index.php/budhi/article/viewFile/540/537 accessed 7 March 2019.

59 Acharya Shrivatsa Goswami, "Krishna Rasalila for Environment Protection," *Journal of Dharma* 37, 2 (April-June 2012), 239.

60 Seeta Lakhani, *Primary Hinduism* (Chennai: Sri Ramakrishna Math, 2009), 24.

of the body. *Gopas* and *gopīs* need many sticks to herd and graze the cows, but Kṛṣṇa needs one reed to make the cows to follow him. Cows symbolically indicate senses. As the cows eat grass so the senses find food in the worldly pleasures. Kṛṣṇa is the one who brings our senses to control through his flute music. The flute pulls us within our self to realize who we are and pushes us to involve ourselves in the society. Flute soothes and touches us so that we begin to soothe and touch others in their cacophonic life-experiences. The famous expression, "Nero fiddled as Rome burned" conveys utter failures of Nero in doing his duties and responsibilities. But the music of Kṛṣṇa's flute reminds us to be other-centred. It is always Kṛṣṇa takes the initiative to play with our flute of life. The wish of each flute has to be:

> You took this broken reed, my Lord,
> And lo a flute was born.
> You put it to your lips, my Lord,
> And lo a symphony flowed.
> Like the flutters of a butterfly's wings,
> Like water over liquid pearls,
> Like dancing rays of sunlight gold,
> Like the flow of fluid honey,
> Thy lips slid over the reed and made it whole.
> At thy feet I place this hollow reed,
> Thine to do as you will.
> *Vanamali*! My only Love!
> *Vanamali*! My Lord! My God![61]

Conclusion

The *Sanskrit-English Dictionary* of Sir Monier Williams gives the meaning of the word *veṇā* as 'joining of a river' or 'joining Kṛṣṇa.' The melody of the *veṇu* unites all those who listen to it to a transcendental realm of Kṛṣṇa. It brings about a fusion between divine and human. The *Vṛndāvana* is the meeting place of heaven and earth in the persons of Kṛṣṇa and cowherd friends. Kṛṣṇa involves in the daily chores of all cowherds and withdraws himself by being invisible within the fraction of a second. It is nothing but the path of the playful which establishes bond between divine and human realms. Kṛṣṇa invites everyone to make their lives a continuous melody. He fills the world with the music of the flute. All of us and the world itself, is a flute. Kṛṣṇa plays it and he plays it with love and spontaneity. As the popular Bengali saying goes, "*kānu*

61 *Mataji Devi Vanamali, In the Lost City of Sri Krishna: The Story of Ancient Dwaraka* (Toronto: Inner Traditions, 2018), EPUB File http://library1.org/_ads/F171751EA71693C7F244F72CDB73B1F5 accessed 7 April 2019.

binā gīta nāhi" i.e., "Without Kṛṣṇa there is no song."[62] In addition to this it can also be asserted that 'without love there is no flute melody.'

Bibliography

Apte, V. S. *The Student's Sanskrit-English Dictionary* (Delhi: Sri Satguru Publications, 1991).

Ayyar, A. S. P. Sri Krishna: *The Darling of Humanity.* Madras: The Madras Law Journal Office, 1952.

Banerjee, P. *The Life of Krishna in Indian Art.* New Delhi: National Museum, 1978.

Caṇḍīdāsa, Baṛu. *Śrīkṛṣṇakīrtana (Singing the Glory of Lord Krishna).* Translated by M. H. Klaiman. California: Scholars Press, 1984.

Chinmayananda, Swami. *Taittirīya Upaniṣad* (Mumbai: Central Chinmaya Mission Trust, 2013.

Das, HG Amarendra. "*Why does Krishna play the flute.*" Yasoda-dulal das (Dec 28, 2017): https://www.youtube.com/watch?v=W1-sxiqRj7U (accessed 26 March 2019).

Dasa, Gopiparanadhana. *Sri Brhad-bhagavatamrta.* Vol. III. The Bhaktivedanta Book Trust International, Inc., 2015.

Dimock, Edward C. and Denise Levertov, trans. *In Praise of Krishna: Songs from the Bengali. Garden City*, N. J.: Doubleday & Co., 1967.

Encyclopedia of Hinduism. Vol.4. New Delhi: India Heritage Research Foundation, 2010.

Entwistle, Alan W. *Braj Centre of Krishna Pilgrimage.* Groningen: Egbert Forsten, 1987.

Giriraj Dasa, *Krishna's flutes.* Gurgaon: 21st February 2015. Blog article, For the Pleasure of Lord Krishna. http://www.forthepleasureoflordkrishna.com/2015/02/21/krishnas-flutes/ (accessed 9 April 2019).

Goswami, Acharya Shrivatsa. "Krishna Rasalila for Environment Protection." *Journal of Dharma*, no. 37, 2 (April-June 2012): 235-241.

Goswami, Tamal Krishna. *A Living Theology of Krishna Bhakti.* New York: Oxford University Press, 2012.

Hawley, John Stratton. *At Play with Krishna.* New Jersey: Princeton University Press, 1981.

Kavirāja, Kṛṣṇadāsa. *Śrī Śrī Caitanya-caritāmṛta.* Trans. Nagendra Kumar Ray. 2nd edition. 6 vols. Calcutta: Nagendra Kumar Ray, 1959.

Kinsley, David R. *The Sword and the Flute: Kālī and Kṛṣṇa.* Delhi: Vikas Publishing House Pvt Ltd., 1975.

Lakhani, Seeta. *Primary Hinduism. Chennai: Sri Ramakrishna Math,* 2009.

Mukundananda, Swami. "Bhagavad Gita: The Song of God" https://www.holy-bhagavad-gita.org/chapter/18/verse/66 (accessed 9 April 2019).

Nandy, Pritish trans. *Krishna, Krishna: The Devotional Songs of Mirabai.* Ghaziabad: Vikas Publishing House Pvt. Ltd., 1982.

Pattanaik, Devadutt. *Shyam: An Illustrated Retelling of the Bhagavata.* Gurgaon: Penguin Random House, 2018.

Prabhupada, A. C. Bhaktivedanta Swami. *Vaniquotes.* https://vaniquotes.org/wiki/There_are_three_kinds_of_flutes_used_by_Krsna._One_is_called_venu,_one_is_called_murali,_and_the_third_is_called_vamsi (accessed 8 March 2019).

Prabhupāda, A.C. Bhaktivedānta Swami. *Kṛṣṇa: The Supreme Personality of Godhead.* Mumbai: The Bhaktivedanta Book Trust, 2002.

62 Kinsley, *The Sword and the Flute*, 78.

Remoto, Danton. "Song of the Flute." *Ateneo Journals Online* 58 (American Theological Library Association, 2016): https://journals.ateneo.edu/ojs//index.php/budhi/article/viewFile/540/537 (accessed 7 March 2019).

Roy, Dilip Kumar and Indira Devi. *The Flute Calls Still*. Bombay: Bharatiya Vidya Bhavan, 1982.

Sarbadhikary, Sukanya. *The Place of Devotion: Siting and Experiencing Divinity in Bengal-Vaishnavism*. Oakland: University of California Press, 2015. https://www.jstor.org/stable/10.1525/j.ctt1ffjn1f.10 (accessed 7 April 2019).

Sheth, Noel. *The Divinity of Krishna*. New Delhi: Munshiram Manoharial Publishers Pvt Ltd., 1984.

Surdas, *The Poems of Surdas*. Editors and translators, S. M. Pandey and Norman H. Zide. Chicago: South Asia Language & Area Centre, University of Chicago, 1963.

The Srimad-Bhagavatam of Krishna-Dwaipayana Vyasa. Trans. J. M. Sanyal. Vol. II. New Delhi: Munshiram Manoharlal Publishers Pvt. Ltd., 1973.

The Upanishads. Vande Mataram Library Trust (VMLT), Gurugram & Sri Aurobindo Foundation for Indian Culture (SAFIC), Sri Aurobindo Society, Puducherry, 2019. https://upanishads.org.in/upanishads/9/3/18 (accessed 9 April 2019).

Vanamali, Mataji Devi. *In the Lost City of Sri Krishna: The Story of Ancient Dwaraka*. Toronto: Inner Traditions, 2018. http://library1.org/_ads/F171751EA71693C7F244F72CDB73B1F5 (accessed 7 April 2019).

Vassanthi. "Kṛṣṇana Koḷalina Bagge Kathe." *Human Value Blog in Kannada* (blog), 28 February 2017, https://saibalsanskaarkannada.wordpress.com/2017/02/28/, accessed on 8 March 2019.

Wadia, Ardaser Sorabjee N. *The Message of Krishna*. London: J. M. Dent & Sons Ltd., 1934.

Williams, M. Monier. *A Sanskrit English Dictionary* (New Delhi: Bharatiya Granth Niketan, 2015).

11

Is Religious Belief Rational and Transformative? A Reformed "Re-visioning"

Chacko Nadakkeveliyil

Abstract

In general, Religions believe in an all-powerful, all-knowing and wholly good God. Many critical thinkers argue that this belief itself is coherent. The problem of incoherence arises from the fact that how is it possible to predicate properties like infinite, transcendent all-knowing and morally perfect to such a being as God? We, humans are only finite and imperfect beings and our knowing is limited. If this is the case, how can we know something about a being like God? How can we apply our limited and incomplete concepts to an infinite and perfect being? The perceived complicatedness of human concepts to refer to a being like God, has led to a heated discussion in analytic philosophy and in philosophy of religion. This paper critically examines scepticism with respect to the referentiality of God based on the "popular view" that Immanuel Kant and his contemporary followers like Gordon Kaufman and John Hick have shown that reference to or thought about such a being as God, even if there is one, is impossible or at least deeply problematic and Alvin Plantinga's reformed "re-visioning" that suggests that our God-Talk is rationally legitimate.

Key words: Religious belief, the "Great Creeds", coherence of religious belief, problem of referentiality, Immanuel Kant's distinction between *noumena* and *phenomena*, Gordon Kaufman, real referent and available referent, William P. Alston, John Hick, Alvin Plantinga, warranted belief, reformed epistemology.

Introduction

One of the most discussed themes in philosophy of religion is the rationality of theistic belief. Whether belief in God is coherent, logically and epistemologically appropriate? Almost all the major religions believe that there is a creator God and He has transcendent existence, infinite power and pervasiveness. On the other hand, we who refer to God, speak about him, attribute cognitive properties to him are finite and temporal. This incurs an epistemological inappropriateness to all references to such an ontogically different being. Taking Christian belief as a default belief, in *Warranted Christian Belief*, Plantinga, the well-known reformed epistemologist argues that theistic belief does not commit any epistemic inappropriateness and incoherence. In this article, we shall critically deliberate Alvin Plantinga's reformed "re-vision" arguments against the incoherency problem attached to the theistic belief as a whole and Christian belief in particular.

1. The Propositional Content of Christian Belief

Before we analyse the question, 'is it rational, justified, and warranted to hold Christian belief' or the intellectual or rational acceptability of Christian belief, we need to discuss a prior issue: what is Christian belief? What does it include? What are its propositional contents? Two important issues are involved here. Firstly, Christian belief is a sort of umbrella concept. It can be applied to a wide verity of beliefs ranging from the extreme conservative positions to highly liberal views. Hence, the important question is: What kind of Christian belief do we want to show here as epistemologically appropriate? Secondly, can our concepts refer to a being like God as understood, believed and worshiped by Christians? In other words: Is Christian belief coherent with our human rational apparatus? Let us begin this discussion of the cognitive uprightness of Christian belief by clarifying these two issues.

2. Christian Belief and its Propositional Components

The term Christian belief means the "Great Creeds" of the main branches of Christian church. It is understood in a broader sense and does not mean the minute faith differences of various individual churches. In other words, Christian belief means "what unites Calvin and Aquinas, Luther and Augustine, Menno Simons and Karl Barth, Mother Teresa and St. Maximus the Confessor, Billy Graham and St. Gregory – classical Christian belief, as we might call it."[1] The "Great Creeds" of the main branches of Christian belief has two components: a theistic component and a uniquely Christian component. The theistic component is common to all the great faith traditions like Islam,

1 Alwin Plantinga, *Warranted Christian Belief*, New York: Oxford University Press, 2000, vii.

Judaism and Christianity etc. It states that there is a being as God. He is a *person* in the sense that God is a being with intellect and will, knowledge and belief, affection and hate, and intention and capability to fulfil what he is indented. God is all-knowing and all-powerful, but at the same time he is perfectly good and wholly loving. This theistic component also says that God in his supreme power created our gigantic universe and continually upholds and providentially guides it.[2]

Besides this common theistic component, "the Great Creed" has also a unique Christian component, something very specific to the Christian belief. This specific Christian component states that "we human beings are somehow mired in rebellion and sin, so that we consequently require deliverance and salvation, and that God has arranged for that deliverance through the sacrificial suffering, death, and resurrection of Jesus Christ, who was both a man and also the second member of the Trinity, the uniquely divine son of God."[3] The propositional content of Christian belief involves both theistic and the unique Christian components.

3. Coherence of Christian Belief in God

Is Christian belief as described above coherent? Can the characteristics and attributes of God as understood by the Christians give a coherent understanding of God? Many philosophers and theologians argue that it cannot. Christians believe that there is an all-powerful, all-knowing and wholly good God, who has created our gigantic world and all its animate and inanimate things, who loves us unconditionally and was willing to send his only son into the world to undergo suffering, humiliation and death to redeem us who were fallen from grace due to sin. Christians not only believe that there *is* such a being, but also that we are able to *address* him in prayer, *refer* to him, *think* and *talk* about him, and *predicate* properties like all-knowing, all-powerful, all-loving and having created the universe, etc to him. Besides, they also believe that this God is infinite, transcendent and ultimate.[4] The problem of incoherence arises from the fact that how is it possible to predicate properties like infinite, transcendent all-knowing and morally perfect to such a being as God? We are finite and imperfect beings and our knowing is limited. If this is the case, how can we know something about a being like God? How can we apply our limited and incomplete concepts to an infinite and perfect being? The perceived complicatedness of human concepts to refer to a being like God, has led to a

2 See, *Warranted Christian Belief*, vii

3 *Warranted Christian Belief*, vii

4 See, *Warranted Christian Belief*, 3-4.

heated discussion in analytic philosophy and in philosophy of religion.[5] Many theologians and philosophers consider that our concepts cannot really apply to God.[6] Therefore, it is argued that even if there exists such a being as God, we cannot think about him, cannot talk about him and cannot ascribe properties to him as normally believers do. If this contention is true, "then strictly speaking, Christian belief, at least as the Christian understands it, is impossible. For Christians believe that there is an infinite, transcendent, ultimate being about whom they hold beliefs; but if our concepts cannot apply to a being of that sort, then there cannot be beliefs about a being of that sort."[7]

According to Plantinga, scepticism with respect to the referentiality of God is based on the belief that Immanuel Kant and his contemporary followers (Gordon Kaufman and John Hick, for instance) have shown that reference to or thought about such a being as God, even if there is one, is impossible or at least deeply problematic.[8] Therefore, in his book, *Warranted Christian Belief* (WCB) Plantinga makes an enquiry into the writings of Kant and the rest of referentialtiy critics to see whether there is something in them to suggest that our concepts really cannot apply to God, or they cannot function the way the ordinary believers use them to refer to God. According to Plantinga those who think or suspect that Kant showed it to be the case, "do not ordinarily develop the point in detail. They either content themselves with a ritual bow in Kant's direction or they do not explain *how* they think these things were shown and what are the arguments establishing them."[9] So he begins his enquiry into the referentiality problem of God by looking into the question: what does it really mean when someone claims that our concepts do not apply to God? State it argumentatively:

(1) If there were an infinite, transcendent, and ultimate being, our concepts could not apply to it.
According to Plantinga, this proposition initially seems to be right, because those who claim this set up "a certain subject for prediction -God- and then declare that our concepts do not apply to this being." If this is the case at least "one of our concepts –being such that our concepts don't apply to it – *does* apply to this being."[10] It means that

5 For the detailed analysis of the problems related to the meaning of religious propositions, See, Joseph M. Bochenski, *The Logic of Religion*, New York: New York University Press, 1965, 96-117.

6 For instance, John Hick is of the opinion that we cannot really comprehend the *Noumena*. We shall discuss this point in the later part of this thesis.

7 *Warranted Christian Belief*, 4.

8 *Warranted Christian Belief*, 5.

9 *Warranted Christian Belief*, 5.

10 See this explanation in Warranted Christian Belief, page numbers 5 and the following.

> there is at least one reference to God possible; one of our concepts can be applied to him. Otherwise the claim (the Proposition 1) itself does not make any sense.[11]

Suppose (1) were a true proposition then it would mean that we have some grasp of the properties such as being infinite, transcendent und ultimate etc. For instance an infinite being is the one that is unlimited with respect to power, knowledge, goodness, love, compassion etc. Similarly a being is transcended, if it is not created, not identical with any being in the universe and not depended on anything for its existence. This shows that we have some idea of what a transcendent and infinite being is. Hence what does the proposition (1) say? Does it say that if there is an infinite being, then none of our concepts, especially concepts like infinity and transcendence could not apply to it? According to Plantinga, it cannot be the case, because we have some idea of these properties; otherwise we will not be able to understand the proposition in question and grasp the meaning of it. Therefore, the proposition (1) possibly means that "these concepts are impossible, incoherent, like concept of a round square, a concept such that we can just see *a priori* that it couldn't apply to anything, that there couldn't be a thing to which it applied," says Plantinga. It means that we have no experience of an all-powerful and all-knowing being to which these properties apply. Therefore these properties cannot be applied to God. If this is the case the proposition (1) could be re-written as follows:

> (1*) If there were an all-powerful, all-knowing being, our concepts *would* apply to it, if we had an experience of such a being.

However Plantinga deems that 'presumably it is not the idea here'.[12] According to him, the best way to understand the idea behind the proposition (1) is to consider it along the line of the argument of John Hick. For Hick, God is a being to whom none of our *positive*, *non-formal* concepts apply because God *an sich* has none of the positive, *non-formal* properties of which we have concepts. He is wholly inaccessible to us. However, this being somehow is the one with which Christians, Muslims, Jews, and others are in touch in their religious practices. But Plantinga thinks that this argument of Hick "isn't good enough; it suffers from serious, indeed fatal difficulties."[13]

---

11 *Warranted Christian Belief*, 6.

12 Plantinga does not explain here why it cannot be the case. Perhaps the reason might be that the point of discussion here is not an evidential/existential question - whether one can have a priori experience of God- but rather epistemological one; whether our concepts really applied to God or not. Hence for Plantinga, the proposition (1*) is not the case of discussion here.

13 This is explained in *Warranted Christian Belief*, 7-8.

However, Plantinga does not give any direct argument here. Instead, he considers that the inspiration for the argument 'that we cannot refer to or think about God, even if there is such a being', comes from the writings of Immanuel Kant. So he first turns to Kant and enquires: Whether he has shown that our concept does not really apply to God or at least that there is undefeatable epistemic problem with our referentially of God. If Kant does not show it, his modern representatives like Kaufman and Hick are simply mistaken to hold the Proposition (1). But, if Kant has shown that there is a serious problem in the traditional Christian belief that there is being such as God and to whom our concepts apply, then Kaufman and Hick will be right in their sceptical claim and in that case the propositions Christians used to express belief in God, like God is all-powerful and all-mighty, Jesus is the son of God, He died and rose from the dead etc will be a "disguised nonsense" without much epistemic worth.[14] Of course, Plantinga's strategy here is not to show that Christian belief is a "disguised nonsense", but to show that there is nothing in Kant's epistemology to recommend that our concepts do not apply to God and hence Hick's sceptical assertion with respect to the referentiality of God is false.[15]

4. Kant and Plantinga's *"Revisioning" of Coherence of Theistic Belief*

One of the known characteristics of Kant is the looming ambiguity of his writings. Therefore, Plantinga is of the opinion that we should not just rely on the established interpretations of Kant to verify whether he held the view that "our concepts can't apply to God". According to Plantinga, contrary to popular sceptical claim, the first thing to note in Kant is that he often writes "as if we *can* perfectly refer to God."[16] Kant seems to suggest that the real issue is not that we cannot *think* about or refer to a being such as God, but that we cannot come to the speculative and metaphysical *knowledge* of God.[17] Therefore his

14 The non-epistemic status of religious belief has been an important idea of logical positivists. Along the same thinking of logical positivists, many argued that the sentences believers ordinary use like 'God loves me', 'God consoles me, when I am sad', 'God has created this universe' etc - do not convey much meaning. These propositions look like that they convey some meaning, but fail to express any meaning in reality. For a detailed discussion of this issue, see Bochenski's, *The Logic of Religion*. See also A.J. Ayer, *Language, Truth and Logic*, New York: Dover Publications, 1946.

15 It is to be noted here that Plantinga does not give any positive argument to show that our concepts can refer to God; but he takes it for granted that they can. What he really argues for is that Kant and his contemporaries do not really prove that we cannot think about God, refer to him, or address him in prayer.

16 *Warranted Christian Belief*, 9.

17 *Warranted Christian Belief*, 9.

aim in the *Critique of Pure Reason* is to curb knowledge[18] to make the room for God-talk. If this is case, it does not make sense to argue that Kant has showed that we cannot think of or refer to God.[19]

However, Plantinga acknowledges that the traditional view that our concepts couldn't apply to God is not a mere fabrication or a thoughtless misunderstanding. It has a strong textual base in *Critique of Pure Reason*; more specifically in the analysis of the 'categories of understanding'. For Kant 'the categories of understanding' are concepts in first place. These concepts are applicable only to the realm of appearance and experience. Beyond the world of *phenomena* and appearances, they do not refer to the things in themselves. If it is the case that the categories of understanding cannot be applied to things *in themselves*, then they do not also refer to God, because he is a being *in excelsis*. When we do this - If we apply our concepts that are limited by the phenomenal world to God - then we commit a categorical mistake. Therefore traditionally, it is argued that in the *Critique of Pure Reason*, Kant has showed that our concepts do not apply to God and hence we cannot refer to God, think about him, or address him prayer.

The traditional sceptical understanding of Kant with respect to referentiality problem is decidedly linked to his ontology; specifically to his categorical distinction between *noumena* and *phenomena* . This raises an interesting question: Are there two words in Kant or only one world? According to Plantinga, the position one takes here is crucial to our question, whether Kant has shown that we cannot refer to or think about a being such as God? The scholars are divided in their opinion here. According to the traditional picture, Kant held the view that there are two fundamentally different kinds of things, constituting two unrelated realms of objects; the word of *phenomena* and the world of *noumena*. Phenomena are things *für uns*.[20] These are things as they appear to us and as we understand them. But *noumena* are the things in themselves (*an sich*) to which we have no direct cognitive access. This distinction shows that "on one hand on this picture, there are tables and chairs, horses and cows, stars and planets, the oak tree in your backyard, just as we ordinarily think. These things really exist and are really there. They are *phenomenally real*, real parts of the world of experience. But they are also *transcendentally ideal*: that is, they are not part of the world as it is independent of human experience. On the other hand, there are the *noumena*, which are transcendentally real. These are the things as they are in

18 See, the preface to second Edition, Bxxx, 29, where Kant has said; "I have therefore found it necessary to deny *knowledge* in order to make room for faith."

19 *Warranted Christian Belief*, 9.

20 This is the Planting's view on how Kant is traditionally understood. I will highlight here only this Plantingan understanding of the traditional two-world picture in Kant. See *Warranted Christian Belief*, 10-30.

themselves; they do not depend for their existence or character upon human beings or human experience. These two realms are disjoint: none of the phenomenal objects is a *noumenon*, and none of the *noumenal* objects is a phenomenon."[21] In the *Critique of Pure Reason*, Kant himself wrote about this categorical distinction.[22]

In nut shell, according to the traditional picture the *phenomenal* world is constructed by us from physical experience of things and from the human intuition to the sense data gained by experience and other evidential facts. Hence phenomenal world is intuited in space and time and depends on us for its existence. On the other hand, the *noumenal* world is not dependent on us and we have no intuition or direct experience of it. However "there is a connection between the two worlds in that something like a causal transaction between the *noumena* and the transcendental ego (itself a *noumenon*) produces in us the given out of which we construct the phenomenal world."[23] This two-world picture is understood in two ways. According to the first way of understanding, at least some of our concepts apply to the things in *themselves* and hence, we can think about them and refer to them. However, when we do this, we do not find real and complete *knowledge* of them, but only predicating properties to them. When we predicate properties to things in *themselves*, we are only making speculations about them. When we predicate more properties to things, it is only a "mere beating of wings against the void."[24] Plantinga calls this understanding, "moderate sub-picture." According to him this "moderate sub-picture" is not satisfactory. Kant considers his work in the *Critique of Pure Reason*, as knowledge and as certain and conclusive. He also seems to tell us about considerable account of the *Dinge*: that they are not limited by time and space, that the phenomenal world is a result of the causal transaction between the *Dinge* and the transcendental ego, that the transcendental ego has no real intuition into the *Dinge an sich*. It means that on one hand Kant seems to say that we cannot extend our intuition into the *Dinge* and when we extend and refer, it does not bring knowledge of the things *an sich*. But on the other hand, he himself predicates properties to them, refers to them and maintains that his explanation is a certain account. Therefore there is an inconsistency with "moderate sub-picture" explanation of reality. It gives "no aid and comfort to the claim that our concepts do not apply to God,"[25] says Plantinga.

Another understanding of the two-world picture is called "the radical sub-picture." According this understanding, we can neither refer to *Ding*

21 *Warranted Christian Belief*, 11.

22 See, Immanuel Kant, A. 249.

23 Note that this is Plantinga's interpretation of Kant. See *Warranted Christian Belief*, 12.

24 *Warranted Christian Belief*, 17.

25 *Warranted Christian Belief*, 18.

(God) nor predicate properties to him. The phenomenal world is a world of appearance and is wholly different from the realm of things in *themselves*, the *noumenal* world. However, the things in *themselve*s somehow impinge on us due to the productive interaction between the *Dinge* and transcendental ego of us, resulting in manifold experiences. We construct the phenomenal object from these manifold experiences by applying concepts. It means that in the "radical sub-picture", concepts are nothing but the rules to construct phenomenal object from the manifold experience.[26] "We may now characterise it as the faculty of rules.... Sensibility gives us forms (of intuition) but understanding gives us rules," says Kant. If concepts are understood in this way – as rules for constructing the phenomenal objects out of manifold of experience, then they cannot be applied to *noumena, Dinge an sich*. Similarly, in the radical sub-picture, our concepts also do not refer to God, because God is a *noumena in excelsis*; he cannot be constructed by applying our concepts to the manifold of experiences. According to Plantinga, this radical sub-picture "has deep incoherence." On one hand, Kant holds that the *Dinge* somehow show themselves to us through manifold experience through transcendental ego. But on the other hand, he maintains that they are not in space and time. How can he refer to the *Dinge* and at the same hold that they are non-temporal and non-spatial? If this picture were really correct, then we should drop the *noumena* altogether, because the reality beyond our phenomenal construction would be practically unthinkable.[27] Hence the "radical sub-picture" does not offer any positive argument for the sceptical assertion that our concepts can't refer to God.

Contrary to the dominant two-world picture, there is another interpretation of Kant which is the position of Plantinga himself. According to this interpretation, there aren't really two worlds in which the *phenomenal* world is seen as distinct from the *noumenal* world. In actuality there is only one world; the world of *noumenal* objects. However there are two distinct ways of understanding and thinking about them; the *phenomenal* and *noumenal*. Therefore "the *phenomena-noumena* distinction is not between two kinds of objects, but, rather between how the things are in themselves and how they appear to us."[28] It means that the distinction is merely two different ways of understanding one and the same thing. Plantinga calls this one-world

---

26 This is the Plantingan understanding of Kant. He calls this understanding the "hart of the radical sub-picture." However Plantinga admits that it should not be seen as the only interpretation of Kant, but rather a possible suggestion one can draw from him; "Aagain, I don't mean to suggest that this is Kant's view, but some of what he says suggests it. (Some of what he says also suggests that it is false; that is part of his charm). See *Warranted Christian Belief*, 19.

27 See, *Warranted Christian Belief*, 19-20.

28 *Warranted Christian Belief*, 12.

understanding of Kant as "the one that more recently has (perhaps) achieved majority status."[29]According to him this model provides a better understanding of Kant and is also the one in agreement with Aristotle and Aquinas.

According to this most accepted one-world picture, our concepts do *refer* to *Dinge*; we can think about them and talk about them, because they are the only objects that really exist and about which we can think and reflect. If this is the case, how could it be that "the categories and our other concepts do not apply to them?" Plantinga asks.[30] If his case succeeds, the same can be also applicable to God - our concepts do apply to God, because what holds for *Dinge* also holds for everything else, argues Plantinga. [31]

In short, according to Plantinga, the analysis of the Kantian ontology does not show that our concepts do not apply to God. Therefore, he concludes the first chapter of *Warranted Christian Belief* with a strong anti-sceptical statement: "it doesn't look like as if there is good reason in Kant or in the neighbourhood of Kant for the conclusion that our concepts do not apply to God, so that we cannot think about him. Contemporary theologians and others sometimes complain that contemporary philosophers of religion often write as if they have never read their Kant. Perhaps the reason they write that

---

29 One of the prominent representatives of the one-world picture is Graham Bird. According to his analysis, "such phrases [e.g., ,transcendental objects and empirical objects'] should be understood to refer not to two different kinds of entity, but instead to two different ways of talking about one and the same thing." See his book, *Kant's Theory of Knowledge*, New York: Humanities Press, 1962, 37. Michael Devitt says that "It is tempting to equate an appearance with the foundationalist's sense datum, taking the thing-in-itself as the unknowable external cause of this mental entity. Kant's writing often encourages this temptation. Nevertheless, scholars seem generally agreed – and have convinced me – that this two-world interpretation is wrong. What Kant intends is the following influential, but rather mysterious, one world view." See his book, *Realism and Truth*, Princeton: Princeton University Press, 1984, 37. There are many more philosophers who are of the same view. See, D.P. Dryer, *Kant's Solution for Verification in Metaphysics*, Toronto: University of Toronto Press, 1966, Chapter 11 Section vi; Henry Allison, *Kant's Transcendental Idealism*, New Haven: Yale University Press, 1983. I am indebted to Plantinga for this explanation. See *Warranted Christian Belief*, 12-13.

30 *Warranted Christian Belief*, 14.

31 It is to be noted here that when I say,I have the concept of *being intelligent*, only if I grasp, apprehend and understand the property of *being intelligent*. So having positive concepts imply the apprehension of the respective properties. In this sense, it can be said that our 'positive concepts' do not apply to things as they are in themselves. This is because there is no positive property we grasp that characterises things as they are in themselves. In this sense, we can say that we cannot ascribe any positive properties to God, because there is no positive property we grasp that characterises God in himself. Hence Plantinga says; "it is not the case that our concepts fail to apply to God in such way that we cannot refer to and think about him. What *would* follow, given that he is a *noumenon* (of course, in this way of thinking, *everything* is a *noumenon*) is that God would not have any of the positive properties of which we have a grasp." See, *Warranted Christian Belief*, 16.

way, however, is not that they have never read their Kant but rather that they *have* read him and remain unconvinced...that Kant actually claimed that our concepts do not apply to God. Alternatively, they may concede that Kant did claim this, but remain unconvinced that he was *right*... Either way, they, they don't think Kant gives us reason to hold that we cannot think about God."[32]

5. Contemporary thinkers and Coherence of Theistic Belief

Having argued that Kant didn't show that our concepts do not refer to God, he asks further: Does any contemporary thinker give us reason to accept such conceptual scepticism? To this, he critically analyses the ideas of the two prominent contemporary sceptical thinkers; Gordon Kaufman and John Hick[33]and says that they also do not give us any positive argument to show the non-referentiality thesis is right and our concepts cannot be applied to God.

Kaufman, one of the prominent anti-exclusivist philosophers says that none of our human concepts refers to God. Central to this non-referentiality thesis is the following argument: "As the Creator or Source of all that is, God is not to be identified with any particular finite reality; as the proper object of ultimate loyalty or faith, God is to be distinguished from every proximate or penultimate value or being. *But if absolutely nothing within our experience can be directly identified as that to which the term "God" properly refers what meaning does or can the word have*?"[34] Plantinga calls this argument as the one that awakes "Kantian echoes." According to him this argument of Kaufman has two claims:[35]

(a) If God is not a finite reality, then absolutely nothing within our experience can be directly identified as that to which the term 'God' properly refers.
(b) If nothing within our experience can be directly identified as that to which the term 'God' properly refers, then the term 'God' doesn't refer to anything, or at least it is problematic when it does.

The first claim (a) means that to apply a term to an object, the object our reference should be directly and immediately available to our experience. Since God is an infinite reality, the term 'God' does not apply to anything within our experience: an infinite and omniscient being is beyond our finite

32 See, *Warranted Christian Belief*, 30.

33 Since I will discuss John Hick at length later, I elaborate only Plantinga's critique on Kaufman here.

34 See, Gordon Kaufman, *God the Problem*, Cambridge: Harvard University Press, 1972, 7. The emphasis is mine.

35 The detailed analysis of Kaufman's thought can be found in Warranted *Christian Belief*, 32-42. For this discussion, I am indebted to this section of Plantinga.

world of experience; we cannot hear him, we cannot touch him and we cannot perceive him. Against this claim, Plantinga argues that how is it that the fact that God is infinite means that we cannot experience him? On the contrary, believers all over the world say that they have experienced God; spoken to him and got a special message from him etc. Plantinga takes here words from Jonathan Edwards and asks, 'are they not then experiencing God'. If they are not true experiences why should great contemporary thinkers like, William P. Alston take it up as an important theme for discussion.[36] The fact that God is infinite with respect to power, knowledge and goodness doesn't follow that he cannot make himself heard or we cannot experience him.

Plantinga calls the claim in the second premise(b) - if nothing within our experience can be directly identified as that to which the term 'God' properly refers, the term 'God' doesn't refer to anything, or at least it is problematic when it does - as "dubious" and unconvincing. The second premise suggests that if a concept does not refer to an immediate object of our experience, it doesn't mean that we cannot understand it or refer to it is problematic. Against it, Plantinga argues that "cosmologist tell us of the Big Bang, an event that occurred several billion years ago in which an explosion of enormous energy caused an expansion from an initial configuration of enormous density. I suppose the Big Bang is not something within our experience, something that can be directly identified as that to which the term 'the Big Bang' correctly refers; does it follow that there is a profound problem with this term?"[37] The meaning and ideas involved in the term 'Big Bang' is highly speculate in nature. We do not have direct and immediate access to the initial singularity or to the explosive cosmic expansion.[38]But the term 'Big Bang' applies to all that happened in the first decisive moments of the beginning of our universe. If there is no particular problem in using this term to the initial status of our universe to which we have no immediate and direct perceptual access, why should we attribute "some special problem in the case of God," ask Plantinga. [39] It is in any case unfair to the theists.

36 Many Christians and Jews believe that God spoke to Moses from the burning bush, to Abraham in a dream and today to people in different ways. According to William P. Alston they should be accepted with proper epistemic merit. See, Alston's book, *Perceiving God: The Epistemology of Religious Experience*, New York: Ethaca, 1993, 34.

37 *Warranted Christian Belief*, 34.

38 For an excellent account of the initial singularity and all what happened in the first few seconds of our universe, see, Stephen Hawking, *A Brief History of Time, From the Big Bang to Black Holes*, New York: Bantam Books,1989;, Heinz Pagels R, *The Cosmic Code: Quantum Physics as the Language of Nature*, Yew York: Bantam Books, 1982; Paul Davis, *God and New Physics*, New York: Penguin Books,1983.

39 *Warranted Christian Belief*, 34

Plantinga firmly believes that the claims of Kaufman's arguments, as explained above do not offer anything to declare that our concepts do not refer to God. Perhaps what he really meant might be the following:

(A) *The "real referent" for God is never accessible to us or in any way open to our observation or experience. It must remain always an unknown X.*[40]

According to Kaufman, when Christians say God has created the universe, He sent his only son Jesus Christ to the world, He redeemed the world through the sacrificial suffering and death of his son etc, they are not referring to the "real referent" of the term "God", but *only* to the "available referent". The "available referent" is simply a human construct – an imaginative creation - to conduct the human action in a morally and metaphysically acceptable way.

Now Plantinga asks, "Do the believers accept the claim (A) of Kaufman?" When they pray it does seem that they are worshiping an illusionary and imaginary being. In all religions the object of worship is real for the believers. Kaufman clarifies that "this fact that the God actually available to people is an imaginative construct, does not necessarily mean that God is "unreal" or "merely" imaginary" or something of that sort. That question remains open for further investigation."[41] According to Plantinga, the claim (A) of Kaufman seems to suggest that on one hand there is this "available referent", an accessible human construct we have in mind when we call upon God. But on the other hand, there is a "real referent" of the term "God", a being to which no cognitive contact is possible and to which we cannot speak. It means that there *might be* a "real referent" and even if there is such a referent, we cannot think about it, speak about it; he is wholly an unknown X. This would mean that when Christian say 'God is almighty and creator of the world' or address him in prayer with different qualifications, they are just referring to the "available referent" of the name God'.

According to Plantinga, this argument of Kaufman is problematic. First, the "available referent" is just a human construct seems to mean that it *wouldn't have existed* before there were human beings. If so, Plantinga argues that "how then did it manage to create the heavens and earth? Could it somehow do this before it existed? In any event, an imaginative construct, a symbol, a

40 See, *God the Problem*, 85.

41 See, *God the Problem*, 86. Does the contention here mean that God does not exist and it is only a human imagination? Kaufman's answer is this: "Does this mean, then, that the conclusion is, after all, that God really does not exist, that He is only figment of our imagination? If those words are intended to put the speculative question about the ultimate nature of things, then, as we have seen, there is a possible way to give an answer." See, *God the Problem*, 111, See also *Warranted Christian Belief*, 36

structure of meanings of some kind is just not the sort of thing that could create the heavens and the earth or, indeed anything else."[42] Moreover "available referent" being an imaginative human construct, can *only* have the properties of being a construct, but it can never have the properties such as being infinite, creator of the world etc. Perhaps, it could be possible that the Christian are mistaken: they are referring to a being that they think has created this world, but in reality they are referring to a being that they themselves have created. According to Plantinga, this could be the case, but "surely a strong argument would be required to this even reasonably possible."[43] Kaufman doesn't offer any such sound arguments for that.

Second, Kaufman's idea of "real referent" is incoherent. For Kaufman, our concepts do not apply to the "real referent"; it is an inaccessible X. If God is an inaccessible X, none of our concepts will apply to him. In that case, this "real referent" also does not have properties like being infinite, existence, being material object or immaterial object and being the creator of the world etc., because these are the properties of which we have concepts. But Kaufman's description entails that at least *one* property applies to the "real referent": it is a being that has no properties of which we have concepts. Therefore, Kaufman's very explanation of the term "real referent" contradicts the very idea itself.[44]

In wake of the staunch criticism, Kaufman seems to have given up the "real referent" idea in his recent writings. However, he still firmly believes that to attribute some qualities, such as infinite, holiness, omnipotence and all-loving, all-knowing etc., to God is epistemically wrong. "To regard God as some kind of describable or knowable object over against us would be at once a degradation of God and a serious category error… Contemporary theological construction needs to be recognized that these terms and concepts do not refer directly to "objects" or "realities" or their qualities and relations, but function rather as the building blocks or reference points which articulate the theistic world-picture or vision of life," says Kaufman. [45]

Why does Kaufman believe that our concepts do not refer to God? According to Plantinga, apart from the epistemological reason, there is also a religious reason. Kaufman, though being a theologian does not believe in God; he thinks that there is no such person as God.[46]However, it does not mean that

42 *Warranted Christian Belief*, 36.

43 *Warranted Christian Belief*, 37.

44 *Warranted Christian Belief*, 38.

45 See, Kaufman, *The Theological Imagination: Constructing the Concept of God*, Philadelphia: Westminster Press, 1981, 244.

46 Kaufman in his article, "Evidentialism: A Theologian's Response" has given three reasons for his contention, why there is no God. First is the emergence of the new consciousness about the significance of religious pluralism. Second, "new theories about the ways in which cultural and linguistic symbolic or conceptual frames shape all our experiencing

religion and its devout practices are meaningless to him. For him, religious practice still has an important social function in human life. Its function is not that of putting us in touch with a being with the properties traditionally ascribed to God or that of enabling us to appropriate the salvation in Jesus Christ. But rather, it should be used to promote *human flourishing, 'human fulfilment and meaning'.*"[47]

According to Plantinga, this way of understanding the function of religion is simply irrelevant. First, it is something like pouring new wine into old wineskins. "What we have here is nothing like the rich, powerful, fragrant wine of the great Christian truths; what we have is something wholly drab, trivial, and insipid. It is not even a matter of throwing out the baby with the bathwater; it is, instead , throwing out the baby and keeping the tepid bathwater, at best a bland, unappetizing potion that is neither hot nor cold and at worst a nauseating brew, fit for neither man or beast," says Plantinga.[48] Second, Kaufman's secular and human centred Christianity is something that can only encourage hypocrisy and dishonesty. This is because here there is no real belief in God, but one should act as if there is God for the well-fare of the society; one should accept Christian faith, but it should mean something else. In short, according to Plantinga, Kaufman's early "real and available referent" distinction and his later socio-functional understanding of religious belief do not offer any decisive argument for the epistemic scepticism with regard to the referentiality of our concepts to God. There is nothing in Kaufman to suggest that our concepts do not refer to God. John Hick is another contemporary thinker who voices similar scepticism. But he is "heavily indebted to Kant," says Plantinga. Hence, the same incoherency problem is also applicable to his view. Subsequently Plantinga claims that there is no serious incoherence in theistic belief in general and Christians' belief in particular.

Conclusion

We have analysed the epistemic problems associated with the theistic belief and Plantinga's "re-visioning" of the coherence of belief in God. I think these arguments and proposals are outstanding epistemic contributions of Plantinga

---

and thinking... have given rise in theologians to a new self-consciousness about the extraordinarily complex and problematic character of all so-called 'religious-truth-claims' including those that are made by Christian faith." Third, Religions are the main cause of suffering and pain in the world. Especially Christian themselves are responsible for more of the evil in the world than they would like to think. See his article "Evidentialism: A Theologian's Response," in *Faith and Philosophy* (January 1989), 30. See also *Warranted Christian Belief*, 39-40.

47 See, *The Theological Imagination*, 34. It is to be noted here that this explanation is Plantinga's understanding of Kaufman. See, *Warranted Christian Belief*, 40.

48 *Warranted Christian Belief*, 42.

to put the rationality of religious belief to the forefront; more accurately they are the grand philosophical arguments to show the epistemic appropriateness of what is specific to theistic belief. However the question still remains; 'did Plantinga succeed in articulating the epistemic coherence of Christian belief adequately'? Though Plantinga has shown that there are in-consistencies in the interpretation of "two worlds" in Immanuel Kant's epistemology and Kaufman's "available and real referent", he still did not give any positive argument to show that we can refer to God *an sich*. The human conceptual inability to apprehend the *nominal* reality of God *in himself* will always remain a problem. Moreover, the plurality of religious truth claims also makes Plantinga's claim weaker. If we can know God and attribute properties to him, the question immediately arises here is this; why there are diverse religious truth claims then? Although religious pluralism does not make Plantinga's arguments irrelevant, it at least challenges Planting's arguments to a greater extend.

12

Towards a Cosmotheandric Spirituality of Work: The Experience of the Sacred in the Secular

Isaac Parackal, OIC

Abstract

Work is a cosmotheandric act which helps humans to live in the 'present' and relates one with all the three dimensions of reality namely divine, human and cosmic. Work as modern *Yajna* (sacrifice) conjoins these three constitutive dimensions of reality. However, the present scenario of work is well characterized by two dilemmas. We witness today a paradoxical situation in the whole world of work. People spend larger chunk of their time for work but they fail to find satisfaction in their life. This has resulted in the degradation of work. People work only for money not for their satisfaction. So, there is an alienation between the worker and work. In this way, the fragmentation of work and the worker, the producer and the product have destroyed the genuine quality of work. R. Panikkar presents work as the worship of modern human being and the worker as the worshipper. Worker as priest of the cosmos acts for the welfare of the whole cosmos. A worker is a contemplative who has to find meaning in his/her work. He/she renounces the result of his/her work (nishkamakarma). Work as an ennobling human activity has to enhance the three dimensions of reality.

Key words: Cosmotheandric vision, alienation, maximum and optimum, sacrifice, worship, ennobling, cosmotheandric act, priest of creation, contemplative, integration, *metanoia, lokasamgraha.*

Introduction

Panikkar's Cosmotheandric vision states that reality is triadic - divine, human and cosmic.[1] These are the irreducible dimensions which constitute reality. Reality is neither one nor many but polarity. In this holistic vision, all the three dimensions of reality-divine, human and cosmic are important and in this way every being is trinitarian. Every being has an abyssal dimension; i.e., both transcendent and immanent. This is the divine dimension of reality. The divine is not an umbrella superimposed over beings but a constitutive principle. Secondly, every being is within the range of consciousness. This is the human dimension. And thirdly, every being stands in the world and shares its secularity. There is nothing which enters human consciousness without once entering into relation with the world. This is the cosmic dimension of reality. There is nothing isolated in this universe. Everything is connected with everything else. In summary, the Cosmotheandric vision is a vision of harmony in which all forces of the universe, from electromagnetic to divine, from angelic to human are intertwined.

Work is a cosmotheandric act which helps humans to live in the 'present' and relates him/her with all the three dimensions of reality. Panikkar presents work as the worship of modern human being and the worker as the worshipper. Worker as priest of the cosmos acts for the welfare of the whole cosmos. By worship or sacrifice, Panikkar means "that act by which we express one way or other the fullness of the human person. It implies devotion, love, i.e., the heart, the emotions, as well as the dedication of our being and the consecration of our lives."[2] Sacrifice is sacred since it effects a breakthrough which rejoins the human and the divine and consequently adds a new dimension to human existence. However, it is also secular for it requires human collaboration and engages the whole world in its performance.[3] Panikkar interprets work as heir to the traditional sacrifice. In this article, let us see how work as a cosmothenadric act conjoins the three dimensions of reality and contributes to the welfare of the whole world.

1. Present Scenario of Work

Panikkar observes that the present scenario of work is well characterized by two dilemmas. We witness today a paradoxical situation in the whole world of work. On the one hand, humans are crazy after work and they spend the larger chunk of their time at the working place. Yet the working place is where people

1 The word "*Cosmotheandric*" is coined from three words: *theos*(divine), *cosmos*(cosmic) and *anthropos*(human).

2 R. Panikkar, *Worship and Secular Man,* London, Longman & Todd, 1973, 47-48.

3 Cf. R. Panikkar, *Vedic Experience Mantramanjari*: *An Anthology of Vedas for Modern Man and Contemporary Celebration*, London, Longmann & Todd, 1977. 277.

generally find themselves out of place and out of mind. Work has been de-humanized and human beings are tired of doing their work and want somehow to get out of it.[4] In this technological era, urbanization is transforming work into bureaucratic patterns of organizations and so modern work is becoming more and more perverse. Work, which is a creative human activity, has been underplayed and seen as 'employment', 'labour' or a 'job'. Labour is an alienating activity.[5] It tends to make people slaves or addicted to work. Panikkar aptly notes: "It looks as if the modern addiction to work is becoming an epidemic for humankind. You have to work because apparently your naked existence has no value; therefore, you must justify your life by usefulness."[6] Human beings consider their working hours a curse rather than a time to become themselves and thereby fulfilling their ultimate needs.[7] The working time seems to so many as a time of slavery and it forces them somehow to get out of time. It has become a routine affair. This has resulted in the degradation of work.

Again, the present day work is not able to make each of us a true '*homo faber'* because what we make is neither our life nor our own happiness. We are in a way chained to the instrument of torture.[8] This is a dangerous signal. One sacrifices one's time through work to earn and not to live. The modern worker is becoming a producer. This has given birth to the reification and objectification of work. In a way, life is subordinated to production.[9] Works may be of many types, but all are homogenized in as much as they are all convertible into money.[10] In this way, the fragmentation of work and the worker, the producer and the product have destroyed the genuine quality of work.

Panikkar observes that in the contemporary world of work humans have almost equated their identity to the profession they have. They do not want to be themselves or known by their name rather they like to be known by their

4 Sudheendra Kulkarni, "Developing A New Theology of Work", *Times of India*, Daily, no. 253, CLXII, (October 12, 1999), 12.

5 R. Panikkar, "Medicine and Religion", *Interculture*, XVII, no.4 (Fall 1994), 6. According to the Marxian ideology, the worker in a capitalist society is used as an instrument of production.

6 R. Panikkar, "The Contemplative Mood", A Challenge to Modernity", *Cross Currents*, XXXIV, (Fall 1981) 265.

7 Work is more than a mere 'need' to be satisfied or conquered. We should cultivate a different attitude to work, which is based neither on money orientations nor on future results.

8 Panikkar, "The Contemplative Mood", 267. Also R. Panikkar, *Invisible Harmony, Essays on Contemplation and responsibility,* ed. Harry James Cargas, Minneapolis, Fortress Press, 1995, 10.

9 R. Panikkar, "The Contemplative Mood", 265.

10 R. Panikkar, "The Contemplative Mood", 265.

profession. In other words, the modern worker is a doctor, a mechanic, an engineer etc. No one likes to be called by one's name but by his/her profession. For modern worker time is money, which is the modern idol, and he/she works for hours in order to get the 'maximum' and not the 'optimum.'[11] The whole preoccupation is to work out one's historical destiny, which is ahead of one(futuristic). Now to realize this, he/she takes the sole motto: "Work now and live later."

2. Work as Worship

In the light of this paradoxical situation, Panikkar's idea of work acquires great significance. It is an accepted fact of experience that our temporal dimension of life is very much related to work. We have seen that worship is an expression of human life and part and parcel of life itself. "An act of worship is an act which allows and enables us to realize our being, to realize the cosmos, to be what really is."[12] In this way, work as worship manifests life authentically. Panikkar says that it is through working within time and space that we are able to transcend our historical predicament and thereby transform time itself.[13] It is in work where time and timefulness meet and enable the worker to enjoy the present and to consecrate his/her life in an authentic way. Today, people are more and more tending towards this sort of attitude. This shows that the genuine experience, which is gained through human work, can be an intelligible and meaningful form of worship for the modern human being. It is in work that the worker can enjoy the present and consecrate his/her life fruitfully. It is 'working' (the act of working) and not 'work' (profession) that is important. According to the well known anecdote, both stonecutter and the master builder were constructing the Cologne Cathedral. The primacy is to the act itself so that work will have to yield its own meaning. The worker acts for its own sake and as Meister Eckhart puts it, he/she acts 'without a why.'[14] Not every love relationship, or any medical service, or each work of art, is automatically a worship, but only those actions which somewhat transcend the intention of private usefulness or egoistic pleasure and intend a collaboration for the welfare of the world.[15] For Panikkar, all kinds of work are important and contribute to the building up of the human community.

---

11 R. Panikkar, "The Contemplative Mood", 268.

12 Panikkar, *Worship and Secular Man,* 48.

13 R. Panikkar, "Time and Sacrifice", *The Study of Time III: Proceedings of the Third Conference of the International Society for the Study of Time, Alpbach-Austria*, ed. J. T. Fraser New York, Springer-Verlag, 1978,702.

14 Panikkar, "The Contemplative Mood", 262.

15 R. Panikkar , "Man as a Ritual Being," *Indian Theological Studies*, VI, no.1 (March-June 1979), 23.

A worker is a contemplative who has to find meaning in his/her work. He/she renounces the result of his/her work: "The contemplative renounces the very results of the work, performing every kind of activity for the sake of act itself and not for what may come out of it."[16] This fundamental aspect of work shows that what is important is not 'what we do' but 'how we do'. In this notion of human work, each moment is important rather than the final achievement. The completion or future is already present in the '*present*'.

Work enables human being to become him/herself fully. It is in and through work, that one realizes one's inner felt needs. Because of this reason, many religious traditions speak of the importance of work for human fulfilment.[17] As in a worship it is through work, one consecrates him/herself and sanctifies the world at large. Work is no longer the task of slaves but of free citizens. It leads one to freedom and happiness.

3. Work as Art

According to Panikkar human work is an art and the worker is an artist. Human being is basically a worker, an artist, a creator and a co-creator in all the fields of the real. Every work is meaningful in itself. It expresses the creativity of the worker and it has an ennobling role. Panikkar elaborates: "A plant will be cultivated because the act of cultivating it is meaningful in itself: a collaboration between the human and the virtual forces of nature, and enhancement of both nature and culture, an ennobling inherent in the act itself. It is neither the act of a slave nor that of a Lord - but that of an artist." [18] Of course, work is done primarily for living but this living means 'to walk in beauty,' to enjoy life, to be open to the beauty of life and nature, etc.[19] Work as a praxis or art is a constitutive activity which springs from the very nature of humans. Creative activity is human's destiny and vocation and not full employment.[20] It is that creativity which makes a worker a contemplative in the modern world. Panikkar explains: "The contemplative does not perform anything in view of obtaining something else. There is place for art because each and every one of the intermediate steps is discovered to be meaningful

16 R. Panikkar, "The Contemplative Mood", 267. This idea is taken from Bhagavad Gīta of Indian tradition which advocates action without looking into the results.

17 Many monastic traditions in the east and west give much importance to work. For example, the Benedictines prescribed work as a spiritual discipline. Their cloister bells sounded not only call the brothers to pray together but also to summon them to common work.

18 R. Panikkar, "The Contemplative Mood", 266

19 R. Panikkar, *The Cosmotheandric Experience*, Scott Eastham ed., Maryknoll, Orbis Books, 1983, 95.

20 R. Panikkar, "Medicine and Religion", 6.

in themselves, just as the tentative sketch or the torso may be as beautiful and complete in its own way as the finished composition."[21]

According to Panikkar genuine work should be like a play not a game.[22] When we play we are totally engrossed in that world and we are concentrated on one thing namely the particular play in which we engage. Work should be an expression of free life and thus of enjoyment. Our action becomes a play when we do it for its own sake. That means, an action must be done for the sake of enjoyment and not with the aim of receiving a reward. The modern human being is always on the go and he/she thinks that the quicker the better in order to gain time. Acceleration is the great discovery of modernity. Panikkar states that "the most important characteristic of techno-centric civilization lies in having introduced acceleration, less in the mathematical-physical than in the global sense: acceleration of rhythms, of times, of all happenings on this earth."[23] Humans want to speed up everything including the natural processes and even the arrival of seasons.[24] In this context, work becomes almost like an end and this end does not give human fulfilment. Instead of helping humans to reach out to their ultimate fulfilment, it gives only temporary satisfaction of their needs.[25] Besides, modern life is a preparation for 'later' or for the time to come. "We are almost trying to speed up the process of life as whole, thereby all the more speeding up the arrival of the *parousia*, the end of the world."[26] We see here a future oriented mentality. Against this modern current, a worker who is a contemplative stops the rush of time in the world and enjoys the 'now' as holistic.[27] He or she realizes that the past, present and future are intertwined into the "*present*."

The workers are those who enjoy their work and not those who consider it as drudgery. The greatest need of humans at this period of history is to create a playful mentality, which has to guide them through all their actions in this world. Work becomes most self-fulfilling and self-transforming when it is done for its own sake. A playful person is one who is able to transcend the limits of this world. While immersed in playful activities we enlarge our horizons and thus transcend our immediate space and time within which we live our daily life. Playfulness is an expression of inner fullness. This is the contemplative

---

21 R. Panikkar, "The Contemplative Mood", 267.

22 Modern games have become almost like wars where the competent will get through and others will be eliminated. Not all have an access to it. The real joy of the act is lost.

23 R. Panikkar, *A Dwelling Place for Wisdom*, Annemarie S. Kidder trans., Delhi, Motilal Banarsidass Publishers, 1993, 26.

24 R. Panikkar, A *Dwelling Place for Wisdom*, 26.

25 R. Panikkar, "The Contemplative Mood:", 266.

26 R. Panikkar, *A Dwelling Place for Wisdom*, 26.

27 R. Panikkar, "The Contemplative Mood", 264.

mood, in which one enjoys the '*tempiternal*' present. The modern worker, who is a contemplative, does not escape time rather he/she lives in the 'present' and acts spontaneously. Contemplatives burn their lives every day. Every day exhausts the entire universe and each moment is a new creation for them.[28]

4. Work as Cosmotheandric Act

Sacrifice is by its very nature a '*theandric*' act, an act in which God and humans have to work together in order that the world (cosmic dimension) can be conserved; it is a cosmic act, because the sustenance of the world depends on it.[29] The refreshing feature of the Vedic way of life is its healthy combination of the sacred and the secular. The intuition of sacrifice demonstrates it.[30] The sacrifice, the sacrificer and the sacrificed meet together in work.[31] Modern work allows one to collaborate in the salvation of the world. Genuine work helps humans to dedicate their time for the preservation and transformation of the world.[32] Panikkar interprets work as the worship of modern human being and the worker as a contemplative who acts for the overall well-being of the whole world. It is nothing but the *lokasamgraha*.[33] Today the modern human being works not for the salvation that he/she is going to achieve in the future eternity. He/she is a contemplative in action for the integral welfare of the whole world, both human and cosmic. In work, one enjoys the true freedom.

Freedom belongs to human creativity, to create oneself and to build up the world. "The experience of contemporary Man finding himself, and moreover believing himself, not master of universe, but in a certain sense its builder, its responsible partner, is a fundamental religious experience."[34] Here worship is not a denial of the human condition but acceptance of it, for this '*theandric*' act faith, hope and love are essentially needed. The main concern of the worker is to promote harmony with the cosmos, communion among all humans and confidence in the divine. This is the sacredness of the secular life where one experiences the splendour of his/her creative freedom.

Human creative freedom is meant for the building up of the universe and for the welfare of the people. Every discovery is the result of human creativity through which reality is revealed. Every revelation is a source of salvation and welfare of humans. Today, Humans is free to create their own destiny and to

28 R. Panikkar, "The Contemplative Mood", 270.

29 R. Panikkar, *Worship and Secular Man,* 34.

30 R. Panikkar, *Vedic Experience*, 276.

31 R. Panikkar, "Time and Sacrifice", 707.

32 R. Panikkar, "Time and Sacrifice", 707.

33 *Loksamgraha* is a Sanskrit word which means the total welfare or maintaining of the world. See R. Panikkar, *Invisible Harmony*, 181.

34 R. Panikkar, *Myth, Faith and Hermeneutics*, New York, Paulist Press, 1979, 452.

fashion the world. This becomes his/her liturgy and worship. For Panikkar, real love of God is service to fellow beings and the loftiest religious service is not to sing the lauds of an invisible creator, but to extol the possibilities of humans themselves.[35]

Today we need to take seriously the world and its concerns, and to act responsibly for the total welfare of the entire human community. This will affirm the basic dignity and freedom of every one. Our actions should be enlightened actions so that through our actions we resonate, radiate and create an atmosphere of spirituality in and around us. This is modern contemplation where the world itself becomes the sanctuary. In this modern type of contemplative life, contemplation itself becomes enlightened action. Panikkar beautifully notes:

What is contemplation? The disciple asked the master. Contemplation is wisdom was the answer. And what is wisdom? Wisdom is to see. And the disciple asks, "to see what"? To see the eagle in the egg, the butterfly in the caterpillar, the saint in the sinner"- was the answer. But seeing is not just looking at the appearances. It is the seeing that brings forth the eagle, the butterfly and the saint. If we do not see the eagle in the egg, the butterfly in the caterpillar and the saint in the sinner, we do not see. We are blind and barren.[36]

One who works for '*lokasamgraha*' is a yogi who is a contemplative in action.[37] Through our actions, we will integrate ourselves, experience the divine and serve the cosmos. Thus, sacred secularity becomes a new paradigm for the religion of this world. Worthy of note here is the Johannine sutra, "The Word was made flesh and dwelt among us" by which the sacred is incarnated in the secular.

5. Worker as Priest and Co-worker of God

Panikkar considers worker as the one who partakes in the creative building up of the society.[38] He holds that worker is the priest of creation and "the sacred hours are not the time of leisure or prayer, but the working hours."[39] He understands that worker sacrifices his/her energy and time for the betterment of the human society and the whole world.[40] Panikkar does not mean that we have to work in order to earn money, but for the maintenance of the universe:

35 R. Panikkar, *Worship and Secular Man*, 51.

36 R. Panikkar, "Cosmic Evolution, Human History and Trinitarian Life", in *Teilhard Review*, XXV, no. 3 (1990), 65.

37 Yogi is a Sanskrit word that means the one who lives a disciplined life in order to attain salvation.

38 R. Panikkar, *Worship and Secular Man*, 89.

39 R. Panikkar, "Time and Sacrifice", 706.

40 R. Panikkar, "Time and Sacrifice", 706.

"We do not work in order to earn money or to acquire commodities, but because human activity is part of human and cosmic life and sustains the entire organism."[41] Worker collaborates in the salvation of the world.[42] For Panikkar, worker finds his/her enjoyment in having been called to play his/her role in the cosmos.[43] The dignity and responsibility of the worker rests in participating with freedom in the continuing creative process of the universe together with the Creator.[44] He concludes, "To be engaged in the perfection of the cosmos is not vanity, but the fullest realisation of the person."[45] Therefore, people who engage in all sorts of work are the priests who sanctify human life. This is the modern religiousness, which generates salvation in and through the world.[46] In short, work is worship and workers are the priests of this age.

Conclusion

Panikkarian vision is a unified vision of reality that calls for the welfare of the whole cosmos. He shows through the broadness of his Cosmotheandric vision that only an integral understanding of reality can save us from the clutches of fragmented ideologies which give birth to disunity among Men. Through the hermeneutics of secularization, we have explained the limitations of worship today. In line with Panikkar's understanding we should change our traditional notions of sacred and secular, time and eternity, work and worship etc. Finally, sacred secularity is suggested as an emerging religiosity in which work is considered as the universal symbol of worship. Work is the worship or the modern sacrifice that leads to the welfare of the cosmos. Today we have to experience the sacredness in the secular by working for *lokasamgraha*, for the survival of the whole world. This depends on a radical *metanoia*, a radical "turning back", a complete "conversion" of mind, heart and spirit."[47] In order to do this human being has to act as a contemplative who lives in the "*present*" and integrates and transforms the world through his/her actions. Let me conclude this article with a universal prayer from our great Sages: *Lokaa Samastha Sukhino Bhavanthu.*[48]

---

41 R. Panikkar, *The Cosmotheandric Experience*, 151.

42 R. Panikkar, "Time and Sacrifice", 707.

43 R. Panikkar, "The Law of *Karman* and The Historical Dimension of Man", *Philosophy East and West*, XXII, no.1 (January 1972), 38.

44 R. Panikkar, „"A New Society for a New Millennium", in *Pilgrims in Dialogue, A New Configuration of Religions for Millennium Community*, ed. A. Kalliath, Bangalore, Dharmaran Publications, 2000, 16.

45 R. Panikkar, *Blessed Simplicity*, New York, Seasbury Press, 1982, 131.

46 R. Panikkar, "Time and Sacrifice", 706.

47 R. Panikkar, "The New Innocence," *Cross Currents*, XXVII (Summer 1977), 7.

48 *Let there be peace and happiness in the whole world.*

Bibliography

Panikkar, Raimundo: *Worship and Secular Man*, London, Longman & Todd, 1973.

________ *Vedic Experience Mantramanjari*: *An Anthology of Vedas for Modern Man and Contemporary Celebration*, London, Longmann & Todd, 1977.

________ *The Cosmotheandric Experience: Emerging Religious Consciousness* (edited with an introduction by Scott Eastham), Maryknoll, Orbis Books, 1983.

________ *Blessed Simplicity: The Monk as Universal Archetype*. New York, Seasbury Press, 1982.

________ *A Dwelling Place for Wisdom* (translated by Annemarie S. Kidder), Delhi, Motilal Banarsidass Publishers, 1993.

________ *Myth, Faith and Hermeneutics*: *Cross-Cultural Studies*, New York, Paulist Press, 1979.

________ *Invisible Harmony: Essays on Contemplation and Responsibility*, (edited by Harry James Cargas) , Minneapolis, Fortress Press, 1995.

________ "Time and Sacrifice: The Sacrifice of Time and the Ritual of Modernity", *The Study of Time III: Proceedings of the Third Conference of the International Society for the Study of Time, Alpbach-Austria*, ed. J. T. Fraser New York, Springer-Verlag, 1978, pp.683-727.

________ "Man as a Ritual Being", *Indian Theological Studies*, VI, no.1 (March-June 1979), pp.1-26.

________ "The Contemplative Mood: A Challenge to Modernity", *Cross Currents*, XXXIV, (Fall 1981), pp. 261-272.

________ "Medicine and Religion", *Interculture*, XXVII, no.4 (Fall 1994), pp.1-39.

________ "New Society for a New Millennium" in *Pilgrims in Dialogue, A New Configuration of Religions for Millennium Community*, ed. A. Kalliath, Bangalore, Dharmaran Publications, 2000, pp. 13-29.

________ "The Law of *Karman* and the Historical Dimension of Man", *Philosophy East and West*, XXII, no.1 (January 1972), 25-43.

________ "Cosmic Evolution, Human History and Trinitarian Life", *Teilhard Review*, XXV, no. 3 (Autumn 1990), pp.61-71.

13

Adaptation of Mosul Fenqitho English Translation in Kurisumala Ashram

Stephen Plathottathil, OIC

Abstract

The article discuses on the liturgical adaptation of Francis Acharya, a trappist monk from Belgium, who migrated to India and founded Kurishumala Ashram at Wagamon, Kottayam, Kerala. He was very much fascinated the Indian cultural heritage and his monastical vision was totally based on Indian cultural heritage. He was able to translate from Syriac into English, a few of the most important liturgical texts. This article highlights his remarkable contributions on his adapted English translation of the Mosul Fenqitho, which is the first attempt in English translation and this translation work points out his unique spirituality and monastical dream.

Key words: Pampakuda Fenqitho; Mosul Fenqitho; qole, madroshe, sughyotho, bo'awotho, Oktoechos etc.

Introduction

Fr. Bede Griffiths, the eminent scholar and author, spent the last years of his life at Shantivanam in Tamil Nadu. Thus, Fr. Francis Acharya became the lone guiding spirit of the Ashram at Kurisumala. In India he embraced the best aspects of Indian spirituality and culture. It is a measure of his total commitment to local adaptation that he acquired a mastery knowledge of Syriac, the original language of the Malankara Syrian liturgy. He was able to translate from Syriac into English a few of the most important liturgical texts such as the Fenqitho, the worship book for feast days throughout the year. In the monastery, the liturgical services are in the Malankara tradition. On an experimental basis, with the official sanction of ecclesiastical authorities, there is an Indianised celebration of the Holy Mass. In this, the chants, ceremonies and symbols are mostly adapted from the Hindu form of worship. This practice bears testimony to the genuine respect and appreciation that Fr. Francis had of Indian culture and religions. He always endeavoured to nurture this attitude in the entire Kurisumala monastic community and to transmit it to the countless devotees of various Christian denominations and other religions who regularly reach the monastery for prayer and meditation. A couple of years before his death, Fr. Francis, who had kept in touch with the monastery of his youth, had the Kurisumala Ashram affiliated to the Trappists.

1. Fenqitho

Fenqitho is the name given to the collection of liturgical texts for the entire year, according to the West Syrian rite of Antioch. The best of the two printed versions was published by the Dominican Fathers in Mosul in seven Folio volumes with some 4000 pages, 16 x 22 cm, 1886-1896. This constitutes one vast, extended meditation on the divine economy of salvation.

Fenqitho is a Greek loanword, derived from *pinakidion* (pinaki,dion)[1], and means a writing tablet, a volume, a book etc. The Syrian Church also uses this word to denote a special book that contains many of the valuable treasures of her faith and spirituality; specifically, Fenqitho is the collection of special prayers and chants for Sundays and the major feasts of the year.

The term 'Fenqitho' as a specific liturgical volume for the choral book is seen for the first time in the 9th century: British Library, Add.14516 contains a collection of Choral services and Homilies for the principal festivals of the whole year *(Fenqitho d-Hudro d-kuleh shaato)*. The contents are similar to those of Brit.Man.Add.14515 and 171902. Baumstark's *Festbrevier der syrischen Jakobiten*, pp.62-68 is a valuable source for the basic study of early Syrian Orthodox Fenqitho manuscripts.[3]

2. Two Editions of West Syrian Fenqitho

The Catholic edition published by Ignatius Gurgis Shelhot (1874-1891) and Ignatius Behnan Benni (1893-1897), Patriarchs of the Syrian Catholic Church

1 Cf. SMITH J.P, *A Compendious Syriac Dictionary*, (Oxford, 1990), p. 451.

2 WRIGHT W., *Catalogue* I, (Cambridge, 1901), p.240-244; BROCK S., "Manuscrits liturgiques en syriaque", in CASSINGENA-TREVEDY F. and JURASZ, I (eds), *Les Liturgies Syriaques* (Études Syriaque 3; Paris, 2006), pp.267-83, especially p.276.

3 BAUMSTARK A., *Festbrevier und Kirchenjahr der syrischen Jakobiten*, Studien zur Geschichte und Kultur des Altertums 3,(1910), pp.62-68.

of Antioch, under the care of the Dominican Friars, at Mosul, Iraq, from 1886 to 1896, runs to seven volumes.

The Syrian Orthodox edition published in 1962-1963 by the late Catholicos Baselios Geevarghese II, at the Mar Julios Press, Pampakuda, Kerala, consists of three volumes only. It is restricted to those parts that are sung by the choir and the congregation, namely, the hymns: *qole*, *madroshe, sughyotho, bo'awotho* with their responses: '*enyone, qonune, kuroke*, arranged for the canonical prayers on Sundays and feast days throughout the year.[4]

There are also several photographic reproductions of modern handwritten Fenqithos produced by the Syrian Orthodox diaspora communities in Europe and North America. These all have many differences in content and are not taken into consideration in this article.

3. Maronite Fenqitho

The Maronites of Lebanon trace their origin back to the late 4th century when a group of disciples gathered around the charismatic figure of St.Maron. They later founded a monastery located midway between Aleppo and Antioch. In the 5th century the monastery vigorously supported the Christological doctrine of the Council of Chalcedon.

By the 8th century, the monks had moved with their band of followers into the remote mountains of Lebanon, where they existed in relative isolation for centuries. This church came into contact with the crusaders in the Middle Ages and underwent progressive Latin influence. Later this latinization was accentuated under Patriarch Joseph Rizzi at the end of the 16th century. But the Office was not so much affected by this.

The Maronite liturgy is of West Syrian origin, but it has been influenced by the East Syrian and Latin traditions. A Maronite edition of the Fenqitho was published in Rome in 1625. After Vatican II, an Arabic translation of a revised monastic office was prepared , beginning in 1973, at the Universitè Saint – Esprit in Kaslik, Lebanon, under the direction of the Monks of the Lebanese Maronite Order. This office has a reduced cursus of Nocturns, Lauds, Sext, Vespers, and Compline, with seasonal propers, and readings daily at *Sapro* and *Ramsho*.[5]

The steady emigration of Maronites from Lebanon in recent years has produced flourishing communities in the Diaspora. In the United States, there are two dioceses. *The Prayer of the Faithful according to the Maronite Liturgical Year*, was translated and adapted for use in the diocese of St Maron, USA, from 'Prière Croyant Selon l'anneé liturgique maronite' edited by Boutros Gemayel, vol-1; Sundays of the Church, Season of Annunciation, and

4 KONATTU ABRAHAM, *West Syriac Fenqitho*, 3 volumes, (Kerala, 1962-1963).

5 Cf. TAFT R., *The Liturgy of the Hours in East and West*, (Collegeville, 1986), pp.243-244.

Birth of our Lord, Season of Epiphany: vol-2; Season of Great Lent, Passion week, season of Resurrection. Vol-3; Season of Resurrection, Season after Pentecost, Season of the Holy Cross. (Brooklyn, Diocese of St Maron, 1982, 1984, 1985).[6]

4. The East Syrian Hudra

The corresponding liturgical book of the East Syrian Church is known as the Hudra or 'cycle'. Indeed this book contains the variable chants of the choir for the divine office and the Mass for the entire cycle of the whole liturgical year.

There are three editions: two of the Catholics,

i. *Breviarum iuxta ritum Syrorum Orientalium, id est Chaldeorum*, 3 volumes, Paris 1886-7/ Rome 1938;
ii. *Breviarum iuxta ritum Syrorum Orientalium, id est Chaldeorum*, 3 volumes abbreviated into 1 volume, Rome 2002;
iii. One of the Church of the East, *Ktaba da-qdam wa-d-batar wa d-hudra wa-d-kashkol wa-d-gazza w-qale d'udrana 'am ktaba d-mazmore*, 3 volumes, Trichur 1960-2[7].

The compilation of the Hudra is traditionally attributed to the Catholicos Patriarch Isho'yab III, of Adiabene (649-659) and his collaborator, the monk Ananisho, and there is no compelling reason for doubting the attribution[8].One reason for the particular importance of the Hudra derives from the fact that it contains a large number of liturgical chants of great theological interest. Indeed after the formal confessions of faith, defined by the Synods of the Church of the East[9] ,the liturgical chants are the most important source for a knowledge of East Syrian theology, and the most ancient of the chants are found precisely in the Hudra.

5. Modern Studies on the Fenqitho

A serious study on Fenqitho as a whole is still not yet done. But there are many articles on particular areas by different liturgical scholars. A series of articles by Mateos J.[10] are of particular value to the study of Fenqitho. His studies of collections of prayers, including *proimia* and *sedre* in the early manuscripts are of special importance. His study of the manuscripts helps us to learn the

---

6 Cf. TAFT R., *The Liturgy of the Hours in East and West*, p.246.

7 For a concordance between the first and the third, see BROCK S., "A Concordance to Bedjan's Breviarium Chaldaicum and Darmo's Hudra", *The Harp* 19,(2006),pp.117-36.

8 BAUMSTARK A., *Geschichte der Syrischen Literatur*,(Bonn ,1922), p.198.

9 CHABOT J. B (ed), *Synodicon Orientale*, (Paris,1902).

10 Published in *OCP* 28 (1962), 33(1967), & 34 (1968).

importance and the place of the manuscript traditions behind the edition of the Mosul Fenqitho.

The contribution of Thekeparampil on the *sedre*[11] is another valuable study of relevance, being concerned with the *sedre* which are important prose prayers in the Mosul Fenqitho.

A considerable number of stanzas of *madroshe* attributed to Ephrem have been identified by Gribomont J.[12] in the Mosul Fenqitho (vols IV-V) as belonging to his Paschal hymns.

Brock has indicated the handling of the genuine *madroshe* by Ephrem in the Mosul Fenqitho[13]. In one of his unpublished articles 'The Fenqitho: A Source for Theologizing in the Syrian Church: The Present State of Study' he provides a source for an introductory study of Fenqitho.

There are many *bote d-hasho* 'stanzas of the Passion' during the Passion week liturgical prayers. A brief general study of these, accompanied by an edition based on the manuscripts of 13th and 16th century in the Berlin collection of Syriac manuscripts has been made by W.Strothmann in his *Syrische Passionlieder.*[14]

Cody in his article entitled "The early history of the Oktoechos in Syria"[15] pointed out the indications of the musical tones in certain early Syriac liturgical traditions.

Sanders in his article "The Beth Gazo or the Octo-Echos of the West Syrian Church"[16] has defined different musical terminologies which are used in the Mosul Fenqitho.

Khouri-Sarkis has written quiet a number of articles describing specific liturgical feasts to be found in the Fenqitho in the periodical *L'Oriente Syrien* (1956-67).

The Syrian Churches have been using Fenqithos of the yearly Cycle from the very early Middle Ages. The prayers and poetic texts for Sundays and feast days are contained in it and it is here that the full depth of the theology of the Syrian Church is displayed.[17] It has magnificent offices for all the

---

11 THEKEPARAMPIL J., *Sedre and Rite of Incense in the West Syrian Liturgy*, Doctoral dissertation in Paris of 1976.

12 GRIBOMONT J,. « La tradition liturgique des hymnes pascales de s.Ephrem », *Parole de l'Orient* 4 (1973), pp.191-246.

13 BROCK S., "The transmission of Ephrem's *madroshe* in the Syriac liturgical tradition" in *Studia Patristica* 33(1997), pp.490-505.

14 Göttinger Orientforschungen, Reihe Syriaca 32; (Wiesbaden, 1989).

15 CODY A., in Garsoian N , Mathews T and Thomson R.W.(eds), *East of Byzantium* (Washington C, 1982), pp.89-144.

16 SANDERS J., in *The Harp* 5, (1992), pp.15-28.

17 *The Book of Common Prayer of the Syrian Church*, (tr.) BEDE GRIFFITHS, (Kurishumala Ashram, 1976), p. xiii.

great festivals of the Christian year, beginning (at the end of October or the beginning of November)[18] with the festival of the consecration of the Church in which the theology of the Church, as the bride of Christ, is unfolded. Then it passes through the season of *Suboro* or Annunciation, which prepares for the feast of Christmas. In the feast of Epiphany, the theology of the incarnation is expressed, with marvellous insight.

During the seasons of Lent (the Great Fast) and Passion week, Easter, Ascension, and Pentecost, in which the central mystery of Christian revelation is re-lived, with a depth of feeling and understanding, which has never been surpassed.

The Fenqitho gives us a deeper awareness of the true meaning of the celebration of the Church's prayer. With the prayer of the Fenqitho we are truly experiencing the Mysteries of the divine dispensation, for it makes unceasing references to them, and in the most poetic and elevating manner.

As the two constituent parts of the divine revelation of God's economy of salvation, it has been rightly observed that the Syrian liturgical tradition remarkably witnesses to the unity of the two Testaments.

The hymns, especially those of St Ephrem, and Jacob of Sarug, display an astonishing perception and sensitivity. These hymns are the best examples to illustrate the revelation of New Testament, not only using the inspired language and thought patterns of the Old Testament, but also by relating simple events of the past, as prefigurations, types, symbols, and mysteries pointing to the realities of the New Testament.

Thus this article is an attempt to provide an introduction to the prayer of Sundays and feast days contained in this large book known as the Fenqitho. The present article comprises four sections. The first section deals with the meaning of the term Fenqitho; the two editions of West Syrian Fenqitho, and their common background and features; the similarities between the East Syrian Hudra, the Maronite Fenqitho, and the West Syrian Fenqithos; and the contributions of Francis Acharya and his adaptations of the Mosul Fenqitho.

Some attention is given to the various manuscripts of the Fenqitho, and its different traditions. There have been three great traditions: Antioch, Edessa and Takrit. There are many examples of the liturgical interaction between these traditions. Because of these different traditions one can easily notice many variations among the Fenqitho manuscripts. The purpose of printing the Mosul Fenqitho was not only to serve the needs of the Church, but also to put an end to the variations between the manuscripts and to achieve uniformity of liturgical usage.

18 This is the beginning of the liturgical year in the West Syrian Churches.

6. English and Malayalam Translations and Adapted Versions

No complete translation of the any of the printed editions of the Fenqitho exists. However, for the Maronite Fenqitho there is an excellent English adaptation for current usage in the Maronite diaspora in America, entitled *The Prayer of the Faithful according to the Maronite Liturgical Year* (3 volumes, Brooklyn NY,1982) and a smaller separate volume simply entitled Fenqitho (1980), which has just the main saints days. The three volume edition was in fact made from the French translation edited by Chor-Bishop (now Bishop) Boutros Gemayel, a noted liturgical scholar. For the Mosul edition there is likewise an excellent English translation by the late Abbot Francis Acharya of the Kurisumala Ashram: volumes II-IV of his "Prayer with the Harp of the Spirit", which have the subtitle "The Crown of the Year" (1982-6). These contain his sensitive translation and adaptation of a large number of the texts for *Ramšo* and *Lilyo* in the Mosul Fenqitho.

7. How has Fr. Francis Acharya Adapted the Mosul Fenqitho?

Kurisumala Ashram[19] in Kerala is one of the monastic communities in the Syro Malankara Catholic Church founded by Fr Francis Mahieu, later known as Francis Acharya–the name given to a Spiritual Guru, like the Russian title 'starets[20]' in 1958 . He has made a partial translation of the Mosul Fenqitho (*PHS*) and adapted to the Indian context. This adapted English translation has been used in the monastery for many years as their liturgy of the Hours. It is undoubtedly one of the most radical and far reaching monastic experiments of time.

8. Adaptations into the Weekly Office

Basically the changes respect the structure of the offices, while suppressing the frequent duplication of liturgical units such as *qolo, or proimion* and *sedro.* In addition the *qolo* texts of the weekly cycles have been enriched with new material, some adjustments have been made in the calendar, a lucernarium is added to *Ramsho* and Indian texts from non-Christian sources have been introduced, experimentally, into the Hours.[21] These are called "Seeds of the Word."[22] At week day *Ramšo,* these texts, chosen because the religious experience they express is similar to what one finds in the Bible, are woven into the first *qolo*. At ferial *Sapro*, the "Seeds" replace the strophes of the morning psalmody, and are chosen not because of similarities with the Judeo - Christian tradition, but to express charisms proper to Indian religious culture.

19 'Ashram' is a Sanskrit word which means a monastery.

20 TAFT R., *The Liturgy of the Hours in East and West*, pp.243-46.

21 ACHARYA F., *PHS*, Vol. 1, p.. 8.

22 A hymn from the sacred writings of India. (ACHARYA F., *PHS*, Vol.1, p.5.)

At ferial *Sapro*, in addition to the "Seeds of the Word" which replace the strophes of the psalmody, a selection has been made from the *qolo* texts in order to reduce repetitions. More surprising is the suppression of the Magnificat, and Pss148-150, if Lauds have been celebrated at *Lilyo*.

The Syrian offices have a double Matins, but it would have been better either to leave the Lauds psalms in *Sapro*, suppressing them at *Lilyo*, or on days when *Lilyo* and *Sapro* are done as one, to simply suppress the second *Sapro* entirely.

9. The Revised Fenqitho Translation

Francis Acharya, founder and first Abbot of the Kurisumala Ashram at Vagamon, Kerala, India has translated Mosul Fenqitho from the original Syriac into English calling it *"Prayer with the Harp of the Spirit"* (*PHS*). Francis Acharya has tried his best to present the Syrian Prayer Service in an abridged form, it being his firm purpose to preserve their authentic features and their distinctive riches.

10. Method of Translation

It is quiet sure that Francis Acharya has done a wonderful service to the liturgy of the West Syrian Church. A single example will illustrate how his translation is sometimes quiet free. Though some of the same footnotes here are illustrated in the 5th chapter, it is given again to show the importance of theological translation.

Esu hu li, w'eno leh. Sbo bi w'labshan wlabshteh
Bnushqoto d'phumeh neshqan. W'lagnuno d'rawmeh dabran[23]
Translation according to Acharya:
Jesus is mine and I am His.
His delight is in me. He spreads his garments over me.
He kisses me with the kisses of his mouth
And takes me to the bridal chamber on high[24].

We translate it literally like this:

Jesus is to me and I am to Him.
He desired me and clothed[25] me and I put on Him.

23 Mosul Fenqitho, *Hudoth Etho*, Night Prayers, Vol. 2, p.38.

24 ACHARYA F., *PHS*, Vol.II, p.31.

25 This simple image of clothing is the Syriac Fathers' favourite way of describing the incarnation. It occurs constantly in the Acts of Judas Thomas. This phrase is frequent in Aphrahat (*Dem*. XXI, 954) beyond such expressions as "the body which he put on from us is the origin of our resurrection" (*Dem*.XXIII,97.19-20). For Ephrem it is Christ's solidarity with the human race through his incarnation. In the hymns Ephrem often speaks of Christ's

With the kisses of His mouth He has kissed me.
And to the Bridal Chamber of His height, He has led[26] me

It is evident that Acharya translated for the worshipping community of Kurisumala, and so he has avoided a very close translation.

11. Francis Acharya's Adaptation of the Mosul Fenqitho

In the evening service, in commemoration of God's work of creation, Acharya has brought out more clearly the celebration of the evening, very commonly observed by the people in India, especially Hindus, with the ritual of lighting the oil lamp, *kuthu vilakku.* And corresponding to the initial Trisagion, he gives the ancient Christian evening hymn, which originated in West Asia and is sometimes attributed to Basil the Great: "Joy–giving light". This is a song of joy for the light that dispels the darkness of the night. It raises our minds to the real Light, the Word, who by his life brings light to every man.

The revised Fenqitho offices appear as follows. At *Ramsho* a light ritual with *Phos hilaron* ("Joyful light") has been prefixed to the service; "Seeds of the Word", have been added to the first *qolo,* and *qole* 1-2 have been joined and somewhat abbreviated. This both tightens and simplifies the structure. In addition the '*enyone* (strophes) of Ps 51 and of vesperal psalms have been expurgated of anti-Jewish expressions, and the *hulolo* and *koruzuto* have been expanded[27].

In *Lilyo* the repetitions of the commemoration of saints, and of *proimion* with *sedro* are reduced, and the Gloria in excelsis, originally the chant of festive morning prayer, is used only on Sundays and feasts.

In festive *Lilyo*, a time for meditation is added at the end of the first two "watches", replacing the repetition of *qolo*, the poetic *madrosho* and the *bo'utho.*

In the place of the deacon's martial, *Stomen kalos*, a Greek acclamation, which passed into the Syriac: "Let us stand well", answered by the congregation, *kyrie eleison*, he has substituted invitatory and exhortative acclamations, "Let us lift up our hearts ....we lift them up to the Lord"

---

body as a garment he put on and also a salvation to all. This leads to the eucharistic sense of Christ's body in the hymns *"De Fide*":

Thy garment , Lord, is a fountain of healing
in thy visible dress dwells by hidden power.

Cf. MURRAY R. , *Symbols of Church and Kingdom,* pp.69-74 .

26 It is the office of *m'dabrono*. It is a title applied both to Christ and to Apostles or Bishops. Here leader is more pastoral than military in the eschatological context. Jesus is our guide and leader on the way to heaven *(kingdom)*. .(Cf MURRAY R., *Symbols of Church and Kingdom*, pp.69-74)

27 TAFT R., *The Liturgy of the Hours in East and West*, pp.243-246.

He has generally chosen the second hymn of Fenqitho, called *qolo,* in preference to the first one called *qubolo*. The prayer for the offering of incense, *'etro*, then comes after this hymn, before the *bo'utho*.

In the translation the "Acclamations before the Gospel" are an enlargement of the *zumoro*[28] of the Fenqitho which consists of a single verse of a psalm chanted with halleluiah. This enlargement adds as a counterpart a verse generally taken from the New Testament.

Similarly the *korozutho*, the intercessions that follow the proclamation of the Gospel, have been considerably enlarged. According to Fr Acharya Francis, this has been done with a view to updating these prayers in the light of the signs of the time. The prayers now show a deeper awareness of the solidarity of all peoples and of the common destiny of the human family.

Many opening prayers and prayers for the offering of incense are new pieces. These have been prepared specifically for Kurisumala's own monastic usage.

The feast of Francis Xavier, the great missionary to Asia, has been introduced by Acharya. For this he has borrowed the framework from the Common of the Confessors (Mosul Fenqitho, Vol. I, p.250). Yet much is his own composition.

The service for the Holy Name of Jesus is his own composition. It celebrates the salvific event of the revelation of the Divine Name. For this he has drawn mainly on the Bible and on the early Syriac tradition. Saints Basil and Gregory are commemorated by the Eucharistic Prayer of the Night vigil, Second watch, the watch of the saints.

In the case of Stephen the First born of the Martyrs, he has provided a Eucharistic Prayer for The First Watch.

The office for the days after the Baptism and Epiphany of our Lord is his own composition though based on material is provided by the Fenqitho. Clearly he wanted to celebrate the feast for eight full days.

For Ephrem the Syrian the MF III, p.393, gives only two 'Eucharistic prayers'. He wanted to compose a full office. For this he has drawn on the writings of Saint Ephrem and on his life, but also on the Common of the Fathers (MF I, p.213).

There is a short prayer service to commemorate the World Day of Peace kept in India on the anniversary of the death of Mahatma Gandhi.[29] When it falls on a Sunday it can be used as intercessions of the evening prayer.

Francis Acharya has added a feast of the most Christ-like Saint, universally venerated, the Messianic King, Mahabali. This is the feast of Onam, celebrated in Kerala, India.

---

28 Means song (*Zumoro*).

29 ACHARYA FRANCIS, *PHS*, Vol. II, p.632.

12. Example of Fr.Francis' Adaptation of Mosul Fenqitho

Ramšo, Sunday of Visitation of Elizabeth to Mary

Mosul edition	***PHS***
(Vol.II,pp.176-181)	(Vol.II, pp.63-69)
p.176 (implied; common intro. pr)	p.63 Common intro. pr.
prayer	*Opening prayers*
Ps 48(47)	Ps 48(47)
Greek '*enyono*'	Response
Oriental '*enyono*'	OMITTED
p.177 Evening Psalms	p.64 Evening Psalms
(Response)	Response
…………	Eucharistic Prayer
Proimion	
pp.177-78 *Sedro*	p.65⇉ not entitled *proimion & sedro*
p. 178 *Qubolo* (with Gloria)	OMITTED
'*Etro*	OMITTED
p.179 *Qolo*	Hymn(with 'Gloria' added after v.2, & 'From age' after v.3)
………	p.66 Prayer for the offering of incense (not the same as '*etro* in Fenqitho p.178)
Bo'utho	p.67 Supplication Song
p.180 *Hulolo*	p.68 Acclamation(expanded)
Gospel Lk 1:39-56	Gospel
p.181 *Koruzutho*	Intercessions(different from Fenqitho)
Prayer	p.69 Concluding prayer (different from Fenqitho)
	Trisagion
	Meditation

Though some of these prayers come from an altogether different cultural and religious tradition: Vedas, Upanishads, Bhagavad Githa, they were found to fit quiet remarkably with the ancient poetry of Christian West Asia. Thus texts from different sources have been brought together, when they were found mutually enlightening.

Conclusion

The above adaptations represent a selection of examples. "The changes do no violence to the structure, nature or genius of their Offices, nor to the Eastern liturgical Spirit. Eastern liturgical books, especially of the divine Office, are not rigid "editiones typicae", but anthologies of material to be used with a certain freedom, though always within the limits of the lived tradition. This is especially true in monastic usage. Eastern monasteries have always been jealous of their particular liturgical uses as set down in their Typika or preserved in the living oral tradition, and one can only applaud the prudent flexibility of Acharya of Kurisumala in adapting the ancient Syrian Offices to the concrete needs of a living, vibrant monastic life in the mountains of India's south west coast."[30]

30 TAFT R., *The Liturgy of the Hours in East and West,* pp.243-246.

PART FOUR

ETHICS AND DHARMA

14

Dharma as the Core Hindu Ethical Category: Semantics, Evolution, and Significance

Henry D'Almeida, SJ

Abstract

The concern of this article is to explore the semantics, evolution and the significance of the core Hindu ethical category' "Dharma." After dealing with the polyvalent and contextual nature of the term, the evolution of the category is elaborated from the Vedic times till the modern period. In the Veda,dharma is understood as cosmic and moral harmony. Upanishads identify it with Satya. Dharmahasras elaborate the sources and kinds as Sadharana and Varnashrama dharmas. It is included in Hindu axiology (Purusharthas). In the Ramayana Lord Rama is identified with the ideal of Dharma. Mahabharata speaks of it as the sustaining force of Society. In the Gita we have Dharma understood as nishkamakarma promoting Lokasangraha. Among the Six orthodox systems Purvamimamsa excusively focuses on Dharma as a Vedic imperative. Vedanta has dharma in the service of promoting soteriological concerns. Among the Modern thinkers Dayananda Saraswati elaborates eleven moral virtues. Vivekananda sees Dharma as universal love and compassion. Gandhi identifies Dharma as Ahimsa. The article concludes with the relevance of Dharma in promoting and nurturing ethics of life in the context of death dealing forces.

Key words: Dharma, purusharthas, axiology, rta, satya, sadachara, atmatushti, sadharanadharma, varna, ashrama, apaddharma, svadharma, nishkamakarma, lokasangraha, karmayoga, abhyudaya, yama, niyama, vedic imperative, categorical imperative, ahimsa.

Introduction

Dharma is the Hindu term for ethics. Morality constitutes an integral part of Hindu tradition. Its practice is directed to the goal of liberation. Even in the Scheme of Hindu axiology known as Puruśārthas it is stated first. According to Crawford 'in the depths of this single word lies an entire civilization'.[1] "Dharma is a very comprehensive term, not only does it include the social, economic, moral and biological duties of man living in society, but it is far deeper in its meaning than these duties. For to create mental and spiritual fellowship among men is the aim of Dharma."[2] In the context of present state of moral ambiguities, the purpose of this paper is to explore the meaning, evolution and significance of Dharma within Hindu tradition.

1. Semantics of Dharma

According to the famous Dharmasastra scholar P.V. Kane: "It is very difficult to say what exact meaning of the word Dharma was in the most ancient period of the vedic language. The word is clearly derived from the root 'dhr' (to uphold, to support, to nourish),[3] Term 'Dharma' defies all attempts at definition."[4] Dharma is polyvalent. We can take the views of Franklin Edgerton regarding the semantic variety of Dharma: "Dharma is propriety, socially approved conduct in relation to one's fellow men or to other living beings (animals or superhuman powers), law, social usage, morality and most of what we mean by religion all fall under this head"[5].

According to Sanskrit – Hindi Dictionary of V. S. Apte the word has the following senses:

1. Duty and following of the duties according to a sect.
2. Law, custom, tradition, order, enactment
3. Religion or moral virtues, goodness, moral acts, one of the few ideals of human existence.
4. The behavior and conduct according to the prescription of the śāstras.
5. Purity, usefulness
6. Morality, ethics

---

1 S. Cromwell Crawford, The Evolution of Hindu Ethical ideals , Arnold- Heinemann, University Press of Hawaii, 1984, introduction.

2 Benjamin Khan, The Concept of Dharma in Valmiki Ramayana, New Delhi, Munshiram Manoharlal, 1983, 23.

3 P.V. Kane, History of Dharmashastra, vol. I, Part I, Bhandarkar Oriental Research Institute , Poona, 1968, 1, 3-4.

4 Benjamin Khan, The Concept of Dharma in Valmiki Ramayana, 35.

5 Franklin Edgerton, "Dominant Ideas in the Formation of Indian culture", Journal of American Oriental Society, 62(3): 151- 156, 151.

7. Nature, temperament, character
8. Basic quality, characteristics, peculiarities
9. Conformity, similarity
10. Yājña
11. Good Company
12. Devotion, Religiosity
13. Procedure
14. Upanisads[6]

Lipner summarizes the semantics of Dharma well:

The word comes from the sankrit root 'dhr' which means to support, to undergird, to establish. Dharma, then is that which 'bears up' in some way or other. In some contexts, e.g. the social or civic, the word could well be translated by law, but not in others. Dharma can have physical, moral, social and religious connotation depending on context. Dharma is that which properly undergirds or establishes something from a certain point of view, prescriptively and descriptively, in fact one often finds that this semantic ambivalence gives an elusive meaning to a term."[7]

The rich meaning of Dharma is further illustrated by Badrinath: "Dharma means that where by whatever lives is sustained, upheld and supported. It is a secular view of life, not a 'religious' one. But it is not secularization either. It cuts across the religious- secular polarity of western thought."[8]

Thus, from the etymological perspective the word 'Dharma' means that which sustains social order.

2. Evolution of 'Dharma'

We shall trace the evolution of this significant category right from the vedic times.

2.1 Dharma in Vedic Times

In the *Rgveda* the most striking moral idea is that of Rta. Rta stands for cosmic order which includes a moral order. It is an intelligence principle that regulates the cosmos as well as the individual.[9] In fact the first products of divine fervor (tapas) were Rta and Satya.[10] In Rgveda Dharma is explicitly connected with

---

6 V.S. Apte, Sankrit Hindi Kosha, Motilal Banarsidass, Delhi, 1966, 489.

7 Julius Lipner, Hindus: Their Religious Beliefs and Practices, London, 1994, 86.

8 Badrinath Chaturvedi, Dharma, India and the World Order, Pahl – Rugenstein, 1993, 86.

9 K R Sundararajan, " Hindu Ethics" in Hinduism ed. by K L Sheshagiri Rao, Panjab University, 1997, 43.

10 Rig Veda 10.190.1 – Rtam ca satyam Cabhiddhat tapaso' dhyajayata.

Rta.[11] Rta also means an inner awareness of what is true based on the scriptural teachings and needs of the duties on hand. When this awareness expresses oneself through words and actions it becomes satya.[12] Rta represents the cosmic form of Dharma while Dharma represents the social form of Rta.[13]

According to R.N. Sharma, "Rta is the metaphysical term of the Vedic ethics. Varnadharma is the sociological basis and ashrama dharma is the psychological basis of vedic ethics."[14] Rta represents the basic truth, harmony, system or eternal moral order of the entire universe. That which is universally true is Rtam and that which is the opposite or false is termed anrtam."[15] According to A. L. Basham Rta is 'the highest flight of Rgvedic thought'.[16]

Living according to Rta was recognized as the way to a full and prosperous life:

> "Sweetly blows the breeze for one who lives according to Rta; rivers flow with sweetness for him" (Rgveda 1.90.6).[17]

According to Kane, Rta has "the rudiments of the later doctrine of the rule of Dharma."[18] Thus we see a comprehensive understanding of dharma covering inner and the outer order.

2.2 Upanisadic Dharma

Upanisads identified Dharma with Satya: "Verily,, that which is righteousness is truth. Therefore they say of a man who speaks the truth, he speaks righteousness, or of a man who speaks the righteousness that he speaks the truth. Verily, both these are the same things."[19] According to Mahānārayana Upanisad (79.7) the entire universe stands on Dharma.[20] The famous convocation address in the Taittiriya Upanisad brings out the ethical character of education: "practice virtue; neglect not the study of the Vedas."[21]

---

11 See Rig Veda 5.15.2, 5.51.2, 5.63.1, 5.63.7, 9.7.1, 9.110.41.

12 Swami Harshananda, A Concise Encyclopedia of Hinduism, Part I, Bangalore, Rama Krishna Math, 2008, 504.

13 R N Sharma, Indian Ethics, Delhi, Surjeet Publications, 1993, 56.

14 Ibid., 15.

15 I C Sharma, Ethical Philosophies of India, Jullandhar, S Nagin & Co., 1964, 71.

16 A L Basham, The Wonder that was India, New York, Grove Press, 1954, 236.

17 John M Koller, The Indian Way, Pearson Prentice Hall, Inc. 2007, 81.

18 P.V. Kane, History of Dharmashastra, vol.III, 42.

19 Br. U. 2.5.12.

20 Dharmo Visvasya jagatah Pratistha

21 Tai. U. 1.11.1 – 4.

We have the famous universal form of Dharma in the Brhadaranyaka Upanisad 1.3.28:

> Lead me from falsehood unto truth
> From darkness lead me unto light
> From death lead me unto immortality.[22]

Further Brhadaranyaka Upanisad identifies Dharma with truth. That which is justice is truth. And justice and truth are the same.[23] According to Chāndogya Upanisad, Dharma has three branches: Performance of sacrifice, study of scriptures and giving gifts. This is the first.[24] Brhadaranyaka Upanisad also extols three comprehensive virtues: self restraint, giving or self sacrifice and compassion.[25]

2.3 Dharmasastras on Dharma

The Dharmasastras and Smrtis give a detailed account of Dharma in terms of sources and kinds. According to Yājñavalkya Smrti (1.7): the vedas, smrtis, usages of goodness, what is agreeable to one's self and desire born of deliberation. These are the traditionally recognized sources of a Dharma.[26]

How does one know what is right? The following means are suggested.

1. Śruti – scriptural guidance
2. Smrti- the tradition
3. Sādācara – example of the elders
4. Ātmatusti – conscience – taht which satisfies the self[27]

---

22 Asato Maa Sad-Gamaya
Tamaso Maa Jyotir-Gamaya
Mrtyor-Maa Amrtam Gamaya

23 Tat Sreyo Rupam Asrjata Dharmam
Tasmat Dharmat param nasty- Yo Vai So Dharmah Satayam Vai Tat (he specially created the Dharma of the form of highest good.. there for there is nothing higher than that – that Dharma is verily Satya).

24 Traiyo Dharma Skandha: Yājño' dhyayanam dānamiti pratamah.

25 Damyata, datta, dayadhvam

26 Swami Harshananda, A Concise Encyclopedia of Hinduism, 507.
Śrutih Smrtih sadacarah svasya ca
Priyamatmanah samyaksakalpajah
Kamo dharamamulam idam smrtam

27 See Manu Smrti 2.6 and 2.12

Manu Smrti classifies dharma as 1) āśrama dharma 2) Varnadharma 3) Sādharanadharmas. Following are the Sādharana dharmas which could be compared to Decalogue of Moses.

1. Steadfastness (Dhairya)
2. Forgiveness (Ksamā)
3. Restraint (Dama)
4. Non Stealing (Caurya- abhāva)
5. Cleanliness (Śauca)
6. Sense control (Indriya – Nigraha)
7. Wisdom (Dhi)
8. Harmony (Vidya)
9. Veracity (Satya)
10. Restraint of anger (akrodha)[28]

Dharamasashastras also deal with the Purusarthas, various sins and expiations and also about samskaras which make one fit for the spiritual journey. According to Manu, one should abandon one's Dharma, if it ends in unhappiness or it has become hateful to the people.[29] Desire and natural material wealth must be rejected if these are contrary to Dharma.[30] Thus we see that Manu has some useful and relevant matters pertaining to societal order.

3.4 Dharma in Ramayana

Rama is depicted as the ideal man whose conduct was in perfect conformity with Dharma as taught and understood them. Rama is described by Valmiki as ' Rāmo vigrahavān dharmah (Rāma is the Dharma Personified). Rama's Dharma was 'to speak the truth and to keep up the promise given under all circumstances.[31]

According to Rāmayana, "Dharma is the cosmic order that is behind everything and is the essence of all. Dharma is order as well as an ideal." Dharma is the prime end in this world and in dharma is established truth" (Ramayana, 2.21.42).[32] Dharma is that which is prescribed by the Vedas and Dharma is that which is forbidden by them[33].

28 S. Cromwell Crawford, The Evolution of Hindu Ethical ideals. 143.

29 Manu Smrti 4.176.

30 Manu Smrti 2.224.

31 Swami Harshananda, A Concise Encyclopedia of Hinduism, 506.

32 Mariasusai Dhavamony, Classical Hinduism, Roma – Universita Gregoriana Editrice, 1982, 339.

Dharmo hi paramo loke

Dharma satyam pratisthitam (Ramayana 2.21.42)

33 Mariasusai Dhavamony, Classical Hinduism, 340.

2.5 Mahabhārata and Dharma

It is an encyclopedia of Dharma. It gives the famous definition of Dharma: Dharma is that which supports (Dhāranād Dharmam ityāhuh). There is description of Varnashrama Dharma. It extols Satya and ahimsā. It also talks of the relaxation of the well- known moral standards and norms in terms of distress and emergencies (āpad dharma). According Mahabharata, "it is dharma that destroys us when destroyed; it is dharma again that protects us when protected by us.[34]

From Gāndharis' famous words the central truths of Mahabhārata are illustrated: Where there is dharma, there is victory.[35] Further the true context of Dharma is given as: "Dharma is non- injury to all creatures; what is conducive to good, non-injury and preservation of all is dharma."[36]

2.6 Dharma in the Bhagavadgītā

The word 'Dharma' clearly stands in the context of doing one's own duty (Svadharma) sincerely: "One's own duty through devoid of merit is preferable to the duty of another well performed. Even death in the performance of one's own duty brings blessedness; Another's duty is fraught with fear (3.35).[37]

According to Gītā Dharma is righteousness, the basis of all purusārthas (18.34). Duty ordained by scriptures as per one's varna and āśrama leading to well- being in this world (abhyudaya) and highest good (nihśśreyasa).[38] Dharma is also synonymous with ātmajñāna (9.3) or karmayoga (2.40).

Bhagavadgītā identifies Kauravas with adharma and Pandavas with dharma. Gītā 16:1-3 describes the virtues as fearlessness, rectitude, purity, perseverance in the path of knowledge and discipline, charity, self control, sacrifice, study of sacred percepts, straight forwardness, doing no harm, truthfulness, equanimity, detachment, peace and no malice, compassion for all, sobriety, gentleness, modesty, guilelessness, fervor, forgiveness, steadiness, cleanliness, freedom from hatred and pride."[39]

The fundamental ethical idea of the Gītā is non-attachment. It contains the spiritual value of non-attachment with the basic factor of human activity and produces a synthesis conducive to spiritual progress. The doctrine

---

34 Dharma eva hato hanti, dharmo raksati raksitah

35 Yato dharmastato jayah

36 Ahimsarthaya bhutanam dhramapravacanam krtam

Yat syad Ahimsayuktah sah hramah (Mahabharata 12.102.12)

37 Jayadayal Goyandka Srimadbhagavadagita tattva vivecani, Gorakpur Press, 1992, 169.

38 See Bhagavadagita 4.8,18.31,1.40,7.11.

39 R De Smet and J Neuner (eds.) Religious Hinduism, Mumbai, St Pauls, 1996. 160.

niskāmakarma (disinterested actions) spiritualizes all actions and makes them a part and parcel of spiritual discipline."[40]

The theory of Gītā is that if actions are performed with the detached mind their consequences do not bind the performed. This distinctly implies that the morality of an action depends not on the external consequences but upon the inner motive".[41]

2.7 Dharma in the Orthodox Systems of Philosophy

2.7.1 Nyāya-Vaiśesika

According to Nyāya,dharma is indicated by the Vedas and justified owing to the reliability of God as the author of the Vedas.Dharma or merit is the result of good works and adharma or demerit results from evil deeds. Kanāda, the founder of Vaiśesika defined dharma as that from which one is associated with worldly success (abhyudaya) and highest good (nihssreyasa).[42] Thus dharma combines both this worldly and other worldly good.

2.7.2 Sāmkhya - Yoga

For Sāmkhya dharma is something that leads one to higher worlds and at the same time increases the predominance of satva in the mind and the body. In contrast the maximization of Dharma on Yoga's account constitutes a unique liberated state: Dharamamegha samādhi[43]. In Yoga, Dharma in the form of Yama[44] and Niyamas[45] are part of means to control the modifications of the mind which is the goal of the Yoga. Yoga tradition regards morality as justified because of its aid in controlling the mind.

2.7.3 Pūrvamīmāmsā and Dharma

According to Pūrvamīmāmsā "Dharma is the desirable goal or result that is indicated by injunctive vedic passages. Dharma means the vedic ritualistic actions leading to happiness here and hereafter."[46] **Pūrvamīmāmsā view**

---

40 K R Sundararajan, " Hindu Ethics" in Hinduism, 55.

41 Ibid., 57.

42 Viśesika Sūtras1.2: Yato' bhyudaya – niśśreya sa siddhih sa Dharamah

43 Shyam Ranganathan, Ethics and the History of Indian Philosophy, Delhi, Motilal Banarsidass, 2007, 276.

44 The Yamas re: Ahimsa (Non- violence), Satya (Truthfullnes), Asteya (Non Stealing), Brahmacarya (celibacy) and aparigraha (Non-covetousness).

45 Niyama has five elements : Sauca (cleanliness), Santosa (contentment), tapas (Penance), Svadhyaya (Scriptural study) and Isvara-pranidhana (surrender to God).

46 Pūrvamīmāmsā Sūtras 1.1.2: Codana laksano' artho' dharmah.

is de-ontological and closely resembles Kant's categorical imperative. Mīmāmsā elaborates three kinds of actions:

1. Kāmya Karmas – which has particular motive or end in view.
2. Pratisiddha Karmas – forbidden actions.
3. Nitya – naimittika Karmas – unconditional duties to be done either daily or on certain specific ceremonial occasions.[47]

2.7.4 Vedānta and Dharma

Realizing the ultimate reality Brahman is the goal of Vedānta. Thus the role of Dharma is only instrumental. According to Advaita Vedānta of Samkara (788CE- 820CE), morality leads a person to think about the self. The sphere of Dharma is only on the vyavaharika (practical) level.[48] In the Visistādvaita system of Ramanuja (1017CE –1137CE), dharma leads and contributes to moksa. 'Attending to one's de- ontic obligations is a sure means of liberation.[49] Madhva (1238 CE–1317 CE) though makes bhakti a sure means of moksa, still insists on Dharma and attending to one's daily duties.

2.8 Some Modern Thinkers on Dharma

From the beginning of the 19 century Dharma underwent significant transformations. There was an attempt to "Ethicize and universalize"[50] Dharma. We shall see the views of some modern thinkers about Dharma. Dayananda Sarasvati (1824CE – 1883CE), the founder of Aryasamaj believes in the eleven moral virtues.[51]

1. Ahimsa (non violence)
2. Dhrti (steadfastness)
3. Ksama (forgiveness)
4. Dama (Self control)
5. Asteya (Avoidance of theft)
6. Sauca (cleanliness)
7. Indriya Nigraha (control of senses)
8. Dhi (wisdom)
9. Vidya (Learning)
10. Satya (truth)
11. Akrodha (restraint of anger)

---

47 Kedar Nath Tiwari, Classical Indian Ethical Thought: A Philosophical Study of Hindu, Jaina and Bauddha Morals , Delhi ,Motilal Banarsidass, 2007, 61.

48 Shyam Ranganathan, Ethics and the History of Indian Philosophy, 340.

49 Ibid.

50 Wilhelm Halbfass, India and Europe: An Essay in understanding, Albany, State University of New York Press, 1998,333.

51 R N Sharma, Indian Ethics, 198.

According to Vivekananda (1863 – 1902 CE), Dharma is the key note of social solidarity.[52] He emphasizes the principle of universal love and compassion born out of the realization that self is the same in all beings. He stresses the Karma Yoga of the Gīta. One should perform actions and fulfill duties without attachment to the fruits there off. One can achieve salvation through moral deeds done in a spirit of detachment.[53]

Gandhi's (1869CE- 1948CE) ethical philosophy is centered on the concept of Ahimsa (Non – vIolence). According to him the Bhagavadgītā which is set up in the back ground of a battle field teaches non – violence. The battle that is mentioned is interpreted as the battle within the mind of human. The Bhagavadgītā advocates the building up of an active moral and spiritual mind.[54] For Gandhi satyagraha is an extension of the principle of non-violence. It consists of three types of positive actions.[55]

1. Non co-operation
2. Civil disobedience
3. Fasting

For Radhakrishnan (1888 CE – 1975 CE), Dharma is essentially a combination of ethics and religion. The goal of dharma, according to him, "a double object of happiness on earth and of salvation."[56] The purpose of ethics is to discipline human nature leading to the realization of the spiritual.[57]" Further Radhakrishnan brings out the relevance of ethical life. Ethical life emphasizes good will, pure love, disinterestedness and non violence as the practical code of conduct.[58]

3.0 Contemporary Significance of Dharma

The underlying principle of Dharma is: every being has a right to live and every individual has the right to order his or her life according to his or her given temperament, capacity and circumstances.[59] Sādharana dharamas as illustrated in the Dharmasastras and accepted by Dayananda Sarasvati have universal application:

---

52 Ibid., 213.

53 Swami Vivekanada, The Complete Works, Vol I, Almora, Advaita Ashram, 1947. 85.

54 K R Sundararajan, " Hindu Ethics" in Hinduism, 60

55 R De Smet and J Neuner (eds.) Religious Hinduism, 304.

56 S Radhakrishnan, Heart of Hinduism, Madras, G A Natesan & Co, 1932, 22.

57 S Radhakrishnan, Indian Philosophy, vol. II, London, George Allen& Unwin, 1923-27, 304

58 S Radhakrishnan, Eastern Religions and Western Thought, Oxford University Press, 1939,83

59 Badrinath Chaturvedi, Dharma, India and the World Order, 3

> One striking feature of Hinduism is that practice takes precedence over belief. What a Hindu does is more important than what a Hindu believes. Hinduism is not creedal. Adherence to Dharma is therefore not an acceptance of certain beliefs, but the practice or performance of certain duties which hare defined in accordance with Dharmic social stratification.[60]

The contextual structure of the Hindu approach to Ethics gives it the flexibility and adaptability necessary for thinking about bioethical dilemmas.[61] "The basic agenda of Bioethics is to prevent evil by advocating principles and proscriptions against behaviours that inflict harm to persons and are sentient creatures. Its fundamental principle is to do no harm – "himsam mā kuru". The vehicle that brings the Hindu ethics into the new world of Bioethics is the notion of Dharma… Dharma is a catalyst for changes; it preserves order in the midst of change and change in the midst of order and thereby always promotes progress."[62]

Dharma, as we have seen plays a pivotal role in the ethico-religious sphere of Hinduism. As a cosmic principle it has integrated the anthropological concerns. In the present context of many moral dilemmas once again we need to harness the ethical resourcefulness of Dharma to bear its imprint upon these issues. After all as Vyasa's succinct summary of Dharma of eighteen Puranas goes:

> Doing good to another is right
> Causing injury to another is wrong.[63]

60 Gavin Flood, An Introduction to Hinduism, Cambridge, 1996, 12.

61 S. Cromwell Crawford, "Hindu Bioethics" in Religious Perspectives in Bioethics ed. by John F Peppin, Mark J Cherry & Anna Iltis, Taylor & Francis, London, 2004, 189.

62 S. Cromwell Crawford, "Hindu Bioethics" in Religious Perspectives in Bioethics, 194.

63 Astadaśa puranesu vyasasya vacanadvayam
Paropākarah Punyāya pāpāya para pīdanam.

15

Deconstruction of Hindu Dharma: Re-Discovering the Spiritual Inner Dynamism of Dharma

George Ayyaneth, OIC

Abstract

There are serious attempts by right-wing political parties to give religious interpretations to the Hindu cultural identity and thereby deconstructing the same to suit their ideology, to procure power. Wherever there has been unholy alliance between religion and politics, it has always resulted in the downfall of the religion. Now India is going through the same painful process which the West has already gone through. Indians have not yet learned to face modernity, a lesson learned in the West only with great pain and many failures. Hindu Dharma is being subverted or deconstructed. Here, subversion or deconstruction means the destructive activities which will lead to the downfall of Hindu Dharma by Hindutva forces themselves. This deconstruction which deviates from the essence of Hindu Dharma will only alienate the coming generation from the so-called Hindu religion of which BJP claims to be the custodians. It will only help in creating a new generation that hates religion. What we need is not the political deconstruction of Hindu Dharma, but a re-discovery of the spiritual inner dynamism of Hindu Dharma.

Key words: Dharma, Hindu dharma, Sanatana dharma, modernity, Hindutva.

The *Gorakshaks* (cow-protection goons) spread unrest in India, instigating mob lynching… Groups of assailants murder innocent people alleging that they have stored, transported or eaten cow meat…The social activists, politicians, media personalities, writers, thinkers, etc., who criticize so-called nationalist political parties and their sister organisations are killed, intimidated, bullied, arrested, shouted down, trolled, etc., by labelling them as antinational or traitors of Hindu Rashtra… Media institutions are threatened through government machineries… National top educational, cultural, economic, defence and security agencies such as UGC, ICHR, NCERT, IIT, FTII, ISRO, CBFC, CBI, NIA, etc., have been filled with *Sangh Parivar* loyalist… Many social activists were arrested and the residences of social activists, such as Fr. Stan Swami SJ, were raided by Police alleging their role in Bhima Koregaon violence.

All in the name of one religion – Hindu, one religious ideology – *Hindutva*, one religious symbol – *cow*, one religious identity – *Hindu nationalism*. The undercurrent of the prevalent condition in India is intertwined with the word "*Hindu*". BJP, the political party, functions and propagates ideas in a way as if the monopoly of speaking authoritatively about the word '*Hindu*', its culture and religion, solely belongs to them. BJP, in fact, ought to thank the British colonials for giving religious attire to the word '*Hindu*'. It is the British who categorised the non-Christians and the non-Muslims into a religious group entitled Hindus. Thereby, thousands of ethnic groups, having Vedic traditions or belief in regional deities or nature worship or Buddhist-Jainist ways, were brought under the single religious label of 'Hindu'. In fact, all these categories differ widely in their beliefs and rituals. It is BJP which now enjoys the fruits of the unification of these ethnic groups which constitute around 80% of the Indian population as they were brought under a single religion by the British. Thus, BJP is playing a political game by which the cultural identity 'Hindu' is given a religious attire, thereby creating a religious majority and transforming them into a vote-bank.

The word '*Hindu*' is mentioned nowhere in Indian scriptures or literary works. Two different opinions persist among historians about its etymology. First, the Persians who shared a common ethnic identity with the Indian Aryans considered those tenants who lived across the *Sindhū* (Indus) river as '*Hindus*'. It was due to the difficulty that they had in pronouncing `*s*´ in their regional language that '*Sindhū*' became '*Hindu*'. Considering this, the word "*Hindu*" itself is foreign. Later, it was the Muslim invaders who first called the land across the river *Sindhū* '*Hindustan*'. Secondly, it is the reference to '*Saptha Sindhu*' in Rig Veda. '*Saptha Sindhū*' means the land of seven great rivers. Here, the word '*Sindhū*' is used in the sense of river. In Vedic Sanskrit the letter `*s*´ is pronounced as `h´. That means '*Sapta Sindhu*' became '*Hapta Hindu*'.

The geographical semantics of the word '*Hindu*' are found in common in both interpretations. The sense of religion is not found anywhere in ancient tradition. The settlements of nomads were always river plains. Later, as they became agrarian societies, various tribes came to be known along with the rivers and their civilizations grew. It was subsequent to this change that the people and the culture of the regions near to the *Sindhū* (Hindu) river came to be known as '*Hindu*', '*Hinduism*', '*Hindu Dharama*', etc. This culture was also shaped by the contributions made by the native aboriginals, Aryans, Persians and many other tribes who existed in these regions during various eras.

It is not in alliance with any one particular religion that the '*Hindu*' culture emerged and continues to grow. The present Hindu culture is a conglomeration of thousands of tribal traditions and ancient Vedic and Persian traditions. Owing to the absence of so-called 'modern science', during ancient times, culture was transmitted orally, through rituals, customs, arts, stories, myths, etc. The moral precepts, truths and practical guidelines in them were known as science (*sastra*). This was always susceptible to change. This is how India owns a tradition enriched with such diversity. It is ever since Sanskrit got prominence that conservatism which resists changes gradually began to tighten its clutches. Yet, the ethnic tribal culture continued to exist in its own glory by overcoming it. Under the monopoly of Sanskrit, the Hindu culture got its own shape. It was called '*Hindu Dharma*', '*Sanathan Dharma*' and so on. Even then, it never had any religious attire. Hindu dharma refers to various ways of righteous living as laid down by seekers of truth. In addition to various such ways like, Vedic, Buddhist, Jain, Parsee, Sikh, etc., Muslim and Christian cultures also joined this stream. The present Indian culture is evolved not from any one religious identity, that is, Hindu. It is like the river Ganges that flows down to the lowlands sometimes as a single entity, but usually as different streams merging and converging to make it a whole.

There are serious attempts by right-wing political parties, especially, by BJP, to give religious interpretations to the Hindu cultural identity and thereby deconstructing the same to suit their ideology, to procure power. This is in immediate and distant future, a challenge to the political existence of India as a country, a country which has its basis in the motto "unity in diversity".

Wherever there has been unholy alliance between religion and politics, it has always resulted in the downfall of the religion. The ultimate loser of this power-play of BJP and *Sangh Parivar*, misusing the identity, symbols, sentiments and traditions of Hindu Dharma for their political gains, will be Hindu Dharma, for that matter, the Hindu Religion itself. In the course of time, we will see the decline of the Hindu Religion, because of BJP's and *Sangh Parivar's* unholy game to convert 80% of the people who fall under the British invented label of Hindu religion, into their vote-bank. It is against this backdrop that we should view the *Gorakshaks'* mob lynching, the appointment of Sangh

Parivar loyalists at the top most positions in public institutions, intimidation and arrest of social activists, rewriting of India's history looking through the prism of extreme Hindutva ideologies for text books, hate speeches against Muslims, Christians and Dalits, moral policing by fringe groups of fanatic Hindu organizations, etc.

Through all these means BJP is trying to establish that they have monopolized the so-called Hindu religion. The official spokespersons of the Hindu religion now are the propagators, beneficiaries and activists of BJP party. The 'Hindu Dharma' is hijacked by the high-tech *Yogis*, *Babas, Swamis, Sanths, Mathajis* anointed by BJP and Sangh Parivar. Earlier it was not the case. The enlightened *Sanysis*, *Swamis* and *Yogis* of monasteries such as Sri Sankaracharya, Sri Ramakrishna, etc., were the true teachers, interpreters and spokespersons of ancient Hindu Dharma. Everybody looked to them for their wise teachings and their teachings were considered as the final word about Hindu Dharma. But, today, no one wants to pay heed to these learned and enlightened people who are true heirs of Hindu Dharma. Their spaces are occupied by frauds who are political puppets in the hands of BJP. These frauds have adopted the noble symbols such as saffron dress and names such as *Yogi, Baba, Mathaji, Swami,* etc. By pitching these people against their opponents, BJP is playing a political game. BJP knows that they will not get the noble, enlightened, learned, great and just people of Hindu Dharma on their side. Here, Hindu Dharma is degraded before the entire world. The world is given an impression that Hindu Dharma means 'cow vigilantism', 'Yogis with political activism', 'high-flying God-men/women', 'commercialized Yoga', 'products in the market with the name of *Rsis* (seers)', like Pathanjali, etc.

The authentic sages, yogis and swamis who lead a life moulded according to the real Hindu Dharma might be deeply wounded by seeing and hearing such things. Their silence has sunken in the political cacophony of frauds. The words of these sages are being pushed into oblivion by the clamouring created by them. BJP is dragging the Hindu Dharma to a huge historical error. These people who are apparently the protectors of Hindu Dharma are, in fact, traitors to Hindu Dharma, causing self-destruction. Wherever there has been unholy alliance between religion and politics, it has always resulted in the downfall of the religion. This is the lesson that history offers.

There was a period in Europe during which Christianity was politically utilized. In order to maintain their power, many rulers forcefully imposed rules, rituals, customs and morality upon the public under the label of Christianity. This unholy alliance caused an aversion to Christianity among the Westerners while they were going through many revolutions. This political abuse has been the reason why a group of people hated Christianity which was the life-breath and root cause of all the prosperity in the West. Many things which those political leaders have done, claiming to promote Christianity, have weakened it in reality.

It is the same historical error that the Hindu Dharma follows in India today. If those politicians insist others about what to eat, what to wear, what to say, whom to love, etc., based on Hindu religion, then it would end up in the downfall of that religion. Though there were many foreign invasions, why then Hindu Dharma could not be ravaged by those invaders? It is because Hindu Dharma had the inner dynamism of diversity, pluralism and inclusiveness. In fact, the languages, cultures, art, literature, music, etc., brought by those invaders only added to the beauty of Hindu Dharma. If this inner dynamism, freedom and spontaneity are lost, then the next generation will fall into the other extreme of counterculture. In simple terms, if somebody is out there to dictate me in the name of Hindu religion, what should be in my frying pan and what should I eat, drink, wear, what language I should speak, what kind of art and music I should make or enjoy, with whom I should make friendship and to whom should I relate, etc., then, the future generation will not only hate that religion, but also a counterculture movement will rise up against this religious fundamentalism and moral policing.

Europe has gone through this phenomenon. The seeds of counterculture in Europe were already sown in the period of Renaissance, from 14th to 17th Century. Then it got momentum by the Reformation in 16th and 17th Centuries. This counterculture got emboldened by the new discoveries, 'isms', ideologies, French Revolution, World Wars, etc., in the period of Enlightenment in 18th and 19th Centuries. Finally, in 20th Century, precisely, the 1960s, counterculture movements became an open threat to mainstream dominant culture and the Catholic Church bore the brunt of these developments. As a result, the hold of Catholic Church on people, political power and state, slowly waned and the number of churchgoers has drastically fallen. The unholy relationship between Church and political power over centuries brought about a hostile attitude towards the Church. People started questioning the misuse of religious sentiments, ethos, symbols, institutions, etc., to amass political power by religious leaders and religious dominance by political leaders. A good number of churchgoers left the Church and adopted materialism or atheism or agnosticism or ultra-secularism. These kinds of developments forced the Church to shed off all political powers from its clutches and to stay away from state politics. Where the separation of State and Religion was most efficiently enforced, that often happened through fierce and painful struggles, sometimes even reaching the verge of civil war. In almost every western European country religious intolerance, bloodshed, 'religious cleansing', extermination of religious minorities was the initial way political and religious powers dealt with those counterculture movements. The 20th century witnessed the total separation of state and religion and the loser in the end was the Church, i.e. religion.

Now India is going through the same painful process which the West has already gone through. Indians have not yet learned to face modernity, a lesson learned in the West only with great pain and many failures. Hindu Dharma is being subverted or deconstructed. Here, subversion or deconstruction means the destructive activities which will lead to the downfall of Hindu Dharma by Hindutva forces themselves. This deconstruction which deviates from the essence of Hindu Dharma will only alienate the coming generation from the so-called Hindu religion of which BJP claims to be the custodians. It will only help in creating a new generation that hates religion. What we need is not the political deconstruction of Hindu Dharma, but a re-discovery of the spiritual inner dynamism of Hindu Dharma.

Reference

Ayyaneth, G. 2016. *Indian Poetics (Kāvya Śāstra) and Narratology Towards the Appreciation of Biblical Narrative*, New York: Peter Lang.

Harrison, Peter (ed.) 2010. *The Cambridge Companion to Science and Religion.* Cambridge: Cambridge University Press.

Lipner, Julius 2010. *Hindus – Their Religious Beliefs and Practices* (2nd edition). London / New York: Routledge Taylor & Francis Group.

16

Hinduism, Dignity and Bioethics: Towards an Egalitarian Moral Concept

J. Charles Davis

Abstract

The central ideas of the human person in Hinduism are: the human is divine and the earthly life is nothing but of the wandering soul temporarily entangled in a body. The self in a human body is the only possibility to get rid of rebirths through knowledge and/or action and/or devotion in order to be united with the divine. To live a dignified life worthy of the divine is imperative for the real self to return to the divine. Hinduism speaks of three kinds of dignities: The *Upaniṣads* accord dignity to the individual self who should strive for unification with the Universal Self. The *Mānavadharmaśāstra* emphasizes the class-dependent social dignity. The *Gītā* relates dignity to the self-less action independent of class. Abortion, suicide, euthanasia and all forms of killings are direct attacks on the human (ātman that equals Brahman in the *Upaniṣads*) and are crimes against the equal moral dignity propagated by the *Bhagavadgītā* and the law of *dharma* which demands right living and universal application of moral duties.

Key words: Hinduism, Atman, Brahman, Dignity, Bioethics

1. An Overview of Hinduism

Hinduism, the major religion of India, is also called the Eternal Religion or Sanathana Dharma which means "the Eternal Law." From the historical point of view, "Hinduism is the dominant religion of the vast Indian subcontinent, and since the beginning of its history has profoundly influenced the lives and thoughts of countless millions of the Indian people from the cradle to grave."[1] From the practical point of view, Hinduism is "a complex set of interrelationships among many sorts of people, belief systems, and practices rather than a single uniformly structured, bureaucratically organized, and centrally codified religion."[2] The developmental stages in the history of Hinduism are: Prehistory or the Pre-Vedic Age up to 1500 BCE, the Vedic Age from 1500 to 600 BCE, when the roots of the religion were in the form of rituals; the Classical Age 600 BCE to 600 CE, when the Vedas[3] including the *Upaniṣads,*[4] the epics (*itihāsas*) of *Rāmāyaṇa*[5] and *Mahābhārata,*[6] and the

---

1 Nikhilananda, *Hinduism*: *Its Meaning for the Liberation of the Spirit* (Madras: Sri Ramakrishna Math, 1982) 19.

2 John Crimes, Sushil Mittal and Gene Thursby, "Hindu Dharma," in: Sushil Mittal and Gene Thursby, (eds.), *Religions of South Asia: An Introduction* (London: Routledge, 2006) 15.

3 The term *Veda* is derived from root ′vid′ which means to know. Literally it is a Book of Knowledge. See Arvind Sharma, *Classical Hindu Thought: An Introduction,* (New Delhi: Oxford University Press, 2000) 194. "The Veda is regarded by some Hindus as a timeless revelation which is not of human authorship (*apaurushya*), is eternal, and contains all knowledge, while others regard it to be the revelation of God. It was received or ′seen′ by the ancient seers (rishis) who communicated it to other men and was put together in its present form by the sage Vyāsa." Ibid. 35. There are four Vedas, namely, *Ṛg Veda, Yajur Veda, Sāma Veda and Atharva Veda*. All of them contain four sections*: Mantra or Samhita, Brāmana, Āranyaka and Upaniṣad.* The Vedas are accepted by all the orthodox systems of Indian philosophy as manuals for ethical conduct.

4 There are more than 200 *Upaniṣads.* They are philosophical texts written by several authors. See S. Radhakrishnan, trans. *The Principal Upanisads* (London: Allen & Unwin, 1968); P. Olivelle, *The Early Upaniṣads: Annotated Text and Translation* (Oxford University Press, 1998); Sharma, *Classical Hindu Thought,* 32: "The word *sad* in Upaniṣads is related to the English word ′sit′ and refers to teachings which were revealed when the students sat *up* close (*upa, ni*) to the masters."

5 *Rāmāyaṇa* depicts the life journey of Rama, one of the avataras (incarnations) of God. It portrays characters of ideal father, ideal servant, ideal brother, ideal wife and ideal king, etc. Traditionally, the authorship is ascribed to Valmiki. See Amaresh Datta, *The Encyclopaedia of Indian Literature,* Volume II (New Delhi: Sahitya Academy, 1988) 1755.

6 Datta, *The Encyclopaedia of Indian Literature,* 1755. Traditionally, the authorship of the *Mahābhārata* is attributed to Vyāsa. It has stories of philosophical nature involving human characters. *Mahābhārata* contains *Bhagavad-Gītā* (also known as Gita) with 700 verses in the present form. The *Bhagavad-Gītā* narrates the conversation between Lord Krishna and prince Arjuna at the start of the great battle of Kurukshetra between the Pandavas and Kauravas. The Pandava prince Arjuna was filled with doubt on the battlefield. Realizing that his enemies are his own relatives, beloved friends and revered teachers, he turns to his charioteer and guide Krishna for advice. Krishna explains "the four goals of human life. The essential idea in the reply which Krishna offered to Arjuna was that through the discharge

Purāṇas[7] were written and ritualism gradually took the form of philosophical thoughts. This was also the period of the reform movements of Jainism[8] and Buddhism;[9] the Medieval Age from 600 CE to 1600 CE, when six major philosophical schools (*Darśanas: Sāṃkhya, Yoga, Mīmāṃsā, Vedānta, Vaiśeṣika,* and *Nyāya* are selective commentaries on the *Vedas* including the *Upaniṣads*) and *bhakti* (devotional) traditions (*Vaiṣṇavism and Śaivism)* took a systematic form; and finally, the Modern Age from 1600 CE onwards, when the rise and fall of two great empires, the Muslim Mughal and Christian British took place.[10] The texts of the classical Hinduism (600 BCE to 600 CE) are considered to be canonical Scriptures and contain doctrines, worship traditions, social systems, cultural customs and legal codes that are common to and accepted by all orthodox schools. They have greatly influenced the social and religious life of India. They hold great respect for life of the foetus as well as of the pregnant woman, and abortion is strongly condemned. Julius J.

---

of the duties of one's station without thought of fruit one was on the way to salvation." John McKenzie, *Hindu Ethics: A Historical and Critical Essay* (Oxford: Oxford University, 1922) 125. As it is found within the *Mahābhārata,* the *Bhagavad-Gītā* is considered to be *smṛti* texts. However, it is also attributed to the fifth Veda, thus, categorizing it in the *Śruti or revealed texts.*

7 The *Purāṇas* are post-Vedic texts. They contain a complete narrative of the history of the Universe from creation to destruction, genealogies of the kings, heroes and demigods, and descriptions of the Hindu cosmology and geography. Axel Michaels, *Der Hinduismus: Geschichte und Gegenwart* ((München: Verlag C. H. Beck, 1998) 76: "Die *Purāṇas* ("Alte Geschichten") sind metrische Sanskrittexte, die Mythen, Kosmologien, Heiligenlegenden, Genealogien, Rechtliches, Wissenschaftliches und Historisches enthalten… Nach indischer Tradition gibt es 18 große (*mahāpurāṇas*) und zahlreiche kleine Purāṇas (*upapurāṇas*), wobei die Zählungen variieren."

8 Helmuth von Glasenapp and Shridhar B. Shrotri, *Jainism: an Indian religion of salvation* (1999) 24: "Jainism was established by Parsva around 800 BC." Paul Dundas, *The Jains* (2002), 17: "Jainism ... flourished in the Ganges basin from around the eighth or seventh centuries BC." J. L. Brockington, *The Sacred Thread: A Short History of Hinduism,* second edition (New York/New Delhi: OUP, 2000), 80-82.

9 Buddhism developed in North India between the mid-6th and the mid-4th centuries BCE. See Axel Michaels, *Der Hinduismus,* 53-54; Brockington, *The Sacred Thread: A Short History of Hinduism,* 76-80.

10 See John Crimes et al, "Hindu Dharma," 20-28. Some authors have a slightly different division of five historical ages. For example, Arvind Sharma classifies broadly into four periods: Vedic and pre-Vedic Hinduism: third millennium to *circa* eighth century BCE, Classical Hinduism: eighth century BCE to *circa* 1000 BCE, Medieval Hinduism: 1000-1800 BCE and Modern Hinduism: 1800-. Arvind Sharma has added Darśanas (philosophical literatures of six schools) to the classical period. See Katherine K. Young, "The Discourses on Hindu Medical Ethics," in: Robert B. Baker and Laurence B. McCullough, (eds.) *The Cambridge World History of Medical Ethics* (New York: Cambridge University Press, 2009), 175-184, 175.

Lipner, of Indo-Czech origin and Professor of Hinduism and the Comparative Study of Religion at the University of Cambridge, remarks with authority:

> [T]here can be no doubt that it was from about 600 B.C.E. to 600 C.E. that the definitive Hindu view on the moral status of the unborn in connection with abortion was developed and established. This is a view which, in its essentials, remained unchanged through succeeding centuries and which continues to exert a powerful influence on the contemporary Hindu mind.[11]

The classical Hindu view relies on Sanskrit texts ranging from 600 BCE. to 600 CE. The Sanskrit texts of this period are the two widely accepted canonical scriptural forms of *Śruti* texts and *Smṛti* texts.[12] *Śruti* texts include the four *Vedas*, the *Brāhmaṇas,*[13] the Āranyakas,[14] and the *Upaniṣads*. *Smṛti* texts include the *purāṇas* and the great epic *Mahābhārata* (and within it, the *Bhagavad-Gītā*) - a compendium similar to the *purāṇas,* some writings on law - *Dharmaśāstras*[15]and Dharmasūtras,[16] and the (Āyurvedic) medical works of

---

11 Julius J. Lipner, "The Classical Hindu View on Abortion and the Moral Status of the Unborn," in: Harold G. Coward, Julius J. Lipner and Katherine K. Young, (eds.) *Hindu Ethics: Purity, Abortion, and Euthanasia,* 41-70 (Delhi: Sri Satguru Publications, 1991) 42. Though Lipner points c. 600 BCE as the beginning of the classical period, many authors begin it from the year c. 800 B.C.E.

12 The *Śruti* (that which has been heard) texts hold primacy as revelatory texts, and *Smṛti* (that which is remembered) texts are the second level tradition of scriptures. "When any school of thought refers to *Śruti to prove something it implies that it refers to a form of divine knowledge which cannot be questioned." Narendra Nath Bhattacharyya, A Glossary of Indian Religious Terms and Concepts (New Delhi: Manohar Publishers, 1990²) Reprint 1999, 150.*

13 The *Brāhmaṇas* are commentaries on four *Vedas.* They contain the guidelines for rituals. See Arvind Sharma, *Classical Hindu Thought,* 194. Axel Michaels, *Der Hinduismus,* 70: "Den Schlussteil der Brāhmaṇas bilden die Āranyakas („Wildnistexte"), die jene Ausdeutungen des Opferrituals enthalten, die wegen ihrer magischen Gefährlichkeit außerhalb der Siedlungen gelehrt werden mußten."

14 The Āranyakas discuss sacrifices and proper performances of rituals (orthopraxy). See Arvind Sharma, *Classical Hindu Thought,* 194. 197.

15 *Dharmaśāstras* are primarily a product of the Brahmanical tradition and represent the elaborate scholastic system of an expert tradition. See Patrick Olivelle, *Manu's Code of Law: A Critical Edition and Translation of the Mānava-Dharmaśāstra* (New York: Oxford UP, 2005) 64. *Dharmaśāstras* were taken by the early British colonial administrators to be the law of the land for Hindus in India. See J. Duncan M. Derrett, "The Administration of Hindu Law by the British," *Comparative Studies in Society and History* 4/1 (1961) 10-52.

16 *Dharmasūtras* are the first four texts of the *Dharmaśāstra* traditions and they focus on the idea of *dharma*, the principal guide by which Hindus strive to live their lives. The *Dharmasūtras* are written in concise prose, leaving much up to the educated reader to interpret. See Patrick Olivelle, *Dharmasūtras: The Law Codes of Ancient India* (New York: Oxford World Classics, 1999) xxi.

Caraka and *Suśruta Saṃhitās*.[17] These literatures have great significance for the religious life of most Hindus. The six major schools (*Darśanas*) focus on themes such as *Bráhman*,[18] Ātman,[19] *Dharma*,[20] *Mokṣa*[21] (liberation), etc. The *Advaita Vedānta* School is monistic and the only reality for it is *Brahman*. Everything else is illusion. Acharya Ramanuja taught a qualified monism in his *Vishishtadvaita*. *Sāṃkhya*, *Yoga, Vaiśeṣika*, and *Nyāya* systems are dualistic and affirm that the universe is composed of matter and spirit. The *Mīmāṃsā* system is basically atheistic. These six schools belong to the orthodox Hinduism due to their acceptance of the authority of the *Vedas*. They are also called *āstika schools of thought or simply darshanas* (*Darśanas*). There are three *nāstika or* heterodox schools of thought in the Indian philosophy. They are Buddhism, Jainism and the *Cārvāka system (a sceptical materialist school)*. They are called *nāstika or heterodox for the reason that they do not accept the Vedas as authoritative. Buddhism and Jainism were reform movements of Hinduism but became independent religions. Hinduism, Jainism and Buddhism have common themes, such as, ahiṃsā, dharma, mokṣa,* etc.

---

17 The Caraka Saṃhitā is an early Āyurvedic (Medical) text on internal medicine and is believed to be the oldest of the three ancient treatises of Āyurveda (science of longevity), whose texts are probably written from 3rd B.C.E to 6th C.E. It is also considered the fifth Veda of the Hindus. The Suśruta Saṃhitā is the other medical treatise in antiquity. Suśruta was a surgeon. See I. A. Menon and H. F. Haberman, "Dermatological writings of ancient India," *Medical History* 13/4 (October 1969) 387-392, 387-8.

18 *Bráhman* is the Ultimate Reality or Supreme God or Soul or Spirit in the philosophies of India. see Arvind Sharma, *Classical Hindu Thought,* Chapter III, on "Brahman," 43-61, 46.

19 *Ātman* is the individual self. The term is also used to identify with the "Universal Spirit," the Absolute Brahman. (Atman is generally translated into English as the true "Self"). See the phrase: "die Lehre von der Identität von Einzelseele (Ātman) und dem Absoluten (Brahman)," in: Axel Michaels, *Der Hinduismus,* 70. See Madeleine Biardeau, *Hinduism: The Anthropology of a Civilization,* Richard Nice (trans.) (New Delhi: Oxford University Press, 2002) 17: "Ātman (literally, ʹselfʹ), i.e. the immortal principle which, in man, is destined to be released from the body, from all embodiment, and at last attains perfect identity with *Brahman*."

20 *Dharma* is understood as the universal principle of law, order, harmony, and truth. In the *Ṛgveda*, the belief, that a natural justice and harmony pervades the natural world, becomes manifest in the concept of *ṛta,* similar to the Western concept of *logos*. While *ṛta* is understood as the natural order, *dharma* is considered to be the foundational truth of the universe. Thus, *dharma* is understood as the duty of human beings to achieve the *ṛta* in the universe. *Dharma* is the socio-ethical vehicle to maintain law and order of the universe in the *Upaniṣads*. For an elaborative study: see Arvind Sharma, *Classical Hindu Thought,* Chapter XIII "Dharma," 101-108. Gavin Flood, *An Introduction to Hinduism* (New Delhi: Foundation Books, 1998), Ch. 3 on "Dharma," 51-74.

21 *Mokṣa* is the ultimate aim of human life. *Mukti* and *nirvāna* are different terms used for *mokṣa. while Nirvāna or Nibbhāna* is specifically used in Buddhism. See Chapter XV on "Mokṣa," 113-118, in: Arvind Sharma, *Classical Hindu Thought,* 113f.

Among the six philosophical schools of thoughts, the *Sāṃkhya* system had a dualistic understanding of humans as component of *puruṣa* and *prakriti* (ātman/self and matter/body), both of which are real but ontologically distinct; while one of the *Vedānta* schools, *Advaitavedānta* (not two but one) considered ātman (namely, Brahman Himself) resides in an illusionary (*māyā*) world of existence, and liberation consists in realizing that the human (ātman) is nothing but Brahman Himself; another school *Viśiṣtadvaita* (qualified non-dualism), had a similar non-dualistic ontology that humans are real but distinct manifold expressions of Brahman; yet another school *Dvaitavedānta* (not one but two) considered Brahman and ātman(s) eternally distinct (the one eternal Self and the many selves). The non-Vedantic medieval schools of *Vaiṣṇavism, Tantrism and* Śaivism understood the self to be either the Lord Himself or the replication of the Lord. Within *Vaiṣṇavism there are different schools with differences in understanding the nature of ontologies between the Lord and the self. Similarly, within* Śaivism there were monistic (Kashmir) Śaivism and dualistic Śaiva Siddhānta – viewing the Lord and the soul eternally distinct. *Vaiṣṇavism and* Śaivism were mostly devotional.[22] Depending on the nature of ontologies of ātman in relation to Brahman, these schools had different epistemologies and ways of life to attain liberation.

In the modern period since 1600 CE, having experienced Christianity and Islam, scholars reformed and revolutionized Hinduism. Main reformers were Rammohan Roy (1772-1833), Dayananda Sarasvati (1824-1883), Paramahamsa Ramakrishna (1836-1886), Swami Vivekananda (1863-1902), M. K. Gandhi (1869-1948), Rabindranath Tagore (1861-1941), etc. Their aim was to revive the richness of Hinduism and safeguard it from external influences. Rammohan Roy tried to restore and purify Hinduism by returning to the Upanishads. His movement Brahmo Samāj fought against icon worships and condemned immoral practices of child-marriage and widow-burning (*suttee, Witwenverbrennung). Similarly, Dayananda Sarasvati advocated radical reforms, such as eradication of child-marriage. His movement Ārya Samāj promoted Sanskrit as significant and Hindi as national language, was not open to pluralism and advocated an aggressive Hindu nationalism. The movement reconverted Muslims and Christians back to Hinduism through the ceremony of purification (*śuddhi). Ramakrishna and Vivekananda advocated the Hinduism of tolerance and accommodation. They saw innate divinity in all human beings. Their philosophy was fundamentally *vedantic. Vivekananda brought Hinduism to the world at par with Christianity, Islam, Judaism and Buddhism. Vivekananda's Neo-Vedānta vision of Hinduism is pluralistic and accepts all religions as aspects of one Truth. Vivekananda held a spiritual superiority of the East. He did accommodate the material, technological and*

22 See Gavin Flood, *An Introduction to Hinduism*, 103-249.

scientific superiority of the West into his school for mutual learning. He was strong proponent of karma yoga, the yoga of action or good works. Vivekananda is to be credited for a great number of schools, colleges and hospitals run by the Ramakrishna Mission throughout India.[23]

2. The Hindu View of the Human Person

The *Ṛgveda* mentions Manu as "the first man, the ancestor of the human race..."[24] The *Upaniṣads* call the ultimate highest Being by different names: *Puruṣa* (Person), *Brahman* (the Absolute), and *Ātman* (Self). These terms are synonymously used to denote humans (*puruṣa* and *ātman* "Thou art *Brahman*") as well. "This whole world is Brahman; the self is Brahman," opens the *Māṇḍūkya Upaniṣad* (1.1). Brahman (God) is the eternal Being as well as the source of the whole universe, including the innermost self (*ātman*) of humans. The Śatapatha Brāhmaṇa (10.6.3) makes a distinction between the *Brahman* and the created world: "Brahman is called ′this whole′ world, which also transcends the world, for it is ′greater than the great′ and indwells the human soul..."[25] The central ideas of the human person are: the human is divine; the earthly life is nothing but of the wandering soul temporarily entangled in a body. The self in a human body is the only possibility to get rid of rebirths through knowledge and/or action and/or devotion in order to be united with the divine. To live a dignified life worthy of the divine is imperative for the real self to return to the divine.

The microcosmic human being (puruṣa, pronounced as purusha, meaning human) is a prototype of the macrocosmic Puruṣa (Brahman). Cosmos and humans are nothing but the dismembered body of Puruṣa. The One (*Brahman*) and the Many (cosmos and humans) are essentially the same.[26] The term Ātman is used in the *Vedas* to denote the animating principle (soul), which is the

---

23 See Gavin Flood, *An Introduction to Hinduism*, 250-273.

24 S. Cromwell Crawford, "Hindu Ethics for Modern Life," in: S. Cromwell Crawford (ed.), *World Religions and Global Ethics* (New York, Paragon House, 1999) 113.

25 Mariasusai Dhavamony, *Classical Hinduism.* Vol.15, Documenta Missionalia (Rome: Editrice Pontificia Universita Gregoriana, 1982), 56. See also *Katha Upaniṣad* 2.20: "The Self, smaller than small, greater than great, is hidden in the heart of that creature. A man who is free from desires and free from grief, sees the majesty of the Self by the grace of the Creator." Quoted from: Max Müller, *The Upanishads*, Part 2. In: *Sacred Books of the East 15* (1879),11. Hereafter *The Sacred Books of the East* as *SBE*. *Chāndogya Upaniṣad* 3.14.3-4; "He is my self within the heart, smaller than a corn of rice, smaller than a corn of barley, smaller than a mustard seed, smaller than a canary seed or the kernel of a canary seed. He also is my self within the heart, greater than the earth, greater than the sky, greater than heaven, greater than all these worlds." Quoted from: Max Müller (trans.), *The Upanishads*, Part 1. In: Max Müller (ed.), *Sacred Books of the East* 01 (Oxford: The Clarendon Press, 1879) 48.

26 *Ṛgveda* 10.90.1-7. See Dhavamony, *Classical Hinduism,* 115.

replica of Brahman (the same Puruṣa Himself). Thus, the human body and soul have their origin in Brahman. The soul, after death, goes back to Brahman to dwell and to live higher.[27] All created beings are parts of *Brahman,* and ātman is the soul that connects Brahman (God), humans and cosmos. The *Upaniṣads* use the term puruṣa synonymously "for the individual human person, Cosmic Person, the Personal Absolute, the impersonal Ground of the objective universe and of the human persons."[28] The World-Soul (ātman) is *Brahman* Himself. The universal spirit of *ātman* is present in every human *(puruṣa)* being, hence the human life is divine, divine in its fullness. Human life becomes fully one with the divine when it attains union with the *Paramātmā.*[29] This cosmic view of Hinduism calls for the coexistence of all creatures under the Vedic principle of *Vasudev Kutumbhakam*, meaning, "the Universe is One Family." This principle is a guiding ethos for Hindus to seek universal harmony through acceptance and tolerance, as the divine is present in every human being and no one is superior or inferior to the other and all are spiritually united.

The *Upaniṣads* describe four stages: "*waking*, *dream*[-ing] *sleep*, *deep sleep* (i.e. dreamless sleep in which the soul becomes temporarily one with Brahman and enjoys a corresponding unsurpassable bliss), and finally the fourth state in which the disappearance of the manifold universe and the union with Brahman takes place in *perfect consciousness*."[30] The epic *Mahābhārata* believed in "a Supreme Being, called Person (Puruṣa) or Self (*Ātman*) or the Absolute (*Brahman*), who emanates and reabsorbs both material nature (*prakṛti*) and souls (puruṣas)."[31] The ātman [person or self] which is an eternal principle in reality, is entangled with the body which produces actions of both good and bad. The immortal soul (ātman) becomes incarnate in bodily existence and goes through various stages of the life-cycle until it becomes united again with *Brahman*. The *Bhagavad-Gītā*, the pearl texts of the

27 *Ṛgveda* 10.58.1. Quoted in: Dhavamony, *Classical Hinduism,* 117.

28 Dhavamony, *Classical Hinduism*,124.

29 *Paramatman* or *Paramātmā* is the Absolute Atman or Supreme Soul or Spirit (also known as *Supersoul* or *Oversoul*) in the Vedanta and Yoga philosophies of India. He is the ultimate Brahman.

30 Dhavamony, *Classical Hinduism*, 125. Italics mine. G. Gispert-Sauch, in his article "The Concept of Person and Indian Thought," in: A. Amaladass, Sebasti L. Raj, Jose Elampassery (eds.), *Philosophy and Human Development,* 27-43 (Madras: Satya Nilayam Publications, 1986) 31, says that the traditional Indian metaphysics "believes that consciousness is found in all living beings," and "conceives of the basic substratum of the human being as rational, or preferably as conscious, or of the nature of the knowledge: *cit, caitanya, svayamjyotiṣtva* (self-luminosity)." See also R. De Smet, "Persona, Anima, Atman," *The Philosophical Quarterly,* XXX: 4 (1958) 259-60; R. De Smet, *The Indian Understanding of Man* (Presidential Address to the History of Philosophy Section of the 44th Session of the Indian Philosophical Congress, 1970), Reprinted in *Indian Ecclesiastical Studies* 3 (1971) 5-9.

31 Dhavamony, *Classical Hinduism*, 128.

Mahābhārata, states that the individual self is immortal, static, timeless and eternal and "is indissolubly connected with a given human personality when it transmigrates from body to body."[32] Through greed, hatred and ignorance of mind (a constituent of the body), the ātman is alienated from the *Brahman* and is subjected to the *Samsara,* the wheel of birth and rebirth.

The human being is essentially a spiritual self (*ātman* or soul) without any connection with the empirical body. The spiritual self is either identical with or partly an attribute of the Absolute Being (Brahman). In the spatio-temporal sphere, the self is imprisoned in the material body. The new body of the psychosomatic self depends on the kind of action performed in the previous birth. It is called the law of *karma,*[33] that leads to the cycle of rebirth (*saṁsāra*). The concept of *karma* is important to understand Hindu ethics, as *karma* has direct effect on human lives. A human being becomes what he does. The law of *karma* does not compromise the free will.[34] The law of *karma* does not mean a predetermination. There is human will and freedom which can change one's own *karma.*[35] The soul of a Hindu is said to be wandering on earth entangled in a material body seeking liberation from the bondage of *karma* and the cycle of rebirth *samsara.* If the individual soul (ātman) gets rid of this condition, it will return to its original stage, i.e., become identical with or similar to or one with *Brahman.* This is the basic understanding of the human condition and salvation in Hinduism. Hinduism does not consider the present bodily life as negative, since only in and through a life in the human form is a soul capable

32 Dhavamony, *Classical Hinduism*, 130.

33 *Karma* literally means action. The law of karma is a doctrine, according to which all actions, good and bad, produce consequences in the life of the person who acts. See "karma," in: Narendra Nath Bhattacharyya, *A Glossary of Indian Religious Terms and Concepts,* 81. Arvind Sharma, *Classical Hindu Thought*, Ch.XII: "Karma," 98-102.

34 Rambachan writes that "the law of karma emphasizes free will and insists upon responsibility. If my past actions have led to my present condition, then by control of my present actions, I will be able to influence my future condition. Karma places the responsibility squarely on our shoulders since it does not propose a power outside ourselves which is responsible for our individual and collective destinies." A. Rambachan, *The Hindu Vision* (India, Delhi: Motilal Banarsidass 1992) 21. Further a scholar in Hinduism, Sivananda gives an analogy of bowman and arrow from the Vedantic literature, "The bowman has already sent an arrow and it has left his hand. He cannot recall it. He is about to shoot another arrow. The bundle of arrows in his quiver on his back is the Sanchita, the arrow he has shot is Prarabha and the arrow which is about to shoot from his bow is Agami. Of these, he has perfect control over the Sanchita and the Agami, but he must surely work out his Prarabdha. The past which has begun to take effect he has to experience." Swami Sivananda, *All about Hinduism* (Shivananda Nagar: Divine Life Society, 1988), 75.

35 Sivananda says, "The supremacy of free will is not compromised by the Law of Karma. You can make your karma what you choose. You can rise to a very high state of perfection. You can become Indian, you may become a perfect Yogin. You can change your character, thoughts and action." *All about Hinduism,* 77.

of pursuing liberation. Liberation is either to be totally identical or to be united with the Brahman or to participate in the bliss of the Lord (*saccidānanda).* There are at least three different paths *(margas or yogas)* to liberation through action *(karma),* knowledge *(jnana)* or devotion (*bhakti).* Through one of these *margas* or together, a Hindu may attain liberation *(mokṣa)* from clutches of bondage while living (*jīvanmukti*) or after death (*videhamukti*). A liberated Hindu attains salvation and is never born again after death.

There are four aims of human life (*puruṣārthas)*: *artha* (success/wealth), *kāma* (passion/desire), *dharma* (virtue/righteousness) and *mokṣa (salvation or liberation or self-perfection).* The ultimate aim (*mokṣa)* of a Hindu is the union with Brahman, while the other three aims of life, namely, *dharma, artha* and *kāma* are centered on earthly life. To pursue the aims of life (*puruṣārthas*), every Hindu passes through four stages (**āśramas**) of life: i) student (*brahmacārya*); ii) householder (*gṛhasthya*); iii) forest-dweller (*vānaprastha*); iv) hermit (*sannyāsa*). Hindu ethics (dharma) speak of three essential duties: i) **Āśrama-dharma**; ii) *Varṇa-dharma*; iii) *Sādhāraṇa-dharma.* The **āśrama-dharma** refers to personal duties through the four stages of life. The *varṇa-dharma* means the duties of the individuals towards the community. The *sādhāraṇa-dharma* is the duties of humans to all members of the human community and the cosmos. When values, duties and rights are in conflict, the common good (*s***ādhāraṇa-dharma**) takes precedence over the individual good (**āśrama-dharma**) and the community good (*varṇa-dharma*). Thus, *sādhāraṇa-dharma* defines the boundaries of other *dharmas.* Generally, preserving of life is to be given precedence over individual and community ethics, for the self is superior to ethics. However, the *Bhagavad-Gītā*, which is held highly by Hindus as the sacred text dealing with real-life dilemma,[36] teaches that the practice of *dharma* leads to salvation, even if it involves violence in war. Dharma stood above *ahimsa* in cases of self-defence.[37] However, the sacredness of human life is always held high. There are scriptural references in the *Manusmṛti*[38] to

36 Brockington, *The Sacred Thread*, 56.

37 Brockington, *The Sacred Thread*, 56ff.

38 *Manusmṛti is one of the Dharmaśāstras.* It is generally known as the Laws of Manu and mentions the *dharma* of the four social classes. Known also as *Mānava-Dharmaśāstra,* it is the most important and earliest metrical work of the *Dharmaśāstra* textual tradition of Hinduism. It was first translated into English in 1794 by Sir William Jones, an English Orientalist and judge of the British Supreme Court of Judicature in Calcutta. [Jones′ translation is available online as *The Institutes of Hindu Law or The Ordinances of Manu*, Calcutta: Sewell & Debrett, 1796.] The text is a discourse by Manu, the progenitor of mankind to a group of seers, or rishis, who beseech him to tell them the "law of all the social classes" (1.2).

the *varṇa*[39] (caste) system. However, modern Hindu philosophers, such as, Swami Harshananda, Arvind Sharma and Mahatma Gandhi, interpret it as a mere social stratification. Swami Harshananda says: "The fourfold varṇa system goes back to the *Ṛgvedasaṃhitās* (vide 8.35.16.7; 1.10.8.7.) itself. To make a living by choosing a profession as per one's desire and aptitude is a common phenomenon seen in all civilized societies. It is the duty of the society to provide suitable opportunities for its members to choose and pursue those vocations that agree with their nature. This is the philosophy behind the varṇa system. The Vedas, including the *Puruṣasūkta (wherein this fourfold division of the society has been enunciated very clearly) have only recognized its existence and not created it.*"[40]

Mahatma Gandhi said that the caste system "has nothing to do with superiority and inferiority," but is "a healthy division of work based on birth ... It is purely a question of duty... He who performs the duty of a Brahmin will easily become one in the next incarnation."[41] As Crawford notes, "it was not long before the original class structure was replaced by the law of heredity, and an ironclad caste system took on all marks and trappings of superiority and inferiority in respect to food, clothing, language, ceremonials, social intercourse, marriage, and occupation."[42] However, the existence

---

39 Varṇa literally means colour ("Farbe"). It is associated with "Kastengruppe." Varṇa refers to the categorization of the Hindu society by four classes. Four or chatur varṇas are mentioned in ancient texts in the following descending order: *Brāhmins* (priests); *Kṣatriyas* (warriors and rulers); *Vaiśyas* (agriculturists and merchants); *Śūdras* (service providers and artisans). People outside the four varnas were considered outcastes or untouchables. *Varna-ashrama-dharma* meant the duties of four varṇas. See A. A. Macdonell and A. B. Keith, *Vedic Index of Names and Subjects,* 1, 3rd Reprint (Delhi/Varanasi/Patna: Indian Texts Series, 1967) 247sqq.

40 Swami Harshananda, *An Introduction to Hindu Culture: Ancient and Medieval* (Bangalore: Ramakrishna Math, 1998) 20. He says, "In the early Vedic period, this division of labour might have taken place on voluntary basis. ... In course of time, each of these varṇas – from brāhminas to the sūdras – acquired hierarchical superiority over the succeeding ones. Though this was a natural process based on guṇa (aptitude) and karma (vocation chosen as per that aptitude), it was more a general rule and an ideal one at that. Hence, birth in a varṇa became an easier and a more practicable principle to fix up the varṇa of that individual. This was the beginning of the jāti or the caste system wherein the varṇa got automatically fixed by birth (jāti = birth)" (21). See also Arvind Sharma, *Classical Hindu Thought: An Introduction,* 166-167.

41 M. K. Gandhi, *Young India* (September 22, 1927): 12-3-25, 23-4-25. Though varṇa-dharma had much to do with the division of labour according to four groups in the Vedic times, it got into a discriminative class system somewhere down the history. There is no unanimous explanation. Nevertheless, the caste system prevails in today's India with discriminative aspects due to socio-political and economic factors and cultural beliefs.

42 S. C. Crawford, *Hindu Bioethics for the Twenty-first Century* (Albany: State Uni of NY Press, 2003), 18.

of four *varṇas* originally did not dilute the moral significance of all human beings. Social stratification does not cancel out the fundamental human rights. Personal (*svadharma*) and universal (**sādhāraṇa-dharma**) duties, values and virtues were to be practiced by all irrespective of their belongingness to any caste (*varṇa*). *Varṇa-dharma* did not contradict with the fundamental principle of right to the life even if it mattered the life of a member of a lower caste. At the level of morality, everyone was considered equal. Social untouchability of the outcastes has been abolished in India by law through Article 17 of the Constitution since 1950.[43]

According to Hindu worldview, one needs to be more holistic and realistic in executing dharmic duties. It is more than mere observance of the *Moralität.* As Rambachan says, "in Hindu mythology, the symbol of dharma is the bull, whose four feet are truth *(satya),* purity *(sauca),* compassion *(daya)* and charity *(dana).* While there is no infallible way of determining dharma, a pure mind, intent on truth and blessed with compassion and charity, is the most reliable guide in our quest for it."[44] When there was the question of personal survival involving the intrinsic worth of human life, even *Manusmṛti* (which has been attributed by many to be the cause for the caste system) said that a hungry person could steal[45] food when all other measures failed. Likewise, the *Dharamśāstras* permit perjury to save life as an act of dharma. The cardinal virtues of Hinduism are: *ahiṃsā (non-violence), satya* (truth)*, asteya* (non-stealing)*, brahamacarya* (abstinence)*, and aparigraha* (non-greed).[46]

---

43 The purity measures of food and places, like temple-worship, have been practiced at the level of social and religious interactions. Of late, people from lower castes are permitted to enter the temple and offer pujas. There are attempts to abolish the caste system itself constitutionally. Justices Dalveer Bhandari and A. K. Patnaik of the Supreme Court of India advocated that "'untouchability' which is a symptom of the malaise of Casteism cannot be eradicated without the abolition of the Caste-system itself afflicting Indian Society." See "Abolition of Untouchability in India." Retrieved on 24.08.2018 from https://indianpeoplescogress.worpress.com/2015/02/15/abolition-of-untouchability-in-india/.

44 Rambachan, *The Hindu Vision*, 19.

45 See Crawford, *Hindu Bioethics,* 27. This is similar to the idea of Cardinal Frings (1887-1978) who spoke in his *Silvesterpredigt* (Köln: 31. December 1946): "Wir leben in Zeiten, da in der Not auch der einzelne das wird nehmen dürfen, was er zur Erhaltung seines Lebens und seiner Gesundheit notwendig hat, wenn er es auf andere Weise, durch seine Arbeit oder durch Bitten, nicht erlangen kann." Dieser Akt von "Mundraub" und "Kohlenklau" wurde "fringsen" genannt. Frings aber sagt weiter: "Aber ich glaube, dass in vielen Fällen weit darüber hinausgegangen worden ist. Und da gibt es nur einen Weg: unverzüglich unrechtes Gut zurückgeben, sonst gibt es keine Verzeihung bei Gott." See Ute Becker, *Die Chronik: Geschichte des 20. Jahrhunderts bis heute,* (Gütersloh/München: Wissenmedia Verlag, 2006), 333.

46 *Manusmṛti* 10: 63. See Alexander P. Varghese, *India: History, Religion, Vision and Contribution to the World* (New Delhi: Atlantic Publishers and Distributers P. Ltd., 2008), 246-247.

All Vedic or Upanishadic or Vedantic or Śaiva Siddhāntic or Tantric understanding of anthropology considers humans to reflect the Brahman or the Lord Himself, and there is divine presence in everyone. The sanctity was always held high without compromise. The sacredness of human life prohibited abortion. The fundamental ontology of the human being as God Himself or as a part of God did not find any compromise at any time of the history of Hinduism. In this regard, Hinduism appears to be a logical and synchronized religion despite having many different sects or traditions or schools within. There is divinity in all human beings, and liberation means the identification or union with the Brahman, though differences do exist regarding the nature of the union with the Supreme Lord, Brahman.

In Vedic traditions and later Hindu systems, there is a firm faith in the inviolable eternal cosmic-moral order *Ṛta*. The word *ṛta* stands for the unerring order found in the universe. It is the cosmic-moral order and the regulative law in the universe. As Radhakrishnan says, "Hinduism recognizes the rule of law not only in outward nature, but also in the world of mind and morals. *Ṛta* manifests itself equally in nature and human society."[47] An ethical life will lead to liberation. *Ṛta* is the order harmonizing gods and humans and enjoins a set of moral principles to be followed by humans in their social conduct. One such important principle is the principle of *satya* (truth). *Ṛta* entails *satya* (truth) as a moral value to be followed by humans in thought, speech and action. Thus, the idea of sin is primarily viewed as transgression of *ṛta* and alienation from gods and fellow humans. As Illa Ravi explains, "while *ṛta* fosters and preserves life, *anṛta* or transgression of the law, it is believed, leads to decay and death which is called *nirriti*."[48] In the post-Vedic period, the concept of *dharma* became the foundational ethical category and took over from the organic unity of *ṛta,* and shifted more toward the human dimension.[49] Dharma, the Sanskrit word, simply means "to hold," and signifies "that which upholds or embodies law, custom, and religion; and is analogous to the concept of 'Natural Law' in Christian ethics."[50] "*Dharma* holds together the universe and its laws, inanimate and living beings, and human beings and

47 Radhakrishnan, *The Hindu View of Life*, (London: Allen and Unwin Ltd, 1927), 73.

48 Illa Ravi, *Foundations of Indian Ethics: With Special Reference to Manu Smṛti, Jaimini Sutras and Bhagavad-Gita* (New Delhi: Kaveri Books, 2002), 45.

49 While *ṛta* is the natural order, *dharma* is the foundational truth of the universe. *Dharma* is the human duty to achieve *ṛta* in the universe. It is the socio-ethical vehicle to maintain law and order, harmony and unity. See Swami Bhaskarananda, "Hindu Ethics," (Chapter XII) in: *The Essentials of Hinduism: A Comprehensive Overview of the World's Oldest Religion* (Chennai: Sri Ramakrishna Math, 1998) 97-102.

50 Crawford, *Hindu Bioethics*, 11.

society in which they live."[51] *Dharma* is expressed through rites of passage in the human body by way of patterning human behaviour and its transformations over time through maturation to eventual death. Body is the center of human development and *dharma* is the vehicle to attain salvation as emphasized by D. M. Levin:

> Religion is a tradition of rituals which bind and fasten the body: it binds us to the performance of special tasks, special postures, gestures and movements; it dedicates the body to the incarnation of a spiritual life, promising that the body's careful adherence to such strict regulations will not be experienced, in the end, as its restriction, but rather, on the contrary, as its dream of health, well-being and liberation.[52]

Contrary to the assertions of the materialists, "a human being is the conglomeration of several parts, apparently different from one another, but acting cohesively for a common purpose, that of the jīvātman or the individual soul (a conscious entity) inhabiting them. They are: the physical body including the sense-organs, the faculty of speech, the mind and the spirit. … It is a balanced development and harmonious combination of all the limbs and faculties that conduces not only to the health of the body but also to the well-being of the personality as a whole."[53] Swami Bhaskarananda enlightens: "The body is the primary instrument to practice religion or dharma. The body therefore has to be taken care of. Hindu scriptures also teach that the body is the temple of God, because the soul or the indwelling Divine Self resides in it."[54] Purity of body is held high in Hindu culture.

In the popular usage, *dharma* means duty or justice or morality. Sivananda tells us that, "anything that helps to unite all and develop pure divine love and universal brotherhood is Dharma. Anything that creates discord, split and disharmony and ferments hatred is Adharma."[55] The whole creation is interconnected and interdependent under the umbrella of *dharma*. *Dharma* is

---

51 S. Rama Rao Pappu, "Hindu Ethics," in: Robin Rinehart (ed.), *Contemporary Hinduism: Ritual, Culture and Practice,* Ch. V, 155-178 (Oxford: ABC-Clio, 2004) 162.

52 D. M. Levin, *The Body's Recollection of Being* (London: Routledge, 1985) 180ff. See Gavin Flood, "Rites of Passage," in: Paul Browen (ed.), *Themes and Issues in Hinduism* (London/Washington: Cassel, 1998) 254-276. Gavin Flood notes ("Rites of Passsage," 258): "There are of course gender issues here, in that male and female bodies are constrained by *saṃskāras* in different ways or by different, gender-specific, rites, but throughout India, women have undergone rites of passage based on oral or folk (*laukika*) traditions." See also V. K. Duvvury, *Play, Symbolism and Ritual: A Study of Tamil Brahmin Women's Rites of Passage* (New York/Oxford: Oxford University Press, 1991) 102; J. Leslie, *(Roles and Rituals for Hindu Women* (London: Pinter Publishers, 1991), 1.

53 Harshananda, *An Introduction to Hindu Culture*, 7.

54 Bhaskarananda, *The Essentials of Hinduism*, 187. (Sharīramādyam khalu dharmasādhanam)

55 Sivananda, *All about Hinduism*, 38.

the cosmic law that maintains the eternal order of the universe. Hindu ethicists believe that ""the nature of things" is fixed and unchangeable, and therefore dharma grounded in the nature of things is eternal."[56] Sivananda says: "Dharma is the heart of Hindu ethics. God is the center of Dharma."[57] *Dharma* cannot be violated by non-human animals but by humans who are endowed with free will. As Rinehart notes, "does the sun ever violate its dharma to rise in the east? Does the cow ever violate its dharma to be gentile? … It is only the human beings who, because of their free will, sometimes choose to violate their dharma."[58] While *dharma* could mean a virtue or cosmic law or moral order or anything that is ethical, it is a human duty to observe *dharma* and maintain cosmic, social and moral order in the world.

3. The Dignities of the Human Life

3.1. Sanctity = Dignity of the Individual Self

The *Upaniṣads,* the *Manusmṛti* (the Law of Manu) and the *Bhagavadgītā* suggest that "human dignity in Hinduism is an ambiguous and perhaps even paradoxical concept: on the one hand, all living beings (not solely human beings) are thought to possess *inherent* dignity, but on the other hand we find that in the social realm dignity appears in *degrees*."[59] The *Upaniṣads* contain two fundamental doctrines in a dialogical form: "the teaching of ātman and brahman – explaining the identity of Self and Universal Whole – and the doctrine of reincarnation or metempsychosis."[60] The self, ātman, is everywhere and one with all things, the Whole, essentially with "*brahman* – the life power which suffuses the universe and is the ground of all material things."[61] The Hindu view towards human life is very positive and sacrosanct. The sanctity of life is an essential element in Hindu worldview that considers the human as sacred and as a living creature with a moral value. Every human life is essentially sacred because all creatures are manifestations of *Brahman*, the Supreme Being. *Īśa Upaniṣad (also known as Īśāvāsya Upaniṣad) begins with the statement, "isavasyam idom sarvam," (verse 1.1.), meaning that the whole universe is the dwelling place of Brahman. According to the Bṛhadāranyaka Upaniṣad* (1.4.10), "everything that is, is Brahman." The *Chandogya Upaniṣad* (v. 6.8.7) of the Sāmaveda has one of the *Mahāvākyas* (Great Pronouncements

56 Pappu, "Hindu Ethics," 166.

57 Sivananda, *All about Hinduism*, 37.

58 Quoted in: Pappu, "Hindu Ethics," 166.

59 Jens Braarvig, "Hinduism: The Universal Self in a Class Society," in: Marcus Düwell, Jens Braarvig, Roger Brownsword and Dietmar Mieth (eds.), *The Cambridge Handbook of Human Dignity* (Cambridge: Cambridge University Press, 2014) 163-169, 163.

60 Braarvig, "Hinduism: The Universal Self in a Class Society," 163.

61 Braarvig, "Hinduism: The Universal Self in a Class Society," 163.

or Statements), namely, "*Tat Tvam Asi*," which means, "Thou art that," signifying that the Ultimate Reality, the *Brahman,* the Individual *Self* (*jiva*), and the *Ātman* are identical. The *Māṇḍūkya Upaniṣad* (1.2) of the *Atharvaveda* has another *Mahāvākya,* "Ayam Atma Brahma," which means "this Self (*Ātman*) is Brahman."[62] The *Mahāvākyas* or Great Sayings state clearly that God is present in every human being. The presence of Brahman makes human life sacred. This understanding is akin to the Christian belief that the human being is created in the very image and likeness of God (Gen. 1:28). Therefore, irrespective of their caste, by the fact of the presence of Brahman, every (*Ātman*) human being is sacred and deserves special reverence and honour. Sanctity is accorded from the very beginning of every human life from conception, when ***ātman***, the replication of Brahman, enters in it. That is why, to protect progenies and celebrate their sacredness, Hindus have a number of *saṃskāras* (sacraments) "for sanctifying the body, mind and intellect of an individual."[63] Unlike the Christian sacraments only after birth, Hindu sacraments begin right at the conception of life. Antenatal and postnatal *saṃskāras* are part and parcel of Hindu life.[64]

> The affirmation of the fundamental divinity of the human being makes it the object of special reverence and respect. All forms of violence towards human beings, therefore, go against the true spirit of Hinduism. Fundamentalism and religious intolerance leading to atrocities against others in the name of God and religion are negations of one of the cardinal principles of the Hindu religion. More than a temple, mosques and churches, the human being is the living temple of God. To desecrate this temple by thought, word or deed is indeed to commit sacrilege against the one true God known by different names.[65]

The *Nine Beliefs of Hinduism,* a tract published by the Himalayan Academy of San Francisco states, "Hindus believe that all life is sacred, to be loved and revered, and therefore practice *ahiṃsā,* or nonviolence."[66]

62 *Īśa Upaniṣad* 1.1. in: *SBE*, 1.1.310; *Bṛhadāranyaka Upaniṣad* (4.10), in: *SBE*, 15.2.88; *Chandogya Upaniṣad,* 6.8.7, in *SBE*, 1.1.101; *Māṇḍūkya Upaniṣad,* 1.2. in: S. Radhakrishnan, *The Principal Upanishads,* 1968; R. Panikkar, *The Vedic experience: Mantramañjarī: an anthology of the Vedas for modern man and contemporary celebration* (Delhi, Varanasi, Patna: Motilal Banarsidass, 2001), 697–701.

63 R. Pandey, *Hindu Saṃskāras* (Delhi: MLBD, 1969) 16.

64 Laale, "Embryology and Abortion in Indian Antiquity," 248, footnote 8. For the ritual aspects of the antenatal *saṃskāras,* see R. B. Pandey, *Hindu Saṃskāras. Socio-Religious Study of the Hindu Sacraments* (Delhi, Varanasi, Patna: Motilal Banarsidass, 1969), 48-77.

65 Quoted in: *Varghese, India: History, Religion, Vision*, 245-46.

66 Available at [http://www.himalayanacademy.com/basics/nineb/]. Retrieved on 24.08.2018. They cite a number of classical texts: For example, *Mahabharata* XVIII:116.37-41: Ahimsa is the highest dharma. Ahimsa is the greatest gift. Ahimsa is the highest self-control.

Destruction of any life was considered as an offence or *hiṃṣa.* Abortion would be a *hiṃṣa* – an injury done to the embryo.[67] Katherine Young notes, "This idea [*ahiṃsā], along with the importance of human life provides the opportunity to work out karma.* Hindus should protect a fetus, because sheer living allows bad karmas to come to fruition, thereby improving destiny. The moral and spiritual dimensions of human life, of course, improve destiny even more."[68] Traditional Hinduism had a consistent stance with regard to respect for all human life. Every life was sacred and sacrosanct from the moment of conception. Love of life and all the elements which go to make life meaningful and ethical was a predominant characteristic of Hindu thought.

Human beings, other living things and gods are not in essence distinct selves: "When a human being intuits his true self – ātman – he becomes one with *brahman*: he manifests *brahman* as his true self, becomes one with the Universal Whole. This Universal Whole, however, is par excellence present in the priestly class, the brahmin (in Sanskrit, *brāmaṇa).*"[69] Salvation does not depend on the (im)moral character of one's actions (karma). It is ultimately a union with the *brahman*. Until the human attains the enlightened knowledge of his real self, s/he repeatedly dies and is physically reborn along with meritorious and unmeritorious karmas:

> The wise one – he is not born, he does not die; he has not come from anywhere; he has not become anyone. He is unborn and eternal, primeval and everlasting. And he is not killed, when the body is killed. If the killer thinks he kills; If the killer thinks he is killed; Both of them do not understand. He neither kills, nor is he killed (*Kaṭha-Upaniṣad*: 2, 18, 19).

Hinduism cannot consider the human bodily life negatively, because precisely the human bodily life is the only means to attain salvation. The killing

---

Ahimsa is the highest sacrifice. Ahimsa is the highest power. Ahimsa is the highest friend. Ahimsa is the highest truth. Ahimsa is the highest teaching. They indicate the fundamental Hippocratic Oath of "Do no harm." Mit der hinduistischen Ethik verbindet man vor allem das Prinzip *ahiṃsā* im Sinne der Gewaltlosigkeit und des Respekts vor dem Leben. Aus diesem Prinzip ergibt sich dann auch folgerichtig wie die Wertschätzung des Menschen, zumal das Leben selbst göttlichen Ursprungs ist.

67 See Julius J. Lipner, "On Abortion and the Moral Status of the Unborn," 59.

68 Katherine K. Young, "The Status of the Fetus in Scriptural Hinduism," in: *Der Umgang mit vorgeburtlichem Leben in anderen Kulturen.* 51-62. Tagungsdokumentation, Jahrestagung des Nationalen Ethikrates 2003 (Berlin: Nationaler Ethikrat, 2004) 55. See also Katherine K. Young, "The Discourses on Hindu Medical Ethics," 175-184; Harold G. Coward, Julius J. Lipner and Katherine K. Young, (eds.) *Hindu Ethics: Purity, Abortion, and Euthanasia* (Delhi: Sri Satguru Publications, 1991); Katherine K. Young, "Euthanasia: Traditional Hindu Views and the Contemporary Debate," in: Harold G. Coward et.al, *Hindu Ethics* (Delhi-India: Sai Satguru Publications, 1991) 71-130.

69 Braarvig, "Hinduism: The Universal Self in a Class Society," 164.

in the above cited text does not refer to the killing of an innocent person but to actions in war. It only refers to the fact that the soul, not the body, is the real self. That is why, a wise man is able to achieve liberation from the circles of rebirths by a supreme knowledge of the self through asceticism and meditation. The concept of dignity in the *Upaniṣads* consists in attaining salvation through union with the Universal Self, *Brahman*. It is an individualistic dignity. Concomitantly, dignity is not a social or legal affair.[70]

3.2. The Graded Class-Dependent Social Dignity but Equal Moral Dignity before Law

The *Mānavadharmaśāstra* or *Manusmṛti,[71] which stems from a period later than the Vedas, speaks of a mythical figure Manu, the wise law-giver, who teaches the universal laws, which express that "dignity is dependent on social status."*[72]. Manu received the universal laws from the creator, the Self-Existent Lord (*svayaṃbhūr bhagavān*), who created four distinct social classes among humans together with the world: "For the growth of these worlds, moreover, he produced from his mouth, arms, thighs, and feet, the Brahmin, Kṣatriya, the Vaiśya, and the Śūdra" (I: 31). There are demarcations in the society: "These castes are hierarchically ordered: the priests form the class all others have to serve; the warrior aristocracy provides the king; the military and government officials; the traders and farmers come thereafter; the lowest class is made up by the servants and slaves. All classes have their own and very strict codes of conduct; ... The wisdom of the Veda, the traditional sacrificial hymns and the foundation of all rites, is accessible to all except the lowest class; which means slaves and servants cannot partake in any socially respected activity."[73]

Social discriminative stratifications deprived opportunities and entered into the religious life, too: "it [also] means that those belonging to lower classes will have difficulty in achieving liberation from the round of rebirth, the unification with *brahman*: the life of the man of learning or the aristocrat is regarded as 'purer' than those of people belonging to lower classes – although *in principle* every individual possesses basic dignity, from the perspective of the social system dignity comes in degrees."[74] The concept of *karma* is invoked to justify the strict class distinctions: "The situation in which a person finds himself is wholly dependent on his past actions: differences, privileges

70 Braarvig, "Hinduism: The Universal Self in a Class Society," 165.

71 See P. Olivelle, *Manu's Code of Law: A Critical Edition and Translation of the Mānavadharmaśāstra* (Oxford: Oxford University Press, 2005).

72 Braarvig, "Hinduism: The Universal Self in a Class Society," 165. See L. Dumont, *Homo Hierarchicus: Essai sur le système des castes* (Paris: Gallimard, 1966).

73 Braarvig, "Hinduism: The Universal Self in a Class Society," 166.

74 Braarvig, "Hinduism: The Universal Self in a Class Society," 166.

and hardships of various sorts are explained and justified on the basis of the idea that there are products of one's previous lives."[75] The class in which a person is born is his own responsibility. Class distinctions are reflected in social relationships, marriages, law and legal proceedings. Punishments for moral transgressions, social crimes and unlawful behaviour were applicable to members of all castes as a form of *purification* but are socially *graded* in accordance with the social class. For example, the punishment of a brahmin for the crime of murder is milder than that of the lower classes.[76] The moral value of any human life is same but the punishments to the offender varied according to the castes. In the modern Indian legal system, gradations in punishments do not exist anymore. Everybody is considered equal before the law.

3.3. An Egalitarian Moral Concept of Human Dignity

The *Bhagavadgītā* (lit. Song of the Lord), also called simply *Gītā,* is a small book within the great epic *Mahābhārata* that stems from the last millennium BCE, is foundational basis for the later Hindu religious thought. The *Bhagavadgītā* supersedes the positions of the *Upaniṣads* (wholly unrelated to laws/duties) and the *Mānavadharmaśāstra* or *Manusmṛti* (solely in terms of class-dependent norms):

> [I]n the *Gītā,* we find an account of dignity which integrates the aim of unification with God and the practice of sacrifice with the concept of moral action. To become united with God, to find salvation from the circle of rebirth, is to do one's duty as a sacrifice to God: only when one renounces all personal gain, is motivated purely by devotion to God – doing one's duty because it is one's duty – may an action be truly valuable and dignified.
>
> The *Gītā* grants a religious identity and dignity to the individual, regardless of the class to which he (or even she; the text is written in gender-neutral terms) belongs – provided that duties are performed from pure motives, from devotion, and are not in any way inspired by personal gain.
>
> It is only in the *Gītā* that dignity becomes something resembling an egalitarian moral concept: dignity is related to self-less action and in that quality is independent from class.[77]

The *Gītā* emphasizes that "actions committed in order to find liberation from the circle of rebirth are sufficient to unify one with God but only those actions which are truly self-less will let the individual participate in the divine

75 Braarvig, "Hinduism: The Universal Self in a Class Society," 166.

76 See Braarvig, "Hinduism: The Universal Self in a Class Society," 166.

77 Braarvig, "Hinduism: The Universal Self in a Class Society," 167, 168.

essence. Only then is one freed all *dharmas*, duties and laws,"[78] as its text by a divine incarnation says: "Be Me-minded, devoted to Me; Worship Me, revere me; And to Me alone shalt thou go; truly to thee I promise it – (because) you art dear to me. Abandoning all (other) duties, Go to Me as thy sole refuge; From all evils I thee Shall rescue: be not grieved!" (XIII: 65-6). The *Bhagavadgītā* is historically credited for the ground of religious rights of each individual, while it emphasizes the littleness of the human existence compared to the greatness of the truly divine.

3. The Hindu Understanding of Dignity

Human dignity is an immense inferred theme in the Indian traditions of Hinduism (ca. 2500 BCE), Jainism (b. 6th cent. BCE), Buddhism (b. 5th cent. BCE.) and Sikhism (b. 15th cent. BCE). In these religions, humans are fully developed persons from the moment of conception. Fundamental to the Indian traditions is the notion of Karma and the belief in rebirth that each person is repeatedly reborn so that the soul may be purified until it is ultimately able to attain liberation from this world and salvation in the next world.[79] Marriage, progeny and sacredness of human life are held high. In fact, everything that exists is sacred and deserves protection. Humans have the highest form of consciousness and thus have duties towards other creatures including humans. The idea of dignified position of humans is found in all these religions, though the term human dignity itself may be an alien in these traditions that entered Indian legal traditions through interaction with the Western world of philosophy and politics. There are three kinds of dignities in Hinduism:[80]

> In the *Upaniṣads*, … dignity is related to the individual self who should strive for unification with the Universal Self, where dignity lacks a social or moral connotation.
>
> In the *Mānavadharmaśāstra,* the social dimension of dignity is strongly emphasized in the sense that the concept becomes class-dependent (although in principle all who achieve liberation from the circle of rebirth command respect).
>
> In the *Gītā,* ... dignity becomes something resembling an egalitarian moral concept: dignity is related to self-less action and in that quality is independent from class.
>
> All in all, we can say that, in the Hindu tradition, dignity appears as an ambiguous and even paradoxical concept; sometimes it appears as an

78 Braarvig, "Hinduism: The Universal Self in a Class Society," 168.

79 Radhakrishnan, *The Principal Upanisads,* 113-145; Harold Coward and Tejinder Sidhu, "Bioethics for Clinicians: 19. Hinduism and Sikhism," *Canadian Medical Association Journal*, 163:9 (2000) 1167-1170.

80 Braarvig, "Hinduism: The Universal Self in a Class Society," 168.

inherent attribute of the individual, sometimes it is dependent on social class, and sometimes a concept related to moral action but is in that quality strongly religious. Taking these traditions together, we see that a type of accentuated individualism coexists with a social system which is programmatically unequal, showing us that a particular anthropology, which ascribes dignity to humans and animals alike, does not necessarily create social conventions that promote the principle of inherent and equal dignity of all human being.

While we might have adequate reasons to challenge the caste system and the inequalities of dignity of humans, the egalitarian moral concept of the inherent dignity of the all creatures proclaimed in the *Bhagavadgītā* has already something unique and substantial to contribute to bioethics. In the moral sense, all humans are equal. Caste-dependent social statuses are purely external and functional.

4. Hindu Bioethics

Abortion, suicide, euthanasia and all forms of killings are direct attacks on the ātman (that equals Brahman in the *Upaniṣads*), and are considered against the equal moral human dignity propagated by the *Bhagavadgītā* and the law of *dharma* which demands right living and universal application of moral duties. The exceptions happen only in self-defence. Crimes create rupture in the sacred ātman as well as in the social harmony. Termination by abortion sends the soul not only of the victim but also of the offenders back into the karmic cycle of rebirth.[81] Suśruta, the surgeon of the early centuries of the common era, known as "Father of Surgery" differentiated the spontaneous abortion (miscarriage) from induced abortions. The former is understandably unavoidable but the later were severely punishable. The *Suśruta Saṃhitā* (3rd to 4th cent. CE) is an authoritative classical text dealing with medical issues with references to another original text from the 2nd or 3rd cent. BCE. This seminal medical document has a section called "The Foetus Astray" (*mūḍhgarbha*) under which there is a chapter titled "Cikitsāsthāna" which deals with the eventuality of aborting the foetus. The chapter begins with the text that "there is nothing as difficult as the delivery of a foetus astray in the womb, for here….

81 See Harold and Sidhu, "Bioethics for Clinicians: 19. Hinduism and Sikhism," 1168; Harold G. Coward, Julius J. Lipner and Katherine K. Young, *Hindu Ethics: Purity, Abortion and Euthanasia* (Albany, NY: University at Albany, State University of New York Press, 1989) 10-11; ; H. Willer Laale, "Embryology and Abortion in Indian Antiquity: A Brief Survey," *Indian Journal of History of Science Vol. 31, No. 3 (1996): 233-258;* Azariah, H. Azariah D.R.J. Macer (eds.), *Bioethics in India. Proceedings of the International Bioethics Workshop in Madras: Biomanagement of Biogeoresources*, 16-19 Jan 1997, University of Madras (Christchurch (NZ): Eubios Ethics Institute, 1998); See J. Charles Davis, *The Ethics of Human Embryonic Stem Cell Research: Proposals for a Legal Framework for India* (New Delhi: Atlantic Publishers and Distributors P. Ltd. 2014) 230-249.

the job must be done ′by feel′... by one hand, without injury to mother or foetus (if possible)."[82] It continues, "if the foetus is alive, one should attempt to remove it from the womb of the mother (alive)."[83] However, the safety of the mother and the unborn must be kept in mind while performing the act. The physician was advised to save both live child and mother with great care and with the chanting of mantras. If the foetus is already dead (*mṛte garbhe*), then it may be removed by cutting (and dismembering, if necessary; *sūtra* 9),[84] but surgery is forbidden when the foetus cannot be safely delivered, "For if (the foetus) be cut one would harm both mother and her offspring. In an irredeemable situation, it is best to cause the miscarriage of the foetus, for no means must be neglected which can prevent the loss of the mother."[85] Only in unavoidable situations or in extreme cases of a medical problem where the mothers' life was in danger and the life of the mother had to be weighed against that of the foetus, an induced abortion or removal of the foetus was permitted.[86] For this reason, the king had to be informed to avoid subsequent charges of homicide.[87] Abortion was thus permissible only as a last resort to save the life of the mother. Suśruta tolerated the destruction of dead or poorly positioned foetuses for the sake of saving the endangered mothers. He performed caesarean operations to save the unborn living children in cases of difficult labour. He removed surgically the living unborn child from the womb of a dead mother.[88] Throughout his work, the lives of both mother and the unborn in the womb are highly respected and are given supreme protection. This rare exception in extreme cases gives more weight to the argument of the moral worth of the unborn. Careful deliberations such as these by an authority like Suśruta should be treated with due consideration.

Notwithstanding the legislation of the Medical Termination of Pregnancy Act (MTPA) of 1971: "For Hindus and Sikhs [Jainas and Buddhists as well] the single most important ethical consideration surrounding the start of life is their belief in karma: that the fetus is not developing into a person but, rather,

82 Quoted in: Lipner, "The Classical Hindu View," 49.

83 Quoted in: Lipner, "The Classical Hindu View," 49.

84 Quoted in: Lipner, "The Classical Hindu View," 49.

85 Quoted in: Lipner, 50, *sūtra* 10-11.

86 Suśruta, *The Suśruta Saṃhitā*, 2.8.9, in: K. K. Bhishagratna (trans.), *The Suśruta Saṃhitā* 2, The Chowkhamba Sanskrit Series 30 (Varanasi: Chowkhamba Sanskrit Series Office, 1963) 2, 58-60. See Laale, 246, 257.

87 Katherine K. Young, "Medical Ethics through the Life Cycle in Hindu India," in: Robert B. Baker and Laurence B. McCullough, (eds.) *The Cambridge World History of Medical Ethics* (Cambridge, New York, et. al: Cambridge University Press, 2009), 101-112, 103.

88 Ibid. Laale, "Embryology and Abortion in Indian Antiquity," 246, 257. See also P. Ray, H. Gupta and M. Roy, *Suśruta Saṃhitā: A Scientific Synopsis,* (New Delhi: Indian National Science Academy, 1980) 22.

is already a person from the moment of conception. Abortion at any stage of fetal development is thus judged to be murder. However, abortion is accepted by Hindus and Sikhs [Jainas and Buddhists as well] if essential to preserve the life of the mother."[89] Unfortunately, the religious prohibition of abortion is overridden by the cultural preference for sons. There are, however, couples who overcome cultural bias against female babies by the strong religious belief in the sanctity of human life. The sex-ratio imbalance with more men and less women among Hindus and Sikhs in India, especially in the states of Punjab and Haryana, indicate a high rate of selective foeticide of female offsprings. Female foeticide is a serious issue and shows a clear gap between religious precept and social practice. This is a moral crime that further perpetrates gender inequality. The religions have a duty to enlighten their followers. On implications of female foeticide, a social activist Sundaramma says:

> While female foeticide is bad in itself, the fact that millions of girls are 'missing' in India has profound human and social implications. If the decline in CSR (child sex ratio) continues for another 20-30 years, the number of marriageable females will be far less than that of the marriageable males. This will lead to the disappearance of the dowry problem and the old practice of giving and taking a bride price will come back into vogue. Polyandry (a woman having more than one husband at a time) may also emerge. Since monogamy is the ideal in India, many men may be required to embrace celibacy. The imbalance in sex ratio may increase violence, including rape, against women. With many men remaining unmarried, prostitution will increase substantially.[90]

The law of *karma* cannot be misused to justify abortion, foeticide, suicide and euthanasia as fate or predestinations similar to social conditions. The Hindus of the classical period were not unaware of such objections. Caraka countered such objections by answering,

> If all life-spans were fixed (willy-nilly by the power of *karma*, abortion notwithstanding), then in search of good health none would employ efficacious remedies or verses, herbs... oblations... fastings.... There would be no disturbed, ferocious, or ill-mannered cattle, elephants... and the like... no anxiety about falling from mountains or (into) rough, impassable waters; and none whose minds were negligent... NO

89 Harold and Sidhu, "Bioethics for Clinicians: 19. Hinduism and Sikhism," 1170; Harold Coward, "World Religions and Reproductive Technologies." in: *Social Values and Attitudes Surrounding New Reproductive Technologies,* Vol 2. (Ottawa: Royal Commission of New Reproductive Technologies, Research Studies, 1993) 454-463.

90 P. Sundaramma, "Does Abortion Law abet Female Foeticide?" *The Hindu* (May 27, 2012). In 2015, there were more than 7.2 million reported abortions besides illegal abortions. see Wm. Robert Johnston, "Historical abortion statistics, India." [www.johnstonsarchive.net]

> VIOLENT ACTS, NO ACTIONS OUT OF PLACE OR UNTIMELY (SUCH AS ABORTION) …
>
> For occurrence of these and the like would not (freely) cause death if the term of all life were fixed and predetermined. Also, the fear of untimely death would not beset those creatures who did not practice the means for fending off fear or untimely death. Undertaking to employ the stories and thoughts of the great seers regarding the prolongation of life would be senseless. Even Indra could not (choose to) slay with his thunderbolt an enemy whose life span was fixed.[91]

Hindus of the classical period made the distinction between "timely" death caused by nature, and "untimely" death caused by humans in the form of abortion, foeticide, infanticide, homicide, suicide and euthanasia.[92] Further, Hinduism would not accept projects such as reproductive cloning, embryonic stem cell research, transhumanism, gene editings and germline altering technologies that are direct attacks on human life and the Brahman Himself. The prime aim of Hindus is to attain liberation and not to get caught up in *karma* endlessly. Since the life in human form is the precious opportunity for the stored (*prārabdha*) *karma* to come to fruition and be liberated, abortion, suicide, and euthanasia or any form of killing except in self-defence or in defence for the security of nation were considered morally wrong by causing an untimely death. If predetermination were to be given as a reason for the untimely death of a person, there would be no place for free choice of human actions, which Hindus believed was necessary in maintaining *dharma*. The

---

91 M. G. Weiss, "Caraka Saṃhitā on Karma," in *Karma and Rebirth in Classical Indian Traditions*, ed. W. D. O´Flaherty (Berkeley: University of California Press, 1980), 95.

92 See Lipner, "The Classical Hindu View," 57; Katherine Young "Euthanasia: Traditional Hindu Views and the Contemporary Debate," 71-130. She writes that the self-willed death (*mors voluntaria religiosa*) was prevalent in traditional Hinduism (Vedic and Upanishadic times), though there was a great appreciation for a long life of hundred years (p.77ff). Jainism was the first to formalize and legitimate the practise of *mors voluntaria heroica* (e.g. in wars) – as a kind of *mors voluntaria religiosa*. (p. 88). Buddha condemned suicide (or self-willed death?) (p. 89). At the time of Mahabharata *mors voluntaria heroica* was highly held as *dharmic,* it takes a fighter into heaven if he died in war (p. 95). In the case of conflict, defensive warfare (*varṇaāśrama-dharma*) took precedence over ahimsa (***sādhāraṇa*-dharma**) (p. 96). The *Bhagavad-Gīta* (8: 5, 6) takes a stand against premature renunciation of action and self-willed death (p. 100f). It disapproves of starving the body (17: 6). The *Manu* (6.31, 49) is ambiguous, but appreciates the liberatated one while living (*jīvanmukta*) to continue to live till natural death occurs (p. 101f). Since the 10th century AD, the religious self-willed death is under criticism (p. 108ff). The *Indian Penal Code* written during the British Raj *condemns suicide inclusive of mors voluntaria religiosa* (p. 113f). Even for a comatose, incompetent person, euthanasia is not permitted (p. 116ff). The Indian Parliament passed a bill in 1987 against *suttee* which became punishable under the law (p. 119).

classical texts do not suggest that they believed in a discriminative law of *karma*, rather used it in the good sense of the term *karma* demanding socio-ethical responsibility for one´s actions. Modern secular India has, through the political separation of the State from religions, abolished discriminations in law and legal proceedings, though the caste system continues to prevail in the social and cultural areas of life. The strict distinctions of the social class do not affect the moral considerations in today's India, though discriminations might exist outside the legal contexts. Law is equal to all. Everyone is equal before the law.[93]

93 Through interactions with the worlds of different socio-political cultures and religions the discriminative caste system will sooner or later, along with its crude institutions, disappear.

17

Holistic Managerial Strategy: Hindu Religious-Ethical Roots to New Workforce Management

Jijo James Indiparambil, CST

Abstract

A high-quality organizational management strategy, beyond its corporate structure, adopts more cooperative labour-management relations. It provides a competitive advantage to the organization to become beneficial for all its stakeholders. In the contemporary Indian business context, the residual traces of ancient religious (and secular) wisdom significantly influence the management policies and approaches, amidst the global convolutions. This article argues for an ethical managerial treatment that goes beyond the materialistic rationality of management and seeks to identify the ethical roots of Indian (Hindu) religious and philosophical thoughts - a holistic management approach - that largely contributes to a new-fangled strategy. The holistic managerial strategy extracted from the Hindu religious traditions focuses on individuals as the unit of analysis for moral judgments, giving employees a significant place, valuing their dignity as human persons. This marks the significance of a humanistic perspective linking altruistic and benevolent behavioural tendencies in workplace and management ethics. This new humanistic-ethical perspective with a holistic managerial strategy provides a significant contribution to the effort to navigate the complexities of individual and organizational management to fetch better industrial relations.

Key words: *Workforce management, holistic management, religious ethics, humanistic approach, Early Hindu thoughts, organizational culture*

Introduction

Organizational management is an adequate, considerate strategy to fulfil unique needs of an organization in order to make it beneficial for all stakeholders. It is a process of effectively leading and directing a company to achieve its objectives, using or controlling its assets and resources beyond its corporate structure. It implies strategies to resolve issues and develop solutions that move a business closer to its desired mission and vision. It relates, however, to a coherent approach to human resource management and encompasses a set of interrelated policies (with ideological and philosophical orientation), forming a business-focused approach to manage people for competitive advantages.[1] These integrated assumptions and beliefs influence the way and purpose of different managerial processes and come to determine factors such as the nature, values, needs and approaches to management. In the contemporary Indian business context, the residual traces of ancient religious (and secular) wisdom significantly influence the management policies and approaches, amidst the global convolutions. After categorizing the dominant modern workforce managerial approaches, this article argues for an ethical managerial treatment that goes beyond the materialistic rationality of management. It then seeks to identify the ethical roots of Indian (Hindu) religious and philosophical thoughts, which we identify as a holistic management approach that largely contributes to a new managerial strategy. This prefers humanistic approach of treating people to its counterparts, commodity approach or machine approach, and directs towards an altruistic, philanthropic workplace behaviors. Hence an adequate assertion of organizational members not merely as "cogs in the machine" but as human beings, as individuals and as social beings.

1. Developments in Modern Workforce Managerial Approaches

Organizational management is the process of using organizational resources, both material and human, to achieve its objectives and goals through planning, organizing, staffing, and leading.[2] It is the art, or science, of achieving goals through people by strategic planning, coordination, directing and controlling of complex decision-making process, ensuring greater productivity and continuous improvement.[3] It possesses the competence and effectiveness in

---

1 *A. Ramaraju, "Human Resource Management Philosophy,"* International Journal of Management *6, no. 1 (2015): 776.*

2 *Andrew J DuBrin,* Essentials of Management, *9th ed. (Mason, OH: South-Western Cengage Learning, 2012), 2.*

3 *Yasin Olum, "Modern Management Theories and Practices," Paper presented at the* 15th East African Central Banking Course, *held on 12th July 2004, at Kenya School of Monetary*

the areas of problem solving, administration, human resource management, and organizational leadership. The term "labor or workforce management" refers to the practice that organizes and harmonizes the workforce to keep the organizational objectives in centre and control the result by maintaining a productive workforce and thus optimize the productivity.[4] It aims to allocate 'just the right' labour talents and numbers of workers in an organization, to meet all requirements and schedules, to minimize costs and to maximize productivity-performances and services. Thus, labour management is a dynamic and life-giving element that aims to ensure the generation, sustenance and growth of a business and the well-being of all concerned through division of labour, effective cooperation, and an increase in workers' productive powers and skills.

Though the history of management goes back several thousand years, it came to be regarded as a formal discipline from the 19th century.[5] The *Scientific Management Theory* of Frederick Taylor –later called *Taylorism* – analyses workflows and tries to improve labour productivity and economic efficiency through the development of a true science, scientific selection, education, the development of workers, and close cooperation between workers and management.[6] However, it is widely being criticized, being accused of dehumanizing workers, exploiting employees unjustly, placing impersonal efficiency above human needs. The *Classical Organizational Theory* arose in reaction to it and includes the *Administrative Management Model* of Henri Fayol, known as *Fayolism*, and the *Bureaucratic Theory* of Max Weber. Henri Fayol preferred management principles to personal traits and argued for a formalized, hierarchical administrative structure, possessing a clear division of labour strategies to achieve organizational goals.[7] Similarly, Max Weber regarded bureaucracy as an ideal form of organizational structure,

---

Studies, 2004, 2.

4 *Arun Kumar and Priyadarshani Singh, "Principles and Practices of Workplace Management in Information Age,"* International Journal of Advanced Research in Management and Social Science *3, no. 4 (2014): 23.*

5 *Richard M. Hodgetts and Steven Altman, "History of Management Thought," in* Management Handbook: Operating Guidelines, Techniques and Practices, *ed. Paul Mali (New York: John Wiley, 1981), 4-5.*

6 *Frederick Winslow Taylor,* The Principles of Scientific Management *(New York: Harper & Brothers Publishers), 130. See also reprinted version, Frederick Winslow Taylor,* The Principles of Scientific Management *(London: Forgotten Books, 2015). Carl Mitcham, ed., "Management,"* Encyclopedia of Science, Technology and Ethics, *vol. 3 (Detroit; Thomson & Gale, 2005), 1152-1153.*

7 *Michael J. Fells, "Fayol Stands the Test of Time,"* Journal of Management History *6, no. 8 (2000): 345-347. See also Ziarab Mahamood, Muhammad Basharat and Zahid Bashir, "Review of Classical Management Theories,"* International Journal of Social Sciences and Education *2, no. 1 (2012): 512-522.*

whereby a good administration is the exercise of control through knowledge and [impersonal] rational authority. He considers this more efficient than personal authority in organizational management.[8] This process has also been criticized, however, for being too focused on administrative requirements, the impersonal machine-like treatment of employees and harsh dependence on rules and policies that make employees feel dehumanized and distrusted.

Discussions about management in the twentieth century raised concerns about the interactions and motivations of individuals in organizations and gave rise to the *Behavioural Theory*, which gave due importance to human relations in management. Researchers like Elton Mayo (importance of human interactions in workplace management), Abraham Maslow (hierarchical need-based analysis of management), and Douglas McGregor (Theory X and Theory Y) acknowledge and illustrate the need to manage human behaviour and relations in the organization. In fact, these theorists introduce the idea of an organizational humanism. These theories emphasize basic and functional human needs, individual or group behaviour, and intra/inter-human relations, and calls for a participatory approach to management, and maintain that employees will be ultimately unresponsive to a controlling style of management. These theories give importance to the social needs of employees, including the need for interpersonal relationships. However, a question always remains: are employees coming to work to seek affection, or affiliation? Management, on this theory, must seek to recognize individual needs and social satisfactions as well as organizational objectives, strive to understand the human aspects of workers, and treat them accordingly.

Recently, a plethora of new management theories and models have emerged. The *systems approach*, being a synthesis and integration of different theories, functions in organizational management by emphasizing the need for systems to adapt to contextual and circumstantial changes and to interrelated subsystems.[9] Another paradigm, the *contingency approach*, also called situational theory, implies that in particular situations, devoid of certain principles, management becomes contingent on the evaluation of an experienced

8 *Mücahit Celik and Edip Dogan, "A Theoretical Approach to the Science of Management,"* International Journal of Humanities and Social Science *1, no. 3 (2011): 67; Ziarab Mahamood, Muhammad Basharat and Zahid Bashir, "Review of Classical Management Theories,"* International Journal of Social Sciences and Education *2, no. 1 (2012): 512-522. Cf. Max Weber,* The Theory of Social and Economic Organization, *trans. A.M. Henderson and Talcott Parsons (New York: The Free Press, [originally in 1921] 2012), 324-406.*

9 *Olum, "Modern Management Theories and Practices," 17. Cf. Christina Mele, Jacqueline Pels and Francesco Polese, "A Brief Review of Systems Theories and Their Managerial Applications,"* Service Science *2, no. 1/2 (2010): 126; Cornell C. Chikere and Jude Nwoka, "The Systems Theory of Management in Modern Day Organizations: A Study of Aldgate Congress Resort Limited Port Harcourt,"* International Journal of Scientific and Research Publications *5, no. 9 (2015): 1.*

manager.[10] In this line, the *team building* approach relies on teamwork and emphasizes the levelling of hierarchies or pyramidal management models.[11] The *lean management* is a recent method that identifies and clarifies what values play a role in workplace processes and adapts to the different situations of organizational and market conditions through functional alternations.[12] It seeks continuous improvements and excellence in the organization by altering the behaviour of its members to improve efficiency and quality.

These theories and models have been developed in view of the many contextual differences and complexities that mark modern management situations and reveal that no single managerial strategy can always be effectively applied to all situations in organizations. Despite there being constant factors across contexts, specific features of the culture will always do much to shape the problems face, and thus addressing these problems will always depend on the particulars of the given context. This situation makes it necessary for managers to look for different strategies at different times and in different situations with different persons. Apart from the rational economic view and mechanized concentration on employees, our discussion must include the ethical perspective in order to make clear employees, as human beings with self-worth and self-actualization and having different perspectives, aspirations, potentials and needs, cannot be managed like the other resources an organization may have.[13] It is therefore crucial that employees be approached from an ethical perspective rather than an economic or technocratic perspective.

2. Ethics in Business and in Workplace Management

Ethics in business is not only a concern in terms of profits or compliance in the domain of risk management but also requires that personal ethics be integrated into a corporate context, which is itself of course enmeshed with social relations.[14] Reaching beyond the concerns about law and compliance, ethics is about the moral character of people and of culture. In business contexts, ethics is the art or discipline of discerning the *Right*, the *Good*, and the *Fitting Action* to take in a given situation.[15] It helps to shape the business

---

10 *Olum, "Modern Management Theories and Practices," 18.*

11 *Olum, "Modern Management Theories and Practices," 19.*

12 *Łukasz Dekier, "The Origins and Evolution of Lean Management System,"* Journal of International Studies *5, no 1 (2012): 49.*

13 *Abdelkarim Kitana, "Overview of the Managerial Thoughts and Theories from the History: Classical Management Theory to Modern Management Theory,"* Indian Journal of Management Science *6, no.1 (2016): 20.*

14 *David W. Miller and Michael J. Thate, "Are Business Ethics Relevant?" in* Economics as a Moral Science, *eds. Peter Rona and Laszlo Zsolnai, 163-173 (Switzerland: Springer, 2017), 163.*

15 *Miller and Thate, "Are Business Ethics Relevant?" 168.*

culture and character of employers and employees through these lenses, and builds integrity encouraging responsible behaviour. It also enhances employee morale, resulting in good corporate reputation. Mollie Painter-Morland opines, "When ethics functions as an integral part of business practice, [...] it informs individuals' perceptions of events from the start and plays an important part in shaping their responses."[16] He observes, "In fact, efforts to formulate unambiguous normative guidelines for the conduct of business may paradoxically cause us to neglect those very aspects of human life that both legality and morality attempt to protect."[17] This also necessitates the idea of 'an ethical culture' to enable one to describe, assess and manage the organizational culture.

Researchers view ethical culture as part of or the subject of organizational culture and as a support to manage ethical risks.[18] As a crucial part of employment, workplace ethics is an ingredient for the success of any organization. It prescribes moral standards to guide both employer (corporate) and employee behaviour and goes beyond the applicable laws to their foundations and the spirit in which they were written.[19] Considering the three sources of workplace ethical codes, namely, - corporate codes of ethics, global codes of ethics, and the business ethics literature, - Mark Schwartz listed six main moral values relevant to the workplace: respect, caring, trustworthiness, responsibility, citizenship and fairness.[20] These values are a foundation for workplace ethical behaviours. An unaffected and unmanipulated commitment to ethics is said to confer three sorts of benefits, namely: within the company, within the business community, and in relation to the wider outside community.[21] Commitment within the company can improve workers' morale, help resolve internal disputes and promote a healthy and secure workplace, while among business communities such commitment can also improve the reputation of a company and thus be an aid in raising venture capital and in defending the company

16 *Mollie Painter-Morland,* Business Ethics as Practice: Ethics as the Everyday Business of Business *(Cambridge: Cambridge University press, 2011), 2.*

17 *Painter-Morland,* Business Ethics as Practice, *3.*

18 *Painter-Morland,* Business Ethics as Practice, *11. Cf. Geert Hofstede, Bram Neuijen, dense daval Ohayv and Geert Sanders, "Measuring Organization Cultures: A Qualitative and Quantitative Study across Twenty Cases,"* Administrative Science Quarterly *35 (1990): 286-316; Linda Klebe Trevino, Kenneth D. Butterfield and Donald L. McCabe, "The Ethical Context in Organizations Influence on Employee attitudes and Behaviours,"* Business Ethics Quarterly *8, no. 3 (1998): 447-476.*

19 *Mark S. Schwartz, "Universal Moral Values for Corporate Codes of Ethics,"* Journal of Business Ethics *59 (2005): 27-44.*

20 *Schwartz, "Universal Moral Values for Corporate Codes of Ethics," 27-44.*

21 *Ronald D. Francis and Mukti Mishra,* Business Ethics: An Indian Perspective *(New Delhi: Tata McGraw Hill, 2011), 31.*

against allegations of impropriety. Committed individuals, both employers and employees alike, with proper execution of ethical policies and practices, can increase workplace ethics in a corporate environment.[22]

When organization's values and ethics becomes compatible with that of individuals, the likelihood of the person remaining in the organization increases.[23] So, the individual's perception of the ethical orientation of a company is very important and is strengthened when individuals and organizations both understand themselves in an ethical context. A positive ethical culture and climate – both individual and organizational – and establishing of a code of conduct for all in the organization produces favourable organizational or business outcomes. An organization is not all about machines and tasks performed, but also about individuals, as persons, who are its primary participants and contributors. In our view, therefore, ethics, as an overarching framework consisting of a set of values and principles that measures individual and communitarian behaviours, is the real foundation on which all actions in the organizational workplaces are and ought to be based. It seeks to identify acceptable moral behaviours in the workplace and achieve individual well-being and corporate growth and development. Workplace ethics can be used to govern and control employee behaviour, normalize or regulate the moral decisions of management, and protect the organization from legal liability. It is therefore an effort to systematically apply ethical principles and moral reasoning to various contexts, with due attention to individual moral character, corporate strategies and values, and management practices to ensure that the objectives of the organization are accomplished.

3. Ethical Management as Beyond Dimension of Managerial Rationality

Managerial rationality is purposeful, goal-directed and an ideological construct that functions to legitimize managerial control.[24] Portrayed as a concern for efficiency and the maximization of profit, this bounded rationality has always been used to legitimize management control over workers.[25] Governance through managerial rationality looks for the most suitable means to ensure business survival and progress by way of a close observation of financial figures and indicators, steps to reduce risks and costs, and the development strategic

22 *Margaret L. Gagne, Joanne H. Gavin and Gregory J. Tully, "Assessing the Costs and Benefits of Ethics: Exploring a Framework,"* Business and Society Review *110, no. 2 (2005): 181-190.*

23 *MaryJo Burchard, "Ethical Dissonance and Response to Destructive Leadership: A Proposed Model,"* Emerging Leadership Journeys *4, no. 1 (2011): 154.*

24 *Stewart R. Clegg and James R. Bailey, eds.,* International Encyclopaedia of Organization Studies, *Vol. 1 (Los Angeles: Sage Publications, 2008), 870.*

25 *Clegg and Bailey,* International Encyclopaedia of Organization Studies, *871.*

action plans, etc.[26] It is a strategic management practice that aims to ensure the sustainability of an organization. However, when the term management is applied to human beings in the same way as to machines, the dimension of care for human beings disappears and the control principle becomes dominant. In line with a Foucauldian concept of power relations managerial rationality consists in watching over and punishing, forgetting the actual handling and training of human persons. Moreover, an exclusivist tendency is observed in many power-centred managerial paradigms and in organizational behaviours. It leads to a neglect of other forms of rationality that are required in an organization and in the organizational workplace.[27]

Johan Verstraeten in this regard refers to 'responsible moral behaviour'[28] that goes beyond a merely rational choice approach in business. The value of business, he argues, is often reduced to shareholder "value" (profit), with ethical considerations subordinated to this. Attention to human rights and moral values depends on market pressures, and thus ethical behaviour is caught in the clutches of this very modern form of bounded rationality, to which a manipulative exercise of power is often linked.[29] When managers are imprisoned within the narrow hermeneutical horizon of modernity with its characteristic forms of manipulative rationality, real innovation in moral behaviour becomes impossible. In a similar way, Amartya Sen writes, "There would be some necessity to go beyond the requirements of rationality in terms of permissive self-scrutiny, and to consider the demands of 'reasonable conduct' towards others."[30] He calls for serious attention to different perspectives and socio-ethical and contextual concerns when taking choices and decisions. and for integrated ethical behaviour in business organizations.

However, managing business organizations in an ethical manner is still a formidable challenge, as such a behavioural pattern is influenced by numerous individual and situational factors.[31] Researchers[32] in this perspective opine

---

26 *Christiane Gebhardt, "The Impact of Managerial Rationality on the Organizational Paradigm. Role Models in the Management of Innovation,"* Technology Analysis & Strategic Management *17, no. 1 (2005): 27.*

27 *Mauksch, "Beyond Managerial Rationality," 166.*

28 *Johan Verstraeten, "Responsible Leadership beyond Managerial Rationality: The Necessity of Reconnecting Ethics and Spirituality," in* Leadership and Business Ethics, *ed. Gabriel Flynn, Vol. 25, 131-147 (Dublin: Springer, 2008), 132.*

29 *Johan Verstraeten, "How Faith Makes a Difference: Business as a Calling or the Christians in Business,"* Estudios Empresariales *113 (2003/3): 56-57.*

30 *Amartya Sen,* The idea of Justice *(London: Penguin Books, 2009), 197.*

31 *John Drummond and Bill Bain, eds.,* Managing Business Ethics *(Oxford: Butterworth-Heinemann, 1996), 56.*

32 *Stead et al., "An Integrative Model for Understanding and Managing Ethical Behaviour," 59-61.*

that along with individual personality traits and backgrounds of socialization, organizational factors also influence the ethical behaviour of employees. Employers must pay attention not only to the content of managerial rational rules, regulations and codes of conduct, but also to the process of determining that content and its implied meanings, circumstantial ingredients, participative environment and the ethical rationality that goes beyond managerial rationality. Employers who act only according to managerial rationality, disregarding the influence of individual ethical reasoning, will be unlikely to promote pro-employee behaviours. Ethics thus becomes an open, integrating and integrated force in workplace management. Adherence to law is thus said to be the lowest common denominator of acceptable behaviour, whereas ethics calls for a step beyond what is prescribed by law in situations of conflict. Since adherence to law is accepted as only a basic prerequisite and cannot ensure total ethical security through law alone, one needs to consider human ethos.

4. An Embedded Religious-Ethical Framework to Managerial Approach

The question now is whether religion and/or spirituality can play an interactive and integrative role in the creation of an adequate ethical framework for workforce management that reaches beyond narrowly legal or regulatory approaches. Since religions have been providing and still provide values and moral principles to millions around the world regardless of demographic or other such differences and discriminations, they have a major impact on value discourses of any kind and religious texts can be sources for ethics in business and politics.[33] Within organizations, along with organizational values, ethical behaviour is perceived as an extension of individual morals and norms, which are also affected by their own religious and spiritual beliefs and practices.[34] Hence an interdependent relationship between religious beliefs and practices and ethical behaviours in organizations. Religious thoughts, whether conscious or not, is said to be a hidden variable that often shapes and informs personal and social ethics. There are number of researches expressing a positive correlation of religion with ethical standards.[35] They argue that in

33 *Victor van Bijlert, "Hinduism, Values and Management,"* Research & Reports, IIAS News Letter *33 (March 2004): 23.*

34 *Sana Moid, "A Theoretical Construct of the Impact of Religious Beliefs on Accounting Practices in the Indian and Global Context,"* NMIMS Management Review *31 (2016): 92. Sarah Drakopoulou-Dodd and Paul Timothy Seaman, "Religion and Enterprise: An Introductory Exploration,"* Entrepreneurship Theory and Practice *23, no. 1 (1998): 71-86.*

35 *Tisha L.N. Emerson and Joseph A. Mckinney, "Importance of Religious Beliefs to Ethical Attitudes in Business,"* Journal of Religion and Business Ethics *1, no. 2 (2010): 2; Patricia L. Smith and Ellwood F. Oakley, "The Value of Ethics Education in Business School Curriculum,"* College Student Journal *30 (1996): 274-83; and Stephen J. Conroy and*

many occasions, religion is perceived as a determinant of the moral values as the moral teachings of every religion approve only ethical actions and do not tolerate unethical behaviour.

A half a century ago, reflecting on religion and business, James W. Culliton stated that religion has something to offer business and both can benefit from knowing each other better.[36] This meaningful and significant influence of religion on business decisions and ethical judgements suggests that "the strength of religious beliefs might result in differences in one's decision making processes when facing business decisions involving ethical issues."[37] It is also widely acknowledged that "religiosity contributes to entrepreneurial success by moderating the relationship between the pursuit of material wealth and resulting personal satisfaction and the personal satisfaction in business is influenced by the belief on the religious values that they follow."[38] Moreover, religious individuals, whose morality is influenced by their religion, generally seem to possess a deep longing to take up larger social responsibilities in the workplace and in business.[39] All these studies show that human religiosity, in whatever dimensions of religious affiliation, activity and belief, can constitute a spirituality among individual employees and enables them to see the world and self in that framework. As such, it influences attitudes and behaviours in organizations.

Researches indicate that religious role expectations, which people internalize as religious self-identity moderated by religious motivational orientations, influence their individual ethical behaviour,[40] and hence there is a positive relationship between religiosity and ethical business or organizational behaviour. Yet some researchers criticize the focus on a narrow link between moral reasoning and religious reasoning. According to them, both are, "Unrelated as they represent two distinct ways of thinking," in which the latter, "Is based upon rational arguments and influenced by cognitive development" and the former, "Is based upon the revelations of religious

---

Tisha L. N. Emerson, "Business Ethics and Religion: Religiosity as a Predictor of Ethical Awareness among Students," Journal of Business Ethics *50, no. 4 (2004): 383-396.*

36 *James W. Culliton, "Business and Religion,"* Harvard Business Review *27, no. 3 (1949): 265.*

37 *Vitell, "The Role of Religiosity in Business and Consumer Ethics," 155.*

38 *Binod Krishna Shrestha, "Religious Ethics and Socially Responsible Behaviours of Small Firms in Nepal,"* Journal of Religion and Business Ethics *3, no. 2 (2017): 1.*

39 *Shrestha, "Religious Ethics and Socially Responsible Behaviours of Small Firms in Nepal," 1.*

40 *Gary R. Weaver and Bradley R. Agle, "Religiosity and Ethical Behaviour in Organizations: A Symbolic Interactionist Perspective,"* Academy of Management Review *27, no. 1 (2002): 77-97.*

authorities."[41] However, most researchers acknowledge a close link between these two constructs, arguing "One's moral reasoning depends, in part, upon the seriousness and character of one's religious commitment."[42] Similarly, examining the relationship between religiousness and ethical orientations of business people, Siu, et al. observe, "Individuals who are more religious were also more oriented toward ethics and ethical issues."[43] This means that an individual's personal religion and religious reasoning, or in other words their religiosity, influences both one's personal characteristics and one's ethical decision-making process.

It is also researched that religion can influence the recognition of ethical issues (moral sensitivity), ethical decisions (moral judgment), intention to act (moral intention), and actual behaviour (moral behaviour).[44] Teachings of all religions highlight religious and ethical norms as the guiding principles of business activities, as they see work in a human-divine partnership model, where human dignity and concern for persons such as justice are crucial.[45] Various religious traditions, spirituality, teachings and practices function as a dynamic tool to develop personal and social ethics as needed to respond to complex situations in the workplace. Though there is a conceptual distinction between religion and spirituality,[46] they do have many functional and substantive commonalities, and the experience of spirituality for many people remain embedded within a religious context.[47] A spiritually healthy workplace has positive influences on employee and organizational performance. It leads people to experience consciousness at a deeper level improving their intuitive skills and encourages teamwork developing more purposeful and compelling

---

41 *Vitell, "The Role of Religiosity in Business and Consumer Ethics," 156.*

42 *Vitell, "The Role of Religiosity in Business and Consumer Ethics," 156. Cf. Justin G. Longenecker, Joseph A. McKinney and Carlos W. Moore, "Religious Intensity, Evangelical Christianity, and Business Ethics: An Empirical Study,"* Journal of Business Ethics *55, no. 4 (2004): 373-86.*

43 *Vitell, "The Role of Religiosity in Business and Consumer Ethics," 160. Cf. Siu et al., "Ethical Evaluations of Business Activities and Personal Religiousness," 233-256.*

44 *Tisha L. N. Emerson and Joseph A. Mckinney, "Importance of Religious Beliefs to Ethical Attitudes in Business,"* Journal of Religion and Business Ethics *1, no. 2 (2010): 1-15.*

45 *Domènec Melé, "Religious Foundations of Business Ethics," in* The Accountable Corporation, *Vol. 2, eds. Mark J. Epstein and Kirk O. Hanson (London: Praeger, 2006), 11-43.*

46 *Peter C. Hill and Gary S. Smith, "Coming to Terms with Spirituality and Religion in the Workplace," in* Handbook of Workplace Spirituality and Organizational Performance, *" eds. Robert A. Giacalone and Carole L. Jurkiewicz (Armonk: M.E. Sharpe, 2003), 231-243.*

47 *Hill and Smith, "Coming to Terms with Spirituality and Religion in the Workplace," 234.*

organizational vision and innovation.[48] In what follows, we explore the Hindu view of moral standards that influence managerial acts in the workplace and thus explain religion and spirituality as central features of many people's lives that regulate how they think and act.

5. The Hindu View of Moral Standards and Holistic Managerial Strategy

Moral standards are generally influenced by several factors, including "Moral principles we accept as part of our upbringing, values passes on to us through heritage and legacy, the religious values that we have imbibed from childhood, the values that were showcased during the period of our education, the behaviour pattern of those who are around us, the explicit and implicit standards of our culture, our life experiences and more importantly, our critical reflections on these experiences."[49] Since religion provides its followers with a set of moral instructions, beliefs, values, traditions and commitments, people perceive and believe that morality also emanates from religion.[50] There is no single source of moral standards in Hinduism, for it encompasses values from various religious beliefs and practices, as illustrated in works such as the *Ramayana, Mahabharata, Bhagavad Gita,* etc. and also accrued from other religious traditions including Buddhism, Sikhism, Jainism, and Zoroastrianism.[51] A strong interrelationship between religious thought and economic activity is foreshadowed in all Indian business scenarios. According to researchers, "The rich culture of India, immersed in spirituality and religion, is focused on intuitive ethical decision making and the rule of man, which sets it apart from the western analytical approach to ethical decision making based on norms and the rule of law."[52] Although religions like Hinduism and Buddhism have individual enlightenment as their predominant consideration,[53] their ethical guidelines and spiritual practices for the enlightened life of all humanity offer

---

48 *Richard D. White, Jr., "Drawing the Line: Religion and Spirituality in the Workplace," in* Handbook of Workplace Spirituality and Organizational Performance,*" eds. Robert A. Giacalone and Carole L. Jurkiewicz, 244-256 (Armonk: M.E. Sharpe, 2003), 244.*

49 *A.C. Fernando,* Business Ethics: An Indian Perspective *(Delhi: Pearson Education, 2009), 31.*

50 *Fernando,* Business Ethics: An Indian Perspective*, 31.*

51 *Colin Fisher and Alan Lovell,* Business Ethics and Values: Individual, Corporate and International Perspectives *(England: Pearson Education, 2009), 442. Fernando,* Business Ethics: An Indian Perspective*, 31.*

52 *Ron Berger and Ram Herstein, "The Evolution of Business Ethics in India,"* International Journal of Social Economics *41, no. 11 (2014): 1075.*

53 *Juliana Essen, "Sufficiency Economy and Santi Asoke: Buddhist Economic Ethics for a Just and Sustainable World,"* Journal of Buddhist Ethics *17 (2010): 70-99. Berger and Herstein, "The Evolution of Business Ethics in India," 1076.*

significant guidance for economic and managerial activities, as these are an inevitable part of human life and well-being.

An ethical principle of the Karma theory of Hinduism, "One is responsible for one's actions and the individual alone must bear the consequences of those actions in the future,"[54] causes individuals to discipline and regulate their activities. Researchers have noted that the "religious enforcement mechanisms" practiced in India emphasize the vitality of applying ethical strands in all areas of life, including business and management.[55] The ethical principles of Hinduism enable organizations to conduct business by adhering to a high personal value system that forms a strong ethical infrastructure for business. All Hindu religious thinking and philosophy leads to the creation of general principles of ethical conduct and ethical management, both seeking individual well-being and organizational development. Though management generally seems to be a universal process, in practice different perceptions must be considered as employees invariably have different cultural and religious backgrounds. They are largely "influenced by attitudes, traits and perceptions which are developed over a period of time as a result of their cultural affiliations, associations with peers, family and their past experiences."[56] This makes it necessary to look for the particulars of contextual management pertinent to each region or country, developed through its religious traditions and practices.

In the Indian management context, we find today residual traces of ancient wisdom as the present practices of trade and business face various and multifaceted complexities of global realities. The traces of ancient wisdom are mainly the compiled treaties by Chanakya, an Indian scholar-practitioner, for human resource practices presented in 'Arthashastra,' the first Indian management writings codified over three millennia before Christ. It presents, "Notions of the financial administration of the state, guiding principles for trade and commerce, as well as the management of people."[57] Along with this, Aryan thoughts and writings called Vedanta also influence the management values in India, which "nurtured an inner private sphere of individualism" including the values of responsibility to others – family, group and society.[58]

54 *Berger and Herstein, "The Evolution of Business Ethics in India," 1077. Cf. Praveen K. Kopalle, Donald R. Lehmann and John U. Farley, "Consumer Expectations and Culture: The Effect of Belief in Karma in India,"* Journal of Consumer Research *37, no. 2 (2010): 251-263*

55 *Berger and Herstein, "The Evolution of Business Ethics in India," 1079. Cf. P. Kanagasabapathi, "Ethics and Values in Indian Economy and Business,"* International Journal of Social Economics *34, no. 9 (2007): 577-585.*

56 *Carl Osunde, Joshi Ashima, Vyas Anup, and Gargh Shankar, "Management Problems and Practices: India and Nigeria,"* Advances in Management *8, no. 1 (2015): 9.*

57 *Chatterjee, "Human Resource Management in India," 92.*

58 *Chatterjee, "Human Resource Management in India," 92-93.*

This is the holistic wisdom identified in Vedantic philosophy that permeates managerial behaviour at all levels of work organisations. It also fosters human capacity for self-transformation and to attain spiritual heights even by facing the challenges and uncertainties of day-to-day lives.[59] This strikes on current managerial mindsets enabling the bonding and mutuality of obligations leading to an altruistic and philanthropic strategic approach.

Today, many are searching for a different, distinctively Indian organizational management model because of the problems created by trying to transfer another country's model of management into India. A dynamic engagement through interdependence and integration is needed and valued in this situation to grasp the overall performance of the workplace and management context. For often, cultural differences are more important and determinative than the commonalities among different countries.[60] For example, "Too much of individualism, the principle of maximization of profits at all costs, little concern for values and a narrow view of life could be some of the major flaws"[61] of Western management model, when it is transferred directly to the more of collectivistic and relationship-based Indian cultural scenario.

Researchers, in this regard, assert that management is predominantly culture specific and derives also from religious and faith practices. For instance, Nigam and Su rightly illustrate that management system in India has its roots in rules and regulations of various dominating empires, different religions, and India's very socio-cultural practice of caste system, British Raj, and more recently the globalization of world economies.[62] To explain this further, any country or region will have a specific set of approaches to life, different economic systems, different predominant cultural frameworks, different spiritual and religious orientations, and differences of temperament, etc., all of which influence business management and decision-making practices.[63] For example, the practice of the caste system, by which people are categorized into different groups – higher or lower – according to the caste into which they are born, brings with it a hierarchical mindset and thus a management model of 'power delegation.' This results in a pattern of centralized authority and top-down decision making.[64] For in line with our precious discussion, this caste system and the continued effects of an old feudalistic tendency, created and prompted by the British Raj promoting inequality in rural and urban population, maintain a hierarchy, status consciousness, power distance and

59 *Chatterjee, "Human Resource Management in India," 92.*

60 *Kanagasabapathi,* Indian Models of Economy, Business and Management, *240.*

61 *Kanagasabapathi,* Indian Models of Economy, Business and Management, *239.*

62 *Nigam and Su, "Management in Emerging versus Developed Countries," 124.*

63 *Kanagasabapathi,* Indian Models of Economy, Business and Management, *238.*

64 *Nigam and Su, "Management in Emerging versus Developed Countries," 126.*

low individualism in the workplace.[65] This practice and the cultural tendencies in the organization strengthen a hierarchical superior-subordinate relationship and thus increase social control over inferiors.

In different texts such as the *Bhagavad Gita*, the *Arthashastra* and the *Thirukkural*, Indians receive knowledge and concepts related to management.[66] These and other ancient Indian literatures, such as various Upanishads, Vedas, and Smrutis, along with the Quran and the Bible, serve as a source of principles and guidelines for the development of good human relations, norms of good governance, and good communication skills.[67] The Indian management style is also marked by different power aspects such as loyalty, affection, respect and bonding based on the above discussed socio-cultural, religious and political traditions and customs. This is because of the Indian inheritance of the *holistic vision* that it pursues in its engagements with others. To further explicate, apart from the managerial presupposition of the West, that the individual is the central unit of reference, Indian culture perceives the individual as merely a component part of larger social institutions such as the family, and thus group efforts are given more importance than individual efforts.[68] Kanagasabapathi in this regard writes that: "Our culture provides us with 'the cosmic vision' which, translated in terms of business, amounts to accepting and owning our social responsibility towards all the stakeholders like share-holders, employees and their union, consumers, society, government, financial institutions, supplier, etc., and beyond, competitors, environment-physical, social, religious, cultural, educational and even the inanimate kingdom."[69] The whole world is thus seen as a family – *Vasudhaiva Kutumbakam* – and when people interact with individuals, groups or organizations, this view predominates, and this holistic or cosmic vision gives a new face to the Indian management philosophy.

The concept *Vasudhaiva Kutumbakam* is a Sanskrit phrase meaning, "the whole world is one single family." Here 'vasudha' means Earth; 'eva' means

---

65 *Debi S. Saini and Pawan S. Budhwar, "HRM in India," in* Managing Human Resources in Asia-Pacific, *ed. Pawan S. Budhwar (London: Routledge, 2004), 120.*

66 *Anindo Bhattacharjee, "Modern Management through Ancient Indian Wisdom: Towards a More Sustainable Paradigm,"* School of Management Science-Purusartha *4, no. 1 (2011): 15; Manish Prasad Rajak, "Ancient Indian Wisdom in Modern Management: A Review of its Scope and Prospects,"* aWEshkar *18, no. 2 (2014): 18-29.*

67 *Kanagasabapathi,* Indian Models of Economy, Business and Management, *242. See also, Yog Raj Singh and Ankur Bhatnagar, "Management and Business Ethics through Indian Scriptures and Traditions," 2012, http://www.managementparadise.com/article/3654/management-and-business-ethics-through-indian-scriptures-and-traditions [accessed March 10, 2018].*

68 *Kanagasabapathi,* Indian Models of Economy, Business and Management, *242 -243.*

69 *Kanagasabapathi,* Indian Models of Economy, Business and Management, *243.*

emphasize and 'kutumbakam' means family. This Sanskrit verse is from Maha Upanishad (Chapter 6, Verse 72), where we read: "*Ayam Bandhurayam Neti Ganana Laghu Chetsam, Udaara Charitaanaam Tu Vasudhaiva Kutumbakam.*" (– "Only small men discriminate saying: One is a relative; the other is a stranger. For those who live magnanimously, the entire world constitutes but a family.")[70] It is also a cultural and spiritual concept as *vasudhaiva* is a state of awareness or consciousness for which love, harmony, co-operation and mutual support from key features. In this concept of universal family-hood, "Individual and collective interests complement each other, and the focus is on caring and sharing and respect for fellow beings."[71] This spiritual and cultural practice is also a defining feature of interpersonal relationships in the organizational workplace. For the sustainability and growth of Indian organizations are deeply rooted in a culture of upward respect, called *Sradha* (loyalty), of downward fondness, called *Sneha* (affection), and of mutual attachment, called *Bandhan* (bonding) that arises through the interaction of loyalty and affection in the organization.[72] These concepts mark the distinctiveness of Indian management models.

The ethical values of ancient India, including *Dharma* (justice righteousness, duty, moral order, virtues), *Artha* (wealth, prosperity, success), *Kama* (worldly desire, pleasure), and *Moksha* (liberation or salvation) constitute the ideals of life, provide a solid ethos for work culture, and offer a broad framework for a new model of organizational management.[73] These values of *Dharma*, *Artha*, *Kama*, and *Moksha* are four *purusharthas* or permissible goals of human life that constitute a way for happy life on earth. *Purusha* is an individual or person and *Artha* means meaning/objective or pursuit and thus objectives of human life is called *purusharthas*. This *purusharthas* is the basis for human life and central to Indian classical ethics. Every human being has to achieve it with detachment and renunciation.[74] For, this fourfold aim of human existence is pertinent to whole practical and day-to-day arenas of human life, and everyone is expected to achieve it disregarding the expectation to get something in return.

In this 21st century, these objectives or ideals – *Dharma* as conscientious living, *Artha* as seeking security, *Kama* as the art of enjoying pleasures, and

---

70 *Shashank Shah and V.E. Ramamoorthy,* Soulful Corporations: A Value-Based Perspective on Corporate Social Responsibility *(New Delhi: Springer, 2014), 249.*

71 *Shah and Ramamoorthy,* Soulful Corporations, *249-250.*

72 *Chatterjee, "Human Resource Management in India," 93-94.*

73 *Alka Mohan Kadam, "Purushartha in 21st Century,"* Online International Interdisciplinary Research Journal *5, no. 4 (2015): 441. Cf., Berger and Herstein, "The Evolution of Business Ethics in India," 1078.*

74 *Kadam, "Purushartha in 21st Century," 441; Berger and Herstein, "The Evolution of Business Ethics in India," 1078.*

Moksha as freedom from all limitations – are becoming more vital, as they can contribute much to an understanding of organizational behaviour as well.[75] *Dharma* and *Artha* allow the generation of wealth or profit so long as it is not done by unjust means. In the same way, *Kama*, the attainment of desired pleasure, invariable looks for cardinal rules and values through the self-disciplined and self-managed efficacy of worldly goods and services. Besides, the concept of *Moksha* in this regard can inform the ideology and philosophy of life in any organization or a corporate body.[76] In the same way, a management model based on these ideals, according to Manish P. Rajak, "stresses on harmonizing the individual goals with the goals of others for bringing harmony in system; such a system would be highly decentralized and depended on every person following Dharma for the attainment of the *Purusarthas*."[77] The *Purusharthas* also, therefore, are held to offer solid ideals of human ethics as important guidelines for managing organizations in modern times.

In these modern times, over against the hierarchical management approach, which often seems antagonistic, a more personal management style is used in many organizational workplaces in India, one which sees all members as associates and thus is friendlier in dealing with each one.[78] The owner-labour relationship is fostered in the context of a higher personal orientation and a fraternal approach that draws employees more closely together, regardless of their professional or socio-economic status. In the Indian non-corporate sector, this 'holistic' management style shows entrepreneur's concern for all parties involved in the firm by means of direct contact with all stakeholders. An entrepreneur, in this regard, takes all risks involved and functions as "a financial expert, a human relations man, a marketing wizard and a production specialist, all at one time"[79] to successfully manage complex situations coming across. Similarly, leaders in the corporate sector in India by and large try to adapt to modern management styles without losing their traditional value systems. Moreover, in the corporate sector, both a higher need for updating operations and services through adoption of the latest technologies and a growing tendency to emulate the West are quite advanced and developed.

---

75 *Kadam, "Purushartha in 21st Century," 445-447.*

76 *Anil Rao Paila and P.S. Rao, "Ethics in Business and Indian Value Systems: Need for Integration in the age of Science and Technology," in* Business Ethics and Human Values, *ed. V.M. Chavan (New Delhi: Excel Books, 2009), 24.*

77 *Rajak, "Ancient Indian Wisdom in Modern Management,"22. It is originally from, Krishan Saigal,* Vedic Management: The Dharmic and Yogic Way *(Delhi: Gyan Publishing House, 2000), 63-100.*

78 *Kanagasabapathi,* Indian Models of Economy, Business and Management, *251.*

79 *Kanagasabapathi,* Indian Models of Economy, Business and Management, *254.*

However, a creative and progressive management model that incorporates the nuances of application and implementation of information and associated technologies will construct and provide for the effective management of the new workforce by focusing on the well-being of employees through a person-centered approach. For the contemporary workplace, with its wealth of information and connectivity, is exemplified perhaps most clearly by the field of IT, job arenas that are horizontally-networked (less hierarchical) and highly-interconnected, and "less command-and-control oriented behaviours, with the big data as key basis of competition, growth and innovation."[80] Researchers have compiled several principles of workforce management, which extends from principles of individual self-development to the principle of contribution to national prosperity.[81] Availing oneself to realize and actualize one's own potential through the responsible utilization of full and equal opportunities given to them, an employee promotes the dignity of labour while also providing for national prosperity by contributing to it with a team spirit. Principles of labour management cooperation, the free flow of communication, fair remuneration incentives and the dignity of labour also all contribute to cordial industrial relations and effective labour management.[82] It is interesting at this juncture to note that Indian work culture and management models are more about performing with a comprehensive or holistic worldview and are invariably humane in practice, functioning in a way that is consistent with Indian religious, socio-cultural and economic orientations.

In a similar manner, India itself, being by its very nature of multiple and outwardly accepting, tolerant and adaptive to diversities, is largely open to imbibing various approaches and management styles. According to Jean-Pierre Lehmann, "The planet needs a sense of moral order, spirituality and an ethical compass. The Indian religious and philosophical traditions can provide a great deal of all three."[83] Therefore, any critical and ethical analyses of work behaviour and progressive workplace or labour management in Indian organizations has to be in tune with its cultural practices and socio-economic and

---

80 *Kumar and Singh, "Principles and Practices of Workplace Management in Information Age," 24.*

81 *Kumar and Singh, "Principles and Practices of Workplace Management in Information Age," 29-31. See also K. Aswathappa,* Human Resource Management: Text and Cases, *7th ed. (New Delhi: McGraw Hill Education [India] Pvt. Ltd., 2013), 26.*

82 *Kumar and Singh, "Principles and Practices of Workplace Management in Information Age," 29-31.*

83 *Jean-Pierre Lehmann, "The Dangers of Monotheism in the Age of Globalization,"* The Globalist, *March 30, 2006. http://www.theglobalist.com/dangers-monotheism-age-globalization/ [accessed March 10, 2018]. See also Kanagasabapathi,* Indian Models of Economy, Business and Management, *280.*

religious traditions and adherences. Therefore, Hinduism contributes to ethical behaviour in the workplace by applying principles of right social behaviour "based on four ideals or goals of life: prosperity, satisfaction of desires, moral duty and spiritual perfection by liberating from a finite existence."[84] These four ideals highlight the human virtues of honesty, righteousness, nonviolence, modesty and purity of heart. This framework enables and engenders the vitality of analyzing deep-rooted behavioural patterns of the modern workplace in Indian organizations and globally, with all its specifics. For the new organizational environment does not exhibit a conventional fixed set of behavioural platforms, but rather a complex, dynamic web where people need to interact with each other for effective work performance.

Conclusion

The holistic managerial strategy extracted from the Hindu religious traditions focuses on individuals as the unit of analysis for moral judgments, giving employees a significant place, valuing their dignity as human persons. This marks the significance of a humanistic perspective linking altruistic and benevolent behavioural tendencies in workplace and management ethics. This new humanistic-ethical perspective with a holistic managerial strategy will provide a significant contribution to the effort to navigate the complexities of individual and organizational management. This leads to both person-centered and altruistic discerning, grounded within the value framework of the rights and interests of both the individual and of society (dignity, autonomy, freedom, choice, coproduction, cooperation, respect for the other, common good, etc.). Complementing various other approaches to humanistic management, such as those centered on human motivations and organizational culture, what we need is a concept of management that emphasizes and orients the human condition and the development of human virtue, and that endorses the unconditional human dignity within an economic context. This approach in fact emphasizes the uniqueness and inviolability of the person and his/her basic relational or communitarian dimensions of life. It takes shape as a reaction against several socio-political and technological tendencies to treat the human being simply as an object, a means, and not an end. As a perspective and an approach, the holistic managerial strategy reacts against the reductionist tendencies deriving from the materialistic ideologies of the managerial rationality. It affirms the centrality of the person, valuing his or her subjectivity, autonomy, dignity and participation, and solidarity participation in a community with an aim of growth and development. It shows, this strategic approach better understands employees as they are, including in terms of their needs and wants, rights and

84 *Shrestha, "Religious Ethics and Socially Responsible Behaviours of Small Firms in Nepal," 4.*

duties, job satisfaction and commitment, relationships with others, individual well-being and organizational development. This type of holistic strategy and management processes has implications for both individual and organizational well-being and can help us to understand the situation of employees who are side-lined from mainstream consideration.

References

Aswathappa, K. *Human Resource Management: Text and Cases*, 7th ed. New Delhi: McGraw Hill Education (India) Pvt. Ltd., 2013.

Berger, Ron and Ram Herstein. "The Evolution of Business Ethics in India." *International Journal of Social Economics* 41, no. 11 (2014): 1073-1086.

Bhattacharjee, Anindo. "Modern Management through Ancient Indian Wisdom: Towards a More Sustainable Paradigm." *School of Management Science-Purusartha* 4, no. 1 (2011): 14-17.

Bijlert, Victor van. "Hinduism, Values and Management." *Research & Reports, IIAS News Letter* 33 (March 2004): 23.

Burchard, MaryJo. "Ethical Dissonance and Response to Destructive Leadership: A Proposed Model." *Emerging Leadership Journeys* 4, no. 1 (2011): 154-176.

Celik, Mücahit and Edip Dogan. "A Theoretical Approach to the Science of Management." *International Journal of Humanities and Social Science* 1, no. 3 (2011): 65-69.

Chattergee, S.R. "Human Resource Management in India: 'Where From' and 'Where To?'." *Research and Practice in Human Resource Management* 15, no. 2 (2007): 92-103.

Chikere, Cornell C.and Jude Nwoka. "The Systems Theory of Management in Modern Day Organizations: A Study of Aldgate Congress Resort Limited Port Harcourt." *International Journal of Scientific and Research Publications* 5, no. 9 (2015): 1-7.

Clegg, Stewart R. and James R. Bailey, eds., *International Encyclopaedia of Organization Studies*, Vol. 1. Los Angeles: Sage Publications, 2008.

Conroy, Stephen J. and Tisha L. N. Emerson. "Business Ethics and Religion: Religiosity as a Predictor of Ethical Awareness among Students." *Journal of Business Ethics* 50, no. 4 (2004): 383-96.

Culliton, James W. "Business and Religion." *Harvard Business Review* 27, no. 3 (1949): 265-271.

Dekier, Łukasz. "The Origins and Evolution of Lean Management System." *Journal of International Studies* 5, no 1 (2012): 46-51.

Drakopoulou-Dodd, Sarah and Paul Timothy Seaman. "Religion and Enterprise: An Introductory Exploration." *Entrepreneurship Theory and Practice* 23, no. 1 (1998): 71-86.

Drummond, John and Bill Bain, eds. *Managing Business Ethics*. Oxford: Butterworth-Heinemann, 1996.

DuBrin, Andrew J. *Essentials of Management*, 9th ed. Mason, OH: South-Western Cengage Learning, 2012.

Emerson, Tisha L. N. and Joseph A. Mckinney. "Importance of Religious Beliefs to Ethical Attitudes in Business." *Journal of Religion and Business Ethics* 1, no. 2 (2010): 1-15.

Emerson, Tisha L. N. and Joseph A. Mckinney. "Importance of Religious Beliefs to Ethical Attitudes in Business." *Journal of Religion and Business Ethics* 1, no. 2 (2010): 1-15.

Essen, Juliana. "Sufficiency Economy and Santi Asoke: Buddhist Economic Ethics for a Just and Sustainable World." *Journal of Buddhist Ethics* 17 (2010): 70-99.

Fells, Michael J. "Fayol Stands the Test of Time." *Journal of Management History* 6, no. 8 (2000): 345-360.

Fernando, A.C. *Business Ethics: An Indian Perspective*. Delhi: Pearson Education, 2009.

Fisher, Colin and Alan Lovell. *Business Ethics and Values: Individual, Corporate and International Perspectives*. England: Pearson Education, 2009.

Francis, Ronald D. and Mukti Mishra. *Business Ethics: An Indian Perspective*. New Delhi: Tata McGraw Hill, 2011.

Gagne, Margaret L., Joanne H. Gavin and Gregory J. Tully. "Assessing the Costs and Benefits of Ethics: Exploring a Framework." *Business and Society Review* 110, no. 2 (2005): 181-190.

Gebhardt, Christiane. "The Impact of Managerial Rationality on the Organizational Paradigm: Role Models in the Management of Innovation." *Technology Analysis & Strategic Management* 17, no. 1 (2005): 21-34.

Hill, Peter C. and Gary S. Smith. "Coming to Terms with Spirituality and Religion in the Workplace." In *Handbook of Workplace Spirituality and Organizational Performance*, eds. Robert A. Giacalone and Carole L. Jurkiewicz, 231-243. Armonk: M.E. Sharpe, 2003.

Hodgetts, Richard M. and Steven Altman. "History of Management Thought." In *Management Handbook: Operating Guidelines, Techniques and Practices*, ed. Paul Mali. New York: John Wiley, 1981.

Hofstede, Geert, BramNeuijen, dense daval Ohayv and Geert Sanders. "Measuring Organization Cultures: A Qualitative and Quantitative Study across Twenty Cases." *Administrative Science Quarterly* 35 (1990): 286-316.

Kadam, Alka Mohan. "Purushartha in 21st Century." *Online International Interdisciplinary Research Journal* 5, no. 4 (2015): 441-448.

Kanagasabapathi, P. "Ethics and Values in Indian Economy and Business." *International Journal of Social Economics* 34, no. 9 (2007): 577-585.

Kitana, Abdelkarim. "Overview of the Managerial Thoughts and Theories from the History: Classical Management Theory to Modern Management Theory." *Indian Journal of Management Science* 6, no.1 (2016): 16-21.

Kopalle, Praveen K., Donald R. Lehmann and John U. Farley. "Consumer Expectations and Culture: The Effect of Belief in Karma in India." *Journal of Consumer Research* 37, no. 2 (2010): 251-263.

Kumar, Arun and Priyadarshani Singh, "Principles and Practices of Workplace Management in Information Age." *International Journal of Advanced Research in Management and Social Science* 3, no. 4 (2014): 21-34.

Lehmann, Jean-Pierre. "The Dangers of Monotheism in the Age of Globalization." *The Globalist*, March 30, 2006. http://www.theglobalist.com/dangers-monotheism-age-globalization/ [accessed March 10, 2018].

Longenecker, Justin G., Joseph A. McKinney and Carlos W. Moore. "Religious Intensity, Evangelical Christianity, and Business Ethics: An Empirical Study." *Journal of Business Ethics* 55, no. 4 (2004): 373-86.

Mahamood, Ziarab, Muhammad Basharat and Zahid Bashir. "Review of Classical Management Theories." *International Journal of Social Sciences and Education* 2, no. 1 (2012): 512-522.

Mele, Christina, Jacqueline Pels and Francesco Polese. "A Brief Review of Systems Theories and Their Managerial Applications." *Service Science* 2, no. 1/2 (2010): 126-135.

Melé, Domènec. "Religious Foundations of Business Ethics." In *The Accountable Corporation*, Vol. 2, eds. Mark J. Epstein and Kirk O. Hanson, 11-43. London: Praeger, 2006.

Miller, David and Michael J. Thate, "Are Business Ethics Relevant?" In *Economics as a Moral Science*, eds. Peter Rona and Laszlo Zsolnai, 163-173. Switzerland: Springer, 2017.

Mitcham, Carl, ed. "Management." *Encyclopedia of Science, Technology and Ethics*, vol. 3, 1150-1155. Detroit: Thomson & Gale, 2005.

Moid, Sana. "A Theoretical Construct of the Impact of Religious Beliefs on Accounting Practices in the Indian and Global Context." *NMIMS Management Review* 31 (2016): 90-103.

Olum, Yasin. "Modern Management Theories and Practices," Paper presented at the 15th East African Central Banking Course, held on 12th July 2004, at Kenya School of Monetary Studies (2004): 1-24.

Osunde, Carl, Joshi Ashima, Vyas Anup, and Gargh Shankar. "Management Problems and Practices: India and Nigeria." *Advances in Management* 8, no. 1 (2015): 9-14.

Paila, Anil Rao and P.S. Rao. "Ethics in Business and Indian Value Systems: Need for Integration in the Age of Science and Technology." In *Business Ethics and Human Values*, eds. V.M. Chavan, 21-28. New Delhi: Excel Books, 2009.

Painter-Morland, Mollie. *Business Ethics as Practice: Ethics as the Everyday Business of Business*. Cambridge: Cambridge University press, 2011.

Rajak, Manish Prasad. "Ancient Indian Wisdom in Modern Management: A Review of its Scope and Prospects." *aWEshkar* 18, no. 2 (2014): 18-29.

Ramaraju, A. "Human Resource Management Philosophy." *International Journal of Management* 6, no. 1 (2015): 776-783.

Saigal, Krishan. *Vedic Management: The Dharmic and Yogic Way*. Delhi: Gyan Publishing House, 2000.

Saini, Debi S. and Pawan S. Budhwar. "HRM in India." In *Managing Human Resources in Asia-Pacific*, ed. Pawan S. Budhwar, 113-140. London: Routledge, 2004.

Schwartz, Mark S. "Universal Moral Values for Corporate Codes of Ethics." *Journal of Business Ethics* 59 (2005): 27-44.

Sen, Amartya. *The Idea of Justice*. London: Penguin Books, 2009.

Shah, Shashank and V. E. Ramamoorthy. *Soulful Corporations: A Value-Based Perspective on Corporate Social Responsibility*. New Delhi: Springer, 2014.

Shrestha, Binod Krishna. "Religious Ethics and Socially Responsible Behaviours of Small Firms in Nepal." *Journal of Religion and Business Ethics* 3, no. 2 (2017): 1-16.

Singh, Yog Raj and Ankur Bhatnagar. "Management and Business Ethics through Indian Scriptures and Traditions." 2012. http://www.managementparadise.com/article/3654/management-and-business-ethics-through-indian-scriptures-and-traditions [accessed March 10, 2018].

Siu, Noel Y. M, John R. Dickinson and Betsy Y. Y. Lee. "Ethical Evaluations of Business Activities and Personal Religiousness." *Teaching Business Ethics* 4, no. 3 (2000): 233-256.

Smith, Patricia L. and Ellwood F. Oakley. "The Value of Ethics Education in Business School Curriculum." *College Student Journal* 30 (1996): 274-283.

Taylor, Frederick Winslow. *The Principles of Scientific Management*. London: Forgotten Books, 2015.

Trevino, Linda Klebe, Kenneth D. Butterfield and Donald L. McCabe. "The Ethical Context in Organizations Influence on Employee attitudes and Behaviours." *Business Ethics Quarterly* 8, no. 3 (1998): 447-476.

Verstraeten, Johan. "How Faith Makes a Difference: Business as a Calling or the Christians in Business." *Estudios Empresariales* 113 (2003/3): 56-68.

Verstraeten, Johan. "Responsible Leadership beyond Managerial Rationality: The Necessity of Reconnecting Ethics and Spirituality." In *Leadership and Business Ethics*, eds. Gabriel Flynn, vol. 25, 131-147, Dublin: Springer, 2008.

Vitell, Scott J. "The Role of Religiosity in Business and Consumer Ethics: A Review of the Literature." *Journal of Business Ethics* 90, no. 2 (2009): 155-167.

Weaver, Gary R. and Bradley R. Agle. "Religiosity and Ethical Behaviour in Organizations: A Symbolic Interactionist Perspective." *Academy of Management Review* 27, no. 1 (2002): 77-97.

Weber, Max. *The Theory of Social and Economic Organization*. Translated by A.M. Henderson and Talcott Parsons. London: Collier Macmillan Publishers, [originally in 1921] 1947; New York: The Free Press, 2012.

White, Richard D. Jr., "Drawing the Line: Religion and Spirituality in the Workplace." In *Handbook of Workplace Spirituality and Organizational Performance*, eds. Robert A. Giacalone and Carole L. Jurkiewicz, 244-256. Armonk: M.E. Sharpe, 2003.

18

The Ethical Dimension in the Social Role of Educator

Nishant Alphonse Irudayadason

Abstract

An attempt to reinstate the ethical dimension in education with a special reference to the social role of the educator is a pressing need of our times when we face the fading away of universal ideals. This researched essay first accounts briefly for the loss of universal ideals that has created an impasse for moral discourse by extensively dealing with the approaches of Kant and Freud to arrive at the reasons for the Statement. Then it deals with the task of the educator by emphasising the need to restore a moral space both for speaking and listening in an attempt to stimulate the desire to learn on the part of the students. Taking inspiration from contemporary thinkers like Paul Ricoeur, this essay tries to show how this moral democratic space becomes inevitable in the novel path of knowledge production.

Key words: Educator, knowledge, freedom, duty, ethics, desire, listening, super-ego, values etc.

Introduction

Nietzsche has called for a revaluation of all values (*Umwertung alles Wertes*)[1] and its effects can be seen today in the rejection of foundational points of reference and the loss of universal ideals, which served as the basis for

1 See Friederich Nietzsche on the Genealogy of Morals

transcendental imperatives. It is not a coincidence that today while many schools of ethics emerge, the universal master-signifiers have become irrelevant. We witness a double movement: On the one hand, multiple forms of religious life coexist, but the cult of reason especially that of scientific rationality prevails on the other hand. The loss of universal ideals has paved way for a dialogical engagement to address many contemporary challenges that resist the principle of a standard application of universal norms. The disarray of the contemporary subject in the face of loss of meaning and emergence of paradoxes tries to place in order the modes of satisfaction drives.

1. The Dominant Modality of Social Bond in the Beginning of the 21st Century

To understand the dominant modality of *social bond* in the beginning of the twenty-first century, we would like to typify three major periods in the history of the West and to assign to each one a dominant psychic structure.

But before that let us focus on the importance of social bond in human life. Behind notion of social bond, there is the idea that the human being cannot exist nor can he make sense in isolation. We know this since Aristotle.[2] Man, he said, is a political being ("*Zon politikon*"). Spinoza[3] affirmed that Being is a totality of relations, taken together in a network of infinite connections (*Nexus infinitus*). Of course, it's not just humans that cannot survive in isolation. All the elements of reality appear to us in interaction. That is why we can say that these elements constitute a world ("*kosmos*"). The more complex an individual is, the greater his dependence on others as a necessary condition for survival. This is what the theory of ecosystem theory accounts for.

The dependence of all living beings on the environment is obvious. The human dependence has some specificities. The totality of interactions that we develop during our existence is located in the field of language beginning with the new born learning to address his nourishing mother to becoming a person capable of creative expression. All these activities mobilize the resources of language. Conservation and the development of human individuals require interaction with each other through mediation of the symbolic. The City (*"Polis"*) is this community of humans who share the same symbolic universe: language, culture, institutions, norms and values. The mediation of language is what denatures all our relations; it separates these relationships from their natural state and gives them symbolic status.

2 Aristotle, *The Politics*, Book I, Chapter 2, 1253a, trans. T. A. Sinchlar (London: Penguin Books, 2000), 59.

3 Benedict de Spinoza, Ethics, Part I, Proposition 28, trans. And ed. Edwin Curley (London: Penguin Books, 1996).

This founding and constitutive symbolism of the social bond has had various figures in the course of human history. For Georges Dumézil, a French anthropologist, far from being homogeneous, the social realm is structured by functions that ensure its orderly functioning. He speaks of three functions: sovereignty ensured by the civil and religious authorities, military power and production ensured essentially by the farmers in traditional societies.[4]

The order of the world depends on respect for the hierarchy of these functions. This Hierarchy was hardly questioned before the eighteenth century. But the combined action of colonial conquests and philosophical reflection on the social order precipitated its collapse. The conquest of new lands produced unprecedented capital accumulation in history. This accumulation of capital, coupled with the evolution of science and technology paved way for the industrial development. The French revolution of 1789 can therefore be viewed as the revolution of bourgeois capitalism against feudalism. With this revolution emerged the claim to the right of private property. This right has become a foundation of our society. This inaugurates in the West what is known as Possessive individualism.[5] Literary Romanticism is one of its avatars, which has the cult of the Self as one of its features. This is the beginning of social fragmentation. It is from that moment that the traditional culture inherited from the Middle Ages (the villages, the extended families, etc.) began to be disintegrated gradually. This has led to the accumulation of capital on the one hand, and the concentration of the work force on the other. What really counts henceforth is the productive profitability. So we enter the realm of calculation, accumulation, counting, accounting and finally digitizing.

The creation of state machinery represented an attempt to regulate this destructive logic of the social bond. So, the repressive and ideological apparatus whose bureaucratic regulation tried to put some order in this anarchy, without giving up the primacy of production has found place. From this perspective, both communism and fascism are regimes based on state terrorism and absolutely ubiquitous bureaucracy that tries to regulate the social functioning in every detail. But these approaches to the social organization have met with failure. The Chernobyl disaster and the fall of the Berlin wall are examples of the bankruptcies of these ideologies and their applications.

Because of the weakening of the sense of belonging to these communities, the question that resurfaces is: who am I? With whom and with what can I identify myself? If nothing else is worth, should I not count more on myself? It is at the heart of my subjectivity, that I would find answer to my questions.

4 Georges Dumézil, "L'idéologie des trois fonctions dans les épopées des peuples indo-européens", in *Mythe et Epopée* (Paris: Gallimard, 1995), 633-634.

5 According to C.B. Macpherson, "possessive individualism" recognizes in each individual that he is solely the owner of himself. See Crawford Brough Macpherson, *The Political Theory of Possesive Individualism: Hobbes to Locke*, (Oxford: Clarendon Press, 1962).

We can call our epoch the age of the return of the subject or "return of the self" to itself to find meaning and value. These reorganizations of the social order do not happen without causing upheavals in the way in which individuals who make up the space of social interconnections find where they are and how they are evolving.

That's why I think we can identify for each era a dominant psychic structure. During the age of the absolute power of the Lord, in which the Prince-Bishop is a modality, women who defy power are branded witches. Their treatment varied from burning them to admitting them in psychiatric hospitals. The non-fiction novel *The Devils of Loudun* by Aldous Huxley in 1952 story is paradigmatic of the treatment of collective hysteria in abbeys first controlled by the Inquisition, then by medicine.[6]

In the industrial era, after the fall of the Prince, the Lord, the religious or civil Sovereign, after the fall of the King-priest, we witness the development of what is called psychosis (schizophrenia or paranoia), whose delusions attempt to restore something of the figure of the divine power. We could say that these paranoid delusions bring to the fore the persecuting power to which the subject devotes himself.

Today, at the age of breaking traditional solidarities, at the age of loss of meaning and the fall of collective ideals, we are left to ourselves. There are several possibilities offered to us, but I would like to highlight only two. The first is the restoration of religious and nationalist ideals through a strong reaffirmation of the collective identity and its corollary, rejection of the other and rejection of difference. We recognize here the figures of racism, xenophobia and fascist nationalisms that rage many countries. The second way to satisfy or respond to this anxiety about meaning is to develop a culture of individual satisfaction of needs, of "my" needs, and this in the name of an imperative of *jouissance*. Both these possibilities, when radicalized, becomes perversion. We are thus dealing with three modalities: hysterical, psychotic and perverse psychic structures.

The new contemporary mode of satisfaction of the drive, called the perversion does not need much effort to accept. The link between this perverse mode of satisfaction and an ethic that is driven by the imperative of the frenzied consumption of goods, characteristic of our contemporary period. The impotence of the state testify that the Ideal Other does not exist. We have to go one step further and recognize in the law of consumption is a new figure of superego. Thus, to ward off the non-existence of the Other the principle of absolute liberalism is established, to which commercialization of bodies is a corollary.

6 See Michel de Certeau, *The Possession at Loudun*, trans. Michael B. Smith (Chicago: University of Chicago Press, 2000).

2. The Dead Ends of the Discourse on Morality

Modern philosophy, especially that of Kant, had attempted to provide a transcendental foundation for morality, with a view to ensuring possibility of a good life beyond the vicissitudes of daily experience. We shall show what impasse does the discourse of pure—pure from all empirical satisfaction lead to. This highest moralizing aim, emerging from educational approach, is not without contradiction, which Freud did not fail to denounce, showing the limits of human ability to receive education and, more broadly, of civilization itself.

2.1 The Kantian Attempt

One of the important contributions of Kant is the construction of a pure subjectivity free of any empirical determination, a purely formal subject capable of being founded in reason, scientific knowledge and moral action. It is the last claim that poses a major problem to Kant. How does a formal subject, emptied of its ontological substance, turns out to be a practical subject? That there is an empirical subject, locatable as an agent of multiple activities in the phenomenal field, hardly poses any problem. The difficulties arise when we recognize that it is the subject of pure reason that must be practical. For Kant, to establish morality means to separate the empirical from the transcendental subject. However, this distinction proved finally unsustainable. Indeed, when it came to basing moral action and establishing the conditions for morality, Kant proposed the moral law as the driving principle and unique object of the will. It was an attempt to think the ethical foundation in all purity. But the concept of purity of practical reason has a contradiction since, determining the faculty of desire, the interest cannot but produce an experience of satisfaction, which is of an empirical order. Kant acknowledged that at this point lies the limit of his moral philosophy. It is therefore impossible to maintain a strict separation between the transcendental subject and the empirical subject. It is because the satisfaction obtained from obeying the moral law is empirical. If this satisfaction is unavoidable, how can we orient our moral judgment? What will be the indication that the maxim that defines the moral value of action is the right one?

Daily experience provides enough evidence to disprove the thesis of natural goodness of human person. But these testimonies do not instruct us on the basis of the judge's opposition to the moral law. To reach this foundation, one must question the concept of evil and its conditions of possibility with regard to the laws of freedom.

There is a necessary arbitration in every human person because of different incentives: the first of these is the moral law itself; the second, desire of senses, for which self-love is the paradigm. The question therefore is, "*which of the two incentives he [man] makes the condition of the other*".[7] Evil consists in the reversal of the hierarchy of incentives, making "incentive of self-love and its inclinations the condition of obedience to the moral law".[8] Kant attributes this reversal to tendency or propensity (*Hang*) of the radical human nature since "this very propensity must in the end be sought in a will which is free".[9]

In the Essay on Radical Evil, Kant emphasizes its essential features: "By propensity (*propensio*), I understand the subjective ground of the possibility of an inclination (habitual craving, *concupiscentia*), so far as mankind in general is liable to it".[10] In a note from the second edition of the work, Kant states that "a propensity [*Hang*] is really only a predisposition to crave a delight, which, when once experienced, arouses in the subject an inclination to it".[11] Let's emphasize the trait of subjectivity which forbids the granting of propensity an ideal or objective status. This is not a condition a priori. But this inclination characterizes human nature in general, which means that we are dealing with a notion of psychology and, more broadly, of anthropology.

Thus, the natural inclination to evil affects the free will. It makes the desire of the senses the maxim to which all the other maxims would be subordinated. This means that at the heart of the moral sovereign, therefore of freedom, may emerge propensity that is of psychological in nature. Let us recall the Kantian analysis of the degrees of propensity to evil: fragility of human nature, powerless to accomplish the Ideal of Good; impurity of the human heart, which mixes the incentive of the law with others external incentives; perversity of the human heart when the hierarchy of motives is reversed.[12] More precisely, this perversion, this inversion of maxims, consists in the fact that every human being has the possibility of choosing, as a rule of his will, self-love as a condition of respect for the moral law. The inclination to evil does not therefore oppose the moral law but subjects it to the respect of the maxim of the love of oneself. The subject is mistaken in morally justifying a maxim that opposes the moral law. We may justify murder in the name of the supreme good. The holy wars, the extermination of the Jews, the destruction of some races are examples of such a perversion.[13] There is always a moral disguise for extermination". As Himmler put it: "We had the moral right, we

7 Immanuel Kant, *Religion within the Limits of Reason Alone*, trans. Theodore M. Greene and Hoyt H. Hudson (New York: Harper and Row, 2008), 31.

8 Ibid, 32.

9 Ibid., 32.

10 Ibid., 23-24.

11 Ibid., 24.

12 Ibid., 25.

13 See Raul Hilberg, *The Destruction of the European Jews* (New York: Yale Univesity Press, 1961).

had the duty to our people, to destroy this people which wanted to destroy us. [...] Altogether however, we can say, that we have fulfilled this most difficult duty for the love of our people. And our spirit, our soul, our character has not suffered injury from it. ".[14]

So we are facing a hierarchical series of traits of human psychology, all witnesses of the impact, at the level of the intelligible act of a will, that is to say at the level of a choice, what Kant calls a "predisposition" to the desire for enjoyment. It is quite remarkable that this happens at the heart of the act of the ethical subject. In affirming the existence of such a tendency to evil, which reaches the root (*Wurzel*) of free will, Kant condemns human person of inability to act morally. As P. Ricœur quite aptly says, "the propensity for evil *affects* the use of freedom, the capacity for acting out of duty—in short, the capacity for actually being autonomous".[15] It is obviously a dramatic questioning of the possibility of the human person to exercise his moral autonomy.

Kant thus comes to enclose the subject of morality between the ideal pure adherence to the moral law and the radical inability to accomplish it. The field of lived moral consciousness is reduced to remorse, a sign of "sensibility" of the subject for the voice of morality. As for the possibility of acting morally, he will require a "miracle" of conversion, an inner revolution, whose fulfilment escapes the proper power of the human person. This conversion of the heart will produce a radical regeneration, a new birth (*Wiedergeburt*). This regeneration cannot happen as a result of human will, especially since it has been perverted at its root. However, this conversion requires the commitment of the subject, without which he would not be recognized as having an ethical value.

This conversion constitutes for Kant a limit to the power of knowledge. No more than the irruption of the inclination to evil at the source of the will, conversion, as rebirth, cannot be the subject of a knowledge (*erkennen*). We can only think (*denken*) these "events". In other words, the moment of intersecting dimensions of the absolute event (emergence of inclination to evil, conversion to good) and of contingent duration (repetitions of the inversion of maxims and remorse, efforts to improve one's morals) cannot be grasped by human intelligence. It is in God alone that absoluteness of the revolution of the heart harmonizes with the indefinite series of progress of the reform of morals. Because it is under the gaze of one who is not limited by time or by the space that the progressive transformation of morals for the sake of good will appear in its unity, as a kind of equivalent to the timelessness of conversion.

---

14 Himmler as cited by Jackson J. Spielvogel, Western Civilization Volume C: Since 1789 (Stanford: Cenage Learning, 2015), 855.

15 Paul Ricœur, *Oneself as Another*, trans. Kathleen Blamey (Chicago: The University of Chicago Press, 1992), 216.

Recourse to a supernatural instance to account for the possibility of liberation of the will in order to adhere to the maxim of morality is a way of acknowledging the impossibility of making empirical subject accord with the ethical subject. Moreover, we are shown the necessity of the postulate for the existence of God for the effective functioning of the moral life. The condition of the divided human subject will be subverted only by a new birth, releasing the moral sovereign from his subjection to evil inclination.

But this new human person is not the one we know. He is thinkable, but only as an ideal. This ideal will support the "progressive reform of the inclination to evil as a perverse way of thinking". The subjective, anthropological spring of this moralization could be admiration, the object of which is "the original moral disposition in us in general". It remains nonetheless evil, "as a natural inclination, [...] that cannot be destroyed by the forces of human beings". Admittedly, the human person can rely on the disposition to the good that is his source. But "assistance from above" is required, of which no knowledge is given to us. Only hope is here, and it does not exempt the finished subject of the efforts of wanting to become a better person. This hope is based on the possibility of a divine complement to human action.

What becomes of desire from this perspective? It can be considered that this is the moral consciousness and its unbridled rigor that would be the desiring instance in the pure state, claiming the renunciation of all empirical satisfaction. Thus, the destruction of the power of propensity to evil would be accompanied by a kind of compensation, since there would be an undivided instance of a pure moral requirement at the heart of the subject, which can be identified as the ideal figure of pure desire, but supported by the Divine Other.

But what happens to the subject when this divine Other loses consistency? Either he is misled by the contemporary conditions imposed on belief, or he is treated by the psychoanalytic cure. For this is "the effect of desperation that analysis allows for so much effort, even the most noble, traditional ethics". Contrary to the Kantian approach, the desire of the psychoanalyst "is not a pure desire". Psychoanalysis leads the subject to separate himself from the primordial signifiers to which he was subjected, signifiers whose value of the ideal was due to their dependence on the desire of the divine Other. In this sense, the psychoanalytic cure frees the subject from chains of the pure desire of the Other. The subversion introduced by the psychoanalyst's desire aims to "get the absolute difference", implying the separation of the subject from the alienating Other. On this point, Lacan is not in agreement with Kant.

2.2 Freudian Criticism of the Civilizing Super-ego

The stalemate that Kantian construction encounters is therefore the emergence of an insatiable instance of moral purity. We have no difficulty in recognizing the Freudian figure of the superego. But the impasse denounced by Freud is exactly this figure. The convening of the so-called internalized civilizer does not in any way guarantee the subject or the community in which he is inscribed to guard against the ravages of the drive to destroy others first and then oneself.

For this, recent history gives sufficient attestation. To stick only to the Christian figure of this superego, it is clear that Christian education (that is, the values promoted by the Gospel message) failed to eradicate the deadly hatred of humans. Ethnocide, homicidal wars, exclusions, banishments, excommunications, have even been preached by those responsible for this education. The silence of Pope Pius XII during the extermination of the Jews by the Nazis, the support of the Catholic Church to the Rwandans authorities who organized the massacre of Tutsi populations, the wars of religion between Catholics and Protestants, from the old French regime to a more recent time in Ireland—all these facts bear witness to a limit to the civilizing.

How to account for this failure, the recurrence of which does not allow us to say that its causes are occasional. The position of Freud is, in this respect, without false pretence.

> We are threatened with suffering from three directions: from our own body, which is doomed to decay and dissolution and which cannot even do without pain and anxiety as warning signals; from the external world, which may rage against us with overwhelming and merciless forces of destruction; and finally from our relations to other men. The suffering which comes from this last source is perhaps more painful to us than any other. We tend to regard it as a kind of gratuitous addition, although it cannot be any less fatefully inevitable than the suffering which comes from elsewhere.[16]

If this threat is not accidental but essential to the human experience, how to account for it? It must be acknowledged that the human nature is not what J.-J. Rousseau thought it to be:

> …men are not gentle creatures who want to be loved, and who at the most can defend themselves if they are attack; they are, on the contrary, creatures among whose instinctual endowments is to be reckoned a powerful share of aggressiveness. As a result, their neighbor is for them not only a potential helper or sexual object, but also someone who tempts them to satisfy their aggressiveness on him, to exploit his capacity for work without compensation, to use him sexually without his consent, to seize his possessions, to humiliate him, to cause him pain, to torture and to kill him. *Homo homini lupus*. Who, in the face of all his experience of life and of history, will have the courage to dispute this assertion?[17]

16 Sigmund Freud, *Civilization and its Discontents*, (New York: Norton, 1961), 77.

17 Ibid, 58.

An impulse of aggression, a mortal force is at work, which seeks to be discharged, if necessary by getting around the obstacles posed by the moral injunctions internalized by the subject. "The existence of this inclination to aggression, which we can detect in ourselves and justly assume to be present in others, is the factor which disturbs our relations with our neighbor and which forces civilization into such a high expenditure [of energy]. In consequence of this primary mutual hostility of human beings, civilized society is perpetually threatened with disintegration. The interest of work in common would not hold it together; instinctual passions are stronger than reasonable interests ".[18]

If the tendency for solidarity is not spontaneous, it is left to the civilization to set up devices capable of reducing tendency for aggression towards the other. "Civilization has to use its utmost efforts in order to set limits to man's aggressive instincts and to hold the manifestations of them in check by psychical reaction-formations. Hence, therefore, the use of methods intended to incite people into identifications and aim-inhibited relations of love, hence the restriction upon sexual life, and hence too the ideal's commandment to love one's neighbour as oneself -- a commandment which is really justified by the fact that nothing else runs so strongly counter to the original nature of man".[19]

Sometimes education and repression, by uniting their efforts, succeed in neutralizing the death drive of members of a given community. The identification of each one with the leader, with the common ideal, produces the mutual identification of brothers who are in solidarity. But the potential for aggression is not diminished and seeks to manifest elsewhere. "It is clearly not easy for man to give up the satisfaction of this inclination to aggression. They do not feel comfortable without it. The advantage which a comparatively small cultural group offers of allowing this instinct an outlet in the form of hostility against intruders is not to be despised. It is always possible to bind together a considerable number of people in love, so long as there are other people left over to receive the manifestations of their aggressiveness ".[20]

Racial hatred and inter-ethnic wars are a way out of this need for satisfying the death drive. "In this respect the Jewish people, scattered everywhere, have rendered most useful services to the civilizations of the countries that have been their hosts; but unfortunately all the massacres of the Jews in the Middle Ages did not suffice to make that period more peaceful and secure for their Christian fellows....".[21] This text is written by Freud in 1929. Its author had foreseen the National-Socialist danger. We can measure today the height of the potential reached by the death drive to the extent of exterminations!

18 Ibid., 59.

19 Ibid., 59.

20 Ibid., 61.

21 Ibid., 61.

3. Position to Adopt as an Educator

The question is whether the hypothesis of a death drive is the last word from the explanation of the fundamental intolerance of human to fellow human. And if so, what position to adopt as educators, as responsible human beings? The importance given today to ethical issues in general and moral education in particular, testifies to the desire to restore some reference points which gives human action a sensible orientation.

In this respect, Paul Ricoeur is perfectly emblematic, as he speaks of ethics "before morality". Thus, in 1990, P. Ricœur suggested to reserve the term "ethics" for the purpose of an accomplished life under the sign of actions considered good, and "moral" for the life under obligation, marked by norms characterized both by a requirement of universality and by an effect of constraint. Ethics is first of all desire for self-fulfilment. This supposes that this self is valued and esteemed estimated. That's why the ethical aim is first of all, a faith in this power-to be oneself, as the subject of one's act, and not only as a product of psychological and social determinations.

Education is this action whose aim is to enable the subject to learn to be recognized by oneself and others, as an "I can" that is realized in various types of activities. Ethics is thus a journey, the journey of an oriented life, a journey from faith in this "I can" to the act that embodies in a real story. We understand that this assertion of self, this embodied self-esteem in action, is strictly dialectical insofar as it calls not only for the recognition of the self by the other, but also for the recognition of the other by oneself. At this stage, the other is my fellow human and calls the movement of solicitude for others. However, this solicitude is not left to the arbitrariness of the impulses of the heart. It is part of a common world, the world of all, whose institution is the guarantor, guaranteeing that everyone has value for others and vice versa.

In this view of oneself, we recognize the importance of research that takes as its object the identity dimension of the subject. The importance of self-esteem in the learning process, such as the development of the biographical approach and especially the autobiographical narrative both for its heuristic and formative values, is a clear testimony to this. This retreat into the private space constitutes a significant loss of universal reference and the insufficiency of the relation to the consumable to find the dimension of the irreducible desire to the need of the subject. Psychoanalysis itself is confined by authors like R. Rorty43, to the sphere of private life, in search of a reconciliation of the self with itself, when it is not engaging in the reduction of the subject to a capable strategist, manoeuvring between the imperatives of the drive, the civilizing super-ego and the harsh external reality!

Now, the question of desire is that of social segregation in the unequal relation to the objects of jouissance. As Ricœur has rightly perceived, the ethical exigency includes justice guaranteed by institutions. This consideration alone raises the idea of taking desire beyond drive satisfaction. It is this beyond that is challenged by relativizing the founding ideals of a community.

Faced with this radical challenge, the field of educational practices has a definite advantage, because it presents this dual characteristic of being deployed in the dimension of love and to be open knowledge which, by its very structure, constitutes its beyond. With regard to the educational activity considered from the ethical point of view, we can say that the subject accomplished in education is no longer to be considered as a beneficiary of a transmitted knowledge, but as subject of action in whom the educational activity is accomplished. This place is the person of the educated. Only then it is possible to locate the essential aspect of educational action, namely the advent of the subject in the first person, as a subject capable of answering for himself. There is a shift of focus from the educator to the educated, now considered as the subject of action. The subject of educational activity does not hail outside of determined social and axiological contexts. But he transcends these contexts and it is important for the educator to present the absolute limit of his intervention. This is the moment when the subject makes a project of himself while he still does not know if he wants this to happen.

This construction of the subject of the act is the effect of an educational transfer work. For the desire of the subject takes form at the heart of the subjective division, which is called by the desire of the Other, the Other whose teacher, on the one hand, the knowledge taught, on the other, can be representatives for the learner. This implies that, far from presenting itself as a compact subject of sediment knowledge to which the subject must submit, the teaching which claims to allow learning must have a dual characteristic. On the one hand, it must reveal its relevance to the question that is at the heart of the process of producing knowledge. On the other hand, it must have a relative incompleteness in order to signify to the learner that his engagement in the process of construction of knowledge is necessary, if he wants this knowledge to make sense for him. This way of teaching requires from the teacher himself a non-dogmatic relation to the knowledge he transmits, that is to say that he does not identify himself with a position of totalizing truth.

The setting of desire in play seems to be a necessary passage for the entry of the subject into a process of formation-transformation. In this respect, the quality of the relationship between the educator and the adult learner is decisive, because it is important that the desire of the subject in formation is mobilized without getting enclosed in a pedagogical transfer but to remain open to new knowledge that will enable him to shape his desire at least partially. This transformation is possible only if the educator does not identify himself with the object of the learner's desire. On the contrary, the educator has to show how the new knowledge can contribute to bringing the subject closer to what causes his desire for learning. The educator introduces himself as a learner subject, divided by a relationship between acquired knowledge and new knowledge. The teacher teaches as a subject learner.

4. Listening and Transmission in Educational Relationship

At the end of our critical reflection on the dead ends of educational ethics, we have proposed a model of educational relationship based on the resources of the subject desiring to initiate a process of learning "new knowledge".

It seems to me that we have one last question to address. If it is true that the division of the subject is structural, the fact remains that the modalities of the contemporary social bond seem to be joining forces to seal it completely. This is the hypothesis we made when we denounced the perverse drift of today's dominant consumerism. It is therefore important to ask ourselves how we can restore a mode of social bond that gives right to this division of the subject. In this respect, listening to the singular subject is an answer, though not exhaustive, but relevant to the malaise in our contemporary civilization. Open to the heart of symbiotic relations, everyone can make his voice heard and can find. This is possible only by listening.

Listening becomes the mode of a new social bond in as much as it contradicts the logic of the imperative of frenzied enjoyment. What is the structure of this operation? It reveals the very condition of the speaking subject with a radical lack manifested in his request for help. It is beyond Oedipus that he discovers that it is not a lack that he must at all cost eliminate, but only the lack which is structural. This lack is not a result of circumstances but that which makes him human. The gradual discovery of something which is irreducible to satisfaction is the effect of an important psychic work. The function of listening is to offer a space for this structural lack to be noticeable in ordinary social experience and particularly in the relationship between the educator and the learner. It is probably from this perspective that the practice of listening becomes significant today not only for the students, but also for the educators who are also confronted with the violence of the imperative of enjoyment.

This wager is about the benefits of communicative action, this wager of conversation, however, is not without producing occasionally a "perverse" effect, namely the illusion that the listening of the child, of the student, the learner, is the whole of the educational relationship. It would be to forget the other pole of the function of the educator: his duty to transmit new knowledge that puts the subject learner in tension with himself and to go beyond his sphere of identity. In this way he will be able to get to work by relying on this fundamental experience of attentive recognition by the other willing to listen to him. Thus we will avoid the demagogic trap of an egocentric education forgetful of the need to go through the other to open up to the knowledge society. This is the challenge of an ethics of education today: to support both the moment of recognition of the subject and to create the conditions for his involvement so that he can open his mind to the otherness of knowledge taken from the opacity of the real, in order to share it in a democratic space governed by an ideal of justice.

19

'Poetic Dwelling as Ecological Mindfulness:' Re-Visiting Heidegger's Deconstruction of Metaphysics Through Technology to Ecology

Jojo Varakukalayil, CST

Abstract

In modern technology metaphysics realizes its ultimate possibility of the subject as domination over reality, and for Martin Heidegger the metaphysical rationality is turned into a technological rationality – a 'logic of domination'. The history of Being, maintains Heidegger, culminates in this technological enframing. From the metaphysics of technological relation he takes us to a 'thinking of Being' (*Seinsdenken*) of ecological relation. In technological thinking the nature is turned into 'standing reserve' and de-worlds the cosmic reality. Technological enframing violates both humanity and nature at its deepest level. Heidegger's thinking of the essence of technology, I argue, challenges us to an 'ecological-conversion (*metanoia*).' Heidegger's thinking of the 'poetically humans dwells' upon the earth is an open invitation of the question of ecology unfolded. The word 'ecology' in its Greek origins is *oikos* (house) and *logos* (letting); and it thus signifies letting be the house be a house only through dwelling. Poetic is the basic capacity for human dwelling in harmony with the entire cosmic milieu where the mode of existence is letting the other be in peaceful justice. The earth is earth only in so far as humans dwell on it. Dwelling is thus the original admission of the poetic where humans remain heedful of the poetic which is the basic capacity for human dwelling. Poetic dwelling is a harmless and kind way of being upon the earth. Poetic dwelling calls forth for an attitude of reverence and respect for the bio-diversity; and thus in poetic dwelling humans emerge to be dwelling 'humanly' upon this habitat as his home. This vocation of a more primal truth brings forth of the true to the beautiful, and accordingly enables humans to be in active alliance with reality - agapeic mindfulness - finding oneself interconnected and shepherd of Being.

Key words: Technology, techne, poetic, dwell, ecology, kindness

"There is a thinking for more rigorous than the conceptual"
- Martin Heidegger

1. Heidegger's Project of the Meaning of Being and *Dasein*

The question of the meaning of Being that struck at the very root of Martin Heidegger's (1889-1976) [1] philosophical career was one of the most central questions that unearthed the meaning of human being (*Dasein*) as well. He has ever finished the project of the meaning of Being in *Being and Time* (1927), rather one finds this remains a lifelong quest in all the different phases of his thinking. This quest was carried out through different ways in Heidegger. Albeit it started with the critique of the western metaphysical tradition he sought of the meaning of Being unravelled through very many ways in the course of his philosophical career.

The course of western philosophical history, for Heidegger, has been characterized by a series of errors that he calls as metaphysics.[2] The western metaphysical pasts are instances of, manifestations of Being (existence), they are not being (existence itself). Heidegger's charge is that western metaphysics, since Plato and Aristotle (we could even say because of them) began well, with the resolve to make an enquiry into existence. But very soon its attention

1 Martin Heidegger (1889-1976) is widely acclaimed as the most outstanding and creative philosopher of the 20th century, not merely for the novelty of his philosophy, but mainly for having brought about a revolution in Western philosophy. Almost every philosopher since Plato and Aristotle, the great milestone philosophers of Western philosophy, continued to philosophize in the same tradition i.e., without any serious change. Heidegger on the other hand stood single-handed against the monolithic structure of Western Philosophy of two millennia, pointed out its deviating growth and proposed a novel approach to philosophy. This ingenious move towards the meaning of Being in Heidegger is presented in his different phases of thought (early, middle and later Heidegger). However his philosophy doesn't remain within the system of thought as in the case of Aristotle or Hegel, rather a movement a way making movement – *be-wegung*. Heidegger went on to point out that this was because the great pre-Socratics, especially Parmenides, were really engaged in the study of Being and not of beings.

2 Martin Heidegger, *Basic Writings* (New York: Harper & Row, 1977).

was distracted, it became enamoured with studying, analyzing and classifying individual existing things (or even God, the Supreme Existent) and forgetting that the original purpose of quest was to focus on Being as such, existence (IM 20). For Heidegger, "Being remains forgotten" (IM 20)[3]. To correct this wrong approach, to lead us back from this misleading path and enable us to find a true path into the very heart of Being, we cannot but break with conventional usages of words (very specially metaphysical terms), for all these have been shot through with connotations of a "oblivion of Being" (IM 20; ID 7).

In Heidegger's contention this tradition of metaphysics began addressing Being as an object of conceptual knowledge and made the mistake of thinking Being *per se* as if it were another being, and that is to say that there is a reification of Being ever since the thinking of Being. This philosophical 'errancy' flourished at the expense of the forgettenness/forgetfulness of Being for the last two millennia. The real question of Being, for Heidegger, was left aside and the Western philosophy was preoccupied with the question of Being as being, i.e., the authentic Being was taken to mean as another thing or object of thought (BT 40). Thus levelling Being to beings. Indeed, as Heidegger never wearied to point out, western-European thought, since the post-Socratic periods has been characterized by oblivion of Being in favour of beings (ID 7). Being itself, as Heidegger interprets it, is not an entity or a thing. (Heidegger, indeed, suggests that poetic language may be the best way to express the meaning of Being which we are to discuss in the later part of this article). This way of fixing of the meaning of Being was the effort of the human minds who controls over the meaning of Being. This tendency of the human effort of thinking - calculative thinking[4] – was doing the wrong to the very meaning of Being itself. Conversely, for Heidegger, true metaphysics should focus on the fact (or, better still, the act) of existence and not on existents, concretely existing things (BT 2). Because Being is 'no-thing', but the event of Being; nevertheless we misconstrue it as being or the existent. Heidegger takes Being as the clearing, the lighting of the 'there' (*da*) in which the entities or particular beings enter into the scene, existents disclose themselves as they are. Heidegger construes human existence as being there or *Dasein*, the ontological name for human being.

Having said this from the earlier phase of Heidegger's critique of the western metaphysical past we understand that this error is most strikingly and

3 Martin Heidegger, *Introduction to Metaphysics* (New Haven: Yale University Press, 1959).

4 Martin Heidegger, *Discourse on Thinking* (New York: Harper & Row Publishers, 1966), 54. Heidegger, in his *Discourse on Thinking* speaks about the distinction between two kinds of thinking, namely, calculative thinking and meditative thinking. Calculative thinking is instrumental and meditative thinking is a way out of the former. A characteristic of the latter could be called as 'releasement'.

destructively transparent in contemporary times in the forms of technology.[5] In order to claim this Heidegger argues that technology as we understand today from its instrumental and anthropological sense of meaning is a way towards ends. In brief, technologies of the modern times remain as instrumental and it is governed by the manipulative reason of the calculative thinking of humans. In such a framework "everywhere we remain unfree and chained to technology, whether we passionately affirm or deny it" (QT, 1) argues Heidegger. Technologies have become the manifestation of the dominant reason that challenges the external world bereft of its meaning as in itself. The environmental world is approached from the point of the material resources ready at hand that can be controlled and used up for the human needs. Such an approach to the natural world has left us into problems that we face with environment today.

Further Heidegger maintains that the modern man remains unfocused or rather left homeless and alienated from him/her self at the wake of the glorification of reason. Faced up with the agony of man from within him/her self there is a devastation happening to humans today. The technological advancement has made certain pronouncements in the destiny of humans today. Contemporary technological and capitalistic society has left humanity as lonely isles. Why? The metaphysical past has left us with the calculative meaning of Being and beings. The idolization Being ever since Plato has become concretized in the modern forms of modern technology as technical-scientific-calculative. The modern mode of approach to the nature was one of stockpile out there for the consumption and controlee of man.

Heidegger's thinking of the meaning of Being leaves us with insights of hope, for Daseins' essential nature is inextricably woven with the essential unfolding of Being. The authenticity of human existence happens for Heidegger in our essential belonging to the happening of Being as it discloses (*aletheuein*).[6] The meaning of human existence at the wake of existentialist

5 Martin Heidegger, "The Question concerning Technology," 1. Heidegger carries out this authentic analysis on the notion of technology which he tried to overcome beyond its instrumental and anthropological understanding to its fundamental meaning as *techne* as bringing forth, to *poiesis*, it is something poetic. He argues that the essence of technology is by no means anything technological. What is most interesting for our analysis is Heidegger's contention of *techne* not as some activities or the skill of the craftsman, but the arts of the mind and the fine arts.

6 There is a shift or turn *(Kehre) in Heidegger's philosophical growth as a thinker of Being. It starts from the epistemological to the ontological – aletheialogical*. There was a shift in the progressive thinking of Heidegger as he realized that he was not fully liberated from the metaphysical Western tradition. In his *Being and Time* Dasein clarifies or discloses Being. But after the shift, Dasein has to be seen in the light of Being. The turn is a movement from the hermeneutical process to the 'aletheialogical' process. In the hermeneutical process, Dasein enables Being to disclose itself whereas in the 'aletheialogical' process, Being is

philosophy was one of the crucial issues that remain un-resolved down to the centuries of western metaphysical thinking. However, later Heidegger thinks a way out of such weight of our being tied it itself to the liberating potential of human being at the neighbourhood of Being. This can be attained from a vantage point of analysing Heidegger's critique of technology, poetry, and thought (PLT). Heidegger's insights on the oblivion of Being is a way to explain the possibility of salvation from such threat that announces the poetic dwelling. Hence, this article carries out the project of investigating Heidegger's deconstruction[7] of technology to poetry and thought to the ecological mindfulness unravelling the ethos of man.

2. Instrumental Reason as the Logic of Domination

One of the first things to catch the eye when it comes to the problematic aspects of our modern and post-modern culture of living is the logic of domination. The logic of domination is mostly expressed in human rationality, that is to say, everything other than the same/ego/self is reduced into the crucible of the whole encompassing reason. The reason is epitomised in modernity as glorification of reason in Cartesian indubitable cogito that hails the reason as the supreme spearhead of human being. The cogito is once and for all certain of its being i.e., the ego cogito undoubtedly exists by virtue of the fact of it as thinking thing that Rene Descartes pronounces in his *Meditations on the First Philosophy*.[8] The modern reason becomes very prominent in its affirmations on truth (truth as correctness) and being. The cult of reason thus leaves no room any being - God, humans, or cosmos - apart from it. Reason understood in this way functions as a panopticon and thus totalizes everything under its vista. This overarching claim of reason in modernity works as instrumental and this is also known as formal, functional, technical, objective-related

---

seen as disclosing itself. After the turn (*kehre*) in his thinking, Being is no more considered from the perspective of human person; on the contrary, human person is seen in the light of Being. He directs his philosophical energy to the thinking of Being, not as an investigation or analysis of it, but as a letting oneself be spoken to by being as to how it presences itself to human person in entities. In short, the revelation of Being in beings as Platonic idea of *ekphanestaton* — the most apparent as the vision of the invisible within the visible. Being is the excess for Heidegger.

7 Deconstruction as construction remains its primary meaning in Heidegger's emplyoing the term originally as *destruktion*. Construing this original meaning of deconstruction Spivak explains that "deconstruction is construction. It's critical intimacy, not critical distance. So you actually speak from inside. That's deconstruction." Gayatri Chakravorty Spivak, Accessed on 30 April 2019. https://lareviewofbooks.org/article/critical-intimacy-interview-gayatri-chakravortyspivak/?fbclid=IwAR1_ytviRmlyIYOILzBrX5lxUq0rYT6EfEVbR0j8Qjw5FKaCbj7AbwQaCdQ#.

8 Rene Descartes, *Meditations on First Philosophy*, Donald A. Cress, Trans. (Cambridge: Hackett Publishing Company, 1993).

rationality at the expense of value rationality. '*Homo mensura'*, the dictum from Protagoras, is the slogan of our times. Man as rational beings become the measure of everything, i.e., the human reason is the arbiter of truth and being.

The problems with rationality lies in its claim to absolutize itself upon every reality where "the values of modern rationality have no connection with the fabric of moral and social relationships; so with the daily life" (SRO 39); thus reason becomes all encompassing where particularity is confused with totality and thus not with thought but with life (CPP 25). There is nothing outside the all encircling reason where the imperialism of reason suppresses the otherness in the universalizing immanence of the Same (*le Meme*) and thereby expelling the violence of Being (*Etre*) (BPW 11). Such logic of domination is manifested in an attitude of violence to nature and reality. This logic of the imperialistic reason is the result of a metaphysical thinking which Heidegger attempted to deconstruct. Such thinking "has its roots in western metaphysics, grew stronger in science, became intense in technology, and got climaxed in globalization" (HEHC 57). Modern technology would not have been there without a metaphysical past as Heidegger looks at it. Given this, modern technology is the outcome of the western metaphysical past that has entangled itself with the question of Being as being, namely, the reification of being.

3. Logic of Domination in Science-Technology

Metaphysical tradition, for Heidegger, starting with Plato and Aristotle, culminates in German idealism and becomes complete in Nietzsche. During the long metaphysical periods of two millennia, it was logic-dominated conceptual philosophy. In the process of conceptualization metaphysics became epistemology with an emphasis on subject-object dichotomy. The subject becomes the arbiter of truth, and the world becomes a 'conceptual' reality for the representing subject, or to the representational cogito. This metaphysical subject has been enjoying an 'intellectual domination over reality. This subjectivist tendency of *domination* grew stronger in science, characterized by 'research' (*foschung*) which calls for rigor in procedure as per a projected plan with mathematical exactitude.

Modern scientific approach gradually prepared the ground for technological attitude, that turned more aggressive expression of scientific thinking. In technology metaphysics realizes its ultimate possibility of the subject's domination over reality. The cry of the technological man of the modernity runs after development at the expense of the relation of the primal truth. It is not an exaggeration to say that without a metaphysical past, there would have come about no technological present. The modern scientific attitude consists in the 'objectification' of reality by the subject's calculative investigation. The modern scientific rationality leads to a calculative thinking and living where shameless reason suspends the primal truth as revealing. One does not dispose oneself to the disclosure or revelation of Being where one is run by the calculative exactitude.

The nature, for a modern scientist, is an 'object' to be analyzed with mathematical exactitude; for the technologist, on the other hand, nature is but a huge source of energy, to be unlocked, transformed, stored up and distributed, to be extracted and exploited. "Modern physics," writes Heidegger "is not experimental physics, because it applies apparatus to the questioning of nature. Rather the reverse is true. Because physics, indeed, already as pure theory, sets nature up to exhibit itself as a coherence of forces calculable in advance, it therefore orders its experiments precisely for the purpose asking whether and how nature reports itself when sets up in this way" (QT 10). In modern science there have developed utilitarian and pragmatic approach to nature where the soul of nature is lost in the technocracy of modern man. It has resulted into the present day ecological crises that have turned to be cancerous and epidemic. Thus the imperialistic reason is not shameful in itself; rather it subdues everything in totalizing – resultantly in representationalism, totalitarianism and scientism. This permits an internal bleeding which happens in our times as the environmental crises. The desertification of the earth would be a result of our internal hollowness. We have abused the nature and have a mistaken perception of the inner meaning, namely, the essence of technology. The metaphysical rationality is turned into technological rationality in which the 'logic of domination' spares not even God; the Divine is 'objectified' and brought under the manipulative control of the humans. Thus along with nature and the humans, the divine, too, has become a victim of the technological culture, characterized by the logic of domination. "What is dangerous," Heidegger writes, "is not technology. Technology is not demonic; but its essence is mysterious. The essence of technology, as a destining of revealing, is the danger" (BW 333).

4. Deconstructing Technology to Ecology

Heidegger deconstructs the meaning of technology. He writes, "[t]he current conception of technology, according to which it is a means and a human activity, can therefore be called instrumental and anthropological definition of technology" (BW 312). This instrumental dentition of technology is uncannily correct. But, for Heidegger, if one inquires step by step into what technology is, one arrives at the essence of technology as revealing. "Technology is no more a means. Technology is a way of revealing" (BW 318) writes, Heidegger. It reveals the realm of the essence of technology, the way of truth; that is, *techne* in its Greek origins means bringing forth, to *poiesis*; it is something poetic

(Ibid).[9] In such an understanding of the meaning of technology from its root word *techne* as bring forth and as *episteme* in Plato and Aristotle, we arrive at the claim of Heidegger that "technology is a mode of revealing. Technology comes to presence in the realm where revealing and unconcealment take place, where *aletheia*, truth, happens" (BW 319). But the danger within the modern technology consists as it is understood as exact science within modern physics.

The logic of domination which is nourished by the metaphysical rationality as exemplified by the technological culture today has brought about devastation of human environment and his/her ecological relation. There is an alienation that has happened to the technological man of the modern times. For Heidegger, "everything depends on our manipulating technology in the proper manner as mean. We will, as we say, 'get' technology 'spiritually in hand.' We will master it. The will to master becomes all the more urgent the more technology threatens to slip from human control" (QT 2). Heidegger's question concerning technology opens forth something very fundaments to questioning itself as he writes "questioning builds a way" (QT 1). The way, of course, for him, is one of thinking. Thinking about technology led him to the essence of technology as *aletheia* as revealing. Hence he argues that "the merely instrumental, merely anthropological definition of technology is therefore untenable" (QT 10). Given this argument of Heidegger we understand that man in the technological age is challenged forth into revealing that concerns nature. It is at this juncture that we find the fertility of later Heidegger's ecological mindfulness. Albeit Heidegger barely talks about ecology in his writings, one could still find the fecundity of such thought. He ever closes the door at it, rather the always welcome! Heidegger's poetic mindfulness takes us very much in to the *ecological recollection*, to such a great degree he is esteemed as the 'philosophical patron' of ecology.

The term 'ecology' is compounded of the Greek root-terms: *oiks* (house) *logos* (letting, gathering); and thus it means 'letting be the house.' This etymological meaning of ecology is to be taken in Heidegger's sense of the hermeneutical.[10] Dwelling becomes one of the very key notions in

9 Marius Geertsema, *Heidegger's Poetic Projection of Being* (Switzerland: Palgrave Macmillan, 2018). In Heidegger's oeuvre, being is essentially dialogical with the poetic and it is not to be taken as strictly tethered poems rather as a type of thinking that refers to the intimation of the future that shapes human thought and behaviour in the light of our finitude. This poetic is a way of Being disclosing as aletheia – that is, an attunement towards nature, oneself, each other and the divine.

10 Drawing inspiration from Husserl's phenomenology, Heidegger shatters down the subject object dichotomy. Heidegger analyses phenomenology in its etymological sense. Phenomenology is made up of *phainamenon* and *logos. Phainamenon* is derived from *phainesthai* that means to show itself and *logos* from *legein* that means letting something be seen as unhidden. Both letting be seen and showing itself are complimentary and related. This method of thinking is the new methodology as hermeneutical phenomenology

later Heidegger. "The fundamental character of dwelling is [the] sparing and preserving" (PLT 147). Dwelling and building holds a significant place in Heidegger as he says building is an original gathering that allows mortals to dwell poetically within the horizon of the truth of Being. Heidegger writes,

> The way in which you are and I am, the manner in which we humans *are* on this earth, is *Bauen*, dwelling. To be a human being means to be on the earth as mortal. It means to dwell. The old word *bauen*, which says that man *is* in so far as he *dwells*, this word *bauen* however *also* means at the same time to cherish and protect, to preserve and care for, specifically to till the soil, to cultivate the vine. Such building only takes care - it tends the growth that ripens into its fruit of its own accord (PLT 145).

The house becomes house only though dwelling. The human abode - the earth - becomes a house when humans dwell on it. The humans have to be 'dwellers' on the earth which is the 'poetical' in Heidegger; and 'dwelling on the earth' implies the mindfulness of the humans beyond calculative thinking/rationality in later Heidegger. Hence to be is to dwell. As there is a primordial openness in to which the bio-diversity shows forth humans must exist ecologically, i.e., human existence becomes a "poetic recollectedness"[11] upon the earth. Humans are humans in so far as s/he lives on earth, under the heavens, in front of the gods, with his/her fellow humans. As mortals we tend the fourfold by saving the earth by letting it be as earth; by receiving heaven as heaven; by awaiting the arrival of the gods, by shepherding themselves, in their own essence. Humans dwell on the earth by being at the neighbourhood of being as the shepherded of being. This is the way to enter in to relation with Being. Humans as mortals are called up on to be dwellers, to be poetic dwellers recalling one's original essence. This poetic dwelling tastes the ecological mindfulness as the fourfoldness in Heidegger.

Ecological relatedness is not something adjacent to the human reality; rather it is a way of being human upon this habitat. From the metaphysics of technological relation, Heidegger leads us to a 'thinking of Being' (*seinsdenken*) of ecological relation. Being, for later Heidegger, is the subject-less activity of the coming-to-be of reality in time and space. The mortals remain open to the coming of Being in receptive opening. It is poetic mindfulness of the mortals. The modes of listening, thanking, gathering, dwelling, releasing, seeing, etc.,

---

in Heidegger's philosophy. However one must be keen in taking Heidegger's method? Not in the sense of the traditional methods of doing philosophy. 'Hermeneutics' for him is not a method, that he employs in his philosophical enterprise, rather it is his philosophy. Heidegger gives a new meaning for 'method'. *'Der Weg heißt griechisch* ***odos; meta*** *heibt 'nach', methodos ist der weg, auf dem wir einer Sache nachgehen: die Methode*." *Der Satz vom Grund* 5 *Aufl* (Pfullingen: Neske, 1978). p. 111.

11 Jojo Varakukalayil, "Cosmic Religiosity as Poetic Recollection," in *Romancing the Sacred*, George Karuvelil (ed.), (Bangalore: ATC Publications, 2007).

are the ways of awaiting its arrival. It evokes humans 'to *dwell* poetically on the earth.' Dwelling upon the earth brings us to this 'ecological musings'. Humans are captivated in to the sense of Being with the call of Being. What does it signify to be poetic dwelling at all?

5. On Poetic Dwelling as Ecological Mindfulness

"*Poetically man dwells* ..." (PLT 213); is borrowed from Holderlin's poem which later Heidegger oft employs to convey the message and essence of technology as revealing, unconcealment – *aletheia*, the manifestation of the primal truth. "The poetical," for Heidegger, "brings the true into the splendor of what Plato in the *Phaedrus* calls to *ekphanestaton*, that which shines forth most purely" (QT 18). He clarifies that today dwelling is often harassed by our work. 'And man's dwelling is supposed to be poetry or poetic?' "The poetic," for Heidegger, "is the way of what first brings man on to the earth, making him belong to it, and thus brings him into dwelling" (PLT 216).[12] It does not assert about man's dwelling conditions today or rather dwelling places. Human existence in terms of dwelling speaks of occupying lodging. The relation to the place of dwelling becomes one of dominance. On the other hand poetic dwelling is an authentic listening to the appeal of language as the home of being. Poetically dwelling, thinking in terms of the key note of this word, does not speak for the meritorious dwelling of man.

The meaning of poetic dwelling would speak for the dwelling of mortals as poetic, which is to say, "Dwelling flies fantastically above reality" (PLT 218). Why does man poetically dwell? Man is called as the image of the God head to look up to the divinities from here below on the earth. This look spans between the sky and earth. This is not to be understood as something *gegenstand* rather "man is man at all only in such spanning" (PLT 221). This is a measuring according to Heidegger in the sense that the God who is unknown manifests as unknown by way of the sky's manifestness; and "this appearance is the measure against which man measures himself" (PLT 223). The poetic in these explanations would suggest that man's dwelling 'on the earth' as mortals spans across the earth and 'beneath the sky' which belongs together. For Heidegger, "their interplay is the span that man traverses at every moment insofar as he is an earthly being" (PLT 223). Being on the earth would be dwelling only insofar as man dwells upon it and thus "in his dwelling lets the earth be as earth" (PLT 227). Poetry admits man to his dwelling into its very nature; and "the poetic is the basic capacity for human dwelling" (PLT 228).

12 This resonates with Richard Kearney's interpretation of 'poetics' as 'an exploration of the human powers to make (*poiesis*) a world in which we may poetically dwell.' Richard Kearney, *Poetics of Imagining, Modern and Post-Modern* (Edinburgh: Edinburgh University Press, 1998), 8.

Nothing is to be excluded from this ecological embrace of the Trinitarian dwelling. Bios-theos-cosmos (theo-anthropo-cosmic) must be the rhythm of being. It brings about a reconciliatory mode of living where the microcosm is in perfect unity with the macrocosm. This poetic mindfulness or recollectedness is a mode of being on the earth. It calls forth for an ecological *metanoia* which could be the paradigm of the Heidegger's approach to the poetic dwelling upon the earth as mortals beneath the divinities. Thus the ecological living calls forth for a poetic dwelling that ordains and consecrates humans to be 'shepherd' being. The dwelling of man here upon the earth as mortals and under the sky beneath the divinities is the poetic dwelling measuring with a measure which calls forth for a "kindness" meaning "with his heart not in his heart" that "the heart turns to give heed to the measure" (PLT226-227), whereupon "man dwells humanly on this earth" (PLT 227). This is the measure of the poetic mindfulness. Heidegger explains,

> The measure consists in the way in which the god who remains unknown is revealed as such by the sky. God's appearance through the sky consists in a disclosing that lets us see what conceals itself, but lets us see it not by seeking to wrest what is concealed out of its concealdness, but only by guarding the concealed it its self-concealment. Thus the unknown god appears as the unknown by way of sky's manifestness. This appearance is the measure against which man measures himself (PLT 220-221).

Then man dwells humanly on this earth – ""the life of man' is a 'dwelling life'" (PLT 229). This is the ecological kindness luxuriant in Heidegger's thinking of the humans on the earth beneath the sky. This poetic existence tells apart man from other beings. Contemporary man should sing the songs of the primal opening of Being revealing and concealing at the neighborhood. The silence chattering of the fourfold sparks the rhythm of Being as it unfolds in 'presencing-absencing'.

6. With poetic mindfulness ...

In tune with Hölderlin Heidegger writes,

> When far the dwellings life of man into the distance goes,
> Where, in that far distance, the grapevine's season glows,
> There too are summer's fields, emptied of their growing,
> And forest looms, its image darkly showing.
> That Nature pains the seasons so complete,
> That she abide, but they glide by so fleet,
> Comes of perfection; then heavens radiant height
> Crowns man, as blossom crown the trees, with light (PLT 227).

Poetic awakening in the human mind of the divine in the cosmos is the provocation of our time that invites forth poetic and *agapeic* kindness. Poetic mindfulness is the agapeic cadence of listening to the voice of the voiceless melody of Being unknown to the "frantic measuring and calculating" (PLT 226) reason, and honouring it with reverence and honesty. It is perennial wisdom too, the primal ground of truth/Being.[13] With Heidegger's mystical enchanting on Being Bede Griffiths intones that this is the task of the centuries to come as the present world order breaks down and a new order emerges from the ashes of the old. It is the spark and sparkling of the intuitive wisdom. Everything has meaning only in line with something beyond and humans as mortals begin to awake to the musings of Being as one opens one's inner eye that the material world, the world of space and time, the heavens above and the divinities as it presences and absences to our senses is nothing but a sign and symbol of a mystery which infinitely transcends it and mysteriously unfolds it. Dwelling poetically man keeps the gods, the earth, and one another safe from the calculating and totalizing gawk of reason.

> To see a world in a grain of sand, and heaven in a wild flower,
> Hold infinity in the palm of your hand, and eternity in an hour!
>
> –William Blake

Works Cited

1. Blake William. "Auguries of Innocence," in *Poets of the English Language*. London: Viking Press, 1950.
2. Descartes, Rene. *Meditations on First Philosophy*. Donald A. Cress, Trans. Cambridge: Hackett Publishing Company, 1993.
3. Einstein, Albert. "Cosmic Religious Feeling," in *Quantum Questions - Mystical Writings of the Worlds Great Physicists*, Ken Wilber, ed. London: New Science Library, 1984.
4. Gayatri Chakravorty Spivak, Accessed on 30 April 2019. https://lareviewofbooks.org/article/critical-intimacy-interview-gayatri-chakravortyspivak/?fbclid=IwAR1_ytviRmlyIYOILzBrX5lxUq0rYT6EfEVbR0j8Qjw5FKaCbj7AbwQaCdQ#.
5. Geertsema, Marius. *Heidegger's Poetic Projection of Being*. Switzerland: Palgrave Macmillan, 2018.
6. Griffiths, Bede. *The Golden String. An Autobiography.* Templegate: Sprinhold Illinois, 1996.
7. McFague, Sallie. *Earth as the Body of God*. Britain: SCM Press Ltd, 1993.
8. Heidegger, Martin. *Being and Time*. Trans. John Macquirre and Edward Robinson. Tubingen: Harper & Row Publishers, 1962.
9. _______. *Poetry, Language and Thought*. Tubingen: Harper & Row Publishers, 1962.
10. _______. *Basic Writings*. New York: Harper & Row, 1977.
11. _______. *Introduction to Metaphysics*. New Haven: Yale University Press, 1959.

13 George Steiner, *Heidegger* (Glasgow: Fontana, 1978), 49. Steiner comments that, "For the Greeks 'being' basically meant this standing presence. Pos-Socratic Greek thought, whether in Platonic idealism or Aristotelian substantiality, never returned to this pure and primal 'ground of being', to this illumination of and through presentness of the existing."

12. _______. *Discourse on Thinking*. New York: Harper & Row Publishers, 1966.
13. Kearney, Richard. *Poetics of Imagining, Modern and Post-Modern*. Edinburgh: Edinburgh University Press, 1998.
14. Levinas, Emmanuel. Totality and Infinity: An Essay on Exteriority. Trans. Alphonso Lingis. Pittsburgh, Pennsylvania: Duquesne University Press, 2007.
15. _______. "The Ego and the Totality." Trans. Alphonso Lingis. In Collected Philosophical Papers, 25-46. Pittsburgh, Pennsylvania: Duquesne University Press, 1998.
16. Panikkar, Raymond. *The Silence of God: The Answer of the Buddha.* New York: Orbis Books, 1989.
17. Puthenpurackal, Johnson. *Human Existence as Home Coming – An Approach in Reflective Phenomenology*. Bangalore: ATC Publications, 2015.
18. Steiner, George. *Heidegger.* Glasgow: Fontana, 1978.
19. Varakukalayil, Jojo. "Research is Adoration," in *Mathavum Chinthayum.* Aluva: St. Joseph's Pontifical Institute, 2006.
20. _______. "Cosmic Religiosity as Poetic Recollection," in *Romancing the Sacred.* George Karuvelil, ed. Bangalore: ATC Publications, 2007.

20

Short-Termism Vs Long Term Vision: The Relevance of Prof. John Vattanky's Indian Philosophy and Western Spirituality to Sustain Our Civilization

Kuruvilla Pandikattu, SJ

Abstract

This article, inspired by Vattanky's prolific writings and life, focusses on the role of long-term thinking based on Indian philosophical thinking and Western spiritual roots After exploring the perils of short-termism, the author looks at some of the cultural works that can promote long term vision. Then we briefly look at the urgent need for the short-term solution based on our larger perspectives, to solve the immediate problem of ecological catastrophe that we are facing today. The article concludes by bringing in the insight of an young Indian child, who promotes such a long term vision.

Key words: Short-termism, Sustainability, Ecological calamity, Present bias, Yugratna Srivastava.

Introduction

This article, inspired by Professor John Vattanky, an eminent Indian thinker and Christian visionary, dwells on the philosophical and theoretical basis of one of our most contemporary challenges. As we know, at the philosophical level Prof. Vattanky has been focusing on the late 12th century Indian mathematician and philosopher from the kingdom of Mithila, Gangesha Upadhyaya,[1] the founder of Navya-Nyāya. Undoubtedly, Vattanky has become the world-authority on Navya-Nyāya. At the spiritual level, he has been exploring St. Ephrem of Nisibis (306-373), Syriac Christian theologican, who is regarded as a Venerable Father in the Eastern Orthodox Church. As a philosopher, thinker and seeker, Prof. Vattanky has made immense contribution to foster the need for sustainable and long-term thinking and acting.

Along with my colleague, Binoy Pichalakkattu, I had had the privilege of bringing out a Festschrift in honour of Professor Vattanky. Titled, *An Indian Ending*,[2] it argued for an Indian way life-style and culture to promote sustainable living, an idea which Professor Vattanky endorsed wholeheartedly. In this article, inspired by him, I look at the pitfalls of short-termism and the need for long-term vision, based on both philosophical wisdom and spiritual depth, which can enable our world to survive, especially in the light of the contemporary ecological problems.

After exploring the perils of short-termism, we look at some of the cultural works that can promote long term vision. Then we briefly look at the need for the short-term solution based on our larger perspectives, to solve the immediate problem of ecological catastrophe that we are facing today. The article concludes by bringing in the insight of a young Indian child, who promotes such a long term vision.

1. Our Greatest Threat: The Perils of Short-Termism

In Shakespeare *Hamlet* the prince of Denmark declares, "The time is out of joint." Today we live in such times. Our perception of time is out of joint. Humanity should be acting to preserve its long-term future. Instead, short-term mindsets and structures dominate. We focus on the urgent and immediate problems, while ignoring other more enduring and life threatening ones like ecological collapse.[3]

In the long span of human history, we did not need to think long-term. "It wasn't very useful when we were avoiding attacks from sabre-toothed tigers,

---

1 Vattanky, John, Nyāyapañcānana B. Viśvanātha, Nyāyapañcānana B. Viśvanātha, and Dinakarabhaṭṭa. *Nyāya Philosophy of Language: Analysis, Text, Translation and Interpretation of Upamāna and Śabda Sections of Kārikāvalī, Muktāvalī and Dinakarī*. Delhi: Sri Satguru Publications, 1995. See also Vattanky, John. *Development of Nyāya theism*. New Delhi: Intercultural Publications, 1993.

2 Kuruvilla Pandikattu and Binoy Pichalakkattu (Eds). *An Indian Ending: Rediscovering the Grandeur of Indian Heritage for a Sustainable Future : Essays in Honour of Professor Dr. John Vattanky SJ on Completing Eighty Years*. 2013

3 For this section, I am grateful to the excellent article of Fisher, Richard. "The Perils of Short-Termism: Civilisation's Greatest Threat." Accessed June 6, 2019. http://www.bbc.com/future/story/20190109-the-perils-of-short-termism-civilisations-greatest-threat. All the quotes in this section are from this article.

desperately foraging for breakfast on the forest floor and surviving extreme weather conditions," writes Richard Fisher, Editor, BBC Future Series. As San Francisco Bay Area-based author and futurist futurist Jamais Casio holds, "In a world of constant, imminent existential threats, the ability to recognise subtle, long-term processes and multi-generational changes wasn't a particularly important adaptive advantage." Today the situation is radically different. No longer do we live a world of "clear, local cause and effect, and the greatest threats to civilisation are happening on the timescale of decades or centuries."

To avoid these dangers, we use our Neolithic mental functions to play evolutionary catch-up. While our minds might be not be wired to deal with long-term threats and priorities in the abstract, they are wired for two significant things : story and emotion. Our predisposition towards story, and the deeply emotional nature of our decision-making, makes art and culture foundational for long-term thinking, ensuing the survival of species.[4]

Our inability to look beyond the latest news cycle could be one of the most dangerous traits of our generation, claims Fisher. We need something very different: "a home for slowing down, delving deep and shifting perspectives."

This article is based on BBC Future Series about the long view of humanity, which urges us to stand back from the daily news cycle in order to "widen the lens of our current place in time." Our goal is to explore what really matters in the broader arc of human history and what it means for our descendants, as well as revealing the hidden patterns shaping our societies in the long term.

a. The Present Bias

How often do we thin about the well-being of these future generations? How often do we contemplate the impact of our decisions for the future generations?

Part of the problem is that the 'now' commands our attention disproportionately. "We are saturated with knowledge and standards of living have mostly never been higher – but today it is difficult to look beyond the next news cycle. If time can be sliced, it is only getting finer, with ever-shorter periods now shaping our world." Fisher paraphrases the investor, Esther Dyson: "in politics the dominant time frame is a term of office, in fashion and culture it's a season, for corporations it's a quarter, on the internet it's minutes, and on the financial markets mere milliseconds."

According to the sociologist Elise Boulding , contemporary society is suffering from "temporal exhaustion." "If one is mentally out of breath all the time from dealing with the present, there is no energy left for imagining the future," she wrote already in 1978. After twenty years, in our relentless,

4 Pembroke, Ella Saltmarshe and Beatrice. "How Art and Culture Can Help Us Rethink Time." Accessed June 7, 2019. http://www.bbc.com/future/story/20190521-how-art-and-culture-can-help-us-rethink-time.

Twitter-fuelled politics, finds no time to talk about larger and more pressing or time-consuming problems like climate change or social inequality .

That's why researchers, artists, technologists and philosophers are converging on the idea that short-termism may be the greatest threat our species is facing this century. They include philosophers arguing the moral case for prioritizing our distant descendants; researchers mapping out the long-term path of *Homo sapiens*; artists creating cultural works that wrestle with time, legacy and the sublime; and Silicon Valley engineers building a giant clock that will tick for 10,000 years.

What these concerned thinkers from diverse fields share is a simple idea: that the longevity of civilisation depends on us extending our frame of reference in time. The survival of our species is based on our ability to consider the future of the world through a much longer lens or wider perspectives. What if we could be altruistic enough to care about people we might never live to see? Then we can break free from the shackles of short-termist ways!

Human beings haven't always had the ability to think in an abstract way about long-term time. In fact, we can live totally in the moment – absorbed by music or fashion– or we can mentally travel forward to imagine scenarios in the distant past or future. It is incredible that we humans have the capacity to "zoom back in your imagination to picture the first acts of our ancestors, and moments later spin the dial to billions of years hence as the Sun engulfs the Earth."

In fact, some researchers argue that this mental time-travel is a vital adaptation that led to our species' indescribable success. According to Thomas Suddendorf of the University of Queensland, humans may be the only animals with this ability: we can create a complex "theatre stage" in our minds with the equivalent of a set, playwright, director and actors, and subsequently describe these imaginary scenes to other people.

"It is a tremendously powerful skill," Suddendorf asserts. "We can imagine situations like what we're going to do tomorrow, next week, where we're going to have a holiday, what career path to pursue, and we can imagine alternative versions of those. And we can evaluate each of them in terms of their likelihood and desirability."

In other words, we have the innate ability to imagine the consequences of our actions in deeper time, but sadly not always the will or the motivation to escape the salience of the present.

Despite our mental faculty to look and plan ahead, we have the inherent weakness in our thinking called "present bias", which favours short-term payoffs over long-term rewards. For example, people are more likely to accept an offer of Rs 100 today, rather than a guarantee of Rs 120 in a week; to smoke cigarettes despite a shortened life; to spend on pleasures, not save for rainy days.

Some psychologists have used the metaphor of a "horse and rider" to describe this tension between our rationality that focusses on the long term benefits and instincsts that suggests instant gratification: the rider knows it's smart to think longer-term, but the horse has its own different urges.

And if we are prone to neglecting the well-being of our own future selves, it's even harder to muster empathy for our future generations. There is nowhere this is more apparent than in the world of politics and economics.

To understand why short-termism has such a hold on our society and how we are governed by the short-term values, imagine the dilemma of a newly-elected politician. She is weighing up whether to spend a few billion dollars on climate change mitigation, pandemic preparation and reducing nuclear waste. She knows that this will be immense value to great-grandchildren. But the immediate benefits will be invisible and the cost painful. Her constituents in the fossil fuel industry also need jobs, the military want funding for national security, and she was elected by promising tax cuts. Thus the dilemma of short-term benefits vs long-term survival strategy.

b. The Philosopher's Challenge

A philosopher can easily propose ethical argument that dismantles the economic reasoning for short-termism. It may work in the long range, or "form the point of eternity," as Barruch Spinoza would hold.

Some philosophers have reasoned that discounting the needs of our descendants is like burying a shard of broken glass in a forest. If a child steps on the glass and cuts themselves today or tomorrow, it seems much worse than a child hurting themselves on the glass a century from now. But ethically, there is no difference between the two.

The philosophical argument for investing in measures to protect the wellbeing of future generations can also be framed, simplistically, by imagining a set of scales, if we compare today's population with unborn person of the future. Today's population of 7.7 billion is large, but very small when we compare it with everybody on Earth who will be born. If *Homo sapiens* survives for tens or thousands of years, that becomes a humongous number of lives to consider. "Trillions of families, relationships, births; countless moments of potential joy, love, friendship and tenderness."

According to some calculations about 100 billion people have lived on our earth in the last 50,000 years. But if we assume average annual birth numbers projected for the 21st Century for the next 50,000 years , then the number of people still to be born will be trillions!

According to the social philosopher Roman Krznaric, failing to value the lives of all these descendants is 'colonising' the future. That is, we deciding that future generations destiny and or non-destiny. "We treat the future as a distant colonial outpost where we dump ecological degradation, nuclear waste, public debt and technological risk" he said.

Krznaric calls this attitude '*tempus nullius*', drawing a parallel with an idea used to justify acts like the British settlement of Australia in the 1700-1800s. According to the legal notion of '*terra nullius*' (nobody's land) the ownership rights of indigenous Aborigines were ignored. Similarly, "we treat the future as 'empty time', where there are no generations", he asserts.

A few governments are, reassuringly, trying to change their ways. For example, Finland and Sweden have parliamentary advisory groups to foster longer-term planning. Hungary has an ombudsman for future generations. There are also various organisations now lobbying politicians to consider future generations from a human rights perspective, particularly in relation to climate change.

Meanwhile, Wales has established "Wellbeing of Future Generations Act," "All decisions taken by the public sector in Wales, including our government, must demonstrate how they are meeting today's needs without compromising the ability of future generations to meet their own."

c. Further Challenges and Trajectories

It's early days though, and while these examples are encouraging, they are also isolated. Unless we get better at ditching our short-termist ways on a global scale, the decisions we make in the early 21st Century could shape the future of our species far more profoundly than we might realise.

And as one group of researchers warned , acts of neglect or stupidity in the present day could possibly threaten civilisation itself. Fisher leads us to early September 2017. The world's attention was focused on various pieces of salient news: Hurricane Irma was brewing in the Caribbean, Donald Trump's administration had announced plans to dismantle an Obama-era immigration policy, and photographers captured Prince George's first day at school.

Around the same time, a small, little-known group of researchers were meeting at a workshop in Gothenburg, Sweden with a goal to look much, much further ahead – far beyond this latest news cycle. Motivated by a moral concern for our descendants, their goal was to discuss the existential risks facing humanity.

The paper presented in the meeting, "Long-term Trajectories of Human Civilisation," attempts to "formalise a scientific and ethical field of study" for thousands of years hence. It reads: "To restrict attention to near-term decades may be akin to the drunk searching for his keys under the streetlight: it may be where empirical study is more robust, but the important part lies elsewhere."

The Trajectories group began with the assumption that, while the future is uncertain, it is not unknown. We can predict many things with reasonable confidence, via observed patterns, repeating events, and established behaviours throughout human history. Their examples: "biology suggests that each mammalian species exists, on average, for roughly 1 million years before it becomes extinct; history shows that humanity has continually colonised new lands and strived to transform our abilities with technology; and the fossil record demonstrates that global extinction events can and do happen."

Extrapolating these patterns into the future allowed them to map out four possible long-term trajectories for our species, according to Fisher:

1. **Status quo** trajectories, in which human civilisation persists in a broadly similar state into the distant future.
2. **Catastrophe** trajectories, in which one or more events cause significant harm to human civilisation.
3. **Technological transformation** trajectories, in which radical technological breakthroughs put human civilisation on a fundamentally different course.
4. **Astronomical** trajectories, in which human civilisation expands beyond its home planet and into the accessible portions of the cosmos.

Following their discussions the Trajectories group concluded that the 'status quo' path would be a pretty unlikely scenario once you get to longer-term timescales. "Instead, civilisation is likely to either end catastrophically or expand dramatically," they write.

So on the optimistic path, merging with some as-yet-unimagined technology or colonising the stars are two scenarios that are entirely possible with the passage of enough time. Both paths could lead to our descendants thriving for millions if not billions of years, spreading out into the Universe or evolving into a more advanced species.

But we also are almost certain to face serious existential risks along the way. Natural disasters have reduced life on Earth continually. What worries the Trajectories researchers more is that today we have added a whole host of additional human-made risks into the mix too – especially the anthropogenic climate change.

Obviously, the researchers can't predict which order any of this will play out. They can predict, though, that it's our trajectory to shape – for better or worse, the decisions we make this century could shape the next one and far beyond. "The stakes are extremely large, and there may be a lot that people today can do to have a positive impact," they write.

The poignant question is: will we?

2. Can We Act to Save Ourselves?

Fisher is deeply troubled by all this. "It's possible that we are at one of the most precarious points of human history. Yet I worry that our power to destroy ourselves is radically outstripping our wisdom and foresight."

How do we avoid sleepwalking into acts that harm future generations, or even worse, precipitating a catastrophe that could threaten our existence as a species? How are enough minds changed to prioritise a longer-term view when so many present-day pressures nudge us towards short-termism?

You can make philosophical and evidence-based arguments for protecting our species and future generations. But sadly, human beings are not rational, at least not always! In spite of the philosophical definition of human being as "rational animal." It is also not that easy. It demands quite a lot of time, energy, effort and foresight!

To foster longer-term thinking that goes against our psychological base instincts, there need to be approaches and arguments that inspire and engage the non-rational part of our brain too, asserts Fisher.[5] That's the thinking behind one new initiative called the Long Time Inquiry, established in the UK, to foster long-term thinking via artistic rather than empirical routes. The founders Ella Saltmarshe and Beatrice Pembroke argue that culture is often relegated in big strategic conversations about the future of humanity and the planet, and that needs to change.

"Culture forms the operating system for our society," they write. "It's foundational to the way science, politics, economics and technology develop. It shapes how we feel, how we empathise and how we connect with each other. It provides the reflective space to navigate complexity and uncertainty."

Moreover, a piece of art – whether it is a painting or a play – has the potential to endure longer than a policy paper or political initiative. Such cultural artefact are often tended, reproduced and preserved as the ages pass, making it one of most enduring legacies a human being can leave for the world.

a. New Cultural Works

Saltmarshe and Pembroke aim to foster and encourage new cultural works about the long-term effects as well as creating a network of like-minded artists, institutions and intellectuals. They have been influenced by a principle called 'Seventh Generation' stewardship, defined by the leaders of the Native American Iroquois Confederacy many centuries ago. "Every decision they took had to keep in mind seven generations hence," explains Saltmarshe. They

5 Because of the need for the emotional aspect, some of us have been pleading that science along cannot tackle this problem. We need to bring in religious commitment, passion and readiness to sacrifice. Thus technology coupled with spirituality and religion can pose answer to the pressing needs of ecological problems.

also point to concepts such as Cathedral Thinking, which refers to the approach of building over multiple generations.

They also propose that the prevalence of short-termism is entwined with our attitude facing our own death. "We've got a hunch that our inability to deal with the future of the world beyond our lifespan is wrapped up with our inability to deal with the fact that our lives will end," they write. "Our denial of our own mortality prevents us from engaging with the long-term future," which will transcend our individual lives.[6]

The Long Time Inquiry will build on the work of various individuals and groups who are using art and other symbolic means to provoke people to think longer-term. For example, in 2014 the artist Katie Paterson began building The Future Library. Here authors submit manuscripts which will be read only 2114. Or there's Longplayer, a musical score that will play for 1,000 years. It is an eerie, but calming, composition seemingly intended to evoke a feeling of religiosity in its listeners.

But perhaps one of the most ambitious symbolic gestures that our generation will create is a special clock buried deep inside a mountain in Texas. It involves a group of Silicon Valley visionaries, a pioneering musician, and the world's richest person – and its story begins in a bad neighbourhood in the late 1970s.

b. The Story of Long Now Foundation

In the 1970s the well known British music producer Brian Eno , on the way to a glamorous dinner party on the suburbs of New York. Going through dilapidated houses and terrible poth-holed roads, he reached the house of the host, which to his surprise, was a glittering, glamorous loft, costing millions of dollars. He asked the super-rich hostess during dinner if she liked living where she did. "Oh sure," she replied, "this is the loveliest place I have ever lived." He realised that what she meant was 'within these four walls'. The dilapidated neighbourhood outside didn't exist for her.

Eno notices the same narrow view everywhere. What's more, this attitude to space also translated to the way this New York glitterati seemed to think about time – not much further than the following week. They were living in what Eno called a 'small here' and a 'short now'. "Everything was exciting, fast, current, and temporary. Enormous buildings came and went, careers rose and crashed in weeks. You rarely got the feeling that anyone had the time to think two years ahead, let alone 10 or a hundred," he noted.

---

6 We have been trying to link ecological calamity with human mortality. "Since I am not able to face my own death, I want to join the "immortality project," causing irrecoverable harm to myself and the environment. See Becker, Ernest. *The Denial of Death*. London: Souvenir Press, 2018

"More and more," he writes, "I find I want to be living in a Big Here and a Long Now." This shocking experience led Eno to work with several other like-minded thinkers to establish the Long Now Foundation, which aims to "provide a counterpoint to today's accelerating culture and help make long-term thinking more common". It runs regular speaker events in San Francisco, and has launched initiatives such as the Rosetta Project, a digital library of all human languages designed to last millennia, or a website called Long Bets, which asks people to stake money on their predictions for the long-term future. Their scope of view is 10,000 years hence, because it was around 10 millennia ago that agriculture became widespread and civilisations began. When talking about dates, they also add an extra 0 in order to capture the notion that our paltry years are dwarfed by a larger timeframe (Year 02019!).

c. 10,000 Year Clock

Of all their projects, however, the most ambitious attempt to break people out of short-term thinking is a symbolic installation – the 60m-tall 10,000 Year Clock, currently being installed in the mountains of Western Texas on land owned by Amazon billionaire Jeff Bezos. The Clock is intended to be a monument that outlasts its creators, ticking for 10,000 years.

In 2018, the first parts of the clock's mechanical architecture were placed inside the limestone cavern. Yet it has been almost two decades in the making. Engineering a mechanism that lasts 10,000 years has stretched designers to answer questions few have tackled before – everything from choosing which ball bearings will slows and wobbles earth's rotation over millenia.

Inside the mountain, a 16-tonne diamond-chainsaw robot has carved a spiral rock staircase, which will snake around the metal cogs and gears of the clock in a central cavity hundreds of feet deep. Engineers recently a manual winding mechanism to power the bells and display dials – but the clock itself will be kept running by the temperature difference from day to night. Air within a tank and bellows at the cavern's top will expand during the day, providing just enough energy to keep a pendulum ticking for centuries.[7]

As the centuries pass, a new, different sequence of bells will play every so often. You can get a sense of what future generations might hear on one of Eno's albums, inspired by the clock. The first track features the sequence of bells that will play 5,000 years from the year he composed it – in the year 07003.

The clock is designed to provoke its visitors to reflect on their place in time. While rationally we can conceive of the deeper future and how our acts affect tomorrow, its creators believe that it will be a wholly different

7 This reminds us eerily of the story published in 1950s. Bradbury, Ray. *There Will Come Soft Rains*. Old Greenwich, Conn: Listening Library, 1976.

experience to stand inside an ancient cavern looking at a clock that will tick for hundreds of lifetimes.

It is useful to remember that such works of art or installations such as the clock can influence people's views and actions in ways that rational, empirical arguments cannot. For example, BBC Future recently explored how the style of imagery deployed to depict climate change can influence the viewer's sense of agency, empathy and willingness to change their behaviour. Similarly, researchers have found that people are more likely to alter their environmental habits if they are asked to engage with climate change through their personal values and experiences rather than hearing scientific arguments from experts.[8]

Our author has mixed feelings about the clock. He wonders what future generations will make it of it, looking back at the period and the place in which it was conceived. It will cost tens of millions of dollars and has developed amidst the dizzying growth of Silicon Valley – and the fortunes and controversies that followed. Still he hopes that the clock will be seen as its makers intended, "a symbol that changes minds about short-term thinking rather than Silicon Valley largesse."

Over 10,000 years, perhaps all of these details will be forgotten anyway. Maybe the clock will mean something entirely different to our descendants, revealing a truth of our age that we can't yet imagine. Like time capsules, often when humanity erects monuments that reach for posterity, these symbols go on to say more about what we value and who we are today than we will ever know ourselves. If the 10,000 Year Clock does hold a hidden truth about us that only our descendants will see, it would be an appropriate legacy for the long-forgotten billionaire and foundation that placed it inside a mountain.

In conclusion, Fisher asks himself: "I understand the dangers of short-termism. I can both rationalise the argument, and feel the need to care more about future generations. But I confess I still struggle with how to translate that to action as an individual. Some days I wonder if I should be eating more ethically. The next I consider sacrificing a trip abroad to reduce my carbon emissions."

We must admit that it is daunting to contemplate how we as individuals might act with kindness and foresight for unborn people. To realise that we are just one in a chain of generations, and accept that while we will one day be forgotten, we owe an ethical obligation to our descendants to leave a better world than the one we inherited ourselves. Truly it is difficult enough extrapolating how my small acts as an individual might affect the wider world and its population today, let alone hundreds of years into the future! Precisely,

8 Here we can see the relevance of the passion based on his spiritual depth, which motivates the life and writings of Prof. Vattanky.

that is what we are challenged to! We need a broader vision, which takes into account our long-term need (not greed!)

3. A Man-Made Ecological Catastrophe

Sir David Attenborough, one of the world's best known naturalists, declared humans to be a "plague on earth," writes Stewart Patrick.[9] Sadly, the man-made ecological catastrophe is unfolding at a gradual, if inexorable, pace in multiple areas of the world. But it is harder to find images akin to a hostage begging for his life, or health workers clad in protective suits, to hold the public's attention and mobilize political support for action. Thus, humanity continues to sleepwalk, as the planet experiences only the sixth major extinction event in its 4.5 billion year history.[10]

On September 30 2014 the World Wildlife Fund (WWF) and partner organizations issued a jaw-dropping report. According to the Living Planet Report 2014, between 1970 and 2010 more than half of all Earth's vertebrates (mammals, birds, reptiles, amphibians, and fish) disappeared, even as the human population nearly doubled from 3.7 to 7 billion. This decline occurred everywhere—on land, in rivers, and in the oceans. The main culprits were habitat destruction and unsustainable resource exploitation through commercial fishing and hunting. The greatest declines occurred in freshwater systems, where populations declined by 76 percent. Latin America alone lost 83 percent of its wildlife—the most dramatic drop globally. "If half the animals died in the London zoo next week it would be front page news. But that is happening in the great outdoors," as one of the reports contributors, Kevin Norris of the Zoological Society of London, told the the Newspaper Guardian.

It is clear by now that Homo sapiens is the most potent invasive species ever. By clearing forests and transforming land for agricultural use and new human settlements, by exploiting and altering water systems, and by polluting the air, rivers, and oceans, we have placed extraordinary pressures on countless species of animals and plants, as well as microorganisms on which natural cycles depend. So an exasperated Sir David Attenborough, declared humans to be a "plague on earth."

The world has just over a decade to get climate change under control, U.N. scientists say. The world stands on the brink of failure when it comes to holding global warming to moderate levels, and nations will need to take

---

9 Patrick, Stewart. "A Man-Made Ecological Catastrophe: More Than Half of All Earth's Vertebrates Have Disappeared." Text. The National Interest, October 10, 2014. https://nationalinterest.org/blog/the-buzz/man-made-ecological-catastrophe-more-half-all-earth%E2%80%99s-11446.

10 See Kuruvilla Pandikattu "Tecnología y valores culturales: Perspectivas desde la India" Concilium, June 2019, 79-90. The title of this section "Man-Made" is purposely used since patriarchy is very much responsible for ecological catastrophe.

"unprecedented" actions to cut their carbon emissions over the next decade, according to a landmark report by the top scientific body studying climate change.[11]

With global emissions showing few signs of slowing, the chance for meeting the most ambitious goals of the 2015 Paris agreement look increasingly slim. To avoid racing past warming of 1.5 degrees Celsius over preindustrial levels would require a "rapid and far-reaching" transformation of human civilization at a magnitude that has never happened before, the group found.

"There is no documented historic precedent" for the sweeping change to energy, transportation and other systems required to reach 1.5 degrees Celsius, the U.N. Intergovernmental Panel on Climate Change (IPCC) claimed in a report requested as part of the 2015 Paris climate agreement.

At the same time, however, the report is being received with hope in some quarters because it affirms that 1.5 degrees Celsius is still possible — if emissions stopped today, for instance, the planet would not reach that temperature. It is also likely to galvanize even stronger climate action by focusing on 1.5 degrees Celsius, rather than 2 degrees, as a target that the world cannot afford to miss.

"Frankly, we've delivered a message to the governments," said Jim Skea, a co-chair of the IPCC panel and professor at Imperial College London, at a press event following the document's release. "It's now their responsibility ... to decide whether they can act on it." He added, "What we've done is said what the world needs to do."

The transformation described in the document is breathtaking, and the speed of change required raises inevitable questions about its feasibility. "Such large transitions pose profound challenges for sustainable management of the various demands on land for human settlements, food, livestock feed, fibre, bioenergy, carbon storage, biodiversity and other ecosystem services," the report states.

Current promises made by countries as part of the Paris climate agreement would lead to about 3 degrees Celsius of warming by the end of the century, and the Trump administration recently released an analysis assuming about 4 degrees Celsius by 2100 if the world takes no action.

Underscoring the difficulty of interpreting what's possible, the IPCC gave two separate numbers in the report for Earth's remaining "carbon budget," or how much carbon dioxide humans can emit and still have a reasonable chance of remaining below 1.5 degrees Celsius. The upshot is that humans are

11 Mooney, Chris, and Brady Dennis. "The World Has Just over a Decade to Get Climate Change under Control, U.N. Scientists Say." *Washington Post*, October 7, 2018, sec. Energy and Environment. https://www.washingtonpost.com/energy-environment/2018/10/08/world-has-only-years-get-climate-change-under-control-un-scientists-say/.

allowed either 10 or 14 years of current emissions, and no more, for a two-thirds or better chance of avoiding 1.5 degrees Celsius.

Meanwhile, the report clearly documents that a warming of 1.5 degrees Celsius would be very damaging and that 2 degrees — which used to be considered a reasonable goal — could approach intolerable in parts of the world.

"1.5 degrees is the new 2 degrees," said Jennifer Morgan, executive director of Greenpeace International. To avoid that, in barely more than 10 years, the world's percentage of electricity from renewables such as solar and wind power would have to jump from the current 24 percent to something more like 50 or 60 percent. Coal and gas plants that remain in operation would need to be equipped with technologies, collectively called carbon capture and storage , that prevent them from emitting carbon dioxide into the air and instead funnel it to be buried underground.

Concluding Story of Two Girls

We are aware of Greta Thunberg, the Swedish teenager whose solo school strike for climate action helped create a global movement, told British MPs in April 2019 that the active support for fossil fuels and airport expansion was "beyond absurd". She added: "This ongoing irresponsible behaviour will no doubt be remembered in history as one of the greatest failures of humankind."

What many of us do not recall is the speech of 13 year old girl Yugratna Srivastava from St Fidelis College, Lucknow and member of Tarumitra at the high-level summit convened by the UN Chief Ban Ki-moon.[12] India was represented by then Foreign Minister S M Krishna and Environment Minister Jairam Ramesh. "We need to call for an action now. We have to protect the earth not just for us but for our future generations," Srivastava told an audience consisting of US President Barack Obama and Chinese President Hu Jintao, on 22 September 2009.

She added:

"We just have present and future in our hands.

Let's act in the present to secure our future.

We have one Mother Earth: Care it and Share it."

She pleaded with the world leaders: "Respected leaders, when you all make policies, please think of a child suffering in greenhouse heat and think of the species craving to survive."

Then she concluded: "A bird can fly in air, a fish can swim in water, a leopard can run far faster. But we the humans have been supernaturally gifted

12 United Nations. "Indian Teenager Seeks Urgent Action from Leaders on Climate Change." Deccan Herald, September 23, 2009. https://www.deccanherald.com/content/26857/indian-teenager-seeks-urgent-action.html.

with mind, a capability to think, change and reform. So come on let us all use these abilities to save our birthplace.... our home.... our mother earth!"

Can we go beyond the immediate and present needs and focus on the long-term needs of our collective humanity? Can we dream together of a humanity beyond the limited present needs and local crisis? Then we can be be long-term both temporally and spatially! We human beings are capable and we will. That is the hope of of all of us, including the great thinker and visionary John Vattanky. Our common religions, arts, technology, science and culture can help us to draw the wisdom for this gigantic life-saving task!